EDUCATION AND ANTHROPOLOGY

Paper and Discussions occasioned by a Conference held at Stanford, California, June 9–14, 1954, under the joint auspices of the School of Education and the Department of Sociology and Anthropology, Stanford University, and the American Anthropological Association.

PARTICIPANTS

Theodore Brameld	Solon T. Kimball
Robert N. Bush	Alfred L. Kroeber
Arthur P. Coladarci	Dorothy Lee
William H. P. Cowley	William E. Martin
Cora DuBois	Margaret Mead
Lawrence K. Frank	I. James Quillen
John Gillin	Fannie R. Shaftel
Paul R. Hanna	Bernard J. Siegel
C. W. M. Hart	George D. Spindler
Jules Henry	Hilda Taba
Felix M. Keesing	Lawrence G. Thomas

EDUCATION AND ANTHROPOLOGY

Edited and with a Foreword by
GEORGE D. SPINDLER

Preface by
LAWRENCE K. FRANK

STANFORD UNIVERSITY PRESS
STANFORD, CALIFORNIA

STANFORD UNIVERSITY PRESS
STANFORD, CALIFORNIA

PUBLISHED IN GREAT BRITAIN AND INDIA
BY GEOFFREY CUMBERLEGE,
OXFORD UNIVERSITY PRESS,
LONDON AND BOMBAY

———

HENRY M. SNYDER & COMPANY, INC.
440 FOURTH AVENUE, NEW YORK 16

W. S. HALL & COMPANY
510 MADISON AVENUE, NEW YORK 22

———

PRINTED AND BOUND IN THE UNITED STATES
OF AMERICA BY STANFORD UNIVERSITY PRESS

Library of Congress Catalog Card Number: 55-9349

FOREWORD

Plans for the conference on interrelationships between education and anthropology reported in this volume began with exploratory conversations with Margaret Mead, David Baerreis, and John Whiting at the meeting of the American Anthropological Association in Philadelphia in 1952. Some of the ideas emerging there were put into motion with letters of inquiry to many anthropologists and educators during the next few months. On the basis of the interest shown in the replies to these letters, and the suggestions made, an application for subsidy for the conference and publication of the results was made to the Carnegie Foundation, and subsequently granted.

With this firm backing, a planning group was established at Stanford University including the following members of the School of Education and Department of Sociology and Anthropology faculties: James Quillen, Felix Keesing, William Cowley, Paul Hanna, John Bartky, Arthur Coladarci, Robert Bush, Bernard Siegel, Fannie Shaftel, and Lawrence Thomas. George Spindler acted as chairman of this planning group, coordinator of the conference, and editor of its results.

In order to broaden the base of the planning operations, subsequent planning meetings were held at the University of Chicago with Sol Tax, Jules Henry, Ralph Tyler, Dorothy Lee, Sherwood Washburn, and Preston Holder, and at the American Anthropological Association meeting at Tucson in 1953 with several different groups of anthropologists. Through these various phases of planning, involving both meetings and correspondence, educators and anthropologists representing ten major universities in widely separate parts of the United States made direct contributions to the development of the project, and many other persons in both disciplines from many other places were involved in some degree. The conference and its results therefore represent no single group of professionals from either discipline or from any single institution in the sense that both participation and conception in planning was as broad as it could feasibly be made. Not all interests or proposals are, to be sure, equally represented. The planning group at Stanford was responsible for mediating the proposals and interests gathered from these many places and persons.

The decision was made early in planning to cast the project in an exploratory framework. We were less interested in what had been done, and its evaluation, than we were in the frontiers of the relationships between these two broad disciplines and their concepts, data, methods, and problems. This volume reflects this exploratory framework in both its strong and weaker points.

Whatever defects in logic, content, or focal areas are represented here, the report of the conference contained in this volume makes interesting reading. It is pregnant with suggestions, hypotheses, and significant tentative judgments that should comprise a meaningful contribution to the development of both education and anthropology—one no less than the other—and to the future of their relationships.

The volume is organized into ten sections, each one comprised of three major parts—a paper within a topical area defined in planning, discussants' comments, and open discussion. The papers have served as springboards for the discussion, not as definitions of limit, so many unanticipated problems and topics are raised. This is one reason why the discussions, as well as the papers, make interesting reading.

The conference was held in comfortable surroundings at Carmel Valley, not far from Stanford University. Every attempt was made to create a situation that would break down interpersonal barriers, so that maximum communication could occur. That these attempts were successful is reflected in the use of first names, and other indications of informality in the discussion. This informal mood has purposely been retained in the edited portion of the transcription included in this volume, so that the reader can perhaps enter vicariously into the group situation, as those who participated directly experienced it.

My editorial commentary cannot close without an expression of personal gratitude to the many people who made this conference, and the volume, possible. The members of the planning group named in this Foreword are all due real credit. James Quillen, John A. Bartky, Felix M. Keesing, Sol Tax, Margaret Mead, and Dorothy Lee must be listed among those whose support and encouragement were particularly crucial in planning and other capacities. I am grateful to E. Adamson Hoebel for his careful reading of the manuscript and his suggestions for the volume. There are, as always, many others who performed large and small services as a contribution to the project, but a special debt of gratitude is owed to the staff that carried the heavy burden of paper and leg work. Barbara Angier, Roland and Marianne Force, Cynthia Shephard, Lynn Gilbert, who acted in various capacities as typists, dittographers, diagram drawers, managers of transcribers, and social expediters, all did yeoman work. Rose Wax, who acted as general secretary and *rapporteur* for the planning and conference, is due a very special thanks. And I am particularly grateful to Louise Spindler for her sustained and invaluable help as editorial assistant.

GEORGE D. SPINDLER
Stanford University

PREFACE

The significance of the papers and four-day conference recorded in this volume may be more clearly recognized if we will recall what has taken place during the past fifty years in education. Beginning about 1900, educational theory and practice and the development of curricula and textbooks have been successively responsive to the contributions coming from various disciplines and professions. Thus education was greatly influenced by the psychologists who studied the learning process as exhibited by laboratory animals, developed a variety of standardized tests and educational measurements, studied the problem of transfer of training, and developed various programs of experimental education that emphasized activities, learning by doing, and a wide range of experiential and noncognitive learning. These contributions from educational psychology were supplemented and enlarged by sociologists and psychiatrists and mental hygiene groups who, through studies of communities and clinical investigations of school children, enlarged the thinking of educators to include the extra–school life and activities of pupils, especially their interpersonal relations with parents and siblings. Child guidance clinics in, or affiliated with, schools and counseling and guidance programs were established for the "problem children," now recognized as one of the school's responsibilities. This concern for the nonacademic aspects of children was furthered by the contributions beginning to come in the nineteen-thirties from studies of child growth and development, which showed that each child undergoes a regular sequence of development, but passes through these sequential changes at his own rate of progress and attains his own individual development. Thus chronological age is not a satisfactory guide to his educational needs and capacities. Also in the middle nineteen-thirties, the Progressive Education Association, generously financed by several large foundations (General Education Board and the Carnegie Corporation) established a series of commissions. The Commission on Secondary Education studied high school programs and produced a number of proposals for revising and enlarging the several subject-matter areas and improving teaching of those subjects. The Committee on Adolescence, organized by this commission, carried on intensive studies of high school students over a four-year period, focusing upon their needs and problems, intellectual and personal, and emphasizing the process of personality development in these years as revealed by these students. In the work of this commission and especially in the activities of the Committee on Adolescence, cultural anthropologists participated, probably for the first time, in planning and directing the studies of adolescents and their school life and also studying the community in which they lived.

The Commission of Relations of School and College conducted an eight-year study of high school students, in thirty secondary schools all over the country. These students were observed and measured during their four-year high school programs and then followed through in their four-year college careers. The findings of this study indicated that many of the assumptions about secondary education and what was required for college work were in need of considerable revision. Moreover, it showed that effective learning takes place when the potentialities of the individual student are recognized and encouraged, as contrasted with the belief in a more or less rigid set of requirements imposed on all students.

These notable contributions began to appear in print just preceding and during the early years of the war. Unfortunately preoccupation with the war situation and the subsequent events has resulted in these significant contributions to education having been overlooked or forgotten, not only by the public, but by many professional educators.

The contributions of cultural anthropologists to education have been both indirect and direct, providing a wider perspective for educational thinking and research and also offering the more specific findings and conceptions developed particularly in the study of culture and personality. These studies of culture and personality began with the Seminar on Impact of Culture on Personality in 1930 at Yale, under the direction of the late Edward Sapir, professor of anthropology, assisted by John Dollard and a number of visiting lecturers, sociologists, psychiatrists, and anthropologists. In 1934 the Hanover Conference on Human Relations carried further these inquiries into the enculturation and socialization of the growing child and formulated an outline which was never published but which served to guide a variety of investigations and educational programs, such as the Commission on Human Relations of the Progressive Education Association. Following this conference, a number of volumes were published presenting this psychocultural approach to personality development and to the understanding of social order and community life.

In the years following these initial explorations, there have been numerous studies of culture and personality by anthropologists and also by psychiatrists, psychoanalysts, and psychologists who have recognized the significance of enculturation in personality development as revealed by observation of children in a variety of cultures, including our own. Also there have been many studies of the ethnic-cultural groups whose children attend public schools where there are frequent clashes. Further, what is known as applied anthropology now comprehends studies by anthropologists of factories, hospitals, military organizations, recreational and leisure-time groups. It has been repeatedly suggested that a school or a school system should be similarly studied to reveal some of the implicit, little-recognized patterns and relationships in educational organizations.

The various explorations and studies carried on in the 'thirties made it clear that education is a continuous process beginning at birth and operating with cumulative intensity as a child grows, develops, and learns to live in the symbolic cultural world of his group traditions and to participate in the social order of which he is a member. These studies have also emphasized that each child is an individual organism with all his inherited capacities: his personality therefore may be viewed as his individualized expression of these organic functions as they have been shaped and patterned by his care, nurture, and education in a culture. More specifically, it has been shown by a variety of observations and intensive studies that each child develops and learns in his own individualized way and continually strives to maintain himself as an individual while living in his social group. Thus it is becoming evident that education must recognize more clearly the problem of how the schools can contribute more effectively to the development of healthy personalities in children and youth, not viewed in terms of fitting the child into an existing set of institutions, as "a good social adjustment." Rather, the schools are confronted with the subtle and complicated task of helping children to grow up in a more or less disorderly social life where almost all our institutions and practices are being rapidly altered and in some cases superseded by new social inventions. This means educating children and youth as personalities who can achieve some degree of orderliness and stability in their lives, despite the weakening of traditional beliefs and patterns by which we have for so long been guided. Approaching the problems of education in this way, we realize that we must become self-consciously aware of what has rarely been recognized by people, namely, that they live in a cultural world of their traditions, the maintenance and improvement of which become the responsibility, in greater or less measure, of every member of that group, who, as a personality, along with all other personalities, constitutes the cultural group. Faced with such questions, the schools, more especially the university departments and schools of education which are largely responsible for the preparation of teachers and the development of teaching materials and practices, should look for whatever insights and understandings may be available from other professions to help them undertake these relatively new and unprecedented educational tasks. The disciplines or professional groups which are most closely associated with these problems are the psychiatric and clinical psychological group and the sociologists and anthropologists who are increasingly focusing their attention on personality in culture, cultural dynamics, and the patterning of interpersonal and group relations. Cultural anthropology has an enormous accumulation of materials on a great variety of different cultures. One of the threshold tasks is to formulate some sort of frame of reference within which the more relevant and significant findings of anthropologists can be made available to the educational group, and, in turn, the educational group can raise those questions for answering which they may appropriately ask the anthropologists to contribute.

This, then, was the two-way situation in which the conference group attempted to communicate, through a series of prepared papers, chiefly by anthropologists, which were then critically examined and discussed primarily by educators. Obviously in a four-day meeting all the relevant questions and exigent problems of education could not be considered or even recognized. Nor was it expected that the conferees at this meeting would in any sense attempt to settle and definitely resolve even those points which were specifically recognized and discussed in the meetings. Readers of this volume therefore should not expect to find pronouncements but rather should look to these papers and the reported discussion as indicating significant areas in education and approaches to contemporary education problems to which anthropologists may offer promising, fruitful leads for further exploration and investigation.

Education in many ways is like medicine; the teacher and the physician are engaged primarily in developing and applying an art based upon scientific knowledge and the best available insights and understandings about the human organism-personality, approached both individually and in groups. Like education, medicine has undergone a succession of changes, such as the displacement of the old humoral doctrine of disease by cellular pathology and the resulting search for pathological lesions and sources of infection. A little later medicine became interested in the so-called normal, or nonpathological, functioning of human organisms as revealed through physiological studies and more especially through endocrinology, which led to an increasing emphasis on glandular disturbance. More recently psychiatrists have shown that many patients have severe emotional disturbances which give rise to a variety of illnesses and dysfunctions, so today medicine has become preoccupied with what are known as psychosomatic ills, calling for recognition of the "person in the patient," with his life history, his family and personality problems. More recently, medicine has become aware that important for diagnosis and treatment is a knowledge of the social-cultural matrix or "field" out of which the patient comes. This later development has reinforced the earlier programs of public health and preventive medicine and given further impetus to a concern for the investigation and, so far as possible, the alteration of the social-economic conditions and circumstances in which people live, work, and play, including their ethnic-cultural tradition.

Today the school is being asked to enlarge its responsibilities and to provide a variety of services, not only to pupils, but to their families, which development goes far beyond the traditional conception of the school as primarily if not exclusively for the teaching of a limited body of subject matter and academic skills. If schools are to meet these new responsibilities and to function not only more effectively but with an awareness of what they are doing to and for our social order, then it is imperative that educational administrators, deans of schools of education, and those engaged in educational research, development of educational materials and new practices, and the training of teachers should look to and accept from all the relevant disciplines whatever they provide as knowledge and guidance needed for these new and more or less complex tasks. Cultural anthropologists, because they have studied so many different cultures and have viewed the educational process as more than formal schooling, beginning from birth and continuing through the life cycle of adults, can make especially relevant and constructive contributions to education today. Moreover, in cultural anthropology we find an almost unique integration of the insights and awareness coming from the clinical studies of personality by psychology, psychiatry, and psychoanalysis together with the findings on many different cultures and social orders. These contributions have an unusual relevance for education, as pointed out by Dean Quillen and by Dr. Spindler in their introductory papers.

This conference and this report will, it is hoped, serve to stimulate and to refocus some of the concerns of educators into the channels suggested in the various papers presented at this meeting. As pointed out earlier, the conference was of necessity limited in scope to what it could undertake in a brief period of four days. It is hoped that further meetings of this kind will be held in the near future to carry on and extend these discussions so that the educational group may press further its search for relevant materials and approaches and in turn the anthropologist may become better acquainted with the thinking and problems of the professional educator. Through such continuing communications it may be expected that both educators and anthropologists will gain and will be better able to carry on their respective professional activities.

Finally, it should be pointed out that this conference, both explicitly and by implication in various papers and discussions, has shown the need for more critical and imaginative thinking in the field of educational philosophy, not only to provide a more relevant, suitable framework for thinking about education, but also to dissipate, if possible, some of the contemporary confusions and controversies engendered by professional educators with widely divergent ideas and conceptions of education and by lay writers and speakers, many of whom are resistant, if not strongly opposed, to any attempts to advance and improve our schools. It is indeed significant how often parents who are extremely solicitous about obtaining the latest and best medical care and treatment for their children demand that their children be taught by the methods and procedures of 1900 or earlier, as if there had been no increase in our knowledge and understanding of children and of the educational process since that date. The anthropologist may be especially helpful in resolving some of these difficulties by showing us how we can wisely and effectively preserve and advance our enduring goal values, by reformulating and transforming our aspirations in the light of new knowledge and new techniques, taking advantage of the new requirements and opportunities offered by our emerging industrial society. Anthropologists also may help us to remember that the strength and the potentialities of a culture are evoked through people's efforts to cope with new situations and to grasp new opportunities by social inventions and a wise vision of traditions. The reorientation of education is urgent so that we and our children can continue to strive for that which we have long sought.

LAWRENCE K. FRANK
New York City

CONTENTS

PARTICIPANTS

THEODORE BRAMELD is Professor of Educational Philosophy, New York University, and member of the staff of the Center for Human Relations Studies. He is author of *Minority Problems in the Public Schools, Patterns of Educational Philosophy*, and other books. He is now engaged in writing an interpretation of the significance of culture theory for educational policy and practice, with the assistance of a grant from the Wenner-Gren Foundation for Anthropological Research.

ROBERT N. BUSH is Associate Professor of Education, Stanford University, and Editor, *California Journal of Secondary Education*. His principal area is secondary education, and his research interests have centered around the problems of school staff personnel. He has been responsible for the development of the Stanford Consultation Service, the work of which features an interdisciplinary team approach (anthropology and sociology, psychology, psychiatry, and education) to the problems of teaching and administration in public and private schools, and is author of *The Teacher-Pupil Relationship*, a volume which draws upon and describes some of this work.

ARTHUR P. COLADARCI is Associate Professor of Education and Psychology, Stanford University. He is author of "The Relative Validity of Topical Areas in Educational Psychology" (*Teacher Ed. Qtly.*), "Are Educational Researchers Prepared to Do Meaningful Research?" (*Calif. J. of Ed. Res.*), "Research Priorities in Educational Administration" (*J. of Ed. Res.*), and other articles in educational and psychology journals.

WILLIAM H. COWLEY is David Jacks Professor of Higher Education at Stanford. After taking his Ph.D. in psychology at the University of Chicago in 1930, he gave most of his attention during nine years at Ohio State University to administration and from 1938 to 1944 served as President of Hamilton College. Since then he has been at Stanford giving all his time to seeking what he calls "a synoptic, integrated overview of American higher education."

CORA DuBOIS is Zemurray Professor at Harvard and Radcliffe, and formerly Director of Research, Institute of International Education. She is a member of the Social Science Research Council Committee on Cross-Cultural Education. She is author of *The People of Alor, Social Forces in Southeast Asia*, and monographs on California Indians and has done field work among American Indians in California, Nevada, Oregon, and Washington, and among the Alorese in the Netherlands Indies.

LAWRENCE K. FRANK was formerly Director, Caroline Zachry Institute of Human Development, New York. He is author of *Society as the Patient, How to Help Your Child in School* (with Mary H. Frank), *Nature and Human Nature: Man's New Image of Himself, Understanding Children's Play* (with Ruth Hartley and Robert Goldenson), *Feelings and Emotions, Individual Development,* several other books, and numerous papers in professional and lay journals.

JOHN GILLIN is Research Professor of Anthropology at the University of North Carolina. He is the author of *The Ways of Man, The Barama River Caribs of British Guiana, Moche: A Peruvian Coastal Community, The Culture of Security in San Carlos, Cultural Sociology* (with J. L. Gillin), *For a Science of Social Man* (with others), and a long list of other anthropological monographs and articles. He has done field work in Algeria, Europe, New Mexico, Northern Wisconsin, British Guiana, Ecuador, Upper Amazon Valley, Peru, Cuba, Colombia, and Guatemala.

PAUL ROBERT HANNA is Lee L. Jacks Professor of Child Education, School of Education, Stanford University, and former Director of the Educational Division, U.S. Mutual Security Agency, Philippine Islands. He is author or editor of many social studies textbooks, spelling textbooks, professional educational books, and official publications of educational organizations.

CHARLES W. M. HART is Professor of Anthropology at the University of Wisconsin. He is author of articles on Australian ethnology and social organization, and on industrial communities in Canada. He has done field work in northern Australia, northern Ontario, and Windsor, Canada.

JULES HENRY is Associate Professor of Anthropology, Washington University, St. Louis, Missouri, Visiting Associate Professor of Anthropology, University of Chicago, and Research Associate, The Sonia Shankman Orthogenic School, University of Chicago. He is author of *Jungle People, Doll Play of Pilagá Indian Children,* "Speech Disturbances in Pilagá Indian Children" (*Amer. J. of Orthopsychiatry*), "Child Rearing, Culture, and the Natural World" (*Psychiatry*). He has done field work among the Apache Indians in Arizona, the Kaingang of Brazil, the Pilagá of Argentina, the Tarahumara of Mexico, and in the public elementary schools in Chicago.

FELIX M. KEESING is Professor of Anthropology and executive head of the Department of Sociology and Anthropology at Stanford University. He has carried on extensive research since 1925 in the Pacific area (Samoa, Philippines, etc.) and among the Menomini Indians of Wisconsin. His main field of research interest, culture change, has included study of educational systems, old and new, among such peoples. He has published a number of books, monographs, and papers, including the report of a seminar conference on anthropology and education held at the University of Hawaii in 1936 (*Education in Pacific Countries*).

SOLON T. KIMBALL is Professor of Education, Department of Social and Philosophical Foundations at Teachers College, Columbia University, and former Chairman of the Department of Sociology and Anthropology, University of Alabama. His publications include *Family and Community in Ireland* (with C. M. Arensburg) and *The Talladega Story: A Study in Community Process* (with Marion Pearsall). He has done community research in Newburyport, Massachusetts; County Clare, Ireland; rural Michigan; Talladega, Alabama; and among the Navaho Indians.

ALFRED L. KROEBER is Emeritus Professor of Anthropology, and formerly Chairman, Department of Anthropology, University of California. He is editor of *Anthropology Today* and author of *Anthropology* (a general text), *Configurations of Cultural Growth, The Concept of Culture* (with Clyde Kluckhohn), *Cultural and Natural Areas of Native North America, The Nature of Culture,* and a long and illustrious list of monographs and articles. He has done field work among many American Indian tribes west of the Mississippi and is a pioneer worker in the ethnology of the California Indians.

DOROTHY LEE is Consultant in Teaching at the Merrill-Palmer School, Detroit, Michigan, formerly Professor of Anthropology, Vassar College. She is author of articles in professional journals on the conceptual and value aspects of culture, and other publications in ethnology. She has done field work in Melanesia, among the Wintu Indians of California, and in public schools in the United States.

WILLIAM E. MARTIN is Associate Professor of Child Development, College of Education, University of Illinois. He is author of *Child Development: The Process of Growing Up in Society* (with Celia B. Stendler), *Readings in Child Development* (with Celia B. Stendler), *Intergroup Education in the Kindergarten and Primary Grades* (with Celia B. Stendler), "Growing Up in an Anxious Age" (*A.S.C.D. Yearbook*, 1952), "The Child in a World of Numbers" (*Childh. Educ.*), "The Development of Values in Children" (*J. Genet. Psychol.*), and a long list of research papers in various psychological journals. He was given the 1953 Award for Outstanding Research by the American Personnel and Guidance Association.

MARGARET MEAD is Associate Curator of Ethnology, American Museum of Natural History, and Adjunct Professor of Anthropology, Columbia University. She has made comparative studies of education in eight different cultures during the last twenty-nine years, and has been continuously interested in the contribution of anthropological findings to education. From among the long list of books, monographs, and articles that she has authored, some of those particularly relevant for the purposes of this volume include *Coming of Age in Samoa, Growing Up in New Guinea,* and *The School in American Culture* (Inglis Lecture).

I. JAMES QUILLEN is Professor of Education and Dean of the School of Education at Stanford University. He was Co-director of the Stanford Social Education Investigation (1938–44), Co-chairman of the Committee on the Function of the Social Studies in General Education (1937–40), President of the National Council for the Social Studies (1944), and an official of the UNESCO Secretariat in Paris, France (1948–49). His professional publications include *The Social Studies in General Education* (with others), *Textbook Improvement and International Understanding,* and *Education for Social Competence* (with Lavone Hanna).

EDUCATION AND ANTHROPOLOGY

FANNIE R. SHAFTEL is Associate Professor of Elementary Education, Stanford University. Her publications include articles in *Educational Leadership, Sociatry, Elementary English Journal, Childhood Education*, a booklet, *Role-Playing. The Problem Story* (Intergroup Education), and "Creating a Good Environment for Learning" (*A.S.C.D., Nat. Ed. Assoc. Yearbook*, 1954). Her special interest is curriculum development, with emphasis on social studies and human relations.

BERNARD J. SIEGEL is Associate Professor of Anthropology, Stanford University. His publications include "Currents of Anthropological Theory and Value Concepts" (*Southwestern J. Anthro.*), "Suggested Factors of Culture Change at Taos Pueblo" (*Proc. 29th Internat. Congress of Americanists*), and "Implications of Social Structure for Economic Change in Brazil" (in *Economic Growth*, Joseph Spengler, ed.). He has done field work in a Syrian community in Boston, at Taos Pueblo, New Mexico, and in communities in Brazil and Portugal.

GEORGE D. SPINDLER holds a joint appointment as Associate Professor in the School of Education, in the Social Foundations area, and in the Department of Sociology and Anthropology, Stanford University. He is author of "American Character in the Military" (*Psychiatry*), "An Experimental Design for the Study of Culture Change" (*Southwestern J. Anthro.*), *Menomini Acculturation*, and other articles in anthropological and educational journals. He has done field work in school systems in coastal California communities, and among the Menomini and Winnebago Indians of Wisconsin.

HILDA TABA is Professor of Education, San Francisco State College, formerly Director, Center of Intergroup Education, University of Chicago, and Director, Intergroup Education in Co-operating Schools, Council on Education. Her publications include *Cultural Attitudes and International Understanding, Intergroup Education in Public Schools, Diagnosing Human Relations Needs, Sociometry and Group Relations, Adolescent Personality and Character Development* (with Robert J. Havighurst), and other articles on human relations in American schools and intergroup education.

LAWRENCE GREGG THOMAS is Associate Professor of Educational Philosophy, Stanford University. He is author of *Mental Tests as Instruments of Science, Education in Wartime and After* (with others), *Syllabus in Philosophy of Education* (with Ganders and Armentrout), and many articles in general education and educational philosophy.

Section I

AN INTRODUCTION TO ANTHROPOLOGY AND EDUCATION

I. James Quillen
Stanford University

Professional educators today face many problems. These problems are produced by such factors as the complexity and heterogeneity of American culture, the rapidity and inco-ordination of cultural change, the effort to provide equality of educational opportunity for all children and youth, the increase in the birth rate, the competition for the tax dollar, current ideological conflict, and conflicting theories of education. Educational problems center in such areas as the cultural role and objectives of education, the organization and administration of the school, the content of education, methods of teaching and learning, the evaluation and guidance of the student, and public relations and the provision of adequate financial support.

In the solution of school problems, professional educators have for some time utilized knowledge from such disciplines as biology, psychology, history, philosophy, and sociology. More recently increasing attention has been directed toward anthropology as a resource for conceptual knowledge and research methods which can contribute directly to the improvement of education. Anthropologists and educators have recognized areas of common interest and concern and have begun to work together on common problems. These co-operative efforts have been limited thus far, but this symposium is an indication both of the significant progress that has been made and of future possibilities. This introductory paper attempts to define some of the problem areas in education where anthropology can make a contribution. The overview by George Spindler, following, maps out some areas in anthropology that are relevant to these problems and surveys the articulation and historical contacts of the two fields.

Education is the instrument through which cultures perpetuate themselves. It is the process through which the members of a society assure themselves that the behavior necessary to continue their culture is learned. Since education is a cultural process, it is important for educators to have a clear conception of the meaning of culture. Confusion over this meaning is an important factor in confusion and conflict concerning the proper role of the school. Here is a basic area where anthropologists can make a significant contribution.

1

The school is concerned with the transmission, conservation, and extension of culture. Cultural transmission and personality formation are perhaps the two most important functions of the school. The anthropologist deals with enculturation, acculturation, and socialization. A knowledge of these processes as they occur in a variety of cultures can help educators to secure a clearer conception of their roles and provide them with a reservoir of tested experience from which they can draw ideas and techniques that may be useful in American schools. An understanding of the relationship between culture and personality will shed light on the nature-nurture conflict in education and contribute to improved guidance and counseling procedures.

For some time there has been considerable conflict in the United States concerning the role of education in the extension and improvement of American culture. This conflict became acute during the depression period and has been intensified by the current concern about communism. George Counts dramatized the issue when he wrote *Dare the School Build a New Social Order?* The problem here concerns the role of the school in cultural innovation. This is another area where the interests of anthropologists and educators converge.

The school is only one educative agency in American culture, and perhaps not the most important. The family, church, young people's organizations, and the media of mass communication all play important roles in the education of the child. In many instances, out-of-school agencies, particularly the mass media, compete with the school for the attention of the child and produce behavioral changes which are contradictory to those which the school is trying to establish. In other instances, out-of-school agencies reinforce the efforts of teachers and other school personnel. If formal education is to be effective, teachers need to understand the role and influence of nonschool educational experiences. Content from anthropology can help greatly toward this end.

Education involves the changing of behavior in a desirable direction. The school is an educational institution specifically established to produce desirable changes in behavior. Educational objectives consist of descriptions of behavior which the school seeks to produce. The over-all objectives of the school are defined by a description of the behavior of the ideal citizen, including his knowledge, values, skills, and abilities. In a heterogeneous culture such as ours, the description of the ideal citizen is difficult, and confusion and conflict concerning educational objectives result. Anthropologists can help educators to develop a conception of the ideal cultural man and can assist in identifying the core values which Americans seek to preserve and perpetuate in an age of conflict.

The school program of study consists of those areas of experience and content which are essential to the development of the desired characteristics of behavior which have been chosen as objectives. The contents and experiences included in the school program are selected from the total range of possibilities which exist in the culture. Intelligent selection can be based only on considerable cultural insight and understanding. If those who make the school curriculum do not understand the changing culture of which they are a part, deadwood will be carried indefinitely in the school program, and there will be important gaps in what is taught and learned. Harold Benjamin showed the proneness of schools to perpetuate outmoded content and experiences in his satire, *The Saber-Tooth Curriculum*.

The complexity, heterogeneity, and rapidity of change in modern culture make the selection of curriculum content particularly difficult. Anthropologists can help educators to understand better their community, nation, and world. The techniques of community study developed by anthropologists can be used by teachers to study their own community.

Methods of teaching and learning are perpetual problems in education. How can methods be used in the classroom that will transfer directly to effectiveness in living outside the school? What methods are most appropriate to the development of democratic citizenship? How can spiritual and moral values best be developed? How can the school produce sound character and wholesome personality? These are questions that many teachers are asking today. Anthropologists can help teachers understand how imitation, participation, communication, and informal methods are used to further enculturation in other cultures. They can also contribute to an understanding of the relationship between cultural motivation, incentives, and values and school learning.

A number of educators and social scientists have been concerned recently about the effects of the cultural experiences of an individual on his performance in intelligence tests. This has resulted in an effort to develop a "culture fair" intelligence test. Teachers need to be helped to see the significance of such activities in the furtherance of equality of educational opportunity.

Closely related to the question of the meaning of the I.Q. is the question of grouping. To what extent is homogeneous grouping in the school compatible with the values of democracy? What is the significance of the variety of cultural backgrounds of American children and youth for grouping and educational methods generally? The heterogeneity of American culture provides an excellent opportunity for the development of intergroup understanding and the improvement of human relations. In this area the concept of race is of special importance. Anthropologists can help clarify the meaning of race and the relationship between race, intelligence, and culture.

Finally, educators have become increasingly concerned about the development of intercultural and international understanding. A number of educators and anthropologists have participated in UNESCO's activities in this area. Educators need to be helped to develop more effective techniques for the study of the ways of living of people of other cultures. In many instances comparative culture studies in the school tend to reinforce prejudice rather than to increase understanding and appreciation. In addition to intercultural and international understanding, educators are concerned with the role of education in the international technical assistance programs. American educational methods are now being exported to other nations. To what extent is this possible and desirable? How can American educators contribute most effectively to the improvement of the ways of living of people of other cultures? These are pressing problems where anthropological knowledge and research can again make a major contribution.

The papers and discussions included in this volume are addressed to some of these problems, and others will emerge out of the cross-disciplinary interchange within the group discussions. It may be anticipated that future studies and similar conferences will provide approaches unanticipated at present.

ANTHROPOLOGY AND EDUCATION:
AN OVERVIEW

GEORGE D. SPINDLER
Stanford University

Though no "educational anthropology" exists at present, and this conference is not aimed at its creation, the purpose of this overview paper is to survey the articulation of these two fields. Education is not listed in *Anthropology Today* (Kroeber, 1953) as a field of application for anthropology. There are only rare instances of self-conscious attention to the mutual relevance of these two fields in the various interdisciplinary symposia. Few professional anthropologists are required by the institutional definition of their positions to interact with professional educationists, and only a handful of joint appointments in education and anthropology exist in American colleges and universities.

Despite this, some educational philosophers cite the concept of culture as most important in their systematic thinking, modern texts used in the training of teachers abound with references to anthropological literature, elementary school teachers include projects on "Peoples in Other Lands" and "Our Indian Friends," and a growing number of departments of anthropology are offering courses with the specific needs of teachers-in-training in mind. But most surprising is the fact that the relations between these two fields have a history in this country extending back to at least 1904, when Hewett wrote his first pieces on education for the *American Anthropologist* (1904, 1905).

These introductory statements suggest that a whole symposium of papers could be devoted to the systematic explication of these sometimes obscure and unacknowledged relationships. Only this overview paper will serve this interest directly. Its purpose is to outline the parts of both anthropology and education as they articulate into one mutually relevant framework of interests, trace briefly the history of such articulations, indicate what anthropologists have written about education and what educators have used of what anthropologists have written, and describe certain potentials and problems that exist in the relationships. It follows upon the introductory statement by Dean Quillen of the problems in education for which anthropological help is sought.

The purpose of this overview is thus sharply different from that of the rest of the papers in this symposium. It is *about* the relations of education and anthropology. The other papers are designed to put into motion some applications of mutual relevance to both fields. They are experimental and question-raising, therefore, since no articulated education-anthropology structure exists from which they could draw. Most of them move well out toward the margins, away from traditional anthropological interests. This is not necessarily good, but it is assuredly inevitable.

Relevant Fields and Interests in Anthropology

Some of anthropology articulates, or can articulate, with education, and some of it does not. Anthropology as the "study of man," with its traditional interests in cultural variability, culture history—both ethnological and archeological—language, race, and human evolution, is admittedly a prime potential contributor to a good general education. While no claim is made here that anthropology should necessarily become the skeleton or the core of a complete "liberal arts" education at the secondary school or college level, it seems clear that no other existing discipline provides an integration, however loose, of so much that is important concerning man and his manifold behaviors. The study of man thus broadly conceived makes it possible to bridge the gap between the human animal and the human being, to conceive of both the relativity and universality of human behavior and propositions about it, to project human affairs upon a time plane that stretches far into the past and future, and turns the focus upon the basic round of life and man's relation to nature.

It is not even necessary, as is often done, to argue that the vicarious cross-cultural experience afforded by an anthropological Cook's tour leads to a better understanding of our own culture. It does or can lead to a more universalistic understanding of human life, and this is more important. Anything else is a by-product.

The implication is clear that anthropology should be used as a contribution to general education more widely than it is. It should not be taught as it is to young anthropologists-in-training or as it usually is at the college level—as an introduction to a discipline—but rather as an introduction to a new perspective on human life. It should also be taught at the secondary school level, possibly under some more conventional and already-existing rubric (Spindler, 1946). It is being taught at the elementary school level when teachers develop lesson units or activities centering on American Indian tribes—but sometimes badly because the teachers have had little or no exposure to anthropology as such and consequently contravene the primary goals of this kind of curriculum design. Anthropologists have been aware of these possible contributions of their field to general education and have written about it (Ehrich, 1947 ; Howells, 1952) but they have only rarely done anything about it, because they conceive of themselves primarily as producers of data and contributors to science and secondarily as teachers or curriculum designers.

In the sense outlined above, all of anthropology is relevant to education.

From this point on, the relationships real and potential are more selective. But these selections need not be made only from the sociocultural side of the discipline. Indeed, the contribution of physical anthropology to education had an early and significant beginning in Montessori's fascinating applications in a "pedagogical anthropology" (Montessori, 1913). To be sure, Maria Montessori, though armed with millimetric tape measures and anthropometers, called for recognition of educable man as a "speaking animal" and a "social animal," and in her practiced philosophy of education anticipated Goldenweiser's arguments for an anthropologically sound and progressive "education for social participation" (Goldenweiser, 1939). But more of Montessori later.

Aside from Montessori the most important contribution of physical anthropology to education has been on the subject of race, and the relationships—or rather the lack of them—between race, culture, and intelligence. Anthropological perspectives on the meaning of race and the myth of racial superiority have been popularized by Ethel Alpenfels in her capacity as staff anthropologist for the Bureau for Intercultural Education, and have become familiar to every well-grounded social studies teacher through this and other agencies. Otto Klineberg has given us the classic treatment on relationships between race, culture, and I.Q. (1935), that has wide circulation in an encapsulated form in a UNESCO pamphlet (1951) and a symposium edited by Linton (1947).

What has not been used sufficiently in education from physical anthropology are the techniques, concepts, and methodology concerning growth patterns, maturational sequences, sexual differences, and glandular processes that could add needed dimensions to the psychosomatic data of educational psychology. Nor have the school plant planners—a new specialization in education—yet consulted the physical anthropologists for ideas, methods, or facts on the anthropometry of the classroom. If anthropologists can design better bucket seats for flying boxcars, they can also design better desks for school children and contribute heretofore unconsidered applications to playground equipment, audio-visual devices, space-to-person ratios, and lavatories.

Directly relevant to the interests of this seminar-conference are the concepts and data of specialized and relatively new fields in anthropology, such as personality in culture and cultural dynamics. In fact, when anthropology-education relations are considered, this is usually where people in both disciplines begin to look first.

For some, interests in cross-cultural education are identical with interests in cross-cultural socialization. This creates confusion. Socialization of the child to human, group-accepted status is a total process of growth and adaptation. The center of the process is the child—adapting to an environment structured by culture, as well as by group size, climate, terrain, ecology, and the peculiar personalities of his always-unique parents or parental surrogates. Education is not this whole process. It is what is done to a child, by whom, under what conditions, and to what purpose. It is the process of transmitting culture—if we can think of culture as including skills, knowledge, attitudes, and values, as well as discrete elements of behavior. It is the culture of the human being—where culture is used as a verb.

There are many books, monographs, and articles by anthropologists reporting research on socialization of the child in environments structured by various cultural sets. The most recent significant comparative research is Whiting and Child's *Child Training and Personality* (1953). There are relatively few studies on education. British anthropologists, with their functional predilections, have provided many of the most useful descriptive analyses of education as cultural transmission in particular cultural settings. One of the better studies by an American anthropologist in terms of application to the who, what, when, where questions has been produced by Pettit, as he summarizes and analyzes education in North American Indian cultures (Pettit, 1946). This work illustrates the kind of thing that needs to be done with more comparative cross-cultural data.

This suggests the relevance of another field of anthropology—traditional ethnography—the factual core of cultural anthropology. Pettit drew his data from ethnographies written by others. The fact that he could do so is a tribute to the inclusiveness of good ethnography. But he had to search for the relevant facts and too often couldn't find them, or could find only indirect allusions to a who, what, when, and how process in cultural transmission. The success of his search indicates that an ethnographic corpus lies waiting to be cannibalized by researchers interested in cross-cultural education, but that more definitive and inclusive categories of observation need to be devised if future reports are to be of maximum use. Ethnography has produced the raw materials for more treatment than has been committed—and it also furnishes the sources for the vicarious "culture shock" that is an essential step in the education of a public school teacher.

That amorphous and loosely defined problem area in anthropology called cultural dynamics is the source of many relevances—most of them potential. If this field is seen as that concerned primarily with processes of culture change and stability, its relation to educationist interests is immediately clear. Change and stability must be mediated by what is transmitted from parent to child in the educative process. This transmission process is not seen as a causative variable—excepting within a limited interaction cycle. But unless this variable intervening between changes in conditions of life and the adaptations of people is understood, the "dynamic" part of cultural dynamics is left unilluminated. And the educative process can be understood better by viewing it as such an intervening variable, for then it is seen as an instrumentality that is sensitive to the cultural and extracultural exigencies under which it operates. Anthropologists have done little systematizing here. Herskovits has supplied one of the few explicit statements in his "Education and Cultural Dynamics" (1943).

One field of interest in anthropology that has realized relatively more of its potential in relation to educational problems is that of social structure.

If the interests here are conceived as broadly relating to group alignments, prestige ranking, status and role interrelationships, and social control in the community context, all of the very useful work of the Warner group and other closely related efforts may be regarded as a contribution from this area. The contributors include, besides Warner, such workers as Allison Davis, Gardner, Dollard, Loeb, Withers, Useem, and many non-anthropologists who have been strongly influenced therein — such as Havighurst, Taba, Hollingshead, the Lynds, *et al.* The relevance of this field to education, particularly with respect to a concept of social class that has been regularized by Warner and his associates, is indicated by two recent special issues of the *Harvard Educational Review* on the subject (1953). No claim is made that this is exclusively an anthropological domain or contribution, but one of the mainsprings driving the interest and its application is fastened to an anthropological pivot.

In this instance the situation as it exists otherwise in the various potential or emergent articulations with education is reversed. More is known about how the educative process is affected by social class and community structure in Jonesville and Elmtown than in the nonliterate societies that are the accustomed habitat of the anthropologists. To be sure, nonliterate societies rarely have social classes in the same sense that Jonesville has, but some do, and all have groups structured into a social organization. Whether this structure is formalized by a widely ramifying kinship system, or by rank, or by a complex political-social system, or is atomistic and individuated—the who, what, when, and why of education will reflect this structure at every turn. For the sake of a clearer concept of education as a sociocultural process something more should be known about these functional interrelationships between educative system, educative process, and social structure in non-Western and particularly smaller, simpler societies.

Relevant Fields and Interests in Education

When the sights are turned on education, it becomes clear that there are more relevant problems and interests than anthropologists could begin to bear appropriate gifts to—even if they were so motivated. Some of the particularly significant problems have been succinctly described by James Quillen. Others have been listed by Fannie Shaftel in a memorandum circulated to the participants in this conference. The discussion below will approach some of these same problems from a different perspective and describe certain interests and fields in education in which these problems occur.

One of the areas within education that most obviously calls for an anthropological contribution is that of the "foundation" fields. These are designated by various names in teachers' colleges and schools of education about the country. The general rubrics are social, psychological, philosophical, historical and comparative, and biological. They represent what is drawn into education as a science, and into education as a professional field, from the behavioral and social sciences, the humanities, and natural sciences, as their data and concepts are used in empirical and logico-deductive analyses of the educative process, and in the training of teachers.

Anthropology has only recently begun to make a significant contribution to these fields, largely because of its newness as an academic discipline. Within the social-behavioral foundations, educational psychology has clearly dominated the scene, partly because of a historical accident that institutionally wedded psychology and education rather early—at least in America — and partly because the problems of educational tests and measurements, principles of learning, and personality development have been naturals for psychological applications. In many teacher-training institutions psychology is still the only behavioral science explicitly recognized in the organization of professional education courses.

Of the various social sciences, education as a professional field has drawn from political science, economics, and jurisprudence, but particularly from sociology. Educational sociology has its own house organ, numerous texts bearing its name, and an impressive pile of research to its credit. Most foundation courses in professional education in the social area are called "educational sociology." In a few places where teachers are trained in America—particularly at Teachers College at Columbia under the leadership of Lyman Bryson and now Solon T. Kimball, at New York University under Ethel Alpenfels, and at Chicago, Harvard, Yale, and Stanford—an explicit anthropological contribution is integrated with those of other social sciences in the foundation program. Hunter College, in New York City, may soon be the site of an unusually wide-ranging curriculum of "foundational" education and anthropology (Rosenstiel 1954), and New York University's School of Education has a long-standing development of this sort. Courses in anthropology are required of teachers-in-training at some universities and colleges where there is no formalized integration of anthropological contributions with the foundation fields in education.

At Stanford, as an illustration of the ways in which anthropology can contribute to the foundation fields in teacher training, relevant materials are presented in three courses: "Social Foundations in Education"; "Cultural Transmission"; and "Social Anthropology in Education." These courses are given under the aegis of a joint appointment in the School of Education and the Department of Sociology and Anthropology, and credit is given in both fields.

"Social Foundations in Education" is required of all upper division education students and all candidates for the Master of Arts degree in education, as well as for the various professional credentials. It combines selected materials from sociology, anthropology, and social psychology. The anthropological contribution lies mainly in a systematic analysis of American cultural patterns and values as they bear directly upon the role and functions of the teacher and public school system. Cross-cultural data are used here for illustrative purposes. Other topical areas covered include social class and education, problems in student-teacher communication, group stereotypes and prejudice in schools, the community context of the school, and the school as a social system.

"Cultural Transmission" is offered as a course for doctoral candidates, and is presented within the advanced social foundations sequence in education. Its coverage includes the construction of a frame of reference for viewing transmission and enculturation processes. This frame of reference is then used in the analysis of these processes in two nonliterate societies, one European society, and American society. The course ends with analysis of case studies of selected types of teachers and their classrooms, and schools, in our society. Sociometric, autobiographic, socioeconomic, observational, and community "social base" data are included in the case study materials.

"Social Anthropology in Education" is a seminar constituted of a majority of advanced graduate students in education and a sprinkling of degree candidates in anthropology and psychology. It has been devoted so far to an analysis of the educative process in nonliterate societies, using standard ethnographic references. A simple outline of educative process is used, with major headings like "teaching personnel," "content taught," "time and sequence of impact," "techniques used," and "formal and informal contexts."

These courses accomplish different things in different ways. An important point in relation to the problem of education-anthropology articulation is that only in the seminar is the greater part of the frame of reference supplied by anthropology; in the other courses it seems essential to provide an integration of selected aspects of sociology and psychology. This is not simply because the titles of the courses are self-determinative. When the educative process is the focus and particularly in our own society, the anthropological frame of reference is not sufficient alone. But it is essential. The core of the contribution is in the attention to culture as a behavioral compulsive, as a perception-directing set of patterns, and in the attention to the variable forms these patterns take. *Cultural awareness* is one vital aim of each course, but not merely generalized cultural awareness; the aim is to create in the teacher an awareness of how culture influences specifically what he does as a teacher, and how to think about, observe, and analyze this influence. Courses in conventional institutionalized anthropology do not serve this same purpose, though they are quite necessary as a first phase of the experiences of the student in training as a professional educator.

This role of anthropology in the foundation fields of education may be regarded as a contribution to teacher training. The conclusion to be drawn is that it does not suffice to throw some standard anthropology courses at the teacher-in-training. By the time he is preparing to be a professional educator, or is improving his already established proficiency, he should have had an introduction to the materials of at least cultural anthropology as a part of his general education. The anthropology he gets in his *pro-*

fessional education should be integrated with the other foundational offerings and used to solve problems in analysis of educative process. Otherwise we are asking him to provide this integration and this application; and most students—in education or otherwise—simply cannot.

There are other parts of the structure of professional education that need, or at least can use, some anthropological help: curriculum construction, for instance, once largely psychology-based, is now beginning to be socioculturally based as well. Elementary school curricula are being reorganized with direct attention to culture content, universal human activities, cultural values, and sequences of culturally patterned experience (Hanna, 1954). The emphasis on intergroup relations and utilization of community resources in the development of social education curricula in elementary schools likewise indicates this shift (Taba, 1950; Willcockson, 1950).

Other relevant interests in education are represented in the problems of educational administration, and the training of professional educational administrators. Cultural awareness is perhaps even more important for the administrator, since he manipulates the setting in which the teacher interacts with students and parents. He must not only have cultural awareness but must also understand the mechanics of culture change, the cultural expectations affecting the leader's role, the concrete as well as idealistic meaning of cultural values, and the social system of the school in the setting of the encompassing community and national social structure. Anthropology has a clear potential utility on the first three scores. In the latter instance sociology supplies more materials perhaps, but does so through community study approaches that are at least claimed to be partly an anthropological invention.

Up to this point the discussion of fields and interests in education relevant to the problem of education-anthropology articulation has centered mainly upon the training and manipulative side of professional education. But education as a professional field is not only concerned with teacher training, teaching, curriculum design, and administration of schools; it has a research base. Probably no social or behavioral science has as great a backlog of research nor encompasses such a high degree of variability of quality of research. The reason for the first is obvious. The reason for the second is partly that education crosscuts every phase of human activity and it is impossible to do good research without a high degree of specialization in the science or discipline treating with selected dimensions within this range. This is very difficult when so much has to be done all at once.

Be that as it may, there are many phases of research within the framework of education that call for anthropological attention. There has been an incorporation of anthropologically based concepts and methods in the studies of social class influences on learning (Davis, 1952), social class and community structures in relation to the social organization of the school and educational opportunities (Warner, Loeb, *et al.*, 1944), and problems of adolescence (Havighurst and Taba, 1949), in the extensive study of the relationships between intelligence and cultural differences by the Chicago group (Eells *et al.*, 1951), and in the studies of social class differences in socialization with their implications for education (Davis and Havighurst, 1947). This interest in social class and learning, and social class and school organization, has been the main stream of influence on research directly relevant to education and stemming from anything that can be regarded as an anthropological source. The main contribution of anthropology, other than in the form of some of the personnel involved, has been in the notion of cultural relativity, and in a functional total-community approach. As for methodology, it is doubtful that many clear claims to contributions can be made by anthropology, other than in a devotion to informants and informal participant observation.

Thus a definite and extensive contribution to research on educational problems, in American society at least, has yet to be made. This is a reflection of the fact that anthropologists have not been very interested in our own society until quite recently. Their proper object of study has been the nonliterate peoples, in their pure or reconstructed form, or as they have struggled for existence under the impact of the industrial-based civilizations.

Anthropologists have been interested and involved with the problem of education in dependent, trust, and colonial territories, and Indian reservations, where nonliterate indigenes have been exposed to a Western-mediated education. But the involvement has been largely in terms of an applied anthropology, in various administrative and consultative capacities, and actual research reports on the processes involved are quite scarce. Felix Keesing has described some of the interesting problems that arise in these contexts in a summary of the content of a seminar conference including educators, anthropologists, sociologists, and government officials on the problems of education in Pacific countries (Keesing, 1937). Margaret Mead has provided a provocative analysis of the feasible educational objectives and the major factors to be taken into account in the twentieth-century education of dependent peoples (1946).

There are many areas of potential application of anthropologically based concepts and methods in educational research in our own society to which attention may some day be given. The roles of teacher and school administrator in American society call for treatment from a cultural point of view that will call attention to some of the excruciating paradoxes projected in the role expectations. The effect of culturally-based values upon teacher perceptions of behavior and personal qualities of students needs to be explicated in a way that the positionally-oriented social class studies have not yet developed. The informal transmission of value orientations and covert culture by teachers and in peer groups has received only preliminary attention. New approaches to the study of the school as a social system need to be devised—perhaps in the manner of the factory system studies that were in part anthropologically inspired. American culture as a specific context of the goals, expectations, and functions of education needs exploration—possibly in the vein of national character approaches.

The conceptual categories and symbolic referents of speech in communication between teacher and child call for a meta-linguistic, language-in-culture application.

Particularly appropriate to traditional anthropological interests is the need for cross-cultural research in education that illuminates the process in our own society indirectly but powerfully. This must be distinguished, as indicated, from primarily psychologically oriented interests in socialization. The educative process—the who, what, when, where, and how of common-human and culturally variable cultural transmission—furnishes understanding of not only basic processes of education but also cultural dynamics, for education thus broadly conceived is culture in motion. Culture is idealized in the educative process. Every teacher, whether mother's brother or Miss Humboldt of Peavey Falls, re-enacts and defends the cultural drama as experienced. As the culture is passed on from one generation to the next in the hands of the teacher, it assumes a patent and rationalized shape. The whole world view is somehow encapsulated in each gesture, admonition, indoctrination, or explanation. And this seems equally true whether physics or sacred dreamtime truths are being taught.

Some of these possibilities are elaborated in various ways in the papers of this conference. Many of them will stay in the state of possibility only. But other approaches and avenues not seen as yet will be opened, perhaps as a result of this conference.

The Routes of Diffusion

Anthropological routes.—Some of the routes of diffusion of concepts and knowledge between education and anthropology have been described. The community structure–educational system stream of influence has been most important. Montessori's influence is another, and of longer standing (1913). Her principal assumptions have been integrated into the framework of modern progressive education. She saw clearly the need for stressing the "organic" relation of the whole child to the environment, emphasized the developmental process so that the child was not seen as a "diminutive adult," anticipated the problem of the differential meaning of school experience to children from various social classes and ethnic groups in her concept of a "regional ethnology" and study of local conditions, called for respect for individual differences in growth and function, demanded that a "scientific pedagogy" concern itself with normal individuals primarily, and developed a "biographical chart" that took the place of the report card and included "antecedents"—vocation of parents, their aesthetic culture, their morality and sentiments and care of children—as well as reports of physical and psychological examinations and on-going observations in the form of "diaries."

Education may contest the characterization of this as an anthropological influence, since Montessori is so clearly a part of the educationist's heritage, but she called her approach a "Pedagogical Anthropology," and used what were regarded, in Italy at least, as anthropological concepts, methods, techniques, and data. Though her cultural anthropology is guilty of what today would be regarded as certain racist errors, and her physical anthropology is now outmoded, her farsighted anticipation of much of the best of the contemporary art and science of education is impressive. Whether this is true because she had genius or because she had an anthropological orientation cannot be divined. She had both.

A history of anthropology-to-education diffusion cannot omit the early contributions of Edgar L. Hewett (1904, 1905). His articles "Anthropology and Education" (1904) and "Ethnic Factors in Education" (1905) in the *American Anthropologist* were the first and almost the last contributions of their kind in that journal. He argued for an "enrichment of the course of study of every public school in the land" through the incorporation of ethnological materials, particularly on culture history not confined to the Western world; called for joint meetings of the national education and anthropology societies to discuss mutual problems; scored culture historians for misuse and lack of use of ethnological data; claimed the clear relevance of an "ethnic psychology" that would contribute to the teacher's understanding of the fact that ". . . Italian and Bohemian, Celt and Hebrew, Anglo-Saxon and African, look upon questions of honor, morality, and decency out of separate ethnic minds . . ."; asked educators to realize that "a civilization imposed from without is usually harmful, often destructive, always undesirable," because the "development of a race must be from within"; and suggested that for all these reasons "normal schools and other institutions for the training of teachers should give a prominent place to the anthropological sciences." The fact that none of his calls was implemented reflects partly an ethnocentrism of American culture, partly the peculiar conservatism of American public education, and particularly the fact that American anthropologists did not have time for much of anything but ethnographic and culture history salvage until the 1930's.

Franz Boas, the dean of American anthropology, clearly saw the relevance of anthropological and educational interests. In his *Anthropology and Modern Life* (1928) he devotes one whole chapter to these interests. He points out that "anthropological research offers, therefore, a means of determining what may be expected of children of different ages, and this knowledge is of considerable value for regulating educational methods." He talks of "normative data for development," sex differences, ethnic differences, and differences in environmental conditions that should be taken into account. He treats of some of the problems of cultural transmission, and points out that "our public schools are hardly conscious of the conflict" between democratic ideas of freedom and flexibility, and coercion; "they instill automatic reactions to symbols by means of patriotic ceremonial, in many cases by indirect religious appeal, and too often through the automatic reactions to the behavior of the teacher that is imitated." He suggests that tradition-based transmission of values and ethics is particularly strong among intellectuals and that the "masses" respond "more quickly and energetically to the demands of the hour than the educated classes . . ."

The writings of Montessori, Hewett, and Boas on anthropology and education have been discussed in some detail because an examination of what anthropologists have written since then reveals that, with some notable exceptions, not much more has been said, and a critical examination of the implementation of their suggestions indicates that no more than a beginning has actually been accomplished.

Articles by anthropologists on this subject have turned up persistently in educational journals and elsewhere for the past twenty-five years. The place of anthropology in a college education, the contributions of anthropology to the training of teachers, the place of primitive education in the history of education are the favorite themes. The articles add to what their forerunners spelled out, but few of them produce clear innovations. Exceptions to this general rule include Mead's suggestive article on education in the perspective of primitive cultures (1943) and her Inglis Lectures, under the title, *The School in American Culture* (1950); Kluckhohn's comments in *Mirror for Man* (1949); Opler's "Cultural Alternatives and Educational Theory" (1947); Goldenweiser's "Culture and Education" (1939); and Herskovits' stimulating discussion in his text, *Man and His Works* (1948). The whole issue of the *American Journal of Sociology* (1943) devoted to "Education and Cultural Dynamics," including articles by Johnson, Redfield, Malinowski, Mekeel, Benedict, Herskovits, Powdermaker, and Embree is an especially outstanding contribution.

It seems clear, upon examination of what has been done, that anthropologists have not been able to say much more than was said fifty years ago by Hewett when they talk about the general relevance of anthropology to general education. This is primarily because there is not much else to say. When the anthropologists have either analyzed their own intimately understood cross-cultural data in the perspective of education in modern society, or vice versa, or have moved over into a direct analysis of the educative process in our society with few methodological or conceptual binders, they have made a definite contribution. But the capital available in these activities has just begun to be utilized.

Educational routes.—Irrespective of the worthy attentions by anthropologists to education, the educators have gone ahead on their own to search out and utilize what seemed relevant to them of the anthropological products. An examination of representative and substantial texts in the psychological, sociocultural, philosophical, and comparative-historical foundations of education used in professional teacher-training institutions about the country reveals a clear shift toward appropriation of social and cultural concepts and data produced by anthropologists.

In educational psychology, for example, the text by Pressey and Robinson (1944) mentions no anthropological references, and uses no cross-cultural data for illustrative purposes. The text edited by Skinner, revised twice, shows an increase of anthropological citations in the last revision (1950). Cole and Bruce, in their 1950 edition, take a strong culture-oriented position, using section headings like "Life Styles as the Product of Cultures," "Diverse Cultures with Their Contrasting Life Styles," "The Culture as Definer of Perceptions, Beliefs, and Behaviors," "The Teacher —an Agent of Culture"; use Samoa, Zuñi, Kwakiutl data as culture case-study materials; and cite extensively literature by Benedict, Davis, Dennis, Kardiner and Linton, Linton alone, Mead, Redfield, Whiting, and Kluck-hohn. Cronbach, in his sparkling new 1954 model for educational psychology texts, draws upon Mead, Davis, Warner, Benedict, and Kluckhohn, among others, and makes considerable reference to cultural pressures, different cultural settings influencing personality development and learning, and formation of social attitudes and values. Martin and Stendler's new text, *Child Development*, intended for use by educators and non-educators both, and already used widely in elementary education and other professional education courses, places a very heavy emphasis on culture-personality relationships. Culture case data are cited for the Alorese, Balinese, Comanche, Japanese, Kwoma, Mentowie, Navaho, Samoans, Sioux, Tanala, Tepoztecans, Yurok, Zuñi, and others. Cultural relativism has found its way into the heart of this book.

In educational sociology—a field that is rapidly being expanded into a sociocultural foundation of education—a like trend is occurring. Cook's book (1950, revised edition), a text of long standing and wide use in educational sociology and social foundations, cites cross-cultural materials infrequently but draws much from the anthropologically influenced community studies on Middletown, St. Denis, Yankee City, and Plainsville. Robbins' *Educational Sociology* (1953) uses many of the same references and refers to writings by Mead, Benedict, Murdock, and Linton for the notion of cultural relativity. Brown's 1954 edition of *Educational Sociology* uses extensive reference to cultural data on the Navaho, Australian tribes, Zuñi, and the Acoma Pueblo, and cites anthropological pieces—by Gillin, Kluckhohn, Wagley, Herskovits, Goldfrank, Redfield, Tylor, Stirling, Warner, Rivers, Linton, Hewett, Mead, Powdermaker, Benedict, and Montague—approximately twice as often as in the 1947 edition.

The trend is not as noticeable in the philosophical and comparative foundations of education—in so far as the limits of the sample of texts permit generalizations. The tendency in these fields has apparently been to utilize highly generalized and Western-limited concepts of culture as an important part of the frame of reference, but to draw relatively little from any of the work by anthropologists in cross-cultural contexts. Brameld has made one of the strongest arguments for a culture base for educational philosophy (1950), but even he cites only a few anthropological works — namely, some by Davis, Kluckhohn, Benedict, Warner, and Herskovits. He is currently engaged in an appraisal of the implications of anthropological concepts and works for educational theory—an activity reflected directly in his paper for this conference.

An over-all summation of the anthropological concepts and data utilized in the contemporary texts in the foundations of education reveals certain general trends. Quite clear is the fact that educators interested in childhood education, elementary curriculum, school-community interrelations, and all of the social and behavioral foundations of education have arrived at the point where an anthropological point of view and, particularly, cross-cultural materials have a positive value for them. They indicate an awareness of culture concepts and cultural data produced by anthropologists by fairly extensive documentations with appropriate literature. They include anthropological references in their recommended reading lists. They consider it desirable to qualify generalizations about learning, cultural transmission, human nature, the functions of education, child growth and development, by invoking the notion of cultural relativity. Some of them incorporate a cultural perspective into their thinking—beyond using cultural relativity as a valued checkative.

The number of concepts relating to culture and culture process is impressive. Anthropologists have no copyright but certainly some possessory rights over them. Values, acculturation, cultural normalcy, cultural diffusion, cultural change, cultural transmission, subcultures, peer culture, folk culture, and even that rather new term—enculturation—ring with authentic familiarity to the anthropologist as they are used by the educationist authors.

But it is also clear that the range of materials being diffused via educationist channels from anthropological sources is in actuality quite limited. The same names and same references keep turning up constantly. A frequency-of-citation chart for the literature examined reveals that Kluckhohn, Mead, Benedict, Davis, West (Carl Withers), and Warner are cited in great disproportion to all others. This suggests that the purveyance of anthropological thinking to education has at most two main disciplinary vehicles—personality and culture, and community studies—and that the mediation of data and concepts is inevitably given an indelible impress by these particular workers. Particularly significant is the fact that it is the relatively most popularized works of these contributors that are cited most frequently. These two tendencies indicate that however useful the contributions and however able the contributors, the educators are not getting a fair and substantial diet of anthropological materials. This will only change when the educators take the next step and get their hands dirty with some of the dust-laden monographs back in the stacks, and when anthropologists exhume their portfolios of esoteria and put them into more publicly usable form. The educators and anthropologists who have respectively done these things already are due some applause.

The Roles of the Anthropologist in the Educational Context

One clear implication in this overview has been that if anthropology is actually going to contribute to education, the anthropologists will have to act at least more than occasionally within the setting of professional education. This is no argument that all anthropologists should. The discipline has many dimensions and interests, and nothing should be permitted to happen in relations with other fields that draws many anthropologists away from the central obligation to do basic research. But anthropologists have always been marked with a certain versatility. If there is a job to do in education some anthropologists will, for one reason or another, be bound to do it. Therefore an explication of some of the roles possible in the context of professional education is in order.

The anthropologist may act as a consultant. Ideally, he should be able to contribute ideas to every division of educational specialization—elementary, secondary, higher education, health, guidance, administration. He contributes, ideally, a widened perspective on human behavior. He sees the educative process as a cultural process, and thus not bounded by formalized, or ritualized lines of specialization or conceptual compartmentalization. He devotes some of his attention to breaking down ethnocentric biases. He is, ideally, not time-bound. He provides objectification of cultural values and, if he is successful, brings educational objectives into appropriate congruence with them. He contributes some useful analytic-descriptive categories, the foremost of which is culture, followed by a train of constructs like cultural transmission, enculturation, role and status, and social organization. To do these things he has to act as a participating member of the groups for which he acts as a consultant, for it is necessary for him to grasp the point of view and problems of those with whom he is consulting. He has already had experience in doing this within a somewhat different setting in his field research.

The anthropologist may do research in education or act as a consulting member of a team that is doing research. He does so with the same perspectives and capabilities that have been outlined above, and in attacks upon problems that fall into areas described previously in this paper. His major contribution lies in the molar approach that characterizes anthropological method. His greatest problem is one of relevance. His problems, definitions, and research values cannot remain exactly the same as they would if he were doing anthropological field research in a nonliterate, or even an acculturating community. He must understand what it is that educators need to know in order both to build a better educational theory and to solve problems of immediate applied relevance. In the research team developed at Stanford under the direction of Robert Bush and known as the Stanford Consultation Service, it was found that a good *modus operandi* was achieved when the educator, psychiatrist, and anthropologist exchanged roles for a time so that each could achieve insight into the other's problems. In this project also, a unique combination of ameliorative case consultation goals and pure research goals has been achieved, so that neither end-point of the value pendulum in educational research is lost. There are frustrations inherent in this procedure, to be sure.

The anthropologist need not necessarily work strictly within the framework of immediate education interests in his cross-disciplinary research. He may elect to confine himself to his own cross-cultural field, chasing down questions on educative process in non-Western societies. Possibly the most significant contributions of anthropology to education via research channels actually lie here.

The anthropologist may act as a teacher in the setting of professional education. Certain propositions concerning this role have already been explicated. His obligation lies mainly in making explicit the cultural assumptions and values that are a substratum of every move in educational action or theorizing. His contribution is particularly critical because education is a sensitive part of the total cultural process, and because in its very nature as an art and science of human cultivation it is loaded with a heavy burden of values. To achieve this contribution he goes to cross-cultural variability first, then turns to our own cultural modes as they bear directly upon the educative process—from the viewpoint of both the learner and the teacher. His aim is to create cultural awareness, which is perhaps even more important than self-awareness in the teacher's sphere of activity and which is pedagogically much more attainable.

Limitations and Reservations

The list of particulars for the roles the anthropologist may assume in the context of professional education is stated in ideal terms. No one anthropologist could do all of these things equally well. Choices have to be made on the basis of personal inclination and necessity.

But other limitations on his functions call for statement. One danger is that the "study of man" can sometimes seem so total that it becomes *the* study of man. One ethnocentrism is substituted for another. The anthropologist's comments seem to glitter like gold—to him at least—because for a time they are new and fresh. He becomes a kind of cultural oracle. But when his stock of illuminating asides on the Upper Pukapuka on the Lower Zambesi runs low he will be forced to take another stance. Then he may be reduced to making broad, conjectural statements that he may confuse as final judgments or substantial generalizations rather than a potential source of hypotheses. He may fool some of the educators some of the time, but he can't fool them all.

Further, the anthropologist's experience with small and relatively integrated societies sometimes gives him an extraordinary naïveté about the complex relations in our own society—a society that he himself may have escaped from—into anthropology. He fails to see complications and looks for integrating features, consistencies, and values where there are none. And as a consequence he may make outlandish pronouncements as to what educators should or should not do.

Beyond this, the anthropologist is not always particularly sophisticated intellectually. He is often not sufficiently familiar with the social and intellectual histories of the great civilizations—including his own. He may have become an anthropologist in order to become an explorer (subconsciously, of course), or buried himself so thoroughly in ethnographies that he has no room in his head for other thoughts. If so, his suggestions to educators would fall short of the mark when he talks about cultural transmission, since he would not know the culture to be transmitted.

And there are limitations inherent in the culture concept. Though the utility of this construct cannot be denied, it is not a theory in itself. It is not sufficiently dynamic, or field-oriented, but tends to contain itself around patterning phenomena that provide form but not function as variables for analysis. This may in fact be part of the reason for the anthropologist's descriptive bias—a limitation that American anthropology is just now getting over. He will usually find in the educational context that he has to turn to other disciplines for concepts and methods in order to do adequate research on or even adequate talking about any single dynamic problem in education in our society. Then perhaps he ceases being an anthropologist and becomes a social scientist with a cross-cultural perspective, and a molar approach to problems.

Conclusion

This overview has been an attempt to present some of the actual and potential articulations between education and anthropology, and is designed to set the stage for the papers and discussions that follow. No attempt can be made to anticipate the many issues and rich content of the conference as a whole. The overview should serve to alert both educators and anthropologists to some of the problems in communication that will prevail. The anthropologists have been asked to do a very difficult thing— to address themselves to problems in a relatively unfamiliar context, using whatever tools and materials they find appropriate. The anthropological identity may be lost in the attempt, or the understandings intended may be lost because the identity is kept. In any event, the anthropologists must use certain criteria of relevance that presumably stem from within anthropology—yet be aware of the perceptual field of the educator audience. The educators must accept the necessity for internal relevance of anthropological material—and yet apply their own criteria for selection and modification of what is offered. This means that both anthropologists and educators must exercise a species of "double awareness" that is always necessary in interdisciplinary efforts but which is rarely exercised sufficiently. The conference is an experiment in this possibility.

References

Boas, Franz. 1928. *Anthropology and Modern Life*. New York: W. W. Norton & Company, Inc.

Brameld, Theodore. 1950. *Patterns of Educational Philosophy*. New York: World Book Co.

Brown, Francis J. 1954. *Educational Sociology*. 2d ed. New York: Prentice-Hall, Inc.

Bryson, Lyman. 1939. "Anthropology and Education," in D. D. Brand, Fred Harvey (eds.), *So Live the Works of Men*. Albuquerque, pp. 107–15.

Cole, Lawrence E., and William F. Bruce. 1950. *Educational Psychology*. New York: World Book Co.

Cook, Lloyd A., and Elaine F. Cook. 1950. *A Sociological Approach to Education*. New York: McGraw-Hill Book Company, Inc.

Cronbach, Lee J. 1954. *Educational Psychology*. New York: Harcourt, Brace and Company.

Davis, Allison. 1952. *Social Class Influences on Learning*. Cambridge: Harvard University Press.

Davis, Allison, and Robert J. Havighurst. 1947. *Father of the Man*. Boston: Houghton Mifflin Company.

Eells, Kenneth, Allison Davis, Robert J. Havighurst, Virgil E. Herrick, and Ralph W. Tyler. 1951. *Intelligence and Cultural Differences*. Chicago: University of Chicago Press.

Ehrich, Robert W. 1947. "The Place of Anthropology in a College Education," *Harvard Educational Review*, XVII, 57–61.

Goldenweiser, Alexander. 1939. "Culture and Education," *Stanford Education Conference*. New York: Social Education.

Hanna, Paul. 1954. "Needed Changes in Elementary Curriculum," paper before the AASA meeting, Atlantic City.

Harvard Educational Review. 1953. "Social Class Structure and American Education," Parts I and II; XXIII, 149–338.

Havighurst, Robert J., and Hilda Taba. 1949. *Adolescent Character and Personality*. New York: John Wiley & Sons, Inc.

Herskovits, Melville J. 1943. "Education and Cultural Dynamics," *American Journal of Sociology*, XLVIII, 109–21.

———. 1948. *Man and His Works*. New York: Alfred A. Knopf, Inc.

Hewett, Edgar L. 1904. "Anthropology and Education," *American Anthropologist*, VI, 574–75.

———. 1905. "Ethnic Factors in Education," *American Anthropologist*, VII, 1–16.

Howells, W. W. 1952. "The Study of Anthropology," *American Anthropologist*, LIV, 1–7.

Johnson, Charles S. (ed.). 1943. "Education and the Cultural Process," *American Journal of Sociology*, XLVIII, 1–136.

Keesing, Felix M. 1937. *Education in Pacific Countries*. Shanghai: Kelly and Walsh.

Klineberg, Otto. 1935. *Racial Differences*. New York: Harper & Brothers.

———. 1947. "Racial Psychology," in Ralph Linton (ed.), *The Science of Man in the World Crisis*. New York: Columbia University Press.

———. 1951. *Race and Psychology*. UNESCO.

Kluckhohn, Clyde. 1949. *Mirror for Man*. New York: McGraw-Hill Book Company, Inc.

Kroeber, A. L. (ed.). 1953. *Anthropology Today*. Chicago: University of Chicago Press.

Martin, William E., and Celia Stendler. 1953. *Child Development*. New York: Harcourt, Brace and Company.

Mead, Margaret. 1943. "Our Educational Emphasis in Primitive Perspective," *American Journal of Sociology*, XLVIII, 633–39.

———. 1946. "Professional Problems of Education in Dependent Countries," *The Journal of Negro Education*, XV, 346–57.

———. 1950. *The School in American Culture*. Cambridge: Harvard University Press.

Montessori, Maria. 1913. *Pedagogical Anthropology*. New York: Frederick Stokes.

Opler, Morris. 1947. "Cultural Alternatives and Educational Theory," *Harvard Educational Review*, XVII, 28–44.

Pettit, George A. 1946. "Primitive Education in North America," *University of California Publications in American Archeology and Ethnology*, XLIII, 1–182.

Pressey, Sidney, and Francis Robinson. 1944. *Psychology and the New Education*. New York: Harper & Brothers.

Robbins, Florence G. 1953. *Educational Sociology*. New York: Henry Holt and Company.

Rosenstiel, Annette. 1954. "Educational Anthropology: A New Approach to Cultural Analysis," *Harvard Educational Review*, XXIV, 28–36.

Skinner, Charles E. (ed.). 1950. *Elementary Educational Psychology*. New York: Prentice-Hall, Inc.

Spindler, G. D. 1946. "Anthropology May Be an Answer," *Journal of Education*, CXXIX, 130–31.

Taba, Hilda, and staff. 1950. *Elementary Curriculum in Intergroup Relations*. Washington, D.C.: American Council on Education.

Warner, W. Lloyd, *et al.* 1949. *Democracy in Jonesville.* New York: Harper & Brothers.
Warner, W. Lloyd, Robert J. Havighurst, and Martin B. Loeb. 1944. *Who Shall Be Educated?* New York: Harper & Brothers.
Whiting, John, and Irvin L. Child. 1953. *Child Training and Personality.* New Haven: Yale University Press.
Willcockson, Mary (ed.). 1950. *Social Education of Young Children.* Washington, D.C.: National Council for the Social Studies, NEA.

FIRST SESSION OF THE CONFERENCE

A CONCEPTION OF EDUCATION

I. James Quillen

Quillen: I thought that I would express very briefly my point of view on education and its relationship to anthropology. I will not attempt to repeat what I said in the paper, but there will be some overlapping in my remarks and the material in the paper.

In the 1890's three interrelated forces converged which tended to place the problem of education in the field of the social sciences. These forces were: (1) the very drastic changes that came in American life in the post-Civil War period, with the development of the industrial-urban cultural pattern in the United States; (2) the development of the social sciences themselves; and (3) the increasing recognition of the social role of education, of the responsibility of education to develop effective citizens and to contribute to the improvement of social well-being. Educators began to stress the social role of education, and the statement was made that there was no true philosophy of education unless it was based on sociology. At the same time, people in the social sciences, particularly in the field of sociology, began to be interested in educational problems. Consequently, in the early 1900's, there emerged a field of study known as educational sociology. It was never pure sociology; it drew from the social sciences as a whole from the beginning, but the field was called educational sociology.

Educational sociology became a part of the teacher training program in most educational institutions. It tended to parallel educational psychology and educational philosophy. In the late 1920's and 1930's more and more interest developed in the child-centered approach to education; as a result both educational philosophy and sociology lost ground in teacher training institutions. But, since the beginning of World War II, there has been a reaffirmation of interest in the social role of education and in value factors in education. This interest, however, is from a new point of view. Most educators now recognize that there is no dichotomy between individual development and social development, that it's not the individual *or* the group, but it's the individual *in* the group, and individual development is produced to a very considerable extent by group interaction. There has emerged in education a personal-social approach, a recognition that the needs, the desires, the goals of the individual are both personal and social, and that, rather than there being an essential conflict between the two, properly conceived they reinforce each other. In the postwar period there has been some tendency, along with the forces in American society moving toward greater equalization and greater concern with group interaction, to go too far in the direction of group participation, and not enough recognition has been given to the importance of individual thought and individual activity. There are two kinds of coercion: the coercion imposed by the individual on the group and the coercion of the group upon the individual. We've become increasingly sensitive to the coercion of the individual on the group, but I don't think we are sufficiently sensitive to the factor of the coercion of the group upon the individual and the danger of increasing conformity in Western culture, in America particularly, to group pressure. But the whole individual-in-group interaction is the major emphasis which is found in most educational thinking at the present time.

Most people in professional education think of education as desirable changes in the behavior of the individual; and in this sense, the family is probably the most important single educational institution. Peer group participation and various other factors are also very important in education. The school as an institution is a deliberately devised environment to produce changes in behavior in a particular direction. The kinds of behavior changes that are thought to be desirable cannot be determined without a consideration of the cultural setting in which the individual is living and in which the school exists, a consideration of the core values of the culture, and the nature of individual growth and development. Educational problems tend to be concerned with an interaction between four basic factors, all of which are closely interrelated: (1) the individual learner; (2) the general cultural setting; (3) the core values of the culture; and (4) the school itself as an institution, including the various participants in the school, the roles and statuses of the participants, etc. In thinking of the over-all function of the school, it seems to me that the essential function of a publicly supported school system is to perpetuate the culture of which it is a part. This is done by perpetuating the core values and by developing in the learner the kinds of behavior which will enable him to participate in the cultural setting as it is and as it is developing, so as to maintain the essential core values that the members of the culture want to maintain. The essence of education, as I see it, from the cultural point of view is cultural perpetuation, including cultural transmission, socialization, and enculturation.

We get our educational objectives by trying to identify the kinds of behavior that are necessary to perpetuate desired values within the kind of cultural setting in which the individual is participating, and of which he and the school are a part. Objectives represent, then, a behavioral description of the kind of individual we are seeking to develop. This statement of educational objectives involves two things: value perception—perceptions of what is felt to be desirable—and cultural selection, that is, selecting from the total range of possible behavior representing the culture that which it is thought desirable to perpetuate. There is another dimension introduced here by the factor of cultural heterogeneity and cultural change. In a changing culture the desirable behavioral patterns may not remain stable, and it is necessary to think of the responsibility of the individual in relation to cultural change.

Following the identification of objectives in the development of the school program, there is the problem of selecting and organizing content and materials. This selection of content and materials is again a selection from the total range of possibilities in the culture. Generally speaking, the problem of selecting and organizing content is to select the content and materials that offer the greatest possibilities for getting the changes in behavior that are desired, and then organizing them effectively so as to take into consideration the needs and basic motivations of the individual and our knowledge of maturation.

In addition to the selection of content and materials, there is the problem of method. This involves directing the child to experiences with the content and the materials in such ways that the desired changes in behavior occur. The problem of method is essentially the problem of creating a situation where the individual learner can have the experiences with the content and materials that present the greatest possibility for him to change his behavior, and then in directing him with regard to his basic feelings, his needs and potentialities, his maturation, and the like, so that the maximum development of the desired changes in behavior is produced.

The next factor in the development of an educational program is the question of appraisal, the determination of the extent to which you have secured the desired changes in behavior. The selection of content, the development of method, and appraisal, all involve the factor of individual differences. This factor feeds back into the biology and psychology of the child and the heterogeneity of the various subcultures from which the children, teachers, and administrators come. All of these things take place in a variety of interrelated cultural settings: a classroom, a school, a neighborhood, a local community, and a larger cultural and social setting, including the county, state, nation, and the whole world. All of these interrelated cultural settings affect the educative process and what happens to the individual learner in terms of changes in behavior.

In relation to the general cultural setting, I've already mentioned some of the factors that I think are particularly significant today. One basic factor is the shift in America from a rural-handicraft to an industrial-urban culture. We have not only had this shift from a rural-handicraft to an industrial-urban culture, but we also have a new kind of industrialization and a new kind of urbanization; an industrialization that is shifting from the specialist to the generalist, from individual semiskilled and skilled laborer to automatic production controlled by electronic devices under the direction of the professional manager and engineer, and an urbanization that is changing from the metropolis to the metropolitan area, with the typical area of urban living being suburbia. Hence, we not only have to think of the shift from a rural-handicraft to an industrial-urban culture, but we also have to think of the basic changes that are occurring in industrial-urban culture itself. Many of these changes are tremendously important for education. Not enough thought is being given at the present time to the effects of the participation of the individual child in the suburban setting on his personality development, and the consequences of these effects for the school.

The rapidity of change is also a tremendously important factor, including inco-ordination in change, the receptivity to material change, the opposition to social and value changes, and the increasing centralization of power in our culture and the changes in the power structure. In my judgment, human beings are gaining greater insight into their problems and are making fewer mistakes proportionately, but at the same time there is greater opportunity to make mistakes, and the consequences of the mistakes are much more threatening than earlier because of the tremendously increased power and the concentration of power. Perhaps most important in our culture is that underlying these factors is an intensification of value conflict, along with the inco-ordination of change, the problems of tension that come from value conflict, and increasing anxiety and fear, producing an essentially antirationalist atmosphere, which is basically antieducational in terms of the Western tradition in education.

Briefly then, this is my conception of education, with the various factors and problems involved in it, and I think that you can see the interrelationship between these and the kinds of problems in which anthropologists are interested.

Along with the developments I have mentioned, there has been a change in the conception of the relationship of the social sciences to education. In the first place, the concept of educational sociology has been broadened and the term itself is decreasing in current use. The term "social foundations" is being more and more used because it is recognized that education should depend not just on sociology but upon all of the social sciences, and very heavily upon social philosophy and anthropology. In addition to the development of the concept of social foundations, there is very recently a great interest in certain institutions in the interdisciplinary approach to educational problems. At Harvard, Yale, Teachers College, the University of Chicago, Stanford, the University of Oregon, and elsewhere, there are now teams of social scientists working with professional educators in an attempt to identify and help solve educational problems.

In the various interdisciplinary approaches and in the development of the social foundations of education, more and more content is being drawn from the field of anthropology. Educators are reading more anthropological literature and using more anthropological concepts and content. However, only a few anthropologists have become directly interested in education. At Stanford, George Spindler has a joint appointment in education and anthropology, and the holding of this conference is an indication of the increased interest in this field. I have the feeling, which is supported by George's paper, that the interest of the educator in anthropological content has not been entirely reciprocated by the anthropologists. What is needed is a more systematic attempt on the part of anthropologists to try to identify the existing knowledge that can be helpful in dealing with educational problems, and also to encourage the development of research that would add to such knowledge. Perhaps because of the profession I am in, as I look at the over-all cultural situation I can't think of anything that is more important than the education of our children and youth, and I personally have great hopes for our deliberations here and what may come from them in the general improvement of professional education and in making a direct contribution to our cultural well-being.

Prospectus

Spindler: I think Dean Quillen has given us a lead, and a projection, almost a propulsion, into what we want to deal with.

I want to say a word about the papers. It has been extremely interesting to me to see them come in. My own reaction has varied, not only from paper to paper, but from day to day as I reread them. And as I began to talk to educators and anthropologists about them I found that this experience was shared by others. I think that this is promising; I think it suggests that people have different positions and therefore different perceptions, and I think it suggests that they will be able to make these positions explicit as they discuss the papers and the topical areas to which the papers lead us.

I think that one of the primary difficulties in communication may be that the anthropologists will tend to look at processes, concepts, and data from the viewpoint of research and theory-building. I think that the educators may be more inclined to look at the same things from the viewpoint of "what can be done now to improve education?" But I think that both groups have the ultimate improvement of society in mind. The anthropologist's goal of ultimate improvement is somewhat more delayed. But it is sometimes difficult for us to communicate, because the anthropologists are talking in the direction of *understanding* at the theoretical level, while the educator will be saying, "Well, so what?" This may not actually happen. If it doesn't, it is because we have a particularly deviant group of anthropologists and educators here.

I would like to say a word concerning the audience we are addressing. As I understand it, we are oriented primarily toward the teachers of teachers. And I think that we have to count on the ideas and hypotheses and the concepts that are developed in the conference being transmitted to the educational community through the teachers of teachers. I define the audience this way because I believe that we are more interested, for purposes of this conference, in formulation than we are in execution; that we are more interested in theory than we are in method, although the two tend to go hand in hand.

And now I think that I ought to indicate what our program will be, so that you will have some idea of where we're going. We're proceeding from the general to the specific and back to the general. This afternoon we are dealing with the overview papers written by Jim Quillen and myself, and I hope that we may be able to discuss a paper that we just received, written by Sol Kimball. Then I hope we can proceed to the paper by Bernard Siegel, because this provides us with a good frame of reference; and from there to John Gillin's paper, because in a sense John's paper fills in some of the concrete material to which Bernard Siegel's models refer. Then we can go on to Cora DuBois' paper on intercultural understanding, since we find that there are some leads developed in the first two papers that will provide a good transition. And from that to Steve Hart's paper on pre- and postpubertal education. This will be an interesting session because I am sure there will be questions raised by both the anthropologists and the educators. And then finally to what I would regard as specializations of interest, that is, the papers by Dorothy Lee and by Jules Henry. The other papers tend in one way or another to take in a rather broad scope of material. These two papers have broad implications, but they deal with specific kinds of problems and are relatively more specialized, and it seems to me that we may best be able to discuss them after we have based some groundwork on the others. Then we should come back to the general; that is, we should attempt to integrate and conceptualize what we have been over. As I see it, there are two phases in this; one of the phases I think will be expedited by using Theodore Brameld's paper as a springboard. This is a paper on a high level of abstraction but one which marshals a great deal of concrete material. In the second phase of this, there will be a session devoted entirely to the purposes of summary, where we will try to obtain some kind of closure on what we have done. This will be under the leadership of Margaret Mead, and should occur on Sunday morning. Then having achieved a sense of closure, hopefully—at least perhaps a sense of closure about not having a sense of closure—we should try to break ourselves loose, raise more questions, and leave in a hopeful state of mind. And I think that the discussion to be organized by Solon T. Kimball on the segregation issue will serve that last purpose. That will bring us up to 4:30 on Sunday afternoon and the end of the conference.

And, last, I wish to say that we are here together because, as Jim Quillen pointed out, our culture is changing; the educator is faced, like any other person caught up in the cultural process at this stage, with some nearly unsolvable kinds of problems. The anthropologist is aware of these problems, is interested in them, is caught up also in the cultural process, and is bringing to the discussion of these problems his knowledge and point of view gained from cross-cultural experience and research. This means that our purpose is to explore approaches to the understanding of the educative process in a changing society. We are exploring with educational and anthropological tools. In doing so, this being exploratory, we are interested in defining new problem areas, developing hypotheses, indicating needed research developments, and hopefully we will help consolidate an emergent application of one social science to the solution of problems in this particular institutionalized part of our own social process—the educational system.

I think that with this it is time to turn the proceedings over to the chairman for the afternoon, who will be Cora DuBois.

OPEN DISCUSSION
What Was Left Out of the Overview?
Mead, Keesing, DuBois (Chairman)

DuBois: I judge that everyone has read these papers. I feel that we are now ready to discuss the matter informally and get the conference moving. I was told by George (Spindler) that at least four people have already commented to him previously on the two papers which are now under consideration: James Quillen's and George Spindler's. Of those who have commented, may I call first on you, Margaret (Mead)?

Mead: I was impressed in reading this overview with the discontinuity that has existed in the interrelationship between education and anthropology, and how much the interplay has been dependent upon personalities rather than upon any on-going institutionalized process of any sort. Perhaps the most striking instance of this is the nonappearance in this overview of all the interdisciplinary contacts between education and anthropology and other sciences, instituted by the General Education Board in the mid-thirties, which were complex and elaborate. This morning I asked Mr. Frank, who was the instigator of the program, what he thought it cost, and he said probably half a million dollars. It dealt with virtually every aspect that is being discussed here: there was a plan for an anthropological study of a school system which Morris Opler undertook to do in Bronxville; there was a plan for the study of the culture and ethos of a particular school which Jeannette Mirsky was to do at Fieldstone; there was a plan to send an anthropologist out to a primitive society to study the induction of youth into the values of that society, which Bernard Mishkin started out to do in Guinea; there was the integration of anthropologists on committees working with teachers of secondary schools; there was the Hanover group, where a whole group of people got together to prepare materials on human relations in the secondary schools; and there was Alice Keliher's big commission to take all these things and put them into shape to be used in the schools. The plan just about covers all the different roles of the anthropologist either in research or as consultant or in interdisciplinary work. Of course, it is represented here, in a way, in the fact that some of us are present at all; in an article Morris Opler wrote fourteen years later; and so forth. But any explicit trace is missing, because these interrelationships were sporadic, sometimes very highly motivated, but they had no place to go afterward. Books were written, people's points of view changed, and undoubtedly we couldn't be doing the sort of thing we are doing today without it. But it looks to me as if we could now aim at a much clearer institutionalization of the relationship between anthropology and education, so that we could depend upon orderly processes; for example, when a particular teachers' college loses an anthropologist it will get another; or if it doesn't have one yet, it will feel it ought to have one. We should institute such processes as more explicit attention to education in the content of courses in the departments of anthropology. If what we do here is not to be lost, not to become one single dramatic effort that has taken a lot of people's thought and time and planning and then goes back into a main stream where you can hardly find it again, such institutionalization is necessary.

Keesing: Much the same as what Margaret (Mead) has said applies in the case of studies of overseas education. We ran a conference in Hawaii of educators and anthropologists in 1936. It was quite a major event, lasting for six weeks and bringing together a group that even included Africanists. The individuals still correspond; the literature still comes out; there have also been efforts to have a follow-up conference, without its being done yet. But it has represented sporadic efforts, not continuous activity; the materials just went back into the general stream of anthropology.

DuBois: We seem to be reviewing right now all of the factors in our favor for making a more organized impact as the result of this conference. I would also assume that we could add the growing sophistication in interdisciplinary inquiries.

Anthropology and the Anthropologist in Teacher Education

Lee, Siegel, Taba, Henry, Spindler, Mead, Frank, Kimball

Lee: What I liked very much about Spindler's paper was his bringing out ways in which a conference such as this could make a definite impact in a teachers' college, for example. He is showing the specific ways in which what we are doing now could be implemented. He describes what he's doing at Stanford, and we know what Sol Kimball, for example, is doing at Columbia. But a number of anthropologists are terrified at the thought of teaching anthropology to people who will not be anthropologists; I think it will be a help if we can see what kinds of things can be taught there. George (Spindler) and Mr. Quillen suggest that the teacher who is passing on culture not only consciously and deliberately but unconsciously and with every gesture that she makes will be helped if she can be aware of what she is passing on. Now, do you just want anthropologists to show her what she is doing, and teach her to be aware? How would you suggest that we do that?

Siegel: One thing that occurs to me in terms of getting things across is simply that we cannot be too concerned about getting across content. The core social sciences, if I may speak of them as such—anthropology, sociology, psychology—almost represent ways of life; they represent ways of looking at wide varieties of phenomena. There is a certain amount of what DuBois has spoken of as affective learning, as opposed to cognitive learning, that I'm afraid would have to come a little late in life if we are concerned with the teacher-training level, but it necessarily would have to come in by way of processing and selecting and interpreting all kinds of events and occurrences that might be termed cultural-anthropological. Exactly how this is to be accomplished I'm not too sure; one thing I'm quite sure of is that it cannot be done in a formal way in the classroom. If there were something analogous in the teacher-training schools to the clinical rounds in the hospitals, it would be a nice way to incorporate the social scientist of one persuasion or another—anthropologist, psychologist, etc.—in a manner which would be meaningful in interpreting things that the student has to come up against all the time.

Taba: Your remarks would indicate that, in the line of practical implementation of this attempt at mutual exploration and integration, an anthropologist in education might be only one and maybe a minor solution. If anthropology has a method of understanding a way of life, then giving teachers one or two courses would be insufficient. Reinterpretation of many other things would be needed, as, for instance, how to diagnose children's behavior, how to select methods of teaching by cultural patterns. Introduction of courses in anthropology would create new barriers and a new task in education of integrating the newly disintegrated.

Shaftel: We've heard how hard it is for anthropologists to get outside of their own culture when studying another. How are we going to help the teacher as a person to get outside of herself, to see what it is she is doing and how much her own cultural orientation determines the choices she makes?

Henry: I think that what Siegel had in mind is just this sort of thing, and I would like to give an example out of my own experience in working in a school system. I used to have lunch with the teacher and chat with her, and our conversation was geared to what had happened in the classroom ten minutes ago. Now it isn't always possible to have anthropologists doing that, but Siegel's observations suggested to me the idea of the presentation of a case in the school—let us say, once a week—which would be discussed, with the rest of the school staff, by somebody skilled in the social sciences. This person would attempt to show, in terms of social science frames of reference, how the case related to social and cultural situations and points of view. I think that such a method, in which the social scientist simply made his contribution along with the rest of the group, in an intensive study of particular cases, would help to make the school staff aware of the significance of their own problems with the children in terms of social science perspectives.

Lee: But I don't want to give up the course in the teachers' training college either. I don't think it has to be a lecture course, but it should be possible to structure a course where the teachers will go through such an experience of another culture, perhaps where certain values, concepts, ways of doing things, approaches, attitudes, will become pointed up but will remain at the same time concrete and embedded in a whole way of life, and will serve as a springboard for discussion to help the teacher to awareness of her own way of life. That would be perhaps changing the teacher as a person to some extent if this course is well presented. I don't think it has to be a course of lectures *about* something.

Spindler: I second your motion, Dorothy (Lee), in the sense that I think there is a role—a very important kind of role—for the anthropologist in the educational context as a teacher. I think I've made the point clear in the overview paper that I don't believe that he teaches anthropology; he teaches *from* anthropology to an educational situation of some kind.

There are three kinds of things that I find seem to produce the most effects in teachers in terms of the goal of cultural awareness. (1) The culture case study; this of course is a traditional approach in anthropology. You provide the student with a vicarious kind of experience and usually that seems to come best from one's own field work because one is able to relate a kind of personality in this foreign setting to a kind of personality the student knows about. This approach seems to help, but it is only a first step; it doesn't do very much good because this material can be so easily externalized. It can be left at an intellectual level and it can be rationalized in or out of any particular problem situation as the student wishes. (2) The type of case treatment where an educator, an anthropologist, and, in our particular case at Stanford,[1] a psychiatrist, go into a school system, take a classroom, a teacher, a whole school, and study the role of the teacher, the culture context that the teacher is working from, the cultural position of the children, the selective perception by the teacher of the different cultural positions of the children, and so on. And you report these data to your students; you analyze the whole case in a perspective that is only partially anthropological. (3) The formal course approach—at Stanford we have a psychological foundations course and one in social foundations. I have taught both and found that in the psychological foundations course the thing that I was after was *self*-awareness; I found that in the other course it was *cultural* awareness. I'll try to explain very briefly what I mean by this. I mean simply that in the case of self-awareness I try to deal with the kinds of emotional conflicts that are within the person, the kinds of emotionalized perceptions that will affect everything that he does. The material is highly personalized through use of group TAT's, among other techniques, and the person gets to the point where he can objectify himself so that he says, "I have hostility toward authority figures"; "I have strong dependency needs"; "I will reject certain kinds of children and accept others." I found this kind of awareness extremely difficult to achieve and found that students could become quite disturbed. By the other kind of awareness, *cultural* awareness, I mean simply this: that the person is aware of the value matrix in which he is caught up. And I found that there were ways of achieving this; that is, rather than simply talking about values, I took some value expressions from students, using such simple devices as open-ended statements: "The individual is . . .; nudity is . . .; popular people are . . .; all men are born . . ." I have a little test of some twenty-five items that I administer and then ask students to do things like describing the ideal American boy and describing the ideal American girl. Then the whole class does a thematic "value" analysis of this material. Having done that, we relate the derived values to what this means in respect to how the teacher will behave when faced with a particular kind of child in a particular kind of social setting. This leads to an expanded cultural awareness. I think that one of the people who is particularly fit to do something like this is an anthropologist, and I think that the place he has to do that is in a course.

Mead: I've experimented for five years in a course at Teachers College that was called "Anthropology and Educational Methods"; and in that

[1] Under the leadership of Dr. Robert N. Bush in the Stanford Consultation Service.

all the students did a project in which they actually analyzed material comparatively (I think perhaps we haven't emphasized so far the importance of comparison). In my course no one was allowed to do a project that didn't compare something with something—either two periods in the same culture, or two cultures; no one was allowed to focus on only one. And they analyzed all sorts of things: television shows and radio shows; they compared *Punch* and *The New Yorker,* or French and American textbooks in elementary education, in a very wide range of materials which were accessible to them, where they had to identify the cultural differences, identify and document. Now I think one reason they did it so well, and a great deal better than most professional anthropology students would (which was quite striking, as they were all Teachers College students, of various degrees of age and sophistication)—one reason it seemed to me that they did such good work was because I taught them about 50 percent of the time by having people who were wrestling with comparable problems (and *hadn't* solved them) come in and give interim reports. They got a sense of work in process, something of course one could give them when talking about his own field work too; one can say, "and I couldn't make any sense of this at all, so I did this and I did this to try and solve this." They were given a chance at an apprenticeship identification with people who were doing the sort of thing they were trying to do. It will depend a little bit on the community or city as to how many people one can find who are in the midst of research, but students must be given a chance to see other people who have not completed the understanding of the cultural element in the situation, but are in the middle of it. They learn to *work with* a cultural analysis instead of taking it pat.

Taba: Now let's not let this obscure the impact that seems to be important to keep in mind. When you talk about changing people—their central values or their cultural values—you're talking about learnings that change slowly and painfully. It's a more profound learning than a new idea, and therefore needs to be done over a longer period of time and in a greater variety of contexts, if it is to get home at all. That means that whatever is taught by way of outside courses needs to be supplemented by similar experiences and similar ideas and similar training in other contexts. There might be a concentrated course such as you have been describing, but in addition there ought to be some re-emphasis of the same idea in making curricula, in teaching, and in treating discipline problems.

There is also the need for a developmental program which places learning experiences in a sequence of maturation. (There are certain things that come first and other things that come later.) This is what Cora DuBois referred to as a total trajectory of learning. In other words, one needs to have a developmental program rather than one short program. A short program, no matter how good, is not enough.

But there is another kind of sequence here which comes from the fact that this learning is both emotional and intellectual. That's one thing that has been discovered research-wise, that experimentation in the intergroup programs in schools brought out very clearly. When I started in 1945, the major idea was that you rammed down concepts, you rammed at prejudice directly. Soon people realized that when you attacked people's emotions and feelings you created defenses and therefore made education more difficult. When we actually started playing with groups of children on this level, it became very evident that you have to combine and alternate the materials with designs and then follow with some conceptualization, and then create new feelings again and follow with new conceptualization, and that the curriculum had to be made up of that kind of rotation.

Lee: It seems to me, however, that the course which Margaret (Mead) described had something in it which produced in the student, if I understood it correctly, a certain ability to get a feed-back, introducing the student to awareness in such a way that awareness itself could be used to make for increased awareness rather than have to be replenished by another course.

Mead: I think that there is a point here that we may not want to go into, but it should at least be mentioned. I do not assume that cultural learning is painful, and my experience with students has not been, on the whole, that they have found it painful; instead, in many instances they found it exceedingly releasing. I think we have overdone the analogy from class consciousness, which as taught in this country is almost always painful and produces a high degree of hostility, and from some of the problems of personality insight, which again have been painful. But in a very large number of cases, recognition of one's own culture and the cultures of other people is something that is sufficiently releasing so that it can go on and on without this mobilized resistance about which Dr. Taba talks, which certainly will come up with certain applications of the social class analysis and some types of personality analyzing.

Martin: In this connection I am aware of some inadequacies on my own part in being a nonanthropologist but trying to introduce cross-cultural material into my own courses. I find—I admit that this is a failure on my part—that the students say, "Oh, isn't this interesting that other people do things differently, bring up their youngsters differently, train and educate them differently. But, so what? They do it their way, and we do it our way." And where do you go from there?

DuBois: While we're on this point—are their degrees of resistance in self- and cultural awareness? Is one as easy and adequate as another? I think Margaret (Mead) has raised an interesting point there. On the other hand, as you indicated, George (Spindler), it can remain on a very intellectual and externalized level, this cultural case history usage. Now, where do we stand on all this?

Mead: One of the basic assumptions that anthropologists have worked with has been that you treat each culture as dignified in itself; it's a kind of theoretical democracy among cultures—granting that the Eskimo did things very simply and the Peruvians did them very complicatedly. Nevertheless, we regarded each culture as having dignity so that one doesn't introduce a hierarchical superordination-subordination set of values.

I always have my students do a long case history back as far as they can go; if they can go four and five generations back, that's fine. Most of them represent many ethnic strains; some of these strains they have not been quite sure about; on the whole, they thought maybe they were skeletons to be kept in the closet. We've experimented with this in high schools, working with adolescents in child care, where we wanted to go back and see what their mothers and their grandmothers did. And we put together European migrants and rural people with the general statement that the whole world was changed from the way it once was. Then we combined that with slides of the way people work in primitive societies. Girls have gone back and interviewed their grandmothers and in the course of this have reaccepted the way in which they were brought up, which before they had been ashamed of. Their pasts had been given dignity. It's not intellectual learning; on the whole, it can be very emotional.

Lee: I had that experience in teaching about primitive groups. One time I did it so badly, or perhaps so well, that they practically needed a psychiatrist. They became so identified with the society they were studying that they resisted everything else; they were going the next term to take another course with another teacher and they hated her, they hated her culture, and I had to work with them to bring them back to themselves. Then later I never did it so extremely; but what I found was what Margaret (Mead) found, that in the beginning they would say, "Oh, how good the Tikopia and the Trobrianders are"; then after a while they would say, "But our culture also has this and this . . . our culture has something good too"; and eventually, instead of feeling pained about their own culture, they would feel good about it.

Spindler: I think then we can say that we wish to move away from mere intellectualization of cultural materials, but this requires, first, an emotional identification of some kind, and then a reobjectification. That is, in order for a person to deal either with himself or with a value system, it has to be objectified so that it becomes a part of the environment. But in order for this to happen, the person first has to become somehow emotionally involved with the process of doing this very thing. So there are several stages in the achievement of this kind of cultural awareness. My original point with respect to the difference between self- and cultural awareness is that it's simply harder to make the self a part of the environment than it is to make a cultural value system a part of the environment.

Quillen: In relation to the aims which you stated, George (Spindler), we not only need to have this feeling of identification plus objectivity, but we also need to get teacher conceptualization. If we're teaching teachers to work with people in the school situation, the teachers themselves not only have to become emotionally identified and objective about their relationships, but they also have to be able to conceptualize their experiences and to find ways to communicate them to pupils in the classroom.

Kimball: I think I might be able to point up this discussion by presenting a case report of my own experiences in the field of education. I am now completing my first year as an anthropologist on the staff at Teachers College in the Department of Social Foundations. In the original interviews for this position better than a year ago, I made very explicit that I was uninformed in the area of professional education. I quickly learned that the interest in my employment related to my skills as an anthropologist and in my ability to bring to educators the principles of anthropology. I found no difficulty in accepting the principle that those who work in professional schools should do so within the objectives of the school with which they associate.

My first introduction to educators in a group was the fall faculty conference. There I discovered that the problems discussed centered primarily around such current issues as student enrollment, graduate student load, and requirements, with the exception of a stimulating discussion on Bestors' recent attack on education. Afterward, I realized that educators have so thoroughly internalized their basic principles that any extended discussion would have been elementary and repetitious for most.

My real initiation into problems of education arose from actually working with others on current issues. One of these relates to the content of a foundations course in social science, where the objective is to relate basic social and cultural principles to education. The discussion of programs and thesis topics for graduate students provided another valuable learning experience. Through these I began to have a clearer understanding of the distinctive points of view which characterize educators.

Another experience that proved very helpful was the occasion when I served as a consultant to an on-going educational research problem. One of the divisions was re-examining methods and concepts, and there was a receptive situation for looking at methods of various disciplines in terms of specific educational problems. It was at this point that anthropological principles could be introduced in terms of the specific problems being considered.

Taba: That was also perhaps the point at which educators began to learn what anthropologists can do.

Do Anthropologists Know Professional Education?

Bush, Siegel, Mead, Hart, Kimball, Cowley

Bush: Sol (Kimball), did you find that there were things that you didn't know anything about? As you said in the beginning, and as I've heard Spindler say many times, "I don't know anything about education." I'd be interested in why you say this. Apparently we are not communicating very well, because I think the educator's idea of the anthropologist is that he has many very important insights about the educative process.

Siegel: I think that what we mean is simply that we don't know what goes on in educational institutions very much; since we haven't been in them we've forgotten what the school looks like, in a sense.

Kimball: And more than that, we don't know the historical depth of all the things that have gone to build education as it is now—its philosophy, the internal divisions, all these kinds of subtle differences which are tremendously important, in seeing why some people do some things one way and some people do them another.

Mead: We don't speak the language. I'm not speaking for myself because I come from a long line of professional educators; maybe it's one reason I'm in this picture. But words like "Montessori," for instance, which I've known ever since I could talk, may be totally strange or at least not value-laden to an anthropologist; and all the fighting jargon that exists in any profession that is in the process of change is all strange; you don't know what the word "integration" means, or you think you do and it means something quite different.

Hart: There's another sense, though, in which the statement that we don't know anything about education is perfectly silly. I would have thought most anthropologists spend a lot of their time educating students in anthropology, and most of this division between educators and anthropologists seems to be phony. Anthropologists spend a lot of their time trying to teach anthropology in an ideal setting—in universities, where they can do as they like in their own anthropology courses to impart this wonderful thing called the anthropological point of view. I hope that somewhere in this conference the anthropologists will be put on the spot as to how they do it. I don't think we're doing a very good job of it.

Kimball: There's a difference between teaching techniques and understanding the historical depth and the assumptions and theories of a whole professional movement. That's what I was trying to say.

Mead: I think the social sciences have suffered for years from the fact that lay people have always thought they understood the whole point. We've always said that the natural sciences have an easier time because the layman doesn't think he understands biology or physics; but when you talk about human beings and social relationships, everybody thinks he understands them. And to think that, because one is an academic professor in a university, one understands the structure, the ethos, the eidos, the language, the functioning, the personality, and everything else about a professional movement like education, I think would be to deny the whole intrinsic style of professional groups.

Cowley: It seems to me that we ought to quit talking at this conference about whether we're educationists or anthropologists. Whatever our backgrounds may be, I'm reminded again and again in discussions of this sort of Jacques Loeb's response to the question whether he was a chemist or a bacteriologist: he didn't know; he studied problems. Now we have a whole series of problems; I should like to see us identify what the educationist has to contribute and what the anthropologist has to contribute. This is the only fruitful way we can attack this, instead of going back and forth and saying, "I'm an anthropologist, I don't know anything about education," or vice versa. These papers bring out certain problems, and it's about the problems that I'd like to talk rather than about whether we're in this discipline, or whether education is a discipline, which I frankly don't believe it is.

Section II

MODELS FOR THE ANALYSIS OF THE EDUCATIVE PROCESS IN AMERICAN COMMUNITIES

BERNARD J. SIEGEL
Stanford University

Introduction

In this paper an attempt will be made to raise certain questions about cultural transmission in the American school and community within appropriate frames of reference. The primary objective will be to analyze the forces which tend to maintain or to distort the explicit cultural elements between their entry into teacher-training institutions and their selection and interpretation by children in the classroom.

The term "model" has been used rather loosely by social scientists in recent years as a close approximation to the terms "frame of reference," and "design." The notion of a model has the advantage, perhaps, of connoting structural properties of the phenomena under investigation, *particularly of creating a familiar image* for the consideration of novel or unfamiliar situations which have properties similar to those of known, or hypothecated, situations. It is in this mood, rather than in the technically more accurate sense of a mathematical model, that I shall use the term. It suggests, simply, a convenient way of thinking about the role of the educational system in the training of the young.

The following remarks are largely exploratory. They are not the result of specific researches carried on by the writer, nor do they constitute a critical appraisal of researches by others. Rather, they reflect the reactions of one anthropologist, with cultural and social-psychological orientations, to the challenging subject matter of this conference. It is hoped that the suggested designs for thinking about these problems will have some constructive value in formulating research projects related to them.

Some Assumptions and Concepts

For purposes of my argument I shall have to make explicit certain assumptions about the nature of the educational community and clarify whatever concepts may be used in the process. To begin with, we mean by the educational community the *formal* school system—sites and interacting members, stated goals, and the role relations in terms of which the goals are translated into action. These, at least, are the primary elements of the system. It is recognized that in the dynamics of activating this system intrusive or intervening factors distort the intent of the formal blueprint in several respects. Principals and teachers may perceive and use their roles in different ways, in relation partly to personality factors and partly to situational conditions. Concerning the latter, the organization might have grown in size, so that patterns of communication, once successful, now break down at several points. Similarly, varying rates in the turnover in personnel can affect the degree of sharing of common goals and values of the institution. Compensatory adjustments for these and other disturbances within the educational community give rise to informal —or at least unintended—sets of relationships and distortions of the formal system. Our contention is not that such resulting forces are unimportant, but rather that their full significance can best be understood by a prior analysis of the organizational design originally intended for the school. Moreover, it is also suggested that the formal system itself will yield useful insights into the processes of transmission and creative alteration of cultural items within the school. Articulating with the focal educational community, moreover, are two additional and important segments of the total community: (1) the centers of higher learning; (2) class and ethnic family units from which the students are drawn. A third segment, the membership of which is recruited from the above categories, is the school board. Presumably board decisions reflect prevailing community attitudes and sentiments, inasmuch as the positions are elective ones. But since the board has direct face-to-face relationships with school executives and operates more in a leadership capacity, it can be considered as an independent force.

The school, looked at from our point of view, is no isolated organization; its operational structure is continually affected by outside environmental forces. It does not set its own goals, nor can it seek to implement them completely independently of other community agencies. The relationship between the educational community and the community as a whole, however, is reciprocal and interacting. The former is not to be visualized as responding unilaterally and automatically to outside forces which impinge upon it. It obviously must make most of its day-by-day decisions and operate *as if it were* an independent organization. Moreover, its explicit goals (to educate the young for certain purposes and in certain ways) are better and more fully understood by the interacting participants than by outside members of the community as a whole. The educational community has its own culture—albeit a dependent and not an autonomous one—including norms for behavior of participants and values underlying and supporting these norms. What happens in the operation of the school system, moreover, may also be expected to work back to affect the values, sentiments, and operations of the tangential segments with which it interacts, i.e., families and teacher-training centers.

Like any other organization, the educational community exhibits certain regularities in the behavior of its members in carrying on the functions of the group. By charting these regularities we can construct a *structure of alignments*, which will also indicate the varying *characteristics* of the different statuses, or positions within the structure. Individuals who occupy certain statuses, for example, are in a position formally to make decisions and to display authority that affects some or all individuals who occupy other statuses. Conversely, the statuses of some will have built into them few or no rights of leadership and decision-making affecting others. The personnel are thus formally organized on a hierarchical (viz., administrator-teacher) and a co-ordinate (viz., teacher-grade) basis.

The school system, conceived as an educational community, has many structural and cultural features in common with other professional com-

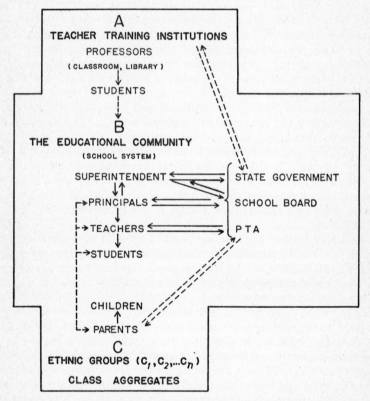

FIGURE I   ACCULTURATIVE FACTORS AFFECTING THE TRANSMISSION OF CULTURAL MATERIALS IN THE SCHOOL SYSTEM

LEGEND: 1. Capital letters, A, B, and C, stand for major collectivities in interaction and their cultures.
2. Arrows signify the direction of authority and main powers for decision making.
3. Dotted arrows indicate intercultural relationships.

munities, viz., the therapeutic community (hospital). Because of the relatively low rank accorded to education as an end-value (in the sense of exciting the young about expanding the frontiers of knowledge), it also differs from the latter. To a considerable extent, education as a value is considered and treated as instrumental to the pursuit of other values (power, wealth, social position). Hence there is much possible ambiguity in the interpretation of its goals and methods within the greater locality. It has different kinds of attractions, interpretations, or repulsions for different segments of the community at large, as well as within the various levels of the educational community itself.

If one accepts these assumed formal characteristics of the school system and its tangential relationships as a point of departure, there are then several possible ways of collecting, organizing, and interpreting data about its operation. We are, of course, particularly interested in how its functioning affects what is taught, and how what is taught is communicated and assimilated. It is the writer's contention—really a guiding hypothesis—that the flow of what is taught is screened, interpreted, and reinterpreted at several levels as a consequence of the carrying networks of role relationships.

One possible model for visualizing the over-all process of transmission would be based upon a theory of organizations (Selznick, 1948, 1949). In view of the specific sociological orientation of this framework, and the fact that it only remotely draws upon or contributes to anthropological understandings of the cultural process, I mention organizational analysis only in passing. There are two relevant models, however, which are closely geared to phenomena of cultural transmission as collated and interpreted by anthropologists. One of these is the familiar process of acculturation. The other is a so-called Channels Theory proposed by Kurt Lewin in a study of food habits. In the remainder of this paper an attempt will be made to analyze each of these in terms of the several dimensions of the problem to which it draws special attention.

The acculturation model.—For our purposes, we may define acculturation as culture change initiated by the continual interaction of two or more autonomous or quasi-autonomous communities,[1] and their cultures. Strictly speaking, the educational community is not autonomous, for it depends upon other collectivities for the recruitment of its personnel and, in part, for the carrying on of its policies. On the other hand, its teachers and administrative officers largely originate in distant localities, and its day-to-day operations are so extensively independent that we perhaps are justified in speaking of it as quasi-autonomous. It is in this sense that industrial concerns, hospitals, and similar social units have been treated as societies for the purposes of sociocultural analysis. We can therefore think of the school system as an organization standing in apposition to other

---

[1] The term "community" is used here in its primitive sense of a group with common interests and common loyalties.

collectivities to which it must adapt, and which in turn it seeks to influence. These multiple relationships can best be summarized by means of the preceding diagram (Fig. 1, page 40), which I shall attempt to explicate in some detail below.

In this schematic presentation only the formal structure of relationships is considered. Informal alignments, such as cliques and less permanent or unrecognized groups, perform important functions for shared needs of individuals arising from the inadequacies of the formal organizations. What these needs are and how urgently they are felt can best be evaluated, it is felt, by prior consideration of formally available channels of cultural transmission.

Each of the collectivities represented by capital letters (A, B, C) may be conceived as exhibiting separate subcultures. We are primarily concerned, then, with the way in which *what is meant to be imparted*—the "educational packages"[2]—to the student-child actually reaches him from its point of origin. The educational packages will be limited in our discussion to the formal contents (textbooks, classroom presentations and materials, teachers' manuals, reading assignments, etc.) originating primarily with the teachers of teachers. It is understood that many attitudes and biases— e.g., on sex morality and cleanliness—are consciously or unconsciously betrayed in the classroom as they are in the home, and that their impact is important to assess. In order to establish some control over the content of what is intended to be learned, I have arbitrarily restricted the problem to the transmission of formal materials, or explicit culture.

The way in which content is transmitted, e.g., from level A to level B, is conditioned theoretically by several factors, such as (1) the degree of consistency of the values in each of the subcultures; (2) the extent of agreement of the members of the collectivities on these values; (3) the kinds of role relations established between participants in the several subcultures (these have also been referred to as "intercultural role relations") (S. S. R. C. Seminar, 1954), and (4) the perception of one's own roles and of content intended for transmission. Although no formal content originates in C, the latter is obviously significant as a third force in affecting what reaches the end products (children) and how it is perceived by them. The picture is structurally not unlike political third-force movements, in which one national unit stands between two other cultural units and must react continuously to the pushes and pulls exerted upon it from both directions.

Teaching members of the academic community tend to share a distinc-

---

[2] The term "educational packages" is not meant to imply unchanging objects or contents that pass ultimately to the child intact. As will become abundantly clear from the text, these packages may change their form and meaning for participants in each of the cultures involved; they may also have different *adjustive functions* for individuals at different levels and hence be *used* by them in different ways for varying ends. What is accented in A may be slighted in B and in C, or vice versa. They may be identified as specific objects, utterances, and the like, but for the above reasons they become different things to carrying categories of individuals who have anything to do with them.

tive set of values which set them apart from other segments of the population. Among other things, they look upon education not only as providing tools for the pursuance of other values, but also as contributing to long-range satisfactions for the individual, or as an end in itself. They are concerned also with innovating both upon the content of what is transmitted and upon the ways in which this can be done. The process is a continuous one, in that the implications of traditional practice and of innovations are constantly subject to assessment and re-evaluation. Hence the understanding which teachers of teachers will have, let us say, of Dewey's pragmatism in relation to education is based upon a broad intellectual grasp and upon viewing its operation in a wide variety of contexts. The same might be said of their grasp of learning theories, of cultural processes, of child growth phases, etc. If we can assume a rather extensive agreement upon values and understandings, at least among the professional educators of any given institution, we should still need to assess the degree of agreement between any two such training institutions. Failing that, we must confine our investigation to the members and teacher-products of specific centers.

In different geographical regions potential grade school personnel probably come from relatively homogeneous sociocultural backgrounds, although this presumption requires verification (Warner, 1944). If this is the case, we might hypothesize (1) a rather high degree of consistency in their understandings of values built into the school system, and (2) broad similarities in the way they perceive their own roles and in the way they internalize their training experience. Should their own backgrounds prove to vary more, as they do in the population as a whole, we should expect the contrary to be the case.

In their role as students in the academic setting, school personnel (actual or potential) are brought into contact with only a part of the cultural reservoir of A, and for a limited period of time (or intermittently for limited periods of time). For this reason, and because they enter with a different set of attitudes and orientation to these ideas, they are apt to evaluate them from a limited (from the point of view of A) perspective. This is the nature of intercultural role relations, namely, that they involve the operation of processes of perceptual selectivity.

As a consequence of this selectivity—the adjustment of new learning to previously internalized patterns of thinking, doing, and believing—we can expect alterations in the educational packages by the time they reach the educational community (B). At the latter point, moreover, a similar process occurs whereby students, the ultimate objects of our inquiry, make further choices about what they learn, for what purposes, and with what commitments.

It is common knowledge that grade school children come from as wide a variety of family backgrounds as there are ethnic and class cultures, although this fact is often slighted in discussions about problems of mass education. One well-known study, at least, has indicated certain implications of primary and secondary school education in America for reinforcing the tendency to freeze the inferior occupational roles of ethnic and racial groups. Thus several technical high schools of California steered members of different minority groups—for example Negroes and Mexicans—into specific curricula and occupational training classes which lead to lower class levels of opportunity. Despite widespread opposition of parents, the vice-principal of one large school virtually segregated Mexican-American girls into domestic science courses which emphasize training in cooking, serving, and housework (Warner, 1944).

In this case there were obvious conflicts of self-conception and conception of others between B and C. The actions of B members cannot be construed as direct applications of marginal participation in A, but rather as special interpretations of what they perceived and selected from it. One might equally wish to know something of the home stresses and motivations which prompt students to elect attending technical high schools in preference to general schools. Several other differences in value orientation and ratings between school and family cultures undoubtedly influence what content is presented in what ways, on the one hand, and how it becomes an object of interest by students, on the other. Among them are conceptions of time—of organizing and economizing time—and of "progressive" self-cultivation, of ranking talents, and so forth.

The cultural (value-interest) forces at work in the contact relations of B and C are several. First, parents and teachers have separate and direct influence upon the children. Second, parent-teacher relations are both formal (P.T.A.) and personal. The intended function of these meetings is to explicate the congruence and conflict of values between the home and school as they are evidenced in the child's patterns of adjustment (viz., living up to ideals of conformity in the classroom). How these relations and interpretations are further communicated to the child—and with what effect on his learning tendencies— is an interesting subject for further investigation. Do the mother and teacher, for example, make the same criticisms and appreciate the same strengths in the child, so that their subsequent interaction with him leads to formation of different attitudes and learning readiness? Or are there conflicting reactions and judgments, such that the child is reinforced in basic behaviorial tendencies in the home, although these tendencies may already be prejudicial to internalizing educational content in the ways intended by the school?

The agreement or clash of explicit purposes between the school personnel and other public agencies, e.g., the school board, is similarly important to assess, as are consequences of classroom experiences (viz., reinforcement of generational conflict between children and parents). It becomes abundantly clear that an answer to the question, "How well does the school accomplish its objectives?" depends not only upon how well teachers and administrators know these objectives and techniques for achieving them; it depends also upon the dynamic interplay of value systems, interests, and shared self-concepts in contact among the several collectivities involved in the formal transmission process.

Although they have been omitted from this discussion, informal peer groups or relatively unstructured relations with age mates admittedly introduce yet another force—other patterns of values, interests, beliefs, attitudes—affecting the perceptual screening and selective learning of the child. Their very presence is evidence of certain lacks, unsatisfied desires, or frustrations within both home and school. It would therefore be desirable to investigate the areas wherein barriers are erected against acceptance of content transmitted within the school, and the effectiveness of leadership within these associations as well as upon the behavior of non-participant children.

The "channels" model.—In 1942 Kurt Lewin directed a project designed to study food habits of a Midwestern town (Lewin, 1951). The general question which he asked was, "How does food get on the table and why?" The answer to this question was conceived in terms of broad and narrow social channels through which food items passed from the points of origin to the table at which they were consumed. The characteristics of the channels and kinds of linkage from one to another were conceptually refined in the process of analysis to account for the adventures of food products, particularly at critical points along the traveled routes. For this purpose, culture was treated as a repetitive process rather than the product of some past history and was conceptualized as being in a state of dynamic equilibrium. "A culture," states Lewin, ". . . is not a static affair but a live process, like a river which moves but still keeps a recognizable form" (Lewin, pp. 172–73).

It is unnecessary to concern ourselves with the details of this specific study, but the frame of reference utilized may have some possible utility for a consideration of cultural transmission in American school systems. As we shall see, the channels model is related to that of acculturation, and simply constitutes a slightly different—and to some, perhaps a more congenial—way of organizing and looking at the same phenomena. Instead of asking how food gets on the table, however, let us substitute the phrase, "How educational packages get into the child and why." The student becomes the focal point of inquiry, and we then attempt to trace the channels through which understandings are molded and pushed in his direction, as he proceeds on his way to becoming a formally finished product. We are, in effect, dealing with the *learning habits* of the child, for they represent sets of behavioral tendencies which are created by a variety of converging forces (see Fig. 2).

The incorporation of new learning by a child is in large measure a product of past habit, what reaches him, the role relations (contexts) in which the flow of materials occurs, and the values and ways of perceiving which underlie these relations. The effectiveness of one or another channel for the child will depend partly on cultural values. Thus, in families where a high value is placed upon formal learning, greater application and better performance may be expected than in those where education as a value ranks low. In other words, children from families of the former type

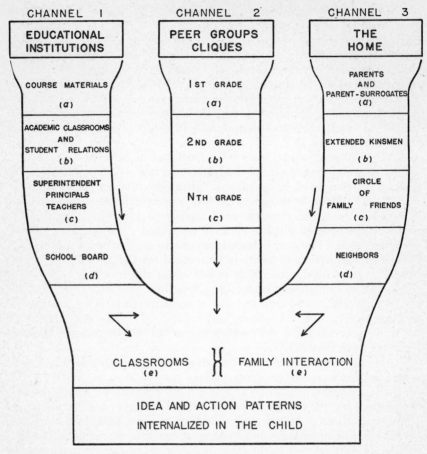

FIGURE 2   CHANNELS THROUGH WHICH EXPLICIT CULTURE
            REACHES THE CHILD

LEGEND: 1. SOLID LINES WITHIN EACH CHANNEL MARK OFF SECTIONS THROUGH WHICH
              CULTURAL CONTENT MUST PASS.

          2. ARROWS INDICATE THE DIRECTION OF STIMULI AND SOCIO — CULTURAL FORCES.

          3. SMALL LETTERS INDICATE SECTIONS WITHIN THE CHANNEL.

will make greater use of channel *1* than will children from those of the
latter type. They may not only take maximum advantage of what is formally presented in the classroom, but may also seek to go beyond it. From
the anthropological point of view we might say that the meaning and functions of learning in channels *1* and *2* are very similar, hence mutually reinforcing.

Many things can happen to the content of what is transmitted in any
channel as it passes from one section to another on its way to the child.

The "gates" are opened by one or more "gatekeepers." In the academic community the form and meaning of transmitted material enter channel *1* through the teachers of teachers. They control what enters, but not completely what happens to the materials since, as we have seen, student trainees may be expected to interpret cultural items in terms of the values they bring into the learning situation. If the ideology of educational training centers emphasizes the values of individual differences in, e.g., rates of learning, the trainee, on the other hand, may value the disciplinary aspects of the process; or else, he may look upon the ideology in special truncated ways. Merely "putting the packages" in the classroom or in the library will not guarantee that the trainee will retain either their meaning or their intended function in this section of the channel.

The teachers and administrators are the principal gatekeepers of what enters into section *B*—the school system itself. The "keys" which they use to open the gates are their own motivations, consisting in part of the *needs fulfilled* by their professional roles (commitment to education as a way of life, interest in child development, in power seeking, or simply as a job situation), and in part by values which they bring from other collectivities.

Meanwhile, similar processes are at work in channels *2* and *3*. The peer group channel is perhaps the most constant and consistent in the kinds of attitudes and action patterns which it instills. Participation itself in such informal relationships, as has been earlier suggested, is an index of unsatisfied needs or frustrations felt within the school system. Leaders are the gatekeepers and control entry of values and understandings shared by other members. The effectiveness of a teacher in having a student "digest" the understandings with which he is presented, we should expect, will vary inversely with the meaning which peer group ties have for the child.

In channel *3* there is similarly relatively high consistency of understandings between the sections through which cultural objects and patterns flow toward the child. Except for purposes of expediency it would be more accurate, also, to depict the sections as co-ordinate rather than linear, since the hierarchy of values, system of beliefs, and behavior patterns of parents or parent surrogates are usually reinforced by kinsmen and family friends, in so far as the latter have meaningful relations with the children. It is unnecessary for our purposes to review known processes of personality development, socialization, and learning which take place within the home and other primary groups outside the school. An awareness of how they dispose the child to respond to stimuli at the point of contact with the educational community is obviously critical, however, as the problem is viewed in this paper.

In the schools themselves the several social channels converge, thus creating a broad stream of *interacting* (not verging) forces. Congruence or conflict of values now can be studied in the interaction of community representatives (board members, school administrators, teachers, and parents). To continue with our analogy, there are several gatekeepers who control the widened and deepened channel; the flow of *educational* packages must compete with that of others. Explicit culture transmitted in the schools has a different weighting from understandings and orientations acquired outside them. At the final gate of this process, therefore, students will further select what they perceive as needed, desirable, anxiety-reducing, and rewarding in other ways. The classroom situation need not exhibit basic agreement with, e.g., family patterns, in order for maximum transmission to occur; it may accomplish the same end for some children because it is an outlet for rebellion against home constrictions and pressures. It would be desirable to ascertain in which kinds of family cultures the one case prevails and in which kinds the other, if indeed any regularity exists in the matter.

In brief, forms of understanding, their content and order of presentation, are blocked, truncated, or expanded, according to changing interpretations at each gate of the channel sections. Most gates require keys, and the keys are crucial in this process. They consist of cultural perception (viz., terms in which people think about education), values (motivations to acquire, subvert, emphasize, or underplay cultural items), and personality dispositions to behavior.

Summary and Conclusions

The foregoing discussion has centered upon the problem of how we can estimate what part of the educational packages—concrete understandings, norms of behavior, and attitudes toward new learning—is actually transmitted to the child in the school system, and with what effectiveness. The sociocultural factors that must be taken into consideration may be conceived a little differently, depending upon the particular frame of reference used for making and organizing observations about the process. In the one case, attention is focused upon the cultures of several communities in interaction: the characteristics of the cultures and the nature of role relations established at points of contact. Backgrounds and contact conditions between the several collectivities constitute the ground and figure, respectively, of the transmission of shared understandings. In the other case, the point of departure is the forces which permit cultural items to move in given forms and with intended meanings and functions through a variety of social agents until they reach the child.

In either event we are concerned essentially with the screening effect of values and learning habits, derived from multiple backgrounds, upon successive reinterpretations and/or reinforcements of behavior patterns. What minimal forms of concrete knowledge, ideology, and behavior norms do academic formulators try to impart to teachers and administrators in training? What functions or consequences for child development do they intend such elements to have as presented, in the light of their own theoretical understandings? To what extent are the intended functions understood and shared in like ways by trainees, and to what extent are they accepted in cult fashion or rejected entirely? The notion of "permissiveness" has certain meanings when interpreted intellectually and critically in terms of psychoanalytic theory (or in terms of some other developmental framework) ; it may be taken over and subsequently imparted quite differently by teachers with deeply ingrained constricted values. Or, again, teachers of teachers may seek in the same way to transmit concepts of personality adjustment based upon certain social psychological theories, only to have them interpreted and conveyed to the child as conformity toward the middle level.

We may expect the same processes to operate in relations of local agencies, families, and children with the educational community. How do values placed upon specific formal materials and upon education itself coincide or conflict? What rank order does the over-all activity have in each group? And, finally, what use does the child make of his school experience in integrating it with extraschool experiences—previously or currently instilled goal orientations, self-conceptions, and role relations? These are illustrative of the central questions which emerge from the above analysis. Answers to them will be possible only in the course of systematic, long-range research programs, in which comparative case studies of each phase of the process become available.

References

Lewin, Kurt. 1951. "Psychological Ecology," Dorwin Cartwright (ed.), in *Field Theory in the Social Sciences*. New York: Harper & Brothers, pp. 170–87.

Selznick, Philip. 1948. "Foundations of the Theory of Organization," *American Sociological Review*, XIII, 25–35.

———. 1949. *TVA and the Grass Roots: A Study in the Sociology of Formal Organization*. Berkeley: University of California Press.

Social Science Research Council Summer Seminar on Acculturation. 1954. "Acculturation: An Exploratory Formulation," *American Anthropologist*, LVI, 973–1002.

Warner, W. L., R. J. Havighurst, M. B. Loeb. 1944. *Who Shall Be Educated? The Challenge of Unequal Opportunities*. New York: Harper & Brothers.

FIRST SESSION OF THE CONFERENCE, CONTINUED

Discussant: F. M. Keesing

Keesing: The paper sets up a series of "models" or "images," and the discussion must test out how far they ring true to the educator. It would not be expected that they would ring 100 percent true, and Bernie (Siegel) protects his position by remarking that he has rather formalized and simplified them for purposes of analysis. The issue concerns their theoretical and methodological helpfulness rather than whether they are minutely accurate as an educator sees them from his professional experience. Bernie also points out that they are not based on research. I found myself not too clear, in reading the materials, how far they derive from his anthropological and social science sophistication as such, or from his personal experience as a parent of two young children, as a teacher of anthropology, or as a citizen in the community. I think all of these elements show in different measures.

The models are concerned primarily with "transmission." To whom? The child. What? Educational "packages." By whom? The paper is dominantly concerned with this dimension. The social structure aspects are presented: the "collectivities" and their interrelationships and interactions, the cultural context including value dimensions. Stress is laid upon the status and role networks involved. But here and there the individual is discussed as being drawn from different backgrounds, sometimes conforming to a role, sometimes behaving idiosyncratically. Role relations and individual variability come out, among other points, in the concept of "gatekeepers"; a concept which stresses an interpretive or sifting function occurring at crucial points in all these interrelations. An "acculturation" model is also introduced. This is, to an extent, an analogy from the conventional acculturation model of anthropology in which two different cultures interact, rather than, as here, two "significant cultural systems," or "subcultures," as John (Gillin) calls them in his paper. There is also a "channels" model.

As a starting point, I would like to raise the question as to whether the social structure dimensions set out in the text, and in the two accompanying diagrams, ring true. Anthropologists might well say to the educator, "We could help you study, with our specialized anthropological tools, the structural aspects of the collectivities, the education community, and so on, as delineated here. But is that new? Or to what extent could the anthropologist make fresh contributions? Do the educators already know their total social structure in the way an anthropologist would look at it?" This seems much more important than the question of whether all the social structure elements are identified, though this may also be considered. It is my impression, having children now in the university and having seen them wrestling for years with homework, that a great deal of the interaction phenomena of the child with the educational process is concerned with the direct relation to teaching materials, so that the textbook writers would need to appear as a dimension of the structure. Or again, teachers' professional associations might come to mind as very important in role-status definition and other educational dimensions. We could probably all name other dimensions of this kind. But you might want as educators to question in other ways Bernie's attempts at a symbolic or structured definition of the collectivities involved.

From the viewpoint of the cultural milieu in which transmission operates, I myself would raise the question as to whether the use of the "acculturation model" by analogy is perhaps the best one. Would it not be better to face the cultural situation directly by setting up a model or models which will illuminate for educators the phenomena of interaction among "subcultures" or "significant cultural systems" within the larger milieu of "a culture" as traditionally defined by anthropologists? The actual text of the paper really amounts to this, and so covers it, but the terminology might cause confusion.

Next, the concept of educational "packages" is an interesting one; we might well want to raise questions relating to that. I myself tend to feel uncomfortable about pushing too far here Lewin's "channels" theory, or any "package" idea as such, as being perhaps overmechanistic and taking inadequate account of the child as an active participant in the interaction process. I would prefer to build upon later communication or information theory, as Jules Henry attempts to do, using the concept of "messages," or whatever you may like to call the interaction behavior. But I think it would be very interesting to follow up with the educators the implications of the "package" idea. The same is true of the "gatekeeper" concept; maybe this, too, is a little mechanistic. How far is it a useful concept? I raise these questions of terminology because I am somewhat worried as to whether the educators would consider the child in these models to be overpassive, or might judge that anthropologists still accept an obsolete theoretical position in which the child tends to be treated as passive in the face of his culture. The second of the model diagrams particularly leaves the child (shown at the bottom of three "channels") as a somewhat passive recipient of varied influences except perhaps for those originating in "peer group" relations.

Another question which obviously interests Bernie, and which we may wish to discuss, is that of tensions between the peer groups and the formal educational transmitters, the teachers and the parents and other collectivities. I have a suspicion that educators might say that this is less so in modern schools than in the school of our own generation; that a teacher would be counted unsuccessful to the extent to which he or she did not align the teaching process with the peer group, so that peer group standards merge at least to a considerable degree with the standards and values that have been set by the teacher. Furthermore, are the peer group–home relationships really in opposition to the extent that is spelled out, in terms of tensions and especially of cause-effect relations?

The problem of constructing diagrams in relation to such problems is of particular interest to me. I would have liked to see Bernie try them out perhaps in three dimensions rather than two. I found it more useful to look at his two diagrams as representing structural "plans" (i.e., from above) rather than "side elevations," particularly so because the hierarchical gradings among the collectivities and in relation to the child when looked at on an up-and-down two-dimensional diagram worried me considerably. Three-dimensional models might serve to show both co-ordinate and hierarchical relations more adequately. The lines and arrows in the diagrams also caught my attention as being sometimes dubious. For example, in Figure 1, the "teacher training institutions" has only one line, apart from the one to the state authority, and that with a downward arrow only to the teacher-to-be in the educational community. Does this mean that there is no interaction upward from the educational community to the teachers college, and no relation between the teachers college and such other collectivities as the ethnic and family milieu? Or again, in Figure 2, the lines and arrows do not show any interaction with attendant "gate-keeping" among the three different channel columns, i.e., the peer groups to the formal educational process groups, and so on. Useful and suggestive as they are, therefore, I believe the educators could have quite a busy time adding to or reorganizing the variables and dimensions involved. Here, too, I must add the reminder that Bernie was primarily concerned with conceptual and methodological questions rather than trying to give the last word on structures, the cultural milieu, the status system, the interaction systems.

DuBois (Chairman): May we go on to Solon's (Kimball) comments before the group takes part so that we will have both of the discussants heard from?

Discussant: Solon T. Kimball

Kimball: There is one comment that I think is of some importance, as regards the first model. Siegal refers to the collectives A, B, and C as exhibiting, or as being, separate subcultures. Now, the first question I will ask is this: Are you dealing with the same order of phenomena in each of these three? The first two categories refer to persons in interacting institutions, but in category C the reference is to classifications of persons, based on behavior. So that C, which is important to the problem, to be of the same order would need to have listed there the kinds of churches, associations, economic and other kinds of institutions which are in the system you are examining. In that connection, although I appreciate that you have a perfect right to do this however you want to, I rather think that you have limited yourself too much. I appreciate that there are reasons for this because if you include too much you get yourself in difficulties. But where you exclude the information organization of systems A and B— the clique behavior and other kinds of informal behavior which occur—you are excluding what may be a very significant part of the total aspects of these two collectives. Where you limit yourself to the transfer of behavior through formal systems, which seems legitimate, you still get yourself into difficulties, because oftentimes these can only be understood as they relate to the perhaps less formal behavior which enters into the picture.

As between the two models, I would say that I found the second model much clearer, sharper, and easier to understand, which may be a function of the difficulties involved in developing your first model. The presentation of the two models has the merit of showing there is more than a single way that a problem of this kind can be approached. Two ways are illustrated for us, with implications that there are additional ways.

OPEN DISCUSSION

The Utility of the Models

DuBois (Chairman), Siegel, Thomas, Taba, Henry, Mead, Martin

DuBois: We've heard from two discussants, both classifiable as anthropologists; it seems to me that we ought to turn to the educators now for a less formal discussion and comment on what this paper has communicated to them, what meaning this has to the educational world. Does anyone want to take that up now?

Thomas: I thought that Fee Keesing's observations showed a very high level of understanding of the problems of education as professional educationists see them. And any nonanthropologists here who wonder about their sharing the same kinds of insights the educators have on this can take their cue from Fee's remarks, and judge themselves.

I have in mind his observation of the possibly too passive role of the child, down at the bottom of Figure 2, his doubts about the package as being an adequate conception of the material as it is reconstructed in the learning process. These are two cases of the very high level of insight which I want to endorse. I have no elaboration to make; I'm delighted to have him in his professional role raise the points.

Siegel: May I respond to that for a moment? I think the point of passivity is a perfectly legitimate one, but actually, I really didn't intend to imply that. The basic emphasis and orientation that I started out with in this paper was that at various levels, at various crucial points in transmission, there is the problem of selectivity, and that two of the most important factors involved in selectivity are those of perception of what is meant to be conveyed, and motivation. I think both of these operate; I accept the fact that these processes are operative with the child as they are with the adult. I think that this particular level of perception, reorganization, reshaping, and internalization goes on within the child. I don't think, however, that that particular point was negated by the model, although it might be obscured by the two-dimensional character of the drawings. I also agree again with Solon's (Kimball) remarks on the importance of things that have been excluded from the paper, particularly the importance of informal organizations. I think that they're extremely important in effect, but one of the reasons I excluded this is because I found myself at a certain point going off on a tangent on this particular issue, and I think it is a subject for a separate paper. I do feel it's useful to take the given framework in its formal sense and try to understand it in terms of its particular goals and its particular processes, and then come back to the implications and reasons for the development of informal structures that emerge along the way. Why do they emerge in the first place, and once having emerged, what are their relations on working back into the functioning of the formal organization?

Martin: Keesing touched on this point; I would like to make it a little more explicit. It worried me a little as I looked at both models to find that these "educational packages" originate with the teacher of teachers, and teachers appear to be the determiners of the cultural content to be transmitted. They seem to do this out of the context of any value matrix; they seem to represent nobody; they do not seem to reflect the needs or wishes of a society or any cultural traditions. I wondered what they were doing out there, standing in splendid isolation.

Siegel: Well, again they don't stand by themselves. This is related to the criticism made by Solon (Kimball) as to the inadequacy, in a sense, of the *C* category in the acculturation model. Obviously, the content of what originally gets transmitted to teachers emerges from a certain context of values and reasons for developing them in the first place. This is something which I think we could develop as a problem in itself. How do they develop? How are they communicated at that level? How are they formalized within the teacher institutions? To what extent are they shared, also, as between one institution and another so that there is a consistency in the creation of the formal elements of organized understandings and content, etc.? These things are certainly all involved in the fact that the academic community formulates these things and presents them in the training of teachers, and does so under certain stresses, with certain motivations and for certain reasons. But we have to start some place.

Martin: It seems to me, once it has been decided what is to be taught, that at least the professional educator decides how best it's to be taught. The method is the problem of the teacher, but the selection of content is not.

Taba: A static diagram tends to convey a wrong impression of anything that is so multidimensional. Maybe a concrete example will help. A static model can only convey the structure, but not the dynamics. One cannot visualize how much the teacher can do with what has been prescribed. I'll describe to you an eighth grade teacher who is teaching civics to Italian lower-class children. She herself is a prissy New Englander who condemns heartily any lacks in English, in cleanliness, in discipline, and in good behavior. She is facing an ethnic group, and she has a task: she has her own objectives and she has something prescribed. Her first major reaction to it is, "These boys and girls don't want to learn; these boys and girls don't have the capacity to learn, but I'll hammer at it anyway. I'll do the best I can to make them write better papers, to make them comprehend the American Constitution, and to accept the school mores— to behave according to the routines and classroom ways." That teacher came packaged, in a sense, from teachers college and from her own cultural learning. But she also is in an environment to which she can learn to make new responses and of which she can make new analyses, especially if helped. And one question that she was helped to ask was, "What were these boys and girls really doing when they were indulging in what I called disciplinary behavior?" She had condemned this behavior. But when she started describing it she discovered she had not looked at it at all. For example, there was the boy who, noticing she had trouble in controlling her class, came up to her and said, "Teacher, if you want me to, I can beat up the whole class." She had thought that boy was just mischievous. Actually, what the boy was saying was something quite different. He was saying first, "Teacher, I want to co-operate with you"; second, "There is a way of controlling this class; I know what it is, and that's beating them up." He was well-intentioned rather than ill-intentioned, but his concrete suggestion was directed by his concept of co-operation. He interpreted the things that she wanted in the light of his culture and his perception of the peer culture in the class. Once the teacher saw that, she had a new orientation to her job and she could begin to reorganize her civics, in spite of the school rules, school board, and prescribed state curriculum. There was a whole lot of latitude in those prescriptions once new dynamics were set in. Your kind of model does not even hint at this possibility. Yet you can misinterpret this structure terribly without considering at the same time these dynamics, which are available to any ordinary public school teacher with a little bit of coaching.

The stuff for relearning was in that very relationship of her to her students. That relationship was more vital than is conveyed by the model; it's not just packaged, it's something done. It isn't as closed as it looks from your scheme.

Henry: I must confess a certain fondness for formal models, and this, it seems to me, satisfies many of the requirements of a good formal model, but I think the position that we take as observers is very important. Dr. Taba takes one position; in your setting up of this formal model you (Siegel) take another position. Now, I think Dr. Taba in what she has said and Dr. Kimball in what he has said have considered themselves as observers within the classroom situation. However, if you consider yourself somewhat removed from this, then your model has very specific meaning to me. Let us think, for example, of the structure of the educational system in the Soviet Union. The teacher-training institutions are made up of individuals of a highly selected group with a very specific kind of ideology. And what is selected then in terms of the Soviet position in the world, how the Soviet Union views itself in the world, how the governing body views the internal structure of the Soviet Union; all these determine who are selected to be teachers. These views will also exercise a certain selectivity over the students. The educational community in a particular Soviet village, let us understand, is more than the teachers; it is also the Young Communist League and other organizations that exercise a more informal pressure on how the school system will operate. The superintendent is also particularly selected. How civics is taught, then, is determined by an over-all picture. When we get closer inside the Soviet classroom, changing our position as observers, then how the particular teacher functions is relevant to what Dr. Taba was saying. But I think we ought not to disregard the excellence of this formal model for considering over-all patterns which determine the types of situations within which the teacher has to operate and the particular content selected for teaching.

Normative or Descriptive?

Brameld, Keesing

Brameld: It might be helpful, in discussion not only of this paper but of other papers following, if we are more self-conscious than we may now be as to the distinction between what we might call *descriptive* models and *normative* models— whether they're written out as models or not. I'm not entirely sure whether the models that are presented here are descriptive or normative in character. I take it that anthropologists are primarily concerned with descriptive models, but educators are not. They are concerned at least as much with normative models. Jim Quillen really implied that when he stressed educational objectives and purposes as part of the educational task. Sometimes Hilda (Taba), for instance, is referring partly to normative models, that is, to what is desirable as well as factual. For surely we're defending the kind of education we believe in, at the same time that we may be describing education as it exists. Now, this acculturative model, and the other one also to a considerable extent, is a descriptive model which I would repudiate normatively. The arrows pointing down, for instance, constitute a hierarchical kind of structure that, from the point of view of what I would call good educational objectives, is undesirable and ought to be opposed. Couldn't we really think of this paper, and also others to be discussed, as a series of models? One type is the descriptive model of what the anthropologist sees as the situation, as he describes it, objectively and scientifically; the other type is the purely normative model which perhaps doesn't exist at all in reality. In between these two extremes we have a whole range of models which are partly descriptive and partly normative; in other words, models in process of being achieved. At the present time, for instance, there are probably a great many American schools that are really not as hierarchical as this model suggests; on the other hand, they're probably not normatively ideal either. A whole series of models is therefore possible—a whole spectrum from the descriptive end to the normative end, and we get confused in our discussion of anthropological descriptions of education, or any other scientific descriptions, by failing to keep the distinction between what is being described, on the one hand, and what is the normatively desirable objective, on the other hand. There is a tendency, I think, to sneak in our value judgments sometimes and to say, "Whatever is, is right," as Alexander Pope said.

Keesing: Could I just say that I never for an instant thought the models presented were "normative"; they were rather more "modal" models. A last point that I had intended to raise in my discussion, but didn't, was, "How does an educator look at these models in view of his needs for evaluation?"

Peer Groups and Their Functions

Taba, Siegel, Spindler, Cowley, Mead, Hart, Coladarci
Henry (Chairman)

Taba: When you look at the chart of the flows here—that is, channel *1, 2,* and *3*—there is the same kind of difficulty of the flows going down each channel, without any indication that there is simultaneously a flow up. We know in education, for example, that the peer groups establish what you might call a climate within which the school materials are or are not acceptable, that is, are or are not motivating forces. A simple example of this is a C-club in one school system, where the requirement of belonging is that nobody is out to get more than C's in courses. That club is definitely influencing the receptivity to the teaching in that school. That is channel 2 influencing what goes on in channel 1; and in reverse you might have to say that channel 1 has to pay attention to what happens in channel 2, because it does have that influence. Or, to take the positive end—if we accept what Riesman says about the American culture becoming an other-oriented culture (that is, people are looking over their shoulders at their peers and asking, What will other people think of me? rather than, What did my mother teach me?), or what other sociologists say about the increase of social distance in families between generations because of increasing rapidity of social change—then it is important for those in channel 1 to think how to create the motivations that will allow us to transmit the American ideals and core values through channel 2, and not depend for transmission entirely on channel 3 and channel 1. If the normal communication of values decreases for the above reasons, then the question in education is how to introduce into channel 2 (the peer groups), which is an open channel, a content more appropriate to maintaining core values of culture than is the present content of adolescent groups. This is the job for all people—schools, social agencies, etc.—who are handling peer groups. From the standpoint of education this crosswise channeling seems to be the important consideration, rather than looking at each one of these channels separately.

Siegel: This would be, I imagine, an exceedingly difficult problem, simply because if all the needs and content that are transmitted and developed in peer groups could be met either in the home or in educational institutions or in any other channel, then presumably peer groups wouldn't develop. And if they do, then the problem of communication would be very difficult. The fact is that peer groups are distinct simply because their members want to be distinct from either the home or any other center of communication. Hence they communicate among themselves.

Spindler: I want to say in respect to this argument that I don't quite understand why we have to think of the effectiveness of teachers as varying inversely with the meaning the peer group might have for the child, because age groups always exist; they are vehicles that can have a variety of kinds of content; if they happen to represent a reciprocal function to frustration within the system, this is an accident of the system; this is not necessarily because of the nature of peer groups as a universal or inevitable social phenomenon.

Henry (Chairman): I would like to say at this point that Dr. Spindler and Dr. Taba both stated issues. It seems to me the problem is, What can anthropology do with such issues? Dr. Taba has stated specifically that sometimes values of the peer group frustrate the purpose of the educational system. The issue is, What is the specific problem that anthropology can formulate, and how can we attack it?

Spindler: It seems to me that this is a legitimate anthropological problem. The age grade or peer group is a type of social phenomenon that has, possibly, universal characteristics. Age grade groups exist wherever there are children. We ought to be able to take such a statement, that we know about or can find out about through our cross-cultural research, and say, "As a universal social phenomenon, what function or varieties of functions do peer groups have in cultural transmission?" and then go back to the model that Bernard (Siegel) has constructed out of anthropological hypotheses and ask new questions or modify the construct.

Cowley: As I understand the question which Mr. Henry has raised, it is, What has the anthropologist to offer in meeting this situation? Now educationists have met such situations. I'll give you a classical example. You talk about the C-grade tradition; when Lowell became president of Harvard in 1909, he found a C-grade tradition that dominated the institution, and he killed it in three years. He did it almost singlehandedly; he did it as an educationist. Now what have the anthropologists to offer? This is historical fact; when he became president of Harvard, only 2 percent of the students were graduating with honors; twenty-four years later 44 percent of the students were making honors. What has the anthropologist to say that can balance what has been done operationally by an educationist without benefit of anthropology?

Mead: I would say the difference would be that for what Lowell did you need a special kind of gifted personality. One of the things we hope to do when we introduce the social sciences or any other science into a situation is to get sufficient mastery over the situation so that it doesn't take the exceptional and unusual person, and it doesn't take a Churchill or a Roosevelt or a President Lowell to deal with it. That would be the difference. Very likely Lowell used a large number of methods that could also be recommended from cross-cultural studies, but what we want to do is to make those more available. For instance, we would attack cross-culturally: under what circumstances is the peer group culture operative —in the period below puberty, or in the period at puberty, or in the period after puberty—and in what ways can we find out from cross-cultural studies whether a graded series of peer groups, such as we are likely to produce by our very narrow age grading in our grade schools, has different effects from wider and more inclusive grading? What can we find out, for instance, from comparing the English, French, American peer group systems in their relations with schools? What are the effects of increasing the heterogeneity within the peer groups? You're more likely to get hazing in a homogeneous, one-sex, one-class peer group, while the increasing heterogeneity by sex and race may alter certain types of sanctions. The answer to that type of question is within the range of cross-cultural research.

Hart: I think one way the anthropologist could grapple with Dr. Taba's question is by remembering that in a lot of our anthropological studies we run into a type of situation where there is a certain amount of competition between institutions in the same culture. And in the form Dr. Taba put her question, I think she is suggesting that, because educationists in America have found that the peer groups are very successful in teaching kids certain things, therefore, if the community at large can use the peer groups as vehicles of transmission, they might be able to teach the kids certain things they are not able to teach in the schools. And if that is what is implied there, I think it's quite wrong. That the peer groups are successful in teaching the kids certain things is true, but peer groups are successful just because parents and teachers don't approve of them. Competition or conflict is an important element in transmission. As soon as the peer groups start teaching things that the parents or school-teachers approve of, the peer group will cease to be a good vehicle of communication of those very things. In most of the discussion of Dr. Siegel's paper, the element of competition between channel *A*, channel *B*, and channel *C* has been neglected.

Henry: I think that Mr. Hart has stated a very important issue. If you are going to use the peer group, then the characteristics of the peer group must be very specifically understood. The peer groups, for example, teach spelling in the schoolroom very differently from the way the teacher teaches the spelling. As you watch spelling taught in a game of spelling baseball, all the elements of competition, rejection, selection, gratification, that peer groups exercise over their members enter specifically into the situation, and this is not the intention of the school curriculum. Now, this would be a contribution that anthropology could make; not to take the peer group simply as a given, but to understand the very specific qualities that the peer group can communicate to the information itself.

Mead: And the peer groups will be different even in different parts of our society. The peer group in rural areas, the peer group in certain foreign-born areas, is a very different phenomenon from the peer group in middleclass, just run-of-the-mill America.

Siegel: I also think that there is a distinction to be made between the informal and the more formalized, quasi-formal peer group as well.

Hart: Well, most of the education in peer groups, I would think, is of an informal character; if you transfer some of the learning of the peer groups to the schools, then you transfer it from the informal to the formal.

Quillen: A number of educators are now trying to make the classroom Group A, utilizing the reciprocal reinforcement that comes from peer group interaction as a basis for the transmission of values and attitudes.

Brameld: I'd like to illustrate that point with just one simple example. New Lincoln School, in New York, has been experimenting for several years with what is called inter-age groups. Instead of having the kind of structure indicated in channel 2, they have set up the curriculum in such a way as to enable the students of three or four different age levels to work together as groups, simply because they think that is in itself a learning experience.

Henry: I am very much interested in the "they." Who are the "they?"

Brameld: By "they" in this case I mean the faculty, who decided to experiment with inter-age groups (the students of three or four different age levels—third, fourth, fifth grades, for instance) on the assumption that peer groups are themselves learning experiences.

Lee: I am confused at this point. As I see it, the classroom situation is based on age grouping, but it has been created by the administration or by the teacher, not by the children themselves, and the motivation is furnished by the teacher and not by the situation. Then you have the peer groups that form themselves outside the school . . .

Quillen: Or inside the school; that's the point. The teachers are trying to use the peer group formation technique within the classroom itself and also outside the school.

Lee: Yes. The teachers use the motivations that come up in a spontaneous, motivated peer group, which does exist already in the schoolroom. Now, what you're suggesting is cutting across the age groups, not forming a peer group any more, but forming something closer to the family grouping, to a group of siblings.

Henry: This is a very general theoretical consideration as to whether operation of the peer groups is, let us say, important or good, or whether breaking down the walls of the peer group and using members of different age groups is the best way to function. In this situation, I see the issue, not as a theoretical issue for anthropologists, but as what anthropology can contribute to clarifying the situation. This is what I think the educators would like to know about.

Mead: But, Jules (Henry), doesn't it mean that what the anthropologists will contribute here is of the order of the sorts of problems that Steve Hart raised? To what extent is the social opposition between the peer group and the parents dynamic, so that in attempting to capture it, you lose the thing that you were attempting to get? Under what circumstances, in what kinds of societies, with what kind of family pattern, does the inter-age group function, under what conditions, and how well? The anthropologist provides the comparative material which makes it possible, at least in part, to answer the question, "Which is best in this situation?"

Taba: You all talk about schools as if they were the same. From a comparative standpoint it's quite evident that the schools in which a middle-class culture is instituted and where the population of the school is predominantly lower-class, you're likely to find that the usual hostility between adolescents and their elders is accentuated, possibly because the socialization process has been a bit too vigorous. There are differences in morale, in spirit, in climate, whatever you call it—and presumably the peer groups have different characteristics too, but we don't know what they are. Nobody seems to be really looking at the school as a piece of indigenous culture. There are some schools in which peer groups completely borrow the social stratification of the surrounding community. There are other schools where this doesn't happen; we don't know why it doesn't, what produces the differences. School just hasn't been studied as a culture phenomenon.

Coladarci: I have a sort of procedural question, Jules (Henry), but I think it's substantive also. I have been thinking in terms of the theme articulated by Spindler and implied in the question posed by Fee (Keesing) earlier, and put to us several times by Hilda (Taba): in what ways can anthropologists help? My own feeling is this: since anthropologists have apparently rarely, maybe with a few exceptions, studied peer groups in the setting with which the educator is faced, the contribution of the anthropologist is a methodological one primarily. The concepts he has may prove fruitful, but at the present time in this particular setting, what I would like to have are some hypotheses with reference to the kinds of problems raised by the educators here and precipitated by the papers read—hypotheses engendered from, if you will, data gathered in whatever context they may have been gathered by the anthropologists, and in light of the unique methodology which the anthropologist has to offer, rather than as assertions of fact about peer groups.

Henry: As I look at the situation, the issue is really not the peer group. The issue is the contribution of anthropology to any particular situation. From statements that have been made here, I see this in different ways: one is, we must understand the internal dynamics of any particular group in order to understand how it functions in any situation, and anthropology can hopefully make some contributions to the understanding of the internal dynamics of the group. The other point, raised by Dr. Mead, is the problem of the boundaries of the peer groups, and what happens when we start to break them down. What contribution can anthropology make to the understanding of the boundaries of any kind of informal group? It seems to me that these issues have been stated implicitly, and it is along these lines that anthropology can make a contribution.

Spindler: May I add that there are substantive questions concerning the structure and function of peer groups in human society that can only be answered by empirical, cross-cultural research; this is an anthropological problem, and the knowledge gained in this approach can be imparted to the educator because it can give him a sense of limits as to those structures and functions—a sense of the *possibilities*, if you will.

Section III

THE SCHOOL IN THE CONTEXT OF THE COMMUNITY

JOHN GILLIN
University of North Carolina

This is a sort of outline of what public school teachers and administrators need to find out, rather than what they need to know, about their own schools in the context of the communities where they live. Considering the variety of communities in the contemporary United States, one would find it impossible in a limited space to supply educational personnel with a "handbook" of knowledge about any and all communities in which they might find themselves. On the other hand, I do not think it would be too difficult for them to discover for themselves most of the necessary facts about their particular communities, provided they have the guidance of certain principles and general information regarding American culture and community structure. The present paper aims to suggest the lines of interest public school teachers and administrators might find it rewarding to follow.

It is easy to say that, in cultural terms, it is the function of the teacher to transmit, or at least to attend or assist in, the transmission of culture to the younger generation. But once the public school educator is actually in a concrete situation, he must face up, either consciously or unconsciously, to questions like the following: What culture and what part of it am I transmitting? To whom? The children are not all alike either psychologically, socially, or culturally; what are the significant differences among them from the pedagogical point of view? And who am I in the eyes of my charges and their elders? That is, how is my role defined locally and how am I rated? These are some of the problems that face any teacher. The fact of psychological differences between pupils has long been recognized in advanced educational circles, and sundry methods of determining intelligence and emotional variations are more or less routinely used as a basis for the application of what are considered psychologically appropriate techniques of instruction.

Formulators of educational policy, however, have lately become aware that the psychological approach alone is not enough, and for this reason they ask for added light from cultural anthropology and cultural sociology. In part this is the result of increasingly convincing data that such "psychological" characteristics as the intelligence quotient (I.Q.) and personality are not entirely innate, but may be culturally and socially conditioned. (Simply as examples, see Davis and Havighurst, 1948, and Henry, 1947.) Likewise, it has been clearly shown on a cross-cultural and cross-community basis that, although certain basic motivations are built into all so-called normal children by their biological heredity, other culturally acquired motivations and attitudes are built into them by their social and cultural background training and experience. Such things as "the desire to learn" and "attitude toward the public school and its personnel" are, so far as modern data go, definitely not biologically transmitted.

One of the first facts the educator must recognize if he is to plan his program in community cultural context is the considerable diversity in pattern among contemporary communities of the United States. Space and time are lacking here to attempt a complete catalogue of variations. Perhaps fundamental from the point of view of cultural anthropology is the fact that the community in which the educator gets a job may be either homogeneous or heterogeneous in culture. The likelihood of obtaining a position in a culturally homogeneous community is relatively slight, because there are comparatively few of them in this country. In general, such communities tend to be small in size (i.e., are rural or small-town) and isolated. There are quite a few such communities, for example, in the Southern mountain region and in the Latter-day Saints areas of Utah and Idaho. In such a situation the teacher will not be confronted by much diversity in the cultural backgrounds of his pupils. Unless he is a native or long-time resident of the community, however, he may find his own role in the community somewhat anomalous, and he should walk carefully until he discovers from local informants what it is supposed to be. Furthermore, he will find that local ideas of the values of an education may be somewhat "backward" in terms of the general culture, and it is not uncommon that the members want to keep their way of life that way— they prefer backward homogeneity to newfangled perversions from the outside. Finally, one must keep in mind that if he finds himself in such a community, he should not think that cultural homogeneity necessarily means lack of internal conflict and rivalry. It merely signifies that the local citizens know and practice only one set or range of customs for solving life's problems, that they agree on one set of values, and that this local culture is available to all members of the community without the interposition of social distinctions other than those assigned to age and sex. Nevertheless, the community may be divided into cliques or even feud groups, with any one of which the outside teacher would be well advised not to become identified. All members of the community may be agreed, for example, that "lying is bad," but they may not hesitate to accuse each other of committing this sin. Or they may know only a limited range of customs for "attacking a person's character," but use them with great gusto on each other.

More important is the heterogeneous community, for this is the type one may expect to find in the great majority of cases in this country. The condition of cultural heterogeneity is, of course, a matter of degree, and one finds considerable variation in this respect. However, for anthropology such a community is essentially a more or less functionally integrated collection of subcultures. If one finds himself in a population or territory possessing a number of cultures that show *no* functional integration, he must conclude that he is not dealing with *a* community, but possibly with several communities in the scientific sense of the term, or even an unorganized and unintegrated congeries of groups with their respective systems of custom. The heterogeneous modern American community consists of a number of socially distinct groups or social categories, each with a system of subculture (including social organization and values) peculiar to itself in the local situation. We call these systems subcultures because, despite their differences, they also all contain certain common or *universal* cultural elements and they all contain patterns of action and organization that permit articulated social relations between the component social groups or categories. Some community universals may be derived from those traits and institutions that are common to all of North American culture, while others may be universal only to the local community. For example, in all United States communities all adults, regardless of their social status and subculture, are required to use English as the language of community-wide discourse and to live with only one spouse at one time. (It is a fact that there are some "foreign" communities on North American soil, such as still unassimilated Indian tribes and immigrant groups. These can be considered North American communities, however, only in the geographical sense.) Likewise there are no communities of United States culture where men do not all wear trousers of a certain pattern with fly front. On the other hand, only in New Orleans is it universal for the whole community to celebrate Shrove Tuesday (Mardi Gras) by participating in street parades and other jollifications of a certain pattern. This is a local universal.

The foregoing are simple examples of patterns that are actually practiced by all sections of the community. One must also consider types of integrating universals that I call value beliefs. They are also sometimes spoken of as moral beliefs, or simply as morals. They have to do with what "should" be done. Sometimes, these value beliefs and the actual practices very nearly coincide. For example, it is universally held in all communities of United States culture that adults "should" be able to read, write, and figure. And the fact is that only a few less than 3 percent of our adult population is illiterate. On the other hand, it is probably a universally held belief in American communities that every voter "should" go to the polls, yet only a fraction of the electorate turns out to register its opinion of, say, a local bond issue. Local universal value beliefs also are often of great interest to the residents. Everyone you talk to in Center City, perhaps, is agreed that the community "should" have a new school plant, but for one reason or another it may be years before this goal is realized, if ever.

I understand that other participants in this conference will deal with certain other subtle aspects of culture, such as implicit and explicit premises, conscious, unverbalizable, and unconscious aspects of culture, the cultural function of symbols, and the like. I shall omit these matters for the present, since my primary purpose is to suggest certain cultural indicators of community integration. To sum up, you have to have some general agreements among the members of the population or you do not have a community. Likewise, a functioning community requires certain mechanisms of internal social adjustment. I shall deal with the latter shortly.

The *types* of subcultures most commonly found in contemporary North American communities are those associated with social classes, with color castes, and with ethnic groups. The *content* of the subcultures may vary from one community or one region of the country to another. Of course it is not true that all communities have divisions based on all three of these criteria.

It comes as a shock to many good Americans to learn that social classes exist in our country, because according to the national credo "no one is supposed to be recognized as any better than anyone else except through his own efforts and abilities." Perhaps "class" is a misleading word, because the divisions we find in American communities lack the rigid, unpassable barriers that separated them in much of Europe and even England of a former day. Nevertheless, an impressive number of social science studies indicate that probably the great majority of United States communities today contain something like a class system. Even though social mobility is permitted, the structure of the system is "played down," and the average person is not clear about the structure. Evidence from a wide variety of communities in different parts of the country shows that the six-class structure depicted by Lloyd Warner and associates for Newburyport, Massachusetts, is by no means universal. In small, rural centers the "upper group" may be no more than a clique of a few families, such as those of the banker and a half-dozen well-to-do merchants and farmers who have a certain wealth and who have been established in the community for a couple of generations or more. The rest of the populace may be common people, although in small communities there are usually a few families, such as James West reports as "people who live like animals" in Plainville, who are "looked down upon" by almost everyone else.

In the present connection the important points are that each such group or category has cultural characteristics not shared with the others, and that special values, often in the form of invidious comparisons, are attached to these characteristics. Furthermore, these status-cultural categories are hierarchically ranked, with those "higher" on the scale accorded proportionately more privileges and rewards—according to a common scale of values—than those in "lower" position. They usually differ in patterns of family behavior and child-rearing, in occupational range of the breadwinners, in the definition of goals and aspirations and the means of achievement. From this it usually follows that the values they attach to education show some degree of variance. The motivations of the children and the attitudes of their parents are formed by the time the children enter the first grade and tend to be maintained at least during the elementary years while the children are under the family and neighborhood controls of their respective status groups.

Warner points out that a variety of studies in New England, the South, and the Middle West show that about 94 percent of public school teachers are either of the middle class or are upward mobile individuals who have assimilated middle-class culture (Warner, 1953, pp. 176–77). If this is true of the country as a whole, and there is reason to think that it is, the average teacher literally does not know from his or her own experience and training what the approved goals of education *are* for those of his pupils who belong either to lower or upper groups. He can find out something about this by background reading and through special courses, and he can get the details in his own community by his personal investigation over a period of time. But once he finds that there are differences in what is expected of education in his community, he is faced with the problem of how to plan his teaching. Should he try to satisfy all comers according to their own class-cultural lights? In cases where the class-cultural expectancies are in opposition to each other, this can only be done by segregating the pupils according to class origin. Should the teacher concentrate merely upon the "common denominators" of the class cultures, leaving the other aspirations of the pupils to be handled by other agencies, such as private schools, clubs, churches, etc.?

Presumably questions such as these will form part of the subject matter of discussion at this conference. At this moment I do not offer suggestions for solution.

What has just been said concerning class subcultures within the total community applies in much the same way to the educational problems of caste and ethnic groups, with certain differences. Color castes and ethnic groups are usually class-stratified within themselves. There is one important difference between them, however. This is that what we call color castes, such as the Negroes and the Nisei, have, class-for-class, practically the same culture as the whites and have taken over parallel class structures. The ethnic groups, on the other hand, in so far as in specific cases they can be considered functioning parts of a community, still preserve significant elements of culture and social organization carried over from their country of origin. I am not referring here to ghettos and Little Italies and the like, peopled by recently arrived immigrants or refugees, for such elements cannot be considered to have full function in community culture or social organization until some assimilation has taken place. I have in mind ethnic groups the members of which are "good Americans," but whose subcultures and social organizations show some variance from the general community pattern. For example, there are in Savannah and Atlanta groups of highly respected Sephardic Jews whose ancestors came to this country two hundred years ago; in Milwaukee are numerous German families whose forebears left the old country shortly after 1848; in California are Spanish families who trace their lineage back to the *coloniaje*; in the South one finds numerous "old Americans" of Scotch-Presbyterian tradition. These people are Americans all right, but they maintain special relations with members of their own groups and they carry on special traditions and values derived from their ancestral cultures.

The educator who finds one or more such groups in his community is again faced with problems. Should it be the objective of the school to "wipe out" these ethnic differences? There is much to be said against such a course, perhaps the least of which is that it would eliminate yet more of the seasoning and flavor from a standardized American way of life that is rapidly showing signs of becoming monotonous. If the children of ethnic groups are to be educated by the school to the American standard, what standard should be selected? Should they be taught the culture of the upper classes, the middle classes, the lower classes, or what?

The decision of the Supreme Court of the United States in May 1954 declared segregation of the races in public schools to be unconstitutional. During the summer of 1953 a South-wide survey of the possible results of this decision was made with funds provided by the Ford Foundation (Ashmore, 1954). This survey indicates that there will probably not be a complete disappearance of segregated schools or pupils, since, because of already existing segregated residential patterns, by "gerrymandering" school districts it will be possible in many cases to send children to schools of their own race. Nevertheless, a sizable number of schools will inevitably have both Negroes and whites—and the teachers must be prepared to deal with race attitudes which the children carry from the home to the school and also with the fact that Negro children will probably never, in this generation at least, be able to occupy the same status positions in adulthood as their white schoolmates.

In the typical heterogeneous American community, the social relations between the constituent subcultural groups and categories are governed by codes, which in large part are often informal and unwritten. The etiquette, for example, of intergroup relations is not standardized throughout the country. More obsequiousness is required of Negroes in certain parts of the South, for instance, than in other regions of the nation. There is less emphasis on certain symbols of status in the Middle West and Far West than in the Northeast and South. Along with the outward patterns of interaction go internalized ideas, attitudes, and rationalizations of the respective statuses. For example, among many lower-class Negro farm tenants in the South there is acceptance of the "natural superiority" of white people and also of upper-class and educated Negroes, whereas lower-class industrial workers in the North seem to be less inclined to agree with the class attitudes of their "social betters."

The teacher must learn to know what these patterns of subculture interaction are in order to establish and maintain contact with the various elements of his community. He must also realize that they are the channels, so to speak, of communication and reciprocal action whereby a certain integration is maintained in the community. Were they, or something serving similar functions, not in operation, the subcultural groups and categories within the community would become mutually isolated and the community would lose whatever cohesion it has. Therefore, the teacher and others who would "reform" such patterns must think in functional terms applied to the community as a whole. This does not mean that educators should not participate in movements for reform and betterment of the community or any portion of it, but it does mean that they should try to assess on an objective basis the results of such endeavors in community-wide context.

In order to carry out his role in the community, the educator should be aware of the *power structure*, which usually cuts across subcultural lines. First, of course, one can inform himself fairly easily of the *formal* power structure—the form of local government, the individuals who hold political positions, the shape and make-up of the various administrative and judicial bodies, such as school boards, housing and sanitation commissions, the courts, the tax assessment system, and so on. This sort of information should be passed on to the pupils so that they may become active participants in the democratic process, and it is also necessary to the educator if he is to be an effective teacher or administrator and a good citizen.

Somewhat more difficult to discover is the *informal* power structure and its personnel. The top power group is not usually composed of criminals, but the members prefer "to keep out of the limelight." One excellent study (Hunter, 1953)[1] and various other evidence indicate that the members of the small, top power group of the community are not necessarily or exclusively members of the top social status categories. Some, although of upper income, are definitely middle class as far as the status symbols and behavior go. The great majority of such individuals, however, do hold controlling interests or responsibilities in the major financial and economic enterprises of the community. In small communities one may find what I have called the "boss man complex"—a single individual rather than a group that holds effective power. Usually the *ostensible* power holders of the community, including elective and appointive officers of responsibility, are effectively controlled by the informal power group. "Nothing gets done" if it meets the disapproval of these effective power holders—so long as they retain their power—and an effort is made to see that any individual who begins to gain prominence or power himself is either brought into line or effectively hamstrung. It is an oversimplification, and perhaps in most cases untrue, to think of the controllers of this informal power structure as venal. Publicly, they are usually of the highest respectability. One reason, however, that they do not ordinarily advertise their power is that their basic goal is to maintain the local economic system

[1] Professor Hunter has collected similar information, which seems to check with that in his book, from a series of representative communities throughout the country, for the "power structure" of the nation as a whole. This material is being readied for publication.

intact and perhaps to expand it. Since this goal might not be rated highest on the list of the population as a whole, or of important segments of it, the counsel of wisdom (from the point of view of the controllers of the economic system) is not to submit the issue to democratic discussion or decision. However, so long as community projects do not seriously interfere with this basic goal, the informal power holders will often permit or even encourage them. A paternalistic view of "welfare" is often entertained, so long as it does not cost the wealthy groups too much and does not "upset the applecart."

In this connection it should be noted that there seems to be a tendency for the members of school boards and other control agencies of education to be drawn from the upper groups of status or power, although school board members themselves usually do not belong to the top inner power group, the members of which have "more important" responsibilities. It is rare for the ordinary schoolteacher to have social relations with members of the school board and their families. Or, if social gestures are made by the latter, it is often in a condescending manner. In many communities, I am told, the school board ignores the teacher as an individual and treats him or her as an "employee." The teacher is often a single person without family in the community and lives on a modest salary. For these reasons, even were there no difference in subcultural backgrounds, teachers would seldom be able to reciprocate socially with members of such groups. Furthermore, school board members are often "conservative" in viewpoint, reflecting either their own class-cultural orientations or those of power groups that control them. Teachers themselves, especially when young, are inclined to reflect the more intellectual and "progressive" values of middle-class culture and are therefore constantly exposed to the risk of being dubbed "radical" by their employers.

Thus the teacher in the great majority of American communities is bound to find differences of opinion, and it may be helpful to recognize that these are to a large extent due to differences in subcultural conditioning and controls. It is not surprising, then, that the teacher often either feels insecure in his or her social role or feels guilty of "compromising" his ideals in order to obtain greater solidarity with various local elements. The teacher as perhaps an "advanced" person of middle-class culture is apt to feel resentful of the "pretensions" of the upper-class people, to regard as "stuffy" the sentiments of the more conservative elements of the community, and to find the manners and attitudes of the lower-class students appalling. This is a dilemma of sorts—and dilemmas are not comfortable. What can be done about it?

In solving this problem I believe that the community role of the school administrators is of first importance. It is my impression that in most public school systems of any size, the administrators—superintendents, principals, and the like—have considered their responsibilities to be mainly toward the school board and other control groups in the community rather than to the teachers. They try to identify with the so-called leaders of the community and very little with their teaching staffs. This is accentuated by the fact that the majority of school administrators are men whereas the greater part of the public school teachers—except athletic coaches and instructors in manual training—are women. The top administrators are usually invited to join luncheon clubs and to take leadership roles in charity campaigns, and the like. And they are often in a position to interact on a common social basis with at least the secondary levels of status and power. Such channels, for reasons already mentioned, are not open to the ordinary teacher.

It would therefore seem that school administrators must be brought to a wider conception of their roles. In addition to their purely administrative duties and their function of liaison with the upper status and power groups, they should likewise "face toward" their teaching staffs. They are in a position to interpret the community, or certain aspects of it, to the teachers and to make contacts and to open channels for the teachers into the realities of community life outside the classroom. Such procedures, devoid of authoritarianism, would, I believe, do much to add to teacher *esprit de corps* and ego-satisfaction, and would decrease the alarming rate at which teachers are leaving the profession.

P.T.A.'s and similar groups, of course, form a link between the teachers and the general population. But it is notorious that they are made up principally of middle-class parents. Neither lower-class nor upper-class family representatives usually participate. It would be possible by properly directed effort to enlarge the scope of such groups. In those neighborhoods and communities in which the school becomes a sort of community center in the evenings, the interest and pride of the adult citizens in the institution seem to be increased.

Finally, the teacher should be encouraged to learn the social and cultural realities of the community on her own account. Here again a permissive and constructive attitude on the part of her administrative superiors is desirable. Also some first-rate courses in teacher-training colleges on the community, personality, and culture would help. It is a curious fact that university and college professors are often persons of prominence, although usually not of top power, in their communities, while the schoolteacher is not often listened to outside the classroom. In part, at least, I believe that this is because university and college administrations not only permit, but actually encourage community participation and leadership on the part of their faculties, whereas such administrative attitudes have hitherto been rare in respect to public school teachers. There is no doubt that the average schoolteacher is or could be an "authority" on many subjects of community interest, and he or she should be recognized as such and given the opportunity to participate more in common concerns.

With respect to the content of classroom teaching, there are common denominators running through the content of all the subcultures of a community, there is consensus about certain precepts of morality, there is agreement on certain common goals and the acceptable techniques for realizing them. These at least should form the basis of instruction.

Beyond these, however, rigidity is to be avoided. In a society such as ours, containing many subcultures among which mobility is permitted, the future citizens must be trained to make choices and to see possibilities within the culture as a whole.[2]

[2] In the following list of references will be found titles of some representative studies of American communities of different types in various parts of the country. Town and rural communities are dealt with by Bell, Blumenthal, Dollard, Hall, Kollmorgen, Leonard and Loomis, MacLeish and Young, Mathews, Moe and Taylor, Nelson, Nixon, Powdermaker, Rubin, Sims, West, Williams, and Wynn. Middle-sized cities are the subject matter of Davis and the Gardners, the Lynds, Warner, *et al.*, Warner and associates. Warner (1953) summarizes work carried on by himself and associates over the past twenty-five years and sets forth their findings on American class systems. Taylor (1945) offers some hints as to how community studies are made. For further information on all of these matters consult up-to-date textbooks on general sociology, educational sociology, urban sociology, or community organization.

References

(*Editorial note*: Dr. Gillin was requested, by several participants in the conference, to furnish a selective list of references on community studies.)

Ashmore, Harry S. 1954. *The Negro and the Schools*. Chapel Hill: University of North Carolina Press.
Bell, Earl H. 1942. *Sublette, Kansas*. (Rural Life Studies, No. 2, U.S. Department of Agriculture.) Washington, D.C.: Government Printing Office.
Blumenthal, Albert. 1932. *Small-Town Stuff*. Chicago: University of Chicago Press.
Davis, Allison, Burleigh B. Gardner, and Mary R. Gardner. 1941. *Deep South*. Chicago: University of Chicago Press.
Davis, Allison, and Robert J. Havighurst. 1948. "The Measurement of Mental Systems," *Scientific Monthly*, LXIV, 301–16.
Dollard, John. 1937. *Caste and Class in a Southern Town*. New Haven: Yale University Press.
Hall, Warren S. 1939. *Tangier Island*. Philadelphia: University of Pennsylvania Press.
Henry, William E. 1947. "The Thematic Apperception Technique in the Study of Culture-Personality Relations," *Genetic Psychology Monographs*, XXXV, 3–135.
Hunter, Floyd. 1953. *Community Power Structure*. Chapel Hill: University of North Carolina Press.
Kollmorgen, W. M. 1942. *The Old Order Amish of Lancaster County, Pennsylvania*. (Rural Life Studies, No. 4, U.S. Department of Agriculture.) Washington, D.C.: Government Printing Office.
Leonard, Olen, and Charles P. Loomis. 1941. *El Cerrito, New Mexico*. (Rural Life Studies, No. 1, U.S. Department of Agriculture.) Washington, D.C.: Government Printing Office.
Lynd, Robert S., and Helen M. Lynd. 1929. *Middletown*. New York: Harcourt, Brace and Company.
———. 1937. *Middletown in Transition*. New York: Harcourt, Brace and Company.
MacLeish, Kenneth, and Kimball Young. 1942. *Landgraf, New Hampshire*. (Rural Life Studies, No. 3, U.S. Department of Agriculture.) Washington, D.C.: Government Printing Office.
Mathews, M. Taylor. 1937. *Experience Worlds of Mountain People*. New York: Columbia University Press.
Moe, E. O., and Carl C. Taylor. 1942. *Irwin, Iowa*. (Rural Life Studies, No. 5, U.S. Department of Agriculture.) Washington, D.C.: Government Printing Office.
Nelson, Lowry. 1930. *The Mormon Village*. Provo: Brigham Young University Press.
Nixon, H. C. 1941. *Possum Trot*. Norman: University of Oklahoma Press.

Powdermaker, Hortense. 1939. *After Freedom: The Portrait of a Community in the Deep South.* New York: Viking Press.
Rubin, Morton. 1951. *Plantation County.* Chapel Hill: University of North Carolina Press.
Sims, N. L. 1912. *Hoosier Village.* New York: Columbia University Press.
Taylor, Carl C. 1945. "Techniques of a Community Study as Applied to Modern Civilized Societies," in Ralph Linton (ed.), *The Science of Man in the World Crisis.* New York: Columbia University Press.
Warner, W. Lloyd. 1953. *American Life: Dream and Reality.* Chicago: University of Chicago Press.
Warner, W. Lloyd, *et al.* 1941–47. *The Yankee Cities Series.* 4 vols. New Haven: Yale University Press.
Warner, W. Lloyd, and associates. 1949. *Democracy in Jonesville.* New York: Harper & Brothers.
West, James. 1945. *Plainville, U.S.A.* New York: Columbia University Press.
Williams, J. M. 1916. *An American Town.* New York: Kempster.
Wynne, Waller. 1943. *Harmony, Georgia.* (Rural Life Studies, No. 6, U.S. Department of Agriculture.) Washington, D.C.: Government Printing Office.

SECOND SESSION OF THE CONFERENCE

Chairman: Jules Henry

Discussant: Robert N. Bush

Bush: As I read Gillin's paper on "The School in the Context of the Community" I felt very much as though he were a fellow educator, in the sense that it confirmed the experiences we have recently been having in our field studies of the school in a community setting. There are several minor points about the paper which I'd like to raise for reaction.

For example, he distinguishes between the culturally homogeneous community and the heterogeneous community and makes the point that probably most communities are culturally heterogeneous. Actually, most of our secondary schools enroll fewer than two hundred pupils, and I suspect that we have many more homogeneous communities, as he defines them, than is suggested.

Gillin reports that 94 percent of teachers are middle-class, upward-mobile individuals and that this incapacitates them as teachers for dealing with other classes. He doesn't use the word "incapacitates," but I gain the impression from reading his materials that their own class pattern prohibits them from effective work and that they are alarmed or at least puzzled and frustrated by what they should do with lower-class and upper-class children in our schools. Since he brings up this issue, I should like to hear him as well as the other anthropologists give us some cues as to what should be done in teaching lower-class children. What kinds of things would likely be most effective? As far as upper-class children are concerned, we don't have many of them in the public schools.

I found extremely interesting his statement concerning the critical position of the administrator in the educational process. This confirms much of the material that we have been gathering in some of our communities. He makes the very good point, confirmed in our materials, that the administrator tends to face the power and the status groups in the community much more than he tends to face the teachers. The question then, as he proposes it, is, Wouldn't it be better for the administrator to face more toward his teachers than to the class of the power and status groups in the community? What little evidence we have suggests that when he attempts to do this, as his teachers expect him to do, he almost inevitably gets into trouble, and very serious trouble, with his community. One of our studies, originally entitled "A Study of Administrative Success," is of a superintendent who had been in his position for about twenty-seven years. He had actually faced the community very successfully, opposing teachers in the raising of salary schedules and the implementation of curricular ideas, and so forth. We had vigorous objections to the study on the part of some advisers, to the effect that this was not administrative success at all. They maintained that this administrator had been able to stay in his position for such a long period of time because he had succumbed, as it were, to the various subcultural pressures and hadn't actually faced the task of improving the educational program, which would have meant facing the teachers more and attempting really to improve the educational process. The administrator is, I think, faced with one of the most difficult tasks in the whole educational system, because he must contend with the great pressures from various segments of the community. One of the most important roles, we find, for the administrator is that of a harmonizer or a stabilizer in an attempt to balance off all these pressures; whereas from an educational standpoint, we say to him, "You ought to be trying to advance and improve the educational program and to implement the kinds of things the teachers are trying to do." When he tries to do this, he frequently finds himself in very severe conflict with a number of the power and status groups that are attempting to maintain the equilibrium in the community. I wonder if we could get some insights from the anthropologist as to what role the administrator might profitably try to perform?

OPEN DISCUSSION

Fair and Unfair Questions for the Anthropologist

Henry (Chairman), Mead, Gillin, Lee, Cowley, Hart, Keesing, Spindler

Henry: Dr. Bush, I feel that some of the questions you asked are unfair, because I do not feel at present that the anthropologist ought to be so vain as to think he can tell the educator what to do. As you talked about the administrative situation, you certainly showed you know a lot more about it than we do. At the present time we cannot be asked what to do about the transmission of culture, or what one should do with the upper- and lower-class children, or how one should advise the administrators on balancing the power groups against the teachers. It seems to me that what the anthropologist can do now is say, "Here is the way to go about finding out what is in the situation."

Mead: Yes. But I would think that one sort of suggestion we could make is, "Look at the general pattern in American culture for administrators." What is the role of administrators with the top of any system, whether it's a government bureau, a factory, or a school—a series of comparable structures which on the whole tend to have many elements in common? During the war, when one of the first international agencies was set up, there was a great deal of confusion introduced because in one of the operations there was a Russian chairman of one section who deviated from the general pattern in Washington, in which the top of the section operated *out* in relation to other people while his administrative assistants operated *in.* He set his administrative assistants to operate out and he stayed home and kept his own little bailiwick, and everybody was hopelessly confused. Now, I would think that one of the sorts of things that an anthropologist can say to the educators is, "There are methods by which the patterns of administrators in educational institutions can be systematically related to other administrative patterns, and it may be that one of the reasons that confusion comes in when the educator attempts to turn toward his administratees instead of out toward other organizations is that he is violating very deep cultural expectations." That seems to me a strictly anthropological answer; we're not giving the answer, but we're saying, "This is a place to look."

Gillin: I should like to see the educators become anthropologists in a way; that is, if they know what to look for, they can find it out in their own communities. That is possibly where anthropologists can be of some help, in giving educators certain general orientations and principles for examining the culture and social organization of their own communities.

Lee: The important thing, it seems to me—perhaps *the* thing that we can contribute in this respect—is to show in what areas there can be awareness of ethnic backgrounds by the teacher. And I'm not speaking of class backgrounds now; ethnic backgrounds come even into the so-called homogeneous schools where you do have a few children who have a different perception from the rest of the children. This is the sort of thing I mean: I don't know how this case will finish, but just before I left Detroit there was the case of a young girl who was undressing to go into the swimming pool and the teaching instructor noticed that she had a great bruise on her arm, and she questioned the girl, till finally the girl, under great pressure and with great agony, broke down and confessed that her brother had bitten her. The teacher then was trying to force her to send her brother to the Juvenile Court because of assault. Now, the girl is a Greek girl; I think that this would run counter to any child perhaps, but certainly for a Greek girl it is really perhaps the worst crime of all to turn an older brother in to the authorities. If teachers were given some kind of awareness of what the cultural background means in situations like that, that is what I think they need.

Cowley: These are some of the awarenesses, but what are the other awarenesses in the situation that the anthropologist thinks the educator should have or know about? Let's take the administrators as a case in point. A lot of work has been done concerning administration by people who aren't anthropologists, and some of it is very important work. I mean the work that's been done by Chester Barnard, for example, the work that's been done at M.I.T., and the work being done at Harvard. It's not anthropological work; but there's a whole series of awarenesses that the person in administration is familiar with because he has a literature about it.

Hart: Dr. Bush's question, which I think Dr. Cowley is also still addressing himself to, seems to me to have a relatively simple answer from an anthropological point of view. And that is, that every social system, anthropologists think, is to some extent stratified, even the allegedly democratic American system. Somewhere in the stratification system you find a character called an administrator, and if you look at his position in the social system—if you just draw a simple diagram and put him in his proper place and look up above him—you will find that he is subject to certain pressures too, and his behavior becomes explicable in terms of these pressures.

Cowley: But you wouldn't stop there, would you?

Hart: Well, theoretically I think you've got to stop pretty much at that point, and say, "Go ahead and try to analyze what the pressures on the administrator are, and if you can understand the pressures on the administrator you will be able to explain his behavior." And you will find that the pressures are such that he has to face toward the community groups rather than toward the teachers.

Keesing: Could we add that this particular approach takes a lot of time? It involves long-term observation and analysis, mainly devoted to small-scale structures—and anthropologists still have to do a lot of learning about handling larger structures, in terms of the necessary statistical sampling, validation, and other operations required. The question is, How many practitioners in these other fields have been willing, and have professional opportunities provided, to do this sort of thing? We haven't more than a handful of community studies to date, nothing like an adequate sample, or again of peer group studies; we talk off the "top of the hat" largely. But I think we must recognize that there are great possibilities here, if only we could define the problems mutually, and on some of them get a team approach. For example, regarding the lines of Bernie's (Siegel) chart drawn between the school, the teachers college, and the state education authorities, I think that you would need on a team a person trained in public administration. The actual fact is that we haven't got depth studies in this mood and manner. By depth I'm thinking in terms of time, in the careful use of informants properly placed in their status roles, of information properly validated by standard anthropological techniques.

Gillin: As an argument for teacher training in anthropology, I would like to point out that some of the big oil companies that send people to South America give their employees courses on the culture of the people they will work with—so that they won't make mistakes. I think that teachers, too, could be given courses which would show them what to look for, just as an anthropologist can take a course in botany, and use it, without becoming a professional botanist. I think that the anthropologist can provide useful material in the following areas : general patterns, a body of theory, methods of getting information.

Mead: The anthropologist certainly cannot give a value dictum, but he can provide material on what difficulties a middle-class person gets into who hasn't had training and who tries to teach a lower-class child, and what the difficulties are if you try to produce homogeneity in certain circumstances. He cannot provide value judgments of what you *ought* to do, but he can suggest what the cost of doing one thing as opposed to another might be.

Hart: Why should the anthropologist be able to give more of such information than the educators themselves can provide? I don't see why the anthropologist has a monopoly on this information.

Mead: He doesn't have a monopoly—if the educator becomes a student of culture. The question is, How can we sensitize people to what they will look for in a community (in much the same way we train students in linguistics by giving them a large number of linguistic forms on the assumption that they will be sensitized to accept different kinds of new situations) so that the teacher learns that there are cultural common denominators—that monogamy is not the only possible pattern, etc.—in other words, learns about cultural styles? You don't have to teach her specifics, but a preparation for looking for patterns. We can teach teachers to ask the right questions, in terms of which they will have to be prepared to do a considerable amount of work.

Gillin: Yes. You learn to discover things for yourself.

Shaftel: Could the anthropologist make a contribution by giving us some studies showing what price is paid when the lower-class child is urged, goaded, or coerced into changing his class status?

Keesing: The literature of forced change and resistance to change would be relevant here. The work so far has been heavily concentrated on acculturative situations, but if it were generalized further it could provide some very rich leads, I'm sure, since so much of the educational process is manipulative in this sense.

Lee: The anthropologist would break down the concept "lower class" in some ways, in ethnic groups as well as in other groups. He would say, for instance: In this group parents want the child to move away from them; in this other group they do not. The "Research in Contemporary Cultures" which Margaret (Mead) has been working on has shown that it is almost the duty of the child of eastern European Jews to go beyond the status of his parents. Other groups were studied where this was not expected of the child. The child would therefore have to pay a different price in different parts of the "lower class" if he wanted to move away.

Spindler: One thing we could do is to use children as informants. I have done this in my own work, asking for information that is not obvious, but in terms of meaning and value orientation. You can ask questions on an intimate level; for example, I have asked such questions as, What kind of house do you live in now? What does it look like? How do you feel about it? One kind of child in his answers gives no evidence of having changed or of desire to change; the answers of another kind of child are quite different. In this way, we get under the skin of the child and look for the culture there, as well as for his aspirations.

Discussant: Hilda Taba

This paper falls into three main divisions: (1) assumptions; (2) discussion of what a teacher needs to know about communities; and (3) some solutions. On the two assumptions: The first one deals with such questions as, What do I transmit? Which parts of the culture do I need to change? The questions raised here are pragmatic questions that the culture itself has to answer. In the practical sense, many educators do answer them—by selecting some things to transmit—but they don't answer them theoretically. If you ask them, "What in a total culture should I transmit and what parts should I change?" everybody would be stumped, including the philosophers.

But probably a fairer and a more important question is involved here: How do I recognize the different types of social learning that come from different types of social-cultural backgrounds, including social class, race, religion, being a newcomer, and many other dimensions? What social learnings do those varieties of subcultures develop? What do children or adults bring to whatever I'm teaching? Where do I need to take over and where can I go with them? This is the problem of linking teaching with social learning in order to make shifts in learning with greater continuity. There are two major tasks in cultural education in school: to fill in the gaps that a particular culture has left in understanding and to alter some learnings which in practical judgments are inconsistent with creating a unity in our culture. Educators depend on the Davis and Warner materials largely because these are the only concrete materials on social learning in modern cultures. A similar analysis of social learning in other subcultures is needed.

Educators need to look at their programs in the light of the fact that education proceeds in a community-cultural context, in which there is a great deal of diversity. This diversity needs to be spelled out in more dimensions than class structure : ethnic culture, regional variations, rural-urban differences, etc. Knowledge of the types of social learnings fostered in these cultural dimensions is especially important in places like California that draw migrants from the whole country, and have an utterly hetero-geneous population. Teachers tend to treat these differences as oddities and as something that one need not take into account in teaching and ap-proaching children and parents.

All of those dimensions have certain common denominators: They foster fear of differences, social distance, tendencies to gain security by exclusiveness, stereotyping, hostility, etc. These patterns of reaction, once learned in one dimension of cultural contrast, tend to be generalized and adopted in reaction to others.

Any deviation from the school culture, which is largely middle-class, creates blocks in communication and therefore in learning. These blocks occur not only because different children hold different values, but also because the same words convey different meanings. A policeman is a different person to a lower-class child than to a middle-class child. Many other common words, such as "family" and "co-operation," have similarly different culturally learned meanings. When teachers are not aware of these differences, teaching becomes merely words in the air, which aren't perceived in the same sense that they were meant to be perceived.

Second, the classroom situations depend for success on adequacy of interpersonal relationships. When the school population includes many culture groups which produce "we-they" divisions, these relationships don't carry what they're supposed to. Even processes like conducting a classroom discussion are blocked when classroom groups are divided. Students tend to attack each other in place of attacking ideas. Group thinking is blocked. There are records of classroom discussions in which most of the time is spent on battling a person rather than dealing with an idea. This is a terrific waste and could be eliminated by greater under-standing of group cleavages and of the ways in which they become ob-stacles to communication, to group participation, and to learning.

On the second question, regarding the extent to which we have func-tionally integrated subcultures, I am again reminded of Riesman's data (*The Lonely Crowd*) showing that we not only have unintegrated sub-cultures, particularly in new areas like California, but also probably have a vast array of lonely people who have no linkages : (1) people who are cut off from their roots, living near neighbors they don't know, in new suburbs which have no real integrative machinery; and (2) the "lonely crowd" completely detached from our culture, e.g., oldsters, whose pro-portion to younger persons is increasing and for whom our culture has never made adequate provision. (We still retire people at 65, even though the average life span has been extended something like ten years.) These are people who don't belong anywhere, who probably turn into bitter at-tackers, and, I rather suspect, our anti-intellectualism of today has a large support in this group.

We need, then to pick from the subcultures what is universal and what's diverse and make available to educators those elements that are most crucial (*a*) to the business of transmitting culture, (*b*) to the business of creating some kind of unified core in our culture, and (c) to the whole business of holding on to what we might call the continuity in culture— not to let the change and the adverse factors get the better of it. The schools have to play a role in it; I'm sure that the family is quite weak in doing it.

Mr. Gillin seems to have omitted one thing in his description of cleavages that the subcultures introduce. One example is the cleavage between the older and younger generations; the psychological distance between generations increases as the culture changes and accelerates. To one concerned with cultural continuity it is frightening to observe how distant great numbers of adolescents are from their parents; parents are not persons at all. They are just givers, blockers, and not people who sometimes get irritated and tired and have all the human feelings. To some adolescents I have studied, parents are as incomprehensible as a foreign culture.

Another problem needing further study and discussion is the psychological factors that go with the status of being a member of a subculture. If the subculture is simultaneously a minority culture, there are definite psychological phenomena that go with it which are rather poorly interpreted. Teachers take such phenomena as a Negro with a chip on his shoulder as objects of hostility and of discipline rather than as objects of understanding. They want to clip it off rather than to understand how it came to be and what one can do about it. There's the whole array of semipsychological, semianthropological problems which need a lot more investigation before schools can do a good job in transmitting and modifying culture. The whole business of the "we-they" feelings requires that these cultural divisions and dimensions produce a clearer statement than the rather surface studies that the so-called interculturalists have produced.

As to the solutions. We have talked a good deal about what administrators can do and how they have to respond to the power structure. There is also another kind of power structure which administrators don't always know how to identify or how to mobilize, and that's the "little Joes" in the community. Being many, they can add up to a power figure. Most school systems need to begin to learn how to marshal the wider community feeling and to use it as a balancing factor against what is usually called the power figures, to whom the specialists in public relations have addressed themselves almost exclusively. School administrators are barely beginning to talk about the problem of channeling the voices of the many "little Joes" in setting school policy and in setting educational goals. The P.T.A. is one illustration. It has been organized strictly around middle-class rituals, such as balancing teacups at teas, listening to lectures, and dressing up nicely. These rituals exclude about 70 percent in every community. Few P.T.A. groups have thought of extending their activities so that they could be comfortable, congenial, interesting, and acceptable to a wider range of people in the community. The same can be said for the ways of marshaling a larger segment of the community for interest, support, and understanding of the schools.

OPEN DISCUSSION

Axiological Questions

Brameld, Gillin, Taba, Quillen, Keesing

Brameld: Before we leave this paper, I'd like to bring up the problem of the "should" questions asked by Mr. Gillin—questions about deciding whether it *should* be the objective of the school to wipe out ethnic differences, *should* children be taught the culture of the upper middle classes, and so on. I would like to make sure that we recognize that these are axiological questions—of normative judgment. And at this point it would we well to bear in mind that there is a whole nest of metacultural and metaeducational assumptions involved in these questions.

Gillin: You say they can't be answered. They are answered; otherwise you can't have an educational policy at all. I don't say that they are answered right, or that anthropologists can answer them better than anybody else would. But somehow or other a decision is made.

Taba: For example, when teachers demand certain behavior and suppress other behavior that has to do with cleanliness, they're answering one question about class culture.

Quillen: There is one point that I would not like to pass, if I understood the statement correctly. You (Brameld) didn't really mean that all axiological questions are metacultural, did you? After all, many questions of value are answered in a cultural context.

Brameld: Yes, they're answered, but the question is whether they are answered "rightly."

Quillen: But your concept of what is right is also culturally determined. You ask the question "ought."

Brameld: The help of social scientists, of the anthropologists particularly, is indispensable to the answer. But should we assume that a complete or adequate answer can be provided by them?

Quillen: I'm talking about the individual's decision apart from the science of anthropology. An individual who has a conception of right and wrong has that conception in a cultural context. What he thinks of as right or wrong is based on a cultural tradition.

Keesing: May I make a statement that would create something of a bridge? It relates to this "should" question, and it also relates to the awareness question (that we never faced directly, I think) as presented by Mr. Cowley. There is a historic controversy in anthropology which is to an extent also the mood of this discussion, in which the question is raised whether the applied anthropologist should go beyond providing descriptive "technical information," which was one of Malinowski's definitions of applied anthropology. The problem as I would interpret it is this—and it may answer some of the difficult questions, I think, of whether the anthropologist holds some magical key that the educator doesn't hold. The anthropologist when he is engaged in scientific activities ordinarily sets up his problem around some problem, historical or other, posed by the science itself. Now, when it comes to applied anthropology he takes a problem that is supplied by the administrator or educator or some other person beyond the science. He must first get a full exposition of that problem by all the technical people concerned—everything they know about it. On this basis he can judge what anthropological methods can contribute. Whatever the problem is—if it's social structure, if it's economic movement of goods—he then brings to bear the particular body of anthropological skills which relate to that problem. It may be best with many of these problems, as Spin (Spindler) and many of the others have found out, to proceed by using a team effort. For other problems an individual effort by the anthropologist is appropriate. Now, here is where the controversy arises: Does he put his technical findings into the hands of the man of action, in this case the educator, and say, "Here's the technical information"? Or should he go a step further and attempt to translate the materials out of his particular jargon and conceptual bias, and say, "Here's an untechnical exposition of my findings"? The "should" question now arises—and I think Margaret (Mead) was indicating that we might in some situations be able to go beyond such steps. The educator might say: "I want to reach this end or goal." The applied anthropologist might then be justified in carrying his technical operations further in the sense of saying: "If you want to reach such an end or goal, this, by our present understandings, is the line of action that you should take as representing the best bet, or the best predictability available; if you were to take these others, on the basis of our present ability to predict, they would lead you further from your goals." Or alternatively if the educator said, "What would be the results of this line of action?" then, if the anthropologist felt well enough informed in terms of predictability, he could say, "If you take this action, thus-and-so is likely to happen; you would increase tension, you would arouse contra-movements, you would turn heterogeneity into greater homogeneity, and so on; by taking other lines of action other results are likely to be forthcoming." In other words, in some action programs anthropologists have felt that they could go beyond descriptive technical information into more interpretive spheres.

Now, on the "should" question in the further sense of cultural "universals" the anthropologists are just feeling their way very gingerly, as for example in the value set on mental health apparently among peoples everywhere. They could offer some broad commonness of value directions that exist for all humans. But such formulations are very tentative, and again do not go to the axiological ends. To sum up, this is essentially a problem in applied anthropology; and I was trying to bring out the fact that all the way the anthropologist and the educator would be team members, not just the anthropologist telling the educator what his problem is or how to solve it. I believe, too, that beyond supplying descriptive technical information there are predictabilities that the anthropologist could provide in the sense of reasonable hypotheses.

THE METHOD OF NATURAL HISTORY AND EDUCATIONAL RESEARCH*

Solon T. Kimball
Columbia Teachers College

One of the characteristics which sets anthropology apart from other social sciences is the extensive utilization of the natural history approach as one of its research methodologies. The anthropologist who does field work has as his first obligation the objective recording of human behavior. Although he may have preference for one of the several schools of anthropological thinking, and though his research may be focused toward some theoretical problem, he remains aware that his finished report must be based upon an accurate and complete presentation of the facts. Only thus may he fulfill his obligation to others so that they may utilize his materials in theoretical or cross-cultural analysis.

These requirements dispose the anthropologist to be inductive in his method of analysis. They also demand of him that he look at the total situation. The traditional anthropological monograph includes sections on physical environment, technology, social organization, and religious behavior. Even if an anthropologist chooses to emphasize one of these aspects over the other, his training has taught him that one cannot understand food, clothing, or housing characteristics except as one knows something about the raw materials available and requirements imposed by the environment for group survival. He also knows that the kind and number of social groups is directly related to environmental and technological characteristics, and finally that religious expression is also related to these other factors.

Much of the field material on which he bases his analyses is drawn directly from observation or informant accounts of human activity in meeting the tasks of daily life. Almost any anthropological monograph could serve as illustration. The one which first comes to mind is the description by Malinowski of the Kula ring in his *Argonauts of the Western Pacific*. Many other works could serve as examples. Their universal characteristic is the description in time and place of human activities and,

---

* *Editorial note*: Dr. Kimball's paper treats explicitly certain methodological problems relevant to both Dr. Siegel's and Dr. Gillin's papers and to the discussion of them and therefore is incuded in this section. No formal discussants were assigned to this paper.

in many instances, the derivation of the cultural and social systems which are revealed in the events described.

This method is substantially the same as that used by the biological ecologist. It has as its goal the search for meaningful relationships between the components present in any given situation. It attempts to uncover the nature of equilibrium and the process of change. It may be contrasted with the other major research methods because its emphasis is upon the natural on-going process. As an example of difference the experimental method creates a controlled situation in which the value and quantity of variables present may or may not have any similarity to a situation found in nature, and hence may have limited applicability in control of natural processes. The natural history method does not exclude use of experimental, statistical, or other techniques; it is just that these are subordinate to its main consideration.

The natural historian utilizes two different but complementary and necessary operations in his scientific procedures. He classifies the phenomena of the observable world on the basis of differences and similarities, and he may, in addition, search for the meaningful relationships that explicate the process which he observes. The latter procedure has been called functional and historically appeared with Darwin. Classification is, of course, taxonomy; it had its roots in classical times and was a necessary first step in science to give order to the apparently endless variation of the natural world.

The natural history method has also been used with considerable success in the study of certain aspects of contemporary civilization. In particular, it has been applied to the study of small groups in community and industry. The primitive counterpart of the small group is "band" organization. Anthropologists have reported upon these social groups from their work in many tribes. They did not anticipate, as Harding has pointed out, that they were pioneering in a field which has recently become so popular. As examples of research in this area I refer to the Banks Wiring Room study in the Hawthorne plant of the Western Electric Company as reported by Roethlisberger and Dickson (1939), and to the study of the street corner gang in an Italian slum in Boston described by Whyte (1943). The emphasis in both researches was the search for relationships within events and thus is illustrative of the functional approach.

Anthropologists who have engaged in the study of modern communities have also utilized the natural history method for some portion of their research activities. Their concern with formal structure, specifically stratification, has led them in the direction of seeking answers to questions which are provided by taxonomic procedures.

Although the natural history method utilizes both taxonomy and functionalism, the distinction between the two is important since the emphasis on one or the other method in any specific research leads to quite different results. Functionalism, as exemplified in the Western Electric and Boston "street corner" studies, gave us a picture of the dynamics of human behavior. There is recorded and analyzed for us the actual behavior in sequential events. On the other hand, taxonomy gives us a classificatory scheme for cataloguing differences in behavior. Both approaches have their uses, but it is suggested that in educational research where it is desired to discover the nature of on-going systems or of the educative process utilization of functional procedures holds greater promise for answering basic questions. Let us consider one problem as an example.

The school system of any specific community is one among several institutions. Its larger habitat is the community, but its specific activities are concentrated within a clearly defined locale. Within each school one may distinguish certain types of persons, related to other persons in certain ways, and carrying out habitual activity. The characteristics alluded to above are commonly known even if they have not been precisely described.

Our central problem, however, is to determine the effect of this system on changes within the child. We are concerned not alone with cultural transmission, but also with cultural acquisition. Some portion of the equipment which the child carries into maturity comes from his experience with school systems. It is our task to determine the character and magnitude of the school influence and to relate it in meaningful ways to other nonschool educative experiences. But the effect of his family and his peers must also be learned.

In ordinary circumstances we would be justified in assuming that the limits of our research could be confined to examining the effect of the events in which the child participates with others. In other societies the socialization process is primarily a function of face-to-face relationships. However, the modern child is subject to a different type of habitat influence. I refer to the mass media of television, radio, and moving pictures. These experiences may be, and often are, of a solitary nature—or at least people are not in face-to-face relationships in the ordinary sense.

A great deal of effort has been devoted to the area of communication research. Attempts have been made to determine specific effects in terms of attitudes and behavior. Very little, if any, of this research has utilized the natural history method. This area of child experience must also be explored.

It is proposed here that understanding of the educative process can be gained only as we focus upon the child in his total habitat. His activities must be viewed in the context of sequential events accompanied by testing devices which measure change. The results should give us the base from which we may modify the environmental situation, if need be, to facilitate cultural transmission. The method of natural history meets the needs of problems which are dynamic in character and certainly has applicability in educational research.[1]

[1] I wish to express my appreciation to Drs. Alfred Kroeber and Conrad Arensberg for their helpful comments on the contents of this paper.

References

Harding, Charles F., III. 1953. "Current Conceptual Trends in Small Group Study: Social and Applied Anthropology," *Autonomous Groups Bulletin*, VIII, 4. New York.
Malinowski, Bronislaw. 1922. *Argonauts of the Western Pacific*. New York: E. P. Dutton and Company.
Roethlisberger, F. J., and William I. Dickson. 1939. *Management and the Worker*. Cambridge: Harvard University Press.
Whyte, William F. 1943. *Street Corner Society*. Chicago: University of Chicago Press.

Discussion

Spindler: We have said as we were going along that Sol's (Kimball) paper did put into motion in a broad sense the methodology from which we were drawing many of our inferences. And Sol has replied, "Yes, but that is not all of it; this is only a part of it." And I think we should take the next few minutes to ask him to answer the question, What is the rest of it? What else is there now that we have not involved ourselves with in the natural history approach as we have talked about the interrelationships in Siegel's paper and how the educator can become aware of the salient characteristics of his community? Could we put that question to you?

Kimball: What I had in mind when I made that statement was certain differences which are a matter more of emphasis and degree than of kind. Keesing has mentioned two or three times the importance of depth and I assume he means depth in time. The natural history approach is one which uses the time factor as one of its dimensions. When one examines a given situation in terms of its actors within the locale where the action occurs, the sequence of action is always within a time span. In the case of a good many social groups, such as the family or clique groups, one may often observe a natural history process of origin, growth, and dissolution.

An aspect which I think is of equal or greater importance, however, and which I do not think has been given sufficient attention is the examination of behavior through events. I have recently had occasion to re-examine a considerable number of community studies with the purpose of determining if my recollections about them were correct. I discovered that, as is often the case, the questions posed determined in considerable measure the answer reported. I discovered that the data were organized topically around such subjects as associations, mobility, or religion, and in addition to being topical they were also taxonomic—reflecting the intense interest in and emphasis upon the question of stratification. Since types are built from similarities and differences in characteristics and it was this focus which gave the researchers the nature of the stratification picture, this meant in a good many instances, persons, per se, were left out of the picture. In particular there was left out of the description the on-going process of human beings in interaction and events. Now, this is one of the reasons why community studies do not provide some of the answers to the problems that have been raised here: They are primarily static in their treatment of structure and do not deal with the dynamic aspects of human beings in a habitat. The taxonomic approach utilized in community studies represents only part of the natural history method, although the roots are distinctly anthropological.

It was my intention in writing this paper to inform the people in education of one of the methodologies in anthropology. Specifically I had in mind three areas of research in which this method seems to me to be particularly applicable. One area, which has already been suggested by two or three people here, was the study of the school system as an on-going institution. Utilizing the natural history method one would study it through the kinds of events which occur, their frequency, who participates, and what happens in these events to determine the kinds of patterns which emerge. One study of considerable importance to the school administrator would be a comparative examination of the natural history of school boards and the relationships of principals and superintendents to school boards. I am certain that some significant regional differences would appear, but the similarities would predominate.

A second area of very considerable importance is the study of clique groups. There is already a good deal of information now available. There is the study by Hollingshead, reported in *Elmtown's Youth*, in which he has one chapter on the clique system of a high school. This has been widely quoted in educational circles. Actually, this particular study by Hollingshead is methodologically deficient in terms of answering some of the questions which have been asked here about peer groups; nor does it give answers to questions about the varieties and kinds of peer groups, their relation to personality, and their relation to different kinds of structures. An adequate study of peer group structure in a high-school system is yet to be done.

Last spring I talked to a group of forty-five principals of schools in the vicinity of New York on this very problem. One of the questions posed was the extent to which they were aware of these groups. All of them indicated an awareness. The next question was the extent to which any of them were utilizing these groups or making any effort administratively to see to what extent the objectives of the school system could be met in some degree by use of these groups. None of them indicated positive use of clique structure, although they often had good knowledge of some of the troublemaker groups, which they watched very carefully. They did not see the relationship between those who were not in the groups and those who were; nor were factors of age, sex, or maturity considered. Thus they lacked a complete picture of the social world with which they were working. Now the natural history method is one which can give answers to the many problems which educators face in the social system of their schools.

The third area in which I think this method is useful is that of the relation of the school system to the community. This problem is related to the models which we discussed this afternoon. There the focus was on the kinds of interrelationships which obtain among persons who participate in school systems and between them and other institutions in the community in terms of time, in terms of status, and in terms of the specific situations in which the relation between natural history and tangent relationship occurs. Since this area has already been discussed there is no need for further elaboration.

The question has been raised in discussion between Mr. Coladarci and myself concerning experimental methods.* I should like to make one comment about this. The natural history method provides the basis for comparative analysis and the opportunity to see a variety of types of groups and group behavior in terms of the variety of situations in which one observes them. Even though you experimentally introduce no specific stimulus into a situation, inevitably such external stimuli arise outside the group at various times. For example, the stabilized relations and behavior of co-eds become suddenly disturbed by the issuance of an order by the Dean of Women. Thus, you have in the on-going process of the relationships of groups in their habitat all kinds of internal and external stimuli arising which provide "natural" experimental situations that may be used to study variability. This doesn't give one all the answers by any means, because a controlled experimental method can, as I think Mr. Coladarci has pointed out, give us answers to problems which are more suited to that approach.

Procedural Problems

DuBois, Spindler, Coladarci

DuBois: I've been bothered by what we're doing or not doing this evening. I detect two main themes between which we've been oscillating. One is, What is the anthropological method? Now we're interested here not in discussing anthropological method per se, I assume, but in discovering what methods used by anthropologists can be usefully transmitted to educators for their own purposes and their own awareness. This is one area of inquiry to which we have returned time and time again. The other general area which has seemed to occupy us this evening has been really, What kinds of research problems can we help phrase which educators can pursue, either by themselves or by hiring teams of social scientists? Now, is this really what we want to do? Are we concerned with the methodology of anthropology that can be transmitted to teachers and with a series of research problems which might be investigated at some other time if the funds, resources, and personnel are available? If this is what we're trying to do, then I think there is a better way of going at it than sitting around and discussing the papers one by one, or having general bull sessions. That is, we sit down in a series of groups and to a degree we effect a draft, let's say.

Spindler: I don't think I can answer Cora DuBois's question, because I find that as the discussion goes along I keep changing my own concept of what we're doing. And that I think in a sense defines the intentions of this whole affair. That is, it is so exploratory that we must shift rather continuously. Now, for instance, Hal Cowley has pointed out that he wants to know what anthropologists have to offer educators. If they haven't anything to offer, he wants to know that. He also said, "Let

* In private discussion.

everybody forget whether he is an anthropologist or an educator and let's talk about problems."

These two statements appear to be somewhat contradictory, but that doesn't bother me. That is, I like this contradiction because it means that we can both address ourselves to such kinds of questions and at the same time stand aside and say, "What did we contribute? Where did we put our weight, if any?" Now when we get through, we have two main trends: First, we have a series of problems that we have addressed ourselves to as intelligent laymen, if nothing else; second, we have a set of rather self-conscious formulations which are semiexperimental in nature that say, "Here is what a discipline has to offer another discipline in an operational field." Now, this still leaves Cora DuBois's question hanging in the air, and I rather guess that it has to be left just there until we get to Sunday morning. We will leave it to Margaret Mead to tie this up and put it into an educational package for our consumption.

Coladarci: I would like to react to George's (Spindler) statement. The ambiguity that Cora (DuBois) sensed doesn't trouble me and I share your orientation. As a matter of fact, I have built myself a very convenient frame of reference, for the moment, which has largely been due to your remarks, Solon (Kimball). It strikes me, as I look forward to the next few days (although this probably will shift completely before we leave tonight) that in the first place there's no such thing as anthropology with the implication that this is some kind of homogeneous mass; it's more of a heterogeneous mass, in terms of interests. If we just sat around talking about problems I'm afraid it would focus on whatever the important anthropologists here—and I suppose there is some hierarchy of importance—think are the important problems. And the same for the educators. I'd rather see it structured in terms of the papers, which represent presumably the heterogeneity of interests among anthropologists. Then my frame of reference is this: Here are various methodologies, one of which happens to be the one Solon (Kimball) has just described; the particular people reading papers have structured, in light of their methodologies and concepts, views that purport to have meaning for education. And, as I read those papers, I am of the thought that they indeed do have such meaning, although we might want to debate them. They do raise issues as anthropologists see them. Whether or not I go home with a nice bag of concepts and models doesn't bother me at all; I don't think that I will and, as a matter of fact, I will be disappointed if I do because there's not that much truth anywhere—for me, at any rate. Again, I'm not troubled by the ambiguities; as a matter of fact, I find the present structure quite convenient; I'm not looking for one-to-one relationships between questions and answers.

Section IV

SOME NOTIONS ON LEARNING INTERCULTURAL UNDERSTANDING

Cora DuBois
Harvard-Radcliffe

Introduction

The original title assigned to this paper was "Intercultural Education and International Understanding." In an attempt to understand what each of these words meant and how they could be related, certain notions emerged that have led to a more modest formulation of the topic. In order to spare the reader the time-consuming confusions through which the writer passed, it will be necessary to present a tentative and preliminary characterization of certain notions and distinctions as they will be used here.

First.—It seems essential to distinguish between intercultural and international. By cultural categories are meant the perceptions, knowledge, values, and attendant behaviors of groups of human beings. National categories, on the other hand, are complex institutional aggregates. Nations and cultures are rarely coterminous. Nations interact systematically through highly structured institutions. However, the system of interaction is of a markedly different order from the system of interaction that operates between individuals of different cultures. Cultural categories are congenial and familiar to anthropologists. They are less equipped to deal with national categories. This paper therefore addresses itself to intercultural rather than international relationships.

One of the common popular fallacies today is the confusion of these two systems. Individuals of different cultures may interact as if they were national (i.e., governmental) representatives. For example, an individual Indian may act toward an individual American as if the latter were the embodiment of military aid to Pakistan. On the other hand, many people today act as if relationships between individuals of different cultures were a direct imperative to relationships between national governments. This viewpoint is held by many advocates of governmentally sponsored programs of cross-cultural study. Cross-cultural study may be "a good thing," but to assume that it will directly and quickly affect international relations is to underestimate the complex forces controlling international relations and to confuse the systems within which peoples and governments relate to each other. The foregoing statements are not the equivalent of saying

89

there is no relationship between these two systems. It is quite possible that they may interlock at many points, but the salient variables of each system are probably discrete.

Second.—Learning is here considered as the process of acquiring a culture; education is the process of imparting it. Intimately related as the two are, we shall be concerned primarily with learning. It is conceived here as a process continuing throughout life but at various tempos. Individuals not only acquire the perceptions, symbols, attitudes, behavior, and values of social aggregates to which they are exposed, but also may acquire a cognitive command of some or all of the systems operative within those social aggregates.

Of considerable importance is the distinction between *affective* and *cognitive* learning. A child for example may absorb from the grandmother who rears him a conservative viewpoint toward life (Mead, 1951, *passim*). But he may also have to learn systems. If he is an individual who has been brought up abroad, or within a family of mixed cultural backgrounds, or even as a bilingual, he may from earliest childhood have acquired varying degrees of bicultural or even multicultural affective learning. If he has not had that sort of early experience in childhood, he may nevertheless learn to learn about cultural differences. An individual whose affective learning endows him with the capacity to relate to people across two or more cultural traditions does not *pari passu* command associated cognitive skills concerning the systems of cultures. Contrariwise, persons who have cognitively learned the systematic aspects of different cultures are not *pari passu* capable of relating themselves interpersonally across cultural lines.

It is suggested that cognitive learning about systems of different cultures is more likely to be applicable to competence in international relations than to competence in intercultural relations. We have all known foreign service personnel who perform their assigned tasks with competence but who never establish contacts with the people of the country in which they are posted. Similarly we have all known acute social analysts who cannot work with informants. On the other hand, we have all known people who lack systematic analytic capacities in any intercultural or international field but have a genius for establishing personal contacts wherever they are. In sum, we must distinguish between affective and cognitive learning in respect to both intercultural and international relationships. Affective learning comes before cognitive learning, although the latter may start very early in life. Both types of learning probably continue through a person's life. It does seem likely, however, that, for most Westerners at least, the weight of affective learning occurs early in the life span and that the weight of cognitive learning occurs later in the life span.

Third.—In the light of the foregoing it may be useful to establish distinctions between intuition, knowledge, and understanding.

"Intuition" is unfortunately a questionable word and one not always in the best repute. However, it is used here, *faut de mieux*, to express the substantive aspect of the affective learning process. It is the series of affective responses, cues, and their attendant values and attitudes absorbed from the outer world by learners. "Knowledge" as used here is contrasted with "intuition" in the sense that knowledge constitutes the substantive aspect of cognitive learning. It is the more or less articulate and articulated command of a structural system. "Understanding" is used to cover the synthesis of intuition and knowledge—in the sense that both the cues and attitudes as well as the comprehension of the structural system can be brought to bear in situational contexts. This is probably what many educators would call "true learning."

Fourth.—To provide certain verbal short cuts a distinction is quite arbitrarily made here between education and educators on the one hand and between schooling and teachers on the other.

Education is both the deliberate inculcation of knowledge, attitudes, and values and the unconscious transmission of modes of perceiving the world. The most important and pervasive type of education is that which occurs in the parent-child relationship. But more precisely, education is practiced by the "formed" in relation to the "unformed" (using these words in the French sense of *formation*). This is a more accurate way of stating the meaning here attached to educator and education, since societies differ greatly in standards of social maturity as well as in the time span and duration considered appropriate for education. Furthermore, in almost all societies there are specialists who transmit their skills, frequently to fellow adults. Therefore education takes highly varied forms. The American Indian elder tells creation myths around the fire at night. Group discussion may be set up in adult education in Chicago. The young Balinese dancer may be physically molded by an experienced performer now too old to dance. The older sibling teaches his junior sibling games and duties. The Ford Foundation sponsors educational radio and television programs requiring the collaboration of many specialists. The Indian holy man has a disciple. The psychoanalyst accepts a patient.

"Teachers" will here mean the type of educator that functions in relation to schools. "Teacher" will therefore be used here in a more limited sense than "educator." Schools are conceived as institutions for the prosecution of education. Schools, as institutions, have a more limited distribution in the world than education. However, where schools occur, they generally involve a teacher and learners, a location, and regular sessions for attendance. In some societies, schools are limited to a particular age group, or to a particular social class. They vary in what is taught and the time required to complete the educational task. They may stress knowledge broadly conceived or the transmission of a limited skill; they may initiate the child into membership in the adult world through the medium of initiation ceremonies or stress the development of individual personality; they may prize "thought" whether rationally or mystically conceived.

Learners in Relation to Intercultural Understanding

It now becomes possible to suggest at least two situational categories within which individuals learn intercultural understanding. Before presenting them, one assumption and five factors should be made explicit that are here considered salient probably in all learning but especially in the learning that is conducive to intercultural understanding

First, it is assumed that the learner must be able to differentiate between the self and the nonself with increasing accuracy in the course of his educational trajectory. This assumption underlies both categories to be discussed. The learner must neither distort the outer world (at least within the boundaries of the reality provided by his culture) nor project the self into the outer world. Genocide and world conquerors are historical realities illustrative of individual "pathologies" of this type that have found social expression. For example, Jewish persecutions rested on the belief of many individuals that the Jews were conspiring to destroy national goals. World conquerors have persuaded the naïve, the timorous, or the helpless that their projective phantasies had external validity.

On the assumption that the distinction between self and nonself is achieved with some regard for external realities, five factors salient in intercultural learning are suggested.

Factor 1.—The learner must find avenues for relating himself to the outer world. An appraisal of the rewards and penalties as well as the various roles open to the learner must be accurately perceived.

The importance of the sequence of relating the self to social reality and to values is clearly indicated in the following quotation, written within theoretical preoccupations quite different from the present one (von Gruenebaum, 1954, p. 1):

A gesture observed acquires meaning only when we know the prayer to which it belongs; and the prayer, in turn, is comprehensible when we understand the sensibilities, the religious attitudes, and the system of faith which demand it and within which it may be judged an appropriate and correct expression of the inner experience of the community and an accepted means of approach to God. The interaction between the causal and the teleological nexus in the genesis of the historical fact (as of any psychological datum) must be noted as another characteristic of methodological importance.

This consideration suggests that an overly permissive educational practice may produce confusion in learners who must adapt to complex and heterogeneous societies. Excessive permissiveness in our society may delay and possibly disorganize the learner's accurate testing of the social reality in which his future rewards and his life chances lie.

Factor 2.—Experience is salient in all learning. If the educational goal is intercultural understanding, the learner must experience intercultural differences in many contexts and in different learning situations.

Factor 3.—Supportive personal relationships facilitate all learning. They are one of the most important channels for learners to internalize motivational and valuational resources in the environment. Such relationships appear to take on added salience in intercultural understanding.

Factor 4.—Timing appears to be crucial to learning. By timing is meant "when" in the life trajectory the learning occurs. The assumption is made that affective learning is the predominant process in childhood and that cognitive learning predominates as the learner matures. We have been told that toilet training prior to myelinization is futile and/or damaging to the infant. The American school system has certain rules of thumb about the appropriate age when a second language should be introduced. State laws vary somewhat on the age at which mechanical judgment has developed to the point where a driving license can be issued. These are timing factors or cultural judgments on timing in respect to learning.

Factor 5.—Duration, as contrasted to timing, is the factor having to do with the length of the learning period. The United States Army, for example, deemed one year an adequate time span for Japanese students to acquire an appreciation of American democracy. Obviously in the West we are preoccupied with time to the extent where we are inclined to see it often as an independent variable. More particularly we are preoccupied with a linear time system. This may well be a culturally determined theme and not a universal category. Nevertheless I have found no way of avoiding linear time as a factor in learning. Both duration and timing in the learning process should provide interesting opportunities for comparative research that are still inadequately explored.

There are undoubtedly other salient factors that should be considered in discussing adequately even two situational contexts relevant to learning intercultural understanding. However, for the moment these five factors alone are used to analyze two gross situational categories.

The bicultural learning situation.—This category is called bicultural for purposes of convenience. It might as easily be conceived as multicultural. It is also conceivable that this notion is applicable to class differences in a society where class ethos are markedly divergent. The interrelation of the five factors in bicultural learning is as follows: The learner is exposed in his early formative years (Factor 4—timing) to cultural differences and bicultural situations. Experience (Factor 2) with cultural differences is provided by the very definition of the category. Whether the learner will have warm supportive relationships (Factor 3) and how long bicultural learning will last (Factor 5) in any individual case are not stated by this crude situational categorization, but at least they can be determined *post factum*. It is in Factor 1, the relation of the self to the outer world and the attendant learning of systems of social rewards and variant roles, that the crucial situation seems to exist. In sum, the learner has had opportunity for affective learning but not necessarily for cognitive learning.

Let us take a fictitious but not improbable case. A boy is born to an American missionary family in India. The parents, absorbed in their responsibilities, turn the infant over in large part to an Indian nurse. He may have a warm supportive relationship with that nurse but much less warmth and support from his parents who are busy with mission tasks. In which world, the Indian or American, will the child ultimately seek relationships and learn the roles open to him and the rewards or penalties entailed? Given the divergent roles of his Indian nurse and his American mother, the inconsistencies between their respective perceptions and values, how will the child learn to place his allegiances? How much confusion will he manifest on this score? The impulse and the tradition of his parents will be to send him to the United States to a "good school" near some member of the family. If the school is indeed a good one, if he makes an early enough transition, his early confusions may be resolved and the way cleared for him to attain bicultural understanding. But to achieve this solution, the affective learning of his early years must be enriched by cognitive learning in the course of his educational career.

A dramatically different illustration of bicultural learning can be suggested. An African village boy has grown up to the age of ten in a moderately acculturated village and has attended a not too "efficient" Western-type village school. He shows aptitude in Western learning. The local administrator and the parents agree to send him two hundred miles away to a boarding school. How do our salient learning factors operate in such a case? Again, cross-cultural experience will not be lacking, but what will be the effect of abrupt transition when he is already ten years old between the boarding school environment and the home village? How will these social discontinuities affect his life trajectory? Will they blur his sense of what constitutes self and nonself? Will they be conducive to regressive formations? How accurately will he be able to compare the two systems of rewards and penalties and the variant roles both in the village and in the other world that is opened to him through a rural African boarding school? And what is the likelihood of his finding in a boarding school those warm supportive personal relationships that we have assumed to be highly important to all learning but particularly to intercultural understanding? Before coming to any conclusion other than the complexity of the situation with which we are dealing, it may be desirable to present a second situational category.

The monocultural learning situation.—In this category the learner is born into a relatively homogeneous social aggregate. Whereas learning to relate the self to the outer world and to acquire a sense of the system of social rewards and variant roles (Factor 1) was suggested as crucial for the bicultural learner, for the monocultural learner let us assume that this factor, relatively speaking, is facilitated. We may also assume that time to learn these matters (Factor 5) is adequate. As in the case of the bicultural learner, the supportive relationship (Factor 3) cannot be predicted. The crucial factors will be the acquisition of cross-cultural experience (Factor 2); what constitutes the best timing for introducing various cross-cultural experiences (Factor 4); and how long a time span must be provided various individuals for cross-cultural learning to occur (Factor 5).

To capsulate the argument so far made, the rough diagram following on the next page is offered.

There is no doubt that such a formulation is intolerably vague and oversimplified. Yet, inadequate as it is, it may further the development of some useful notions.

DISTINCTION BETWEEN SELF AND NONSELF IS ASSUMED

Salient Factors	Bicultural	Monocultural
1. Relation of self to society	Crucial	Facilitated
2. Experience with other culture	Given	Crucial
3. Supportive relationships	Must be determined	Must be determined
4. Timing	Assumed at period of greatest proto-learning	Crucial to intercultural understanding
5. Duration	Must be determined	Crucial to intercultural understanding

Before pursuing such notions, let us turn to some of the very broadest forces that affect the context within which intercultural learning is proceeding in the contemporary world.

Contemporary Conditions of Intercultural Learning

The assumption is made that no numerically significant ethnic group in the contemporary world has escaped either the direct or the indirect influence of the last four centuries of Euro-American cultural expansion. This is as true for the West as for other areas of the world, since the feedback effects on the West of its expansion have exerted great influence upon it. The intercultural contacts of those four centuries have engendered cumulative intercultural learning. In other words, intercultural contacts provide the situational context for intercultural learning. The lessons of the West have been learned, and their implications are often more vigorously pursued in the rest of the world than in the West itself. But education, as the deliberate inculcation of Western knowledge, attitudes, and values started later than the first learning contacts and has had on the whole a somewhat slower rate of acceleration.[1] The Western school system has been slowest of all, with the result that the Western system of schooling as it has been introduced into other cultures is at present, or soon will be, interpreted and restructured by local teachers who have comprehended and accepted Westernization in varying degrees.

Two propositions may now be advanced:

First, in societies undergoing rapid change there will be discrepancies between what the individual learns, what the educators inculcate, and what the schools teach. Probably even in societies that change at relatively slow rates such discrepancies are present, but the proposition here suggested is that the greater the rate of social change, the greater the discrepancies. If this proposition is true, then it follows from our earlier assumption about the rapid rate of social change in the contemporary world that we may

[1] There are exceptions of course. The proselytizing fervor that accompanied Hispanic expansion must be counted as education in the sense in which the word is used here.

expect to find individuals everywhere facing discrepancies between the knowledge, attitudes, and values they have learned, those inculcated by their educators, and those taught in their schools. All learners therefore face to some degree the situation suggested for bicultural learners.

The second proposition is that social tensions are definable in terms of the gap between values and practice, or, if one speaks in terms of individual psychology, between aspirations and resources. Presumably all learning and much social change is attributable to such tension gaps. As social analysts or practitioners we must try to formulate means for determining under what conditions and at what intensity gaps prove intolerable to individuals and have deleterious repercussions on social groups, institutions, or commonly held value systems.

These are certainly not novel ideas. Studies of the social and psychological implications of urbanization point in this direction. Riesman (1950) has given us a provocative statement of discrepancies between values and practices and between inconsistent values in the American scene. Rundblad's (1951) study of Forestville in Sweden reveals the deleterious individual and social results of the gap between aspiration and resources. The contemporary problem of caste in India is another case in point. The sociological concepts of anomie and the marginal man point in the same direction. Individual cases like Kenyatta in Africa and the recent Puerto Rican attempts at assassination are straws in the same wind.

The argument just advanced runs as follows: Euro-American expansion produced intercultural contacts; these in turn triggered intercultural learning in both donor and recipient groups; intercultural learning has accelerated rates of social change; in periods of rapid social change discrepancies will arise between learning, education, and schooling; these discrepancies create individual as well as social tensions that can result in, as well as be the result of, social dysphoria.

The essential problem is to understand the processes of intercultural learning in the individual so that education can be used to diminish the deleterious personal and social tensions such learning may engender. Intercultural understanding is presumed to be a contributing element in reducing social tensions.

Given what has been suggested about learners in relation to intercultural understanding and about contemporary conditions of intercultural learning, the roles of educators and more specifically of teachers can be tentatively explored.

A Valuational Topography of the Functions of Educators and Teachers

In order to provide a preliminary topographic orientation one might suggest that educators function at one extreme of a continuum as transmitters of cultural traditions and values. The teacher of a Koran school and the traditional Chinese teacher of the classics are both examples of this type. But so also are parents who duplicate their own upbringing

in their children. At the other extreme educators may function as innovators and experimenters. Teachers who are concerned with widening
horizons of knowledge and the teaching of intercultural understanding
and who wish to share these interests with their students belong to this
category. But wittingly or unwittingly so also may parents whose educational practice is based as nearly as possible on the latest psychological
theories of child development, or who because of their own confusions
abandon the child to pick up his own values and standards wherever he
may.

Within this general topography persons of essentially traditional and
conservative outlook will argue that the role of the educator should always
be that of transmitter of traditions. Somewhat less tradition-bound individuals might argue that the teacher should be the transmitter of tradition
during periods of rapid social change, that only in this way can brakes
be put upon social changes that outstrip the capacity of individuals to
cope with them. Such individuals might be willing to see the educator
function as an innovator and experimenter during periods of relative social
stability. On the other hand, persons might also argue that during a period
of rapid social change, if the tension gap is not to reach individually
intolerable and socially disruptive proportions, the function of educators
must necessarily be that of innovators. This is precisely the situation, such
persons would argue, in which education must be experimental to keep
abreast of the times and to search out devices that will help human beings
to deal with social tensions. Such persons might also argue that this
type of education also mitigates against social stagnation in periods of
relative social stability. Crudely presented as it is, the following table
serves to illustrate the different value positions just presented:

Value Judgment	Role of Education During Periods of:	
	Rapid Social Change	Slow Social Change
1	Transmitter	Transmitter
2	Transmitter	Innovator
3	Innovator	Innovator

It is now necessary to elaborate this oversimplification. Patently in
no era or area have all educators belonged exclusively to one or another
type. But the important point is that schools have stressed one or another educational philosophy. There are, for example, in the United States
today schools that are concerned with traditional learning and others that
are frankly innovative and interested in educational experimentation. The
Western type of schooling introduced into other cultures is always innovative (but not necessarily experimental) from the viewpoint of those
societies.

Quite apart from value judgments on what should or should not be
the role of educators in relatively stable and in rapidly changing societies,
one possible hypothesis suggests itself. Since no teacher exists in a social
vacuum, interaction between the social milieu and the teacher both as an
individual and in his social role is inescapable. It might therefore be

hypothesized that in periods of relative social stability the major tendency will be for teachers to function as transmitters of tradition, whereas in periods of relatively rapid social change the major tendency will be for them to espouse innovation and/or experimentation. As a subhypothesis it might be suggested that schools will lag behind an educational trend in either direction, on the assumption that organized institutions respond more slowly to changing situations than do individuals.

In connection with this notion it is possible that much of the philosophy of innovation, experimentation, and permissiveness current in certain sectors of American education today reflects the unsureness of teachers, parents, and other educators concerning the relevance and viability of traditional methods and values of training the young for the world in which they will have to live. This bewilderment may be one factor in the reported inclination of parents to place responsibility for bringing up children increasingly on the schools and other institutions external to the home.

Intercultural Understanding as the Goal of the Learner-Educator Relationship

It is probably a safe guess that the vast majority of the people in the world today lack the motives and the opportunity to establish linkages across cultural or class groups, and that many never extend their direct learning beyond what is provided by primary face-to-face groupings, although they are rarely able to escape the indirect effects of the intercultural contacts and learning that characterize the modern world. This contrast between direct and indirect learning may account in part for the psychic satisfaction claimed for life in small communities or tribal groups, whether we are thinking of an American small town or the Pueblo Indians. The psychic strain of life in large social aggregates, whether nations or metropolitan centers, may reflect the same gap between direct and indirect learning.

It can be suggested that there are certain crucial points for learners in the process of relating the self to steadily expanding horizons required by contemporary life. One point is when the learner must make the transition from face-to-face (or potentially face-to-face) groups like the school or the village to secondary groups like the nation, the United Nations, or the Standard Oil Company. The other point is when cross-cultural persons or systems must be related to the self. The affiliational problems for the learner are then:

1. In-group
   a) Primary relationship
   b) Secondary relationship

2. Out-group
   a) Primary relationship
   b) Secondary relationship

The bicultural learner is presumably equipped by early life experiences with resources in primary relationships of both in-group and out-group (1a and 2a). The monocultural learner is presumably equipped by early life experiences only with resources in primary relationships of the in-group (1a). But on the other hand the monocultural learner is presumably better equipped than the bicultural learner to achieve secondary relationships in the in-group (1b).

It is now possible to return to the earlier notions presented in an earlier section, "Learners in Relation to Intercultural Understanding," to see if we can relate them to the question of educators and teachers.

In the monocultural learning situation it was suggested that the three learning factors crucial to intercultural understanding were experience, timing, and duration. The crucial questions, then, are when and for how long should learners be provided cross-cultural experiences, and what types of experience can realistically be provided within the framework of a monocultural educational and schooling system. Let us begin with the transition from in-group primary relationships (1a) to in-group secondary relationships (1b).

It can be suggested that for monocultural learners an important pre-disposer to experience is the existence of a symbol charged with plus values. I do not feel competent to develop this point in any detail, but I would like to suggest that symbols must be of a sort that facilitate the relation of the self to the value and to its internalization. For example, the double-headed eagle, the crown, the swastika, and the jade Buddha seem less obvious channels to self-relatedness than the Great White Father, Mother India, or the Queen. Lincoln and Washington may be better symbols of national life than the flag. There is, however, much to be said for badges of identification, such as a flag, so long as the learner is assisted in distinguishing the badge from the symbol and the symbol from reality, and so long as the symbol remains in the realm of human experience. The dilemma here appears to be twofold. Human symbols facilitate identification, but if they are not clearly and cognitively recognized as symbols, there is the risk that these human symbols may become repositories for projections of unresolved interpersonal relationships with all of the distortions such projections can induce both in the individual's intropsychic economy and in his social and political judgments. The other dilemma is that the symbolic figure must be charged with the desired value. Thus in India, Brahman girls for a month each year between the ages of about seven and thirteen are expected to fast, meditate, and pray on the legendary life of goddesses like Sita in order that they may lead lives of comparable virtue. A human yet frankly symbolic figure with appropriate value charge is provided in an experiential context. The desired value as such is deliberately taught and presumably internalized. One wonders whether equivalent symbols and rituals could be provided that would carry the value of intercultural understanding.

What additional educational experiences may be suggested to carry the monocultural learner outward in a widening sphere of self-relatedness with out-groups, whether primary or secondary (2a and 2b), in such a way that cultural differences can be encountered without threat?

If there is any value in the abstract argument here proposed, the answer would seem to lie in providing quite young monocultural learners with cross-cultural primary face-to-face contacts (2a) in an atmosphere of positive valuation. Teachers, family friends, nurses, and playmates from different class, cultural, and racial backgrounds will presumably afford the best channel for establishing out-group primary relationships. The disappearance of segregation in our schools may be a step in this direction. The unfortunately minuscule teacher-exchange program is another step in such a direction. Undoubtedly far more could be done in this direction by American schools than now is. It seems wise to introduce cultural behavior and values that diverge considerably from those of the monocultural learner, not in terms that stress traditional differences but rather in terms of common problems (Johnson, 1951, p. 86).

Quite apart from face-to-face experiences, the monocultural learner can be introduced quite early to cognitive learning materials that should go far in facilitating both primary and secondary out-group relationships (2a and 2b) throughout life. Chief among these is the study of foreign languages. Differing styles for perceiving and construing the world can be unthreateningly conveyed by the teaching of foreign languages. The almost complete ignorance in this country of languages that are outside the Indo-European stock is startling in a nation with world leadership responsibilities. The drop in even the customary French, Spanish, and German language teaching in the American schools should be a source of grave concern on many scores. Language training is an excellent and unthreatening channel to understanding of the arbitrary quality of symbols and of differing cultural modes of perception. It is probably one of the best educational devices for leading monocultural learners toward intercultural understanding. As a medium serving these purposes it is unfortunately seriously handicapped by the methods and the timing now employed in language teaching (Carroll, 1953, Chap. 6).

In line also with providing monocultural learners cross-cultural experience, educators and school systems can encourage study tours across cultural boundaries. American study abroad as compared with tourism is not only limited but is directed largely to countries where cultural differences are minimal, as in the United Kingdom or France. The experience of travel and study for American learners in Latin-American countries is all too little encouraged by our school system. However, it is important to insist on the importance of competent guidance and interpretation in connection with foreign study and travel (Taba, 1953, *passim*; Kahn, 1954, pp. 459–64). Cross-cultural experience without education is of minimal benefit. It may actually impede intercultural understanding. Experience must be mediated by competent and knowledgeable teaching. This was amply demonstrated by the behavior of most American army personnel overseas, who were ill-prepared to establish contacts with people of other cultures and even less prepared to develop intercultural understanding.

However, it need scarcely be stressed again that a school system can operate only within a social context. The American school system and all educational activities, whether television or psychotherapy, inevitably reflect the American system of social rewards and penalties. Until clear rewards are available for international understanding and the skills that are attendant upon it (e.g., the command of other languages or personal poise when faced with contradictory values and conditions associated with overseas travel and living experience), the school system and educators cannot be expected to alter social attitudes quickly and solely with the tools at their disposal.

We have so far dealt essentially with experience that might be provided the monocultural learner to develop his capacity for intercultural understanding.

By implication both timing and time have at least been touched upon. Both affective and cognitive learning for encouraging both primary and secondary relationships may be introduced early in the educational trajectory. Thus language could easily be introduced in the primary grades, whereas guided study tours would not be feasible before the secondary school. There is much need for precise and practical educational research into the problems of timing and duration in providing learners viable experiences that will lead to intercultural understanding. I would assume that learning opportunities in this area must be many-faceted, reinforcing, and continuing.

Let us now turn to the bicultural learner. If the earlier suggestions have validity, the bicultural learner has greater resources than the monocultural learner in that he has established at least two primary group relationships early in life. The crucial area for the bicultural learner will lie in discovering how to relate the self to at least two secondary groups without being forced to reject one or the other. What has been suggested earlier about symbols applies in the case of the bicultural learner with added emphasis. That symbols should be as culture-free as any symbol can be suggests itself further at this point.

Whereas the educator's problem with the monocultural learner is to stage in cross-cultural experience, his problem with the bicultural learner is to help his pupil discover the differing systems of rewards and the variant roles provided by secondary group relationships in different cultures, and to help him reach a viable adjustment in the face of choice. Here the role of the educator-teacher as a warm supportive figure seems to emerge with even more saliency than in the case of the monocultural learner. Educators and teachers must in their persons provide support to the bicultural learner that the monocultural learner derives from a social milieu whose system of rewards and roles are relatively apparent to him. The bicultural learner must be assisted to select social roles that promise rewards commensurate with his capacities as a learner. Variant social roles and their attendant rewards will need to be stressed in the education of the bicultural learner. But at the same time, in the achievement of these social roles and rewards, he must not have to suppress or reject the alternative cultural resources acquired through his bicultural experience. Probably one of the greatest barriers to the development of intercultural understanding among the foreign-born or second-generation students in the United States has been the rigorous insistence in American schools, until recently, on the exclusive quality of American values. When these were reinforced by the relatively accessible rewards and variant roles offered by American society, the "alienation" of our foreign-born from their own cultural origin and their rejection of it was assured. We appear to have built national solidarity at the expense of intercultural understanding.

The establishment of Western schools, especially boarding schools, and curricula in non-Western societies is likely to constitute an extreme type of cultural discontinuity and may do much to force "either-or" choices on their learners. The native learner is presented with discrepant persons and discrepant values but not with resources for integrating both systems into an expanding concept of the self. The knowledge offered him by teachers is likely to be inadequate to the learning process and need for intercultural understanding. The learner often has no recourse except to select one or the other cultural alternative. His own pattern may close off avenues to international understanding, but the alternative educational pattern gives him no foundation in personal security. By the same token this suggests that the village or community school taught by competent indigenous teachers will provide more accessible channels to the widened identifications than will the boarding school. The ineffectuality of the boarding school program adopted by the United States Bureau of Indian Affairs in facilitating intercultural understanding among American Indians may rest on such considerations. On the other hand, this is the problem created by those non-Western students who select the Western alternative without adequately based learning patterns. The insistence of certain West Africans on a British classical education, whose relevance to their life trajectories is hard to establish, is an example of the repercussions of such discontinuities in learning that may face the bicultural learner when his resources of affective learning and his bicultural primary relationships receive exclusive rather than inclusive treatment in the course of schooling. His efforts to relate the self to secondary groups will be commensurately impaired. Whatever value judgment may be passed on this situation, we must face the probability that discontinuities in the schooling of bicultural learners are conducive to the creation of social marginality.

One final and perhaps gratuitous comment should be added. If we are considering study abroad—whether for the bicultural or monocultural learner—we are presumably concerned with a relatively advanced stage in the learner's educational trajectory. It would appear from recent studies in cross-cultural education that the same salient factors we have selected for younger learners are still operative. The educators and teachers of foreign students can help to introduce ameliorative factors that will enhance the likelihood of the learner emerging not only with a cross-cultural education but with intercultural understanding. These ameliorative factors phrased in terms of foreign students in the United States include: establishing early in the sojourn a warm supportive interpersonal relationship; safeguards against diminished self-esteem derived from attitudes bearing on race and accorded status in the host country (i.e., reduction of social penalties); provisions for schooling that will interlock with past cognitive resources; opportunities to achieve self-related goals (i.e., social rewards); and sufficient time for these processes to occur.

It should be noted that the importance of the time element in adjusting to new cultures is emerging with increasing clarity. Research on foreign students in the United States indicates that stages in learning to adjust to this country can be postulated. For example, "adjustment" seems most satisfactory in the early so-called spectator stage before the individual is genuinely engaged in the demands of a new culture. Later, if the sojourn has lasted more than a year, a deeper but again reasonably satisfactory sense of adjustment is reported. The crucial period for young adults appears to be somewhere between three months and eighteen months (Social Science Research Council, 1953; Lysgaard, 1954). The relevance of these preliminary findings for international understanding seems clear.

So far the learner-educator relationship has been discussed largely in terms of interpersonal relationships, but the social role of the educator in the larger social matrix still requires exploration. If earlier suggestions are valid, intercultural learning is a given in the contemporary world, and in a period of rapid social change discrepancies between learning, education, and schooling are probably inevitable. Educators are faced with the dilemma of choosing whether to become cultural transmitters or experimental innovators. How do such roles affect the learner-educator relationships?

The potentiality for intercultural learning in the contemporary world is, of course, an asset to the expressed value implied in intercultural understanding. The educator who wishes to assist the learners toward that goal has unprecedented opportunities offered by the increasing movement of peoples across cultural and national boundaries, the development of communication systems, new social science insights, and the growth of relevant teaching materials. The issue is to marshal these resources for the learner. "Facts" are understood only to the degree in which their context is comprehended (von Gruenebaum, 1954, p. 1). National and cultural values need not be slighted in the process. The problem is one of placing in-group and out-group cultures in comparative but nonvaluational perspectives. The role of the educator in fostering intercultural understanding is neither that of cultural transmitter nor that of experimental innovator but rather that of cultural translator. The skilled educator will appreciate the gaps on the one hand between learning, education, and schooling, and on the other hand between cultural systems. Differences can be objectively considered. Training should stress that value judgments are relevant only to values and that they are not automatically attached to any subject or system simply because they are different from the familiar or congenial. Teachers and educators have a large responsibility for cultivating rational thinking, objective analysis, and a sharp sense of relevance. The re-emphasis in the last century on man's irrationality has served as a useful corrective to the eighteenth century's overvaluation of reason as arbiter of human affairs. Today, with our unparalleled (though avowedly meager) insights into individual and social dynamics, it is as appropriate to reappraise and to cultivate the human individual's capacity for rational and objective thought and to direct such capacity to valuational choice, as it is to assume that valuational choices reflect early and nonrational conditioning.

Summary and Conclusion

Intercultural understanding results from the ability to bring both intuition (affective learning) and knowledge (cognitive learning) to bear on cross-cultural situations. For a learner to achieve intercultural understanding certain sufficient conditions must exist: Intercultural understanding must have positive value attached to it; rewards should be perceivable for such learning; cultural differences must have been experienced; the experiences must be self-related; the sequences between the self and the learned must be left unresolved. In the monocultural learner the crucial problems are when and for how long to stage in cross-cultural experiences. In the bicultural learner the crucial problem is how to establish the coherent linkages between the self and secondary groupings of two or more cultures. Educators' and teachers' roles in respect to learners are threefold: first, to encourage an expanding system of self-relatedness; second, to supply the affective learning resources essential to intuition; and third, to provide the cognitive-rational materials necessary for systematic knowledge.

Remove supportive personal elements, skip too widely and too early in the learner's life experience over the sequence of expanding self-relatedness, cut too short the time allowed to absorb new ways and objectively appraise new values, fail to provide the opportunities for experiential learning or fail to establish it as a habit of learning, distort or fail to supply systematic cross-cultural knowledge, and the learner is unlikely to achieve international understanding.

For educators and teachers to perform their necessary role in this process, they must themselves possess intercultural understanding, but also they must conceive their function to be neither solely that of cultural transmitters nor solely that of innovators. Rather, their function is to translate cultural realities to individual learners whose capacities and incapacities for intercultural understanding will vary greatly not only between learners but also at various periods in the learner's life.

If we grant that we are somewhat less than perfect educators living in a somewhat less than perfect world, there is cause for considerable optimism that there are even a certain number of people capable of intercultural understanding. It behooves us to recognize that the number of people capable of practicing intercultural understanding today is a numerically small group and that this group does not necessarily embrace all people who make international relations their business. The opinion might even be hazarded that the elite of the so-called underdeveloped countries contains a greater proportion of people who possess intercultural understanding than do more stable and "advanced" Western European nations. The former have usually had to learn languages basically different from their own; they have often had extended foreign study experiences; their educational regimen has often been intercultural in form and content; they have frequently grown up in families where consistent image ideals, traditions, and values laid the ground for a firm internal security system; last, they live in nations whose aspirations are not conducive to complacency, whose international power responsibility breeds fewer anxieties than our own, and whose very national aspirations tend to develop rewards for individuals with intercultural understanding.

If persons possessing intercultural understanding do not seem to be produced automatically by our present system of mass education in the United States, it may be desirable for educators and teachers to recognize that special training for this goal is as necessary as special training for any other leadership specialty. Not only must educators and teachers themselves be trained (or at least selected) for such functions, but they should be concerned with identifying the aptitudes and resources of individual learners for intercultural understanding. The education of the masses is a force as irreversible as interdependence in the contemporary world. But we cannot expect mass education automatically to achieve intercultural understanding.

If, and when, we understand more precisely the nature of the process, its broader extension into a mass education system may be more feasible than it now appears to be.

References

Carroll, John B. 1953. *The Study of Language.* Cambridge: Harvard University Press.

Gruenebaum, G. E. von (ed.). 1954. "Studies in Islamic Cultural History," *American Anthropologist.* Comparative Studies of Cultures and Civilizations, No. 2 (American Anthropological Association), LVI, No. 2, Part 2, Memoir 76.

Johnson, Charles A. 1951. *Education and Cultural Crisis.* New York: The Macmillan Company.

Kahn, Lothar. 1954. "Teachers' Guided Tours Abroad: A Frank Assessment," *Clearing House,* Vol. 28, No. 8, pp. 459–64.

Lysgaard, Sverre. 1954. "Adjustment in a Foreign Society: Norwegian Fulbright Grantees Visiting the United States" (preliminary draft of a paper delivered at the XIV International Congress of Psychology, Montreal, June 7–21, 1954).

Mead, Margaret. 1951. *The School in American Culture.* Inglis Lecture of 1950. Cambridge: Harvard University Press.

Riesman, David. 1950. *The Lonely Crowd: A Study in Changing American Character.* New Haven: Yale University Press.

Rundblad, Bengt G. 1951. "Forestville: A Study of Rural Social Change," Uppsala: Sociologiska Institutionen (mimeographed).

Social Science Research Council: Committee on Cross-Cultural Education. 1953. "Report on the Ithaca Conference: August 8–16" (mimeographed).

Taba, Hilda. 1953. *Cultural Attitudes and International Understanding: An Evaluation of an International Study Tour.* New York: Institute of International Education, Research Program, Occasional Papers, No. 5.

THIRD SESSION OF THE CONFERENCE

Chairman: James Quillen

Quillen: This is an area in which there is considerable interest on the part of people in education.

The area of intercultural education was developed first, I think, under the Bureau of Intercultural Education, which took the broad conception that intercultural education meant practically all kinds of intergroup relations including interracial, which tended to support the assumption that there was a direct connection between race and culture. As a result of this, the concept of intercultural education has been more closely restricted, as Dr. DuBois says, I think properly, in the paper. Intercultural education is now of concern not only in regard to the relationships between cultural groups in the United States, but also in terms of its implications for international relations, which are also treated in this paper.

But there are other types of related problems which have been considered by educators under the general term "intergroup" education. One of the leaders of the intergroup education movement in the United States has been Hilda Taba, and I believe she's going to make some comments on the paper.

Discussant: Hilda Taba

Taba: The problem of learning intercultural or intergroup understanding is analyzed rather well in this paper. I have therefore not tried to reorganize the basic mode of thinking. My comments are devoted to extending some concepts in each category presented in the paper.

First, assumptions re the nature of learning.

The first thing about learning, already partly stated in the paper, is that learning goes on on two levels, which are here called cognitive and affective learning.

Miss DuBois places them in a sequence : Affective learning comes first, at an earlier age, and cognitive learning at a later period of education. To my mind the sequence of affective and cognitive learning is not that of age. Affective learning occurs at all levels of maturity, though its proportionate role probably decreases with age. There is, however, a sequence. Learning is more effective when it begins with a primary experience, and anything really new has to be learned through some kind of starting point. That pertains particularly to learning feelings.

In place of the two types of learning, then, there seem at least four that need to be combined in intercultural learning : the cognitive (conceptual), the affective (feelings, sensitivities), primary (firsthand), and secondary (through symbols and words).

Second, to an educator the general classification of learning into either primary and secondary or cognitive and affective is not sufficient. It is more helpful to distinguish the various behavioral elements of learning, all of which may require in part primary and in part secondary experiences, and all of which may be compounded of both the cognitive and affective elements. Four such behavioral classifications of learning experiences seem relevant to intercultural learning.

a) Learning of concepts and ideas.

b) Extension of sensitivity or capacity to respond to values and feelings different from one's own.

c) Thinking—the capacity to generalize, to relate ideas logically, to infer, to interpret facts and experiences.

d) Social skills—or the tools and techniques of relating oneself to other human beings.

As to cognitive learning—or learning of concepts and ideas—the important thing to remember is that in the area of intercultural or intergroup relations most important concepts are wrought with feelings. Different cultures or different subcultures in the same major culture provide different experiences and therefore also different meanings for the same concept. Furthermore, the meanings of these concepts are culturally conditioned. Therefore cognitive learning without corresponding extension of feelings and sensitivities leads to unreal ideas, to mastery of verbal symbols without understanding, or to different interpretations or certain common symbols for concepts.

For example, the idea of "hardships of immigrants" is without meaning to students in high-school history who have had no experience of hardships. Their feeling reactions to "hardships" need extension before a realistic understanding of this concept can be acquired. This applies to many other commonly used concepts, such as "co-operation" and "democracy." It is difficult to develop these concepts solely by cognitive learning, and different learners bring to them different meanings and feelings, depending on their cultural backgrounds and the corresponding experiences. In intercultural learning the problem of different meanings and feelings being attached to the concepts' symbols is ever-present. Therefore the development of any common meanings of concepts requires extension of sensitivities to the variant meanings. It also requires a sequence in which the acquisition of cognitive elements (e.g., ideas and facts) must alternate with extension of feelings, and each must fructify the other.

Extension of sensitivity also has a developmental sequence that can be thought of as spanning the different age levels. Children start as egocentric creatures who need to learn first to respond to other persons immediately around them. This circle of possible response expands to include the values and feelings of their culture (community, nation, an ethnic group, etc.). In the modern world a more cosmopolitan sensitivity is needed and an ethnocentric orientation is too limiting. Capacity to respond to the "generalized other" (to use Mead's term) is required not only on the national scale, but on the world scale. The trouble at the present time is that while the techniques have shrunk the world, our sensitivities and understandings are not of a corresponding scope. Taylor, in *Richer by Asia*, points out that the common denominator subject to understanding between the Western culture and India is but 5 percent—a mighty thin thread on which to make common decisions or to have communication. If we are to expand this common denominator in intercultural understanding, much more needs to be done toward this aim, and earlier in the learning career than is usual now. Otherwise the uncontrolled experiences in adult life (such as travel) are insufficient, and they are not accessible to a sufficient number of people. The cultural exchange may do for some people, but it would be impossible to educate enough people that way.

Naturally, direct experience is not sufficient. Affective learning is always limited. Only most crucial things can be sampled even by planned extension of experience. From there out, extension by cognitive learning—by inference, by comparison, by analysis—is needed. Here the method of thinking about human beings, about human relations, about institutions, and so on is important. It is at this point that the comparative method about which anthropologists talk is important. This method of comparison needs to extend beyond comparing cultures that are extremely different. It needs to be applied even to minor differences within the culture, such as "This family has bacon for breakfast, and that family has pancakes." Children need to learn early that these different ways of doing many things are equivalent rather than inferior and superior.

Learning how to handle generalizations so as to recognize their limits is also important in intercultural learning. Such phenomena as stereotyping strange cultural groups spring essentially from a tendency to overgeneralize, though an affective element is usually also involved. People stereotype partly because they want to ascribe certain qualities to *all* members of a group, and partly because they have not learned to recognize the limits of generalizations. The interesting thing is that the problem of generalizing has usually been a concern of logicians, of scientists. I would like to propose that they should also be the concern of the first grade, that it is possible to make it the concern of the first grade.

The problem of social skills—that is, the tools and techniques for converting insights, understandings, and attitudes into conduct, of throwing lines across cultural and group barriers—has received little attention from anthropologists and educators alike. Yet, from the practical standpoint of implementing understanding, of developing people who act out their beliefs and understandings, it is crucial to pay attention to methods of relating oneself to persons in a "they" category, of overcoming psychological and cultural distance, of creating communication lines and consensus.

Finally, as to sequence. Miss DuBois mentioned the trajectory for learning, a natural history of learning. I agree with the idea that there is a sequence from an emotional or primary learning to a cognitive learning, and that primary learning has to come first in some shape before the cognitive learning can take place properly. But actually the primary and emotional, and the cognitive and secondary learning need to rotate in shorter trajectory. Learning each new idea requires first some learning of sensitivity followed by some conceptualizing, which in turn gives a new avenue for sensitivity, and so on. Experiments in schools have demonstrated the potency of this type of integrated sequence in intercultural learning. For example, we have tried to break down the separation between social studies, with its emphasis on learning facts, and literature, which cultivates sensitivity vicariously. The use of literature to extend sensitivity to human relations (not only to cultivate aesthetic appreciation) opens a tremendous avenue for aiding understanding of cultures and the development of identification on a broader scale.

The distinction between monocultural and bicultural learning is perhaps oversimplified. There are, of course, difficulties in developing intercultural understanding in completely homogeneous groups because total absence of differences eliminates the possibility of using comparison and contrast as a method of revealing cultural assumptions. But a person with bicultural experience has other problems in developing intercultural understanding, especially if that experience is combined with being a member of a minority culture. He is likely to have had threatening experiences which block his learning. He is also faced with value dilemmas growing out of the conflicts between the expectations of the two cultures.

Miss DuBois has rightly pointed out that a supportive psychological climate is important to effective intercultural learning. However, such support from a teacher alone is ineffective. It must come also from the peer group in which the individual functions. In many classrooms the teacher's support brings forth negative reactions from the peer group. Emotionally difficult learning can come about within a completely supportive environment in which both the teacher and peer group have been mobilized to help the individual. What happened to one third-grade boy who was subject to constant tantrums might serve as an example. He lost control of himself whenever anyone touched him, because he had been severely knocked about by his father, who was a habitual drunkard. The group had to learn not to touch him. Gradually they began to ask how they could teach the boy to be kind. By eliminating hostile reactions to the boy's outbursts and by helping him understand how everyone had some problems beyond his control, the teacher and the other students eventually helped the boy not only to control his reactions, but even to gain a perspective toward his father which made his father's behavior less disturbing to him. This method of mobilizing the group for a supportive relationship toward an individual did something for the boy which no single individual except perhaps a psychiatrist could have done.

The distinction between school teaching and education is perhaps drawn too much in black and white. School education can play a more significant role than people outside education assume. Teachers are learning to plan classroom experiences which are effective in helping students learn feelings, in changing fundamental cultural orientations, and even in changing some aspects of behavior which amount to a change of personality. It is extremely important for any group concerned with affecting education to distinguish between planned education and the accidental accumulation of social learning in an unplanned social experience.

More thought is needed also on the problem of the factors affecting the capacity for intercultural understanding. In this connection the anthropologists would do well to dip into social-psychological research in order to see some fundamental factors which prevent intercultural learning. One series of such factors is analyzed in the studies of authoritarian personality—which fears change, which is threatened by differences, which is afraid of ambiguity in perceptions, which requires clear, black-and-white answers and cannot tolerate an exploratory situation. Such a personality—called "pre-fascist" before they chose the term "authoritarian"—when developed fully, is probably incapable of intercultural learning. More data are needed on what kinds of cultural settings produce the maximum number of that kind of personality and what kind of culture tends to favor nonauthoritarian personality, which has the capacity to accept and to tolerate changes, differences, alternate ways of doing things, and unclear, tentative answers.

Discussant: Lawrence K. Frank

Frank: This paper offers so many points one wants to comment on that it's rather embarrassing to know how to deal with it in a short period. I've picked out some things, some of which will relate to what Hilda (Taba) has just said, and then some other points that will be worth considering here, that relate, not only to this paper, but to the larger question of what cultural anthropology can offer to education. As I've said before, we have to recognize some theory of learning which we ought to try to make explicit, each one of us—not that we can settle our differences here. In addition there are certain conceptions of the way in which the individual is enculturated that we should be explicit about when we talk about intercultural education.

The first point is that the paper makes a very useful and necessary distinction between intercultural and international education. An immense amount of time and money is being spent for programs of education in international relations — which are, I fear, creating what Riesman has called a host of "inside dopesters," the people who know exactly what each nation or its government is going to do, and who can explain the tricks in diplomatic maneuvers and so on, but who may be developing no intercultural understanding whatsoever. Indeed, we may say that this kind of education in international affairs is creating more resentment and suspicion of other people. And yet that is being done all over the country under the auspices of some of our leading agencies for furthering international understanding and improving international relations.

The next point is the question about different types of learning. We cannot work out any agreement on theories of learning at this meeting. We should consider what this paper has offered as two types of learning but use a different terminology. We might think, not of affective and cognitive, but of two kinds of processes in learning which, following discussions in cybernetics, are called the analogical and the digital. The analogical type of learning is that holistic, empathic, intuitive way of learning the meaning, of grasping the basic concepts rather than deriving facts, details, and generalizations from inductive study. It is a way of perceiving or understanding a situation conceptually. Historically, religion, poetry, art, analogical learning all came long before science. This analogical learning, I assume, is what Hilda (Taba) has called primary learning—which Margaret Lowenfeld has also emphasized as early learning. That is, the child, initially at least, perceives and relates himself to the world by a kind of learning process which isn't acquiring facts or knowledge in the ordinary sense; it's a holistic way of grasping, interpreting, understanding, which we may call analogical.

Taba: But it contains knowledge . . .

Frank: Well, if you want to use those terms, but I'd like to keep out of that question for a moment, because I want to try to distinguish the analogical, as contrasted with the logical, the mathematical, the digital process, which is our Western European practice of analyzing, breaking everything down into bits and then trying to put the bits back together. Language, for example, might be looked at as an analogical process; arithmetic would be digital, operating with integers and quantities. A slide rule is an analogical instrument for approximating answers; a calculating machine is usually a digital instrument which gives precise answers in quantitative terms. Metaphors are analogical, logic is digital. Now, it seems to me that the basic learning, the learning that takes place through enculturation of a child early in life, is analogical—the child learns the basic concepts, the patterns of perception of his family traditions in terms of which all his later learning of factual knowledge will be assimilated. We have not recognized this analogical learning as clearly as we should in our learning theory; we believe that we should give children chiefly facts and content without recognizing how important it is for them to get a set of concepts with which to order, interpret, and give meaning to those facts and the generalizations from facts. This analogical learning, as Hilda (Taba) has pointed out and I've often emphasized, is empathic to a large extent, operating with feeling tones which color the learning and often distort the perception. Deutero-learning, as Bateson originally used that term, was primarily concerned with the learning to learn. Now that doesn't mean learning inductive generalizations, or acquiring a kind of summation of many facts and observations. A process of learning to conceptualize and pattern experience occurs in deutero-learning after the child has had some primary analogical, conceptual learning and has recognized how events take place.

Cora (DuBois) has referred to intuition, knowledge, and understanding. We might again say that the intuitive or analogical learning, this basic conceptual formulation, is how a child begins to see the world in terms of meanings and develops concepts which are ways of stabilizing the flux of experience, so that he is not at the mercy of every variation in size, shape, and variety, but can begin to equalize his experiences. Intuition may be seen as this analogical process. Knowledge, then, may be regarded as the product of analytically derived facts, laws, generalizations, and so on, which are always patterned by these prior preconcepts analogically learned. Then understanding to a certain extent might be looked upon as analogical, plus the digital or analytic where the two kinds of learning come together.

I would like to remind you of the terms "ethos" and "eidos," ethos being the group-sanctioned ways of feeling, the sensibilities, the awareness which each culture develops among children; and eidos being the logic, the systematic ways of thinking, the criteria of credibility they employ. It is important here—and later when we discuss Brameld's paper—to emphasize goal values. We communicate an understanding of other cultures to children and adults, to the nonprofessional, by emphasizing each culture as that which is sought, as revealed in its goal values. It's a way of life that people strive to achieve and maintain and perpetuate in their rearing and education of children, always guided by these enduring goal values which generation after generation are maintained and sometimes reformulated in the light of new knowledge, new experience, new sensibilities. This conception of goal values may get us out of some of the axiological difficulties that we are so often caught in when we think of values as something out here, as abstract and superhuman. Instead we may think of "valuing" as a verb, not an abstract noun, and emphasize the goal values as the persistent aspirations of a people—what they are striving for which can be attained only by being changed. Cultures have broken down and disappeared because they couldn't change, because they couldn't reformulate their goal values and make new social inventions to continue striving. Now, what is sought then, in intercultural education, is not only factual knowledge of other people, but more of the empathic, intuitive understanding which the nonprofessional person can accept analogically. I want to contrast here the communication of anthropological facts, know-how, skills, to people who are going to be anthropologists or social scientists, with the communication to the nonprofessional who has to assimilate new ideas, new ways of thinking, into his already existing frame of reference.

That brings us to some further points in the paper which call for comment. For example, consider the distinction between the "me" and the "not-me" which is especially important for all our thinking in education. This distinction takes place quite early in childhood and I believe it happens in this way: The first distinction between "me" and "not-me" is not to recognize and face "reality," as our analysts keep saying. It's to recognize that there is a highly idiomatic, idiosyncratic "not-me": *my* mamma, *my* father, *my* crib, the things that are particularly mine. And then only somewhat later, probably after language comes, does the child begin to recognize, and more or less accept, the consensual "not-me" of the world as defined by his cultural tradition. As Margaret Lowenfeld has emphasized, and as is recognized in some recent work on schizophrenia, this is a crucial transition in personality development; some children find great difficulty in relinquishing the idiomatic "not-me" and accepting the consensual "not-me"; and some may alternate back and forth—as found in some types of mental disorders. Now, recognition of this consensual world of "not-me" marks a distinct transition, from the primary process of relating oneself to the world through direct, sensori-motor activity, to the conceptual, symbolic process. The child begins then to pattern his perceptions and impose meanings on the world, viewing the world according to his basic concepts and then acting toward the world as he has learned to interpret his experiences. That's essentially a transactional process, and it presents to a child a more crucial task than has been recognized, namely, a primary anxiety in early childhood over learning how to create and help to maintain this consensual symbolic world. This is different from the affective anxiety over oral or anal functions which has been emphasized by so many psychiatric formulations. The child has to learn how to recognize that everything has a name and a meaning, learn to put that meaning into objects, situations, and people, and then deal with the meaning which he himself has imposed upon the world or imputed to situations. That is always highly idiomatic; he has somehow to mediate between his private world—his own personal, idiomatic, idiosyncratic interpretation of these prescribed meanings—and what is expected of him by the world. And there is always, I believe, a certain amount of anxiety in that operation, especially at the beginning. Thus when we ask children to recognize other cultures, to accept another way of thinking, another set of perceptions and concepts, we may be creating additional anxiety because they're already concerned with trying to maintain a stable world in terms of their own culturally defined meanings.

Now, the paper also points out that the question of relating oneself to the world is involved. I find it useful to think of the child, from the moment of birth, beginning to maintain a continuing intercourse with the "surround"—to use Sherrington's phrase, "surround," which takes in the animate, the inanimate, the organic, the personal, and the social. We may say that the child becomes a personality by the way he learns to transform organic functions into the patterned, goal-seeking, purposive striving which each culture demands. For example, the child starts breathing from the moment he's born, but very soon he transforms breathing into a social act of speaking, or communication. He transforms elimination into cleanliness, continence, sanitation; he transforms hunger into appetite for certain kinds of food, eaten at specific intervals, so that he is not governed by hunger—but his blood sugar level is regulated by social convention. We see how, to a considerable extent, what we call culture is in individual personalities, and we may recognize the regularities of patterns and relations in a culture, recognize the recurrent frequencies, when we talk about cultures. But when we look at the identifiable individual members of that culture and observe their idiosyncratic performances, then we're talking about personality. Personality is the way in which each member of the group carries on, expresses, and tries to achieve the goal values and life aspirations of his culture, always in his own idiomatic way. If we can make that conception clear, then we may realize that in that process of being enculturated, the individual builds up an image of himself which is his own conception of himself and his relationship to the world of events and especially people. That's a two-way process, a circular, reciprocal relation that we may call a transactional process. Thus we may say that whatever is "internalized" is related to the outside; what is relevant outside is responsive in the child. If a child exhibits hostility, he perceives the world as a threatening, antagonistic place against which he must mobilize whatever resources of defense or offense he has. So we may emphasize the idiosyncratic, perceptual, patterned world in which each child lives as his life space, his private world, which represents both the cultural patterns and his own idiomatic version of these. The formulation of the culture and personality process seems to me to be important—because that's the way we can understand culture dynamically as operating in individuals and all their activities. Each person is striving to live up to those patterns and to carry them out in his own way. This may be called a field theory, recognizing the individual person in the cultural-social field as it is "structured" by him and perceived by him.

It would be useful, and again relevant to this topic, to recognize the process of maturation as both a biological and a psychological process. In psychological theory, the idea of learning has been contrasted with maturation, and maturation is considered to be the biological unfolding more or less independent of learning. The term "maturation" may be used to indicate the biological-psychological process of continually relinquishing, giving up, what one has learned—unlearning in order to learn the next pattern and relation essential for the growing, developing individual. The baby sucks at the breast or the bottle for months: We may note frequency, recency, and reward—according to reinforcement theory he would do nothing but suck for the rest of his life—but he gives up suck-ing, accepts a cup, wants to feed himself, etc. The baby creeps and crawls and gets around, but he gives up such locomotion, learns to stand erect when physiologically ready, and gets a new perspective on the world—through a new perception as he begins to walk around and explore. If we think of the child as undergoing a series of such transitions, then—as emphasized in Hart's paper—how those transitions are managed by each culture facilitates or hampers the child in growing up and using his en-larging capacities.

Mead: And you would include all the way to old age, wouldn't you?

Frank: Oh, yes. Maturation is, or can be, a lifelong process. We're just beginning to identify these transitions—for example, the six-year-old period when the child goes to school calls for a new image of himself; he is no longer Mrs. Jones's little boy, he must give up much of his baby lan-guage, his ways of relating himself to adults, etc. There's an enormous potential for new learning at the six-year-old level, just as there is at puberty, when he must again revise his image of himself and develop new relationships to others, learning the masculine and feminine roles, etc. One of our problems in education is to identify these "learning moments," these crucial transitions, and recognize more clearly where it would be most relevant, appropriate, and congenial to the developmental and matu-rational process to offer a child a chance for the new learning that he's ready and eager for. When, for example, are children ready for inter-cultural education of different kinds? Could we devise a series of expe-riences to help them understand and accept other cultures as ways of life, just helping children to recognize how children in other cultures play, learn, achieve, relate themselves? The problem of motivation and the frequent question of how we can motivate children arises largely because we ignore children's own desire to learn to relate themselves. If we would cease talking about motivation and think of development and maturation, maybe we might be more alert to the learning potentialities of children. Most of our learning theory comes from rats, who have no personalities and no cultures; they have to be motivated by deprivation and press to do what the experimenter wants them to do, usually quite different from their normal ways of living. Human children have aspirations and a ca-pacity for learning to learn.

Mead: I think you're going to have to be careful about those rats, though, in light of last week's discoveries that they have this supersonic language that we haven't tapped yet! They may be telling each other, "This is what the experimenter wants."

Frank: This concept of the child's learning to relate himself to the "surround" involves this relation of oneself to one's social life and a re-ciprocal relationship of society to the individual. We have discussed how the individual must adjust to society; but the way in which society re-gards, treats the individual and relates to him is equally important. This relationship may be congenial and reinforcing, and supporting, or may be conflicting and defeating. In so far as we are becoming a multimodal culture, we will have to think of school programs in terms of a learning process which recognizes how children come to school with their traditional patterns of learning—these different ways of learning which Hilda (Taba) has emphasized—that govern their capacity for accepting and understanding educational material.

This analogical-digital process becomes important for intercultural understanding because there may be certain types of experiences of an analogical type of learning which are initially important; those would then be followed, as I think Hilda was saying, by more of a digital, knowledgeable type of learning. But first the child needs concepts, awareness, empathy, before he can master the knowledge, the facts, the generalizations that have been derived from research and the study of other people, before these can become operationally meaningful to him. Rapid social-cultural change, the disintegration of so many of our traditions, provides an extraordinary opportunity to foster intercultural education. Now we can say to people, "We are in much the same position as all others in the world. We must face the task of renewing our culture by reformulating our goal values, by finding and inventing new patterns for meeting the persistent tasks of life as every other group is now trying to do." That then means that we must try to develop a process whereby we can give pupils from childhood on through adult life an awareness that they're living in a symbolic, cultural world. This means helping people to realize that they're not just organisms adjusting to an environment, but personalities living in a symbolic cultural world with meanings and goal values which are in them—their way of life. That should not be too difficult if we can agree upon the desirability of such a program. Hilda used this idea—which I largely approve—of giving people some awareness of cultural equivalents: that every group of people faces the same persistent life tasks but each cultural group has developed its own ways of meeting these tasks, creating its own symbolic world in which its members have equivalents of what we have and do. We recognize that not only in food but in language—as we say the different words for bread, such as *pan, brot,* etc. Different words are used by different people for the same objectives or equivalents, just as they use different patterns, tools, rituals, for equivalent purposes.

If we recognize that the initial enculturation of the child takes place through interpersonal relationships with a cultural agent — mother or nurse, or someone known more or less intimately—then, much as in psychotherapy, changing a person's ideas or cultural patterns or conceptual formulations may call for some equivalent kind of relationship, either individual or group; a group such as a class very often not only helps the individual to change his ideas, his relationships with people, but may give him the reassurance he needs to change his ideas and assumptions.

To what extent can we use aesthetic experiences for communicating intercultural understanding? Poetry and drama, literature and folklore, music, dance, architecture, and so on may create empathy, communicate insights, develop awareness and respect for other ways of life, because the aesthetic combines, as in the arts, both the ethos and the eidos of a culture and so may communicate what just factual content and logical, rational learning or teaching cannot.

Finally we ought to recognize how important it is for adult education to develop some programs of intercultural education, as contrasted with the frequent programs on international relations. I believe that the adult, who hasn't had any such orientation in the schools, can be helped to recognize that one of our basic problems is to create a world community—approached as an "orchestration of cultural diversities"—as contrasted with a monolithic conception of world order which the totalitarians (and some advocates of world government) apparently want to impose on everybody. Perhaps the Russians and the Americans will be the last to be able to accept that conception of world community; they seem to be more resistant to recognizing other ways of life. It is possible that some of the rigidity and the dislike of other cultures, the belief that the Americans have the only desirable patterns, may be born of the traumatic experiences of being acculturated and being compelled to learn a new culture which so many of our people have undergone. They are not going to give up what they have so painfully mastered and change to something new if they can help it.

Mead: This is also true of the Russians. The bulk of the Russians today have gone through very rapid change, very much like what we had to do with immigrant groups here in the 'twenties.

Frank: In the 'twenties, we attempted to Americanize all our recent immigrants, telling them that everything they believed and did was wrong and must be given up.

Kimball: The change has also been from an agrarian kind of culture to an industrial one. So it's also been a universal thing for Americans, not alone those who have immigrated.

Frank: These are points we should keep fairly focal in our discussion of intercultural education, especially the question of how much of the professional knowledge of cultural anthropology we should try to communicate in intercultural education. When psychiatrists want to talk about mental health, they usually write a book or give a lecture on psychopathology, giving laymen what is primarily professional material in clinical terms. Every professional who tries to communicate with the public feels that he ought to communicate all his professional knowledge and technical terminology, forgetting that the kind of understandings and learnings people need and can grasp may be different. Some simple conceptual formulations of culture, as a way of life, an aspiration toward goal values, a design for living, would help people to see how other people have attempted to meet the common problems of mankind in their own way, with their special knowledge and experience, *vis à vis* their kind of "surround." This might be one way of avoiding the confusions and reducing the resistance that many people have. We can emphasize the goal values of different cultures as crucial. Thus we Western people have emphasized over the centuries, and cherished the belief in, the worth of the individual personality and human dignity. Now, those goal values have been variously stated, formulated, institutionalized in changing patterns. We're changing them rapidly today. For example, mental health experts recognize that human dignity begins at birth, and that loving little children involves acceptance of their individuality. The acceptance of individuality, of individual personality, is one of the insights that we're trying to develop. Each generation has to reformulate these enduring goal values in its own way. If we emphasize, then, the striving to maintain and achieve certain goal values in a symbolic cultural world of meanings and values for which each individual carries responsibility, we can say that today each one of us has the great privilege and equally great responsibility of selecting which of our traditional patterns we're going to perpetuate and which we're going to give up. No group of parents has probably ever before been privileged to look at their traditions this critically, and selectively ask what they are going to perpetuate in rearing their children. Every parent who today says, "I'm not going to perpetuate the belief that everything that has to do with sex is nasty, dirty, and everything below the neck is obscene," is by so much changing our culture. In the same way, every parent who gives up some of the terrorizing, theological beliefs that were long used to indoctrinate children is also changing our culture. We have been operating with a conception of social order as a superhuman system of forces. It will call for long and sustained efforts to replace that closed conception with the concept of society as social order and of culture as in people, with the realization that each person in his decisions and choices, in his sensitivity to our goal values, helps improve and change our culture.

OPEN DISCUSSION

Varieties of and Blocks to Learning to Learn

Brameld, Frank, Shaftel, Mead

Brameld: Your (Frank's) reference to analogical learning reminds me of one of Kilpatrick's favorite theses—what he calls "concomitant learning." They're not the same, perhaps, but there is definitely a relationship between that and what Hilda (Taba) referred to as primary learning.

For Kilpatrick, concomitant learning is at least as important as systematic learning. The school, properly understood, is a place where concomitant learning is as fundamental as what you called analogical learning. And this goes back to Siegel's diagram; for instance, his peer-group learning is a kind of concomitant learning and may be just as important and as much in need of understanding by educators as so-called systematic learning.

I also couldn't help thinking of George Herbert Mead's theory of the self and society—the relationship of the self and the not-self that Miss DuBois refers to and that Larry (Frank) stressed. Mead's *Mind, Self and Society* is a marvelous theoretical formulation of the point of view that I believe is at least implicit in Miss DuBois's paper.

Another item is suggested by Miss DuBois where she refers to symbolization—particularly to the danger of symbols becoming identified with projection. I was reminded there of Ernst Cassirer and his studies of symbolization: for instance, *The Myth of the State*, in which he contends that the greatest single danger of our times is the danger of hypostasizing symbols, of making symbols realities—what Hitler did and what McCarthy has been doing.

Frank: In scientific work, the great danger is of reifying data into entities: where we speak, for example, of "prices" as entities which are changed by the law of supply and demand, forgetting that a price is always an indication of human action in a symbolic world, using rituals like buying and selling.

Mead: Or saying, "Culture *makes* you wear a hat."

Shaftel: I'd like to try to make an application to the early years in the elementary school of some of the things that have been said this morning, and tie this into Bernie's (Siegel) paper yesterday. When we induct the child into the school, we school people have responded to certain pressures that come to us from the C-group, from our school boards, from certain expectations, let's say, within the culture, about what schooling is about, plus our ideas of learning motivation, and have set certain very definite structured pathways by which a child may enter school life and may be successful in school. As a result, we have helped to destroy in the children their ability to develop the kind of a self-concept which enables them to relate easily to others and to a larger world outside, because their first experiences teach them that they are inadequate to meet the demands which the school culture places upon them. We see this very interestingly when we try to study the children who are bright and obviously capable of academic achievement who are not being successful in school. When we try to trace back to their early experiences we find that their motivations, their interests, their ways of relating themselves to the rest of the world were not utilized by the school, and therefore their first experiences in school were failure experiences; and being bright and sensitive they have then concluded either "I must defend myself from this world" or "I am inadequate, I will stop trying." And then we have a kind of personality development which denies the achievement of a kind of self that can be intercultural. I think this is one of the major problems of the school. Teachers are afraid to tackle it. Perhaps one of the things that we need from anthropologists is more help in looking at the school as a culture, and the school as an institution in American culture in terms of the pressures which create this kind of situation. Teachers say over and over again, "I would like to do it differently but *they* won't let me; I can't do it." Or, even in their anxieties— and Bob (Bush) and I have experienced this very graphically in a recent study—these teachers develop a gradual recognition that what they were doing was wrong, but say, "I don't dare do it any other way for these various reasons. . . ."

Frank: May I try to relate this to cognitive learning? At the very beginning of formal education in the school, if we could recognize that children are individuals, with different patterns of awareness, perceptions, and so on, and that if in their first experience of learning they are permitted and encouraged to learn in their individual ways so they would get a feeling of confidence and mastery, then cognitive learning will begin, because they have then learned to learn. But the difficulty which you have pointed out is that we very often defeat them in their first efforts at learning in school, block their learning to learn in their way, because we insist that they must learn in a standardized manner.

Mead: Whole cultures tend to have a style of learning to learn; that is, if we take the different types of learning that have been identified by learning theory—instrumental avoidance, reward and punishment, rote learning, and so forth—we find that cultures tend to institutionalize one form at the expense of another, or various combinations. For instance, one of the things Western European, Anglo-Saxon, North American culture has institutionalized is that if the good thing comes after the bad thing it's virtue and if the bad thing comes after the good thing it's vice. We teach children that in every possible way: Parents say, "If you eat your spinach you can have your ice cream," but nobody ever says, "If you eat your ice cream you can have your spinach." "If you do your lessons you'll have a vacation," but not vice versa, and so on. We build up a notion that a certain sequence of situations is expected in every kind of learning and you identify then the painful in one way, the rewarding in another. And the whole culture sets up a style of learning. Most children in our society have learned the tradition that school is unpleasant. When we reverse that in progressive schools and try to make the school pleasant, we make vacations awful. I've lived through the whole period where, instead of children having a wonderful time all summer doing the things they weren't allowed to do in winter, they did nothing all summer but lie flat with boredom because every single thing that was identified as fun—"what you did in the summer"—had been taken over by the school, but the school had not changed the primary culture or expectation of what was fun and what wasn't fun.

There is fairly good evidence from a great many fields on the idiomatic element in the behavior of each child: Children have from birth different ways of approaching life; some of them approach it more with their mouths, some more with their eyes, some more with their hands. In all probability there's a similar variation in children from any culture in any part of the world in innate capacity, in idiomatic capacity to approach experience, in rhythm, in timing, in type of imagery. The problem here is to recognize that the learning-to-learn style in our culture is much narrower than the range of the entering children, and that even the best educational systems tend to superimpose an arbitrary learning-to-learn pattern instead of a wider and more inclusive one.

Cultural and Personal Crises and Learning Intercultural Understanding

Kimball, Taba, Mead, Siegel, Hart, Frank

Kimball: What about the relationship to the progressive school in crises—if everything is lovely and sweet, is the learning there as effective?

Taba: The crises in learning come because we haven't calculated the psychological bridge or the path from one stage of learning to another. One kind of crisis comes when the learning of an individual for the time being has omitted many important elements that he should have learned and many situations that have those elements in them. The second kind comes at a certain point of discarding old learning in order to take on new learning, when the sequence in that discarding is too rapid and an individual suddenly finds that all of his previous framework is gone before his new framework is yet in shape to provide a way of living, or thinking, or teaching. If this moment comes too abruptly, individuals go through a period of psychological anxiety. We run into such crises in the intercultural workshops where a really fundamental reorientation takes place. It comes around the third or fourth week in a major portion of people in one degree or another, to the extent that some people want to pack up and go home.

Mead: They even break down.

Taba: The main danger is that while we helped pile up new learning, we didn't know how to calculate the tempo of changes in each individual so as to provide him with a suitable transition. We know as yet too little about the various sequences in the individual's learning to provide a systematic, sequential, calculated way of changing a person fundamentally from one way of thinking to another one, or from one way of feeling to another one. And when we play with those feelings in education, as some of us do, we run into the danger of producing crises. These crises do not occur in education concerned only with pouring in knowledge, because such education never produces a fundamental learning.

Kimball: Is it then seen to be desirable that we either minimize or eliminate these crises?

Taba: It's desirable to so time the learnings that they are minimized. You have a series of minor crises but never what you would call a real crisis.

Frank: Instead of talking about crises, couldn't we think of the child as going through a continuous sequence of transitions from birth to old age, that if in these transitions individuals are not provided with some *rite de passage*, so to speak, these transitions may become crises? Couldn't we say that the school ought to provide these *rites de passage* at each of these transitions instead of thinking only of cognitive learning?

Mead: But we can find cultures that do not have to deal with these things as great crises. On the whole, the greater the discontinuity, the greater the need for the crisis ceremonial. Where do you get your big wedding ceremonies?—where virginity is stressed, and so forth. Then you need a wedding that everybody works on for weeks, and a bride with a white veil and all the rest of it. The minute you get an easier approach to coeducation and relations between the sexes instead of separation, you don't need that kind of wedding. That doesn't mean that *rites de passage* don't serve a great purpose. But Hilda (Taba) is saying that we don't need *rites de passage* of the same violence and the same degree of trauma if each step is really related to each other step. The *rite de passage* is the way in which culture deals with the fact that it itself has created this discontinuity in experience.

Frank: We might emphasize, then, in this context the great importance of helping the child to *un*learn. Now some of us would be inclined to say that the test of intelligence is not what a child has learned to do or say but the capacity to reformulate and unlearn, so he can go on learning.

Hart: I've been wanting to say for a long time that anthropologists kid themselves that they understand intercultural learning because they operate across cultural and subcultural lines. Therefore I think the relevant question is how do anthropologists achieve this intercultural understanding themselves, or when? If anybody asked me that, I could name the day and almost the hour when I think I got over the hump from the mono- to the bi-; and it was on the first morning of my first field trip. I think I understood what cross-culture meant then and not before. And the reason I was able to pinpoint the time so accurately is that it was rather shocking, and I suspect that most anthropologists would agree that the transition point from appreciating your own culture to really realizing that another culture can exist as a natural way of life for another bunch of people is a real hump—you feel a bump when you go over it.

Mead: If you learned as an adult; but I learned it at about four because my mother already knew such things and was studying another culture and I was taken along. The first wedding I went to was an Italian wedding and I learned cross-cultural understanding gradually in a family situation because it had already been incorporated as part of the frame of reference around me. Now, I think that what we're talking about here is the difference between something that has to be learned as an adult and has not been part of one's experience (so there is discontinuity and therefore trauma, which is either created itself or we created it for people) and continuity—where these things would not follow.

Can Primary Learning Be Unlearned?
Siegel, Taba, Gillin, Keesing, Frank

Siegel: I think this brings up another point in connection with this core concept of distinctions between reactive dispositions—what has been called analogical learning, primary learning, etc.—and secondary or digital learning. Analogical learning, or reactive dispositions of an emotional sort, involve sets of such dispositions—not any one intuitive way but several intuitive ways—and they are probably patterned in some way that we haven't really studied very adequately; furthermore they are held with different degrees of commitment. The question then arises as to what kinds of such dispositions to act and react are learned with such a strong degree of commitment at such an early age that the intercultural learning which we are stressing here becomes a next-to-impossible task to achieve. In other words, by the time you get the child he has such a commitment to a way of reacting, a disposition to react, that there's almost nothing you can do about it. I refer again to the studies that were mentioned on the authoritarian personality: To what extent is this inability to tolerate ambiguity so completely a matter of emotional commitment at what age, so that beyond that point it becomes almost impossible to change this set of dispositions?

Taba: I have experimented with that from the first grade up to the twelfth grade, and with teachers from age eighteen to sixty, and I have completely discarded the notion that age has anything to do with it. It is a degree of commitment in the first place and a degree of organization of skills and ways around that commitment. A strong commitment which is not the center of one's life can be revised with less of a crisis than if it is such a center. However, this matter is idiosyncratic and we know too little about it yet. There is no real description in literature of that kind of thing. I remember two instances that might illustrate this problem. In one workshop we had a Catholic girl from the South. She was also a Southern lady and she had a club foot which had made her a bit insecure and sensitive about herself. For her, the crisis was produced by a simple thing that usually doesn't arouse much of a ripple. It was a lecture by Pauck on comparative religion, in which he remarked that each religion had to institutionalize itself into a church and by doing that it created a dilemma between its spiritual mission and a temporal mission. It had to adopt, for example, advertising methods that were contrary to the spiritual message. That girl went into a crisis at that point and really went through a whole day of emotional upset.

Another example is of a person who is a fairly capable teacher with a rigid personality. She could learn everything about intercultural education and the methods that go with it, but she could not conduct an open discussion because she had so strongly organized all of her personal conduct around clear logical answers. She found it difficult to raise the kinds of questions which would open up further questions, to allow the students to play out their present feelings and uncertainties, and to let this process continue without expecting final answers. She tried it for three years, without success.

Gillin: It seems to me that it may be important from an educational point of view to distinguish between primary and secondary drives (or acquired drives, if you wish). We have a good many cultures where children suck nipples until they're five or six years old; in our culture, of course, the mother heavily rewards the child for changing to some other mode of behavior. The evidence, to me, doesn't indicate that the previous behavior, for example, suckling, is unlearned. What you have is a substitution of new behavioral response, often with new motivation. The phenomenon of retrogression, for example, shows that the individual can go back to his earlier learned motivation and responses. The important thing about acquired drives—and this ties up with the goals and aspirations— is that apparently people become motivated by certain types of acquired drives with the anticipation of reward, and the reward has to be actually demonstrated; the subject has to "see" it pretty clearly.

The child has got built into him already a lot of acquired drives before he comes to school, which have been rewarding. What so often happens is that the school has not been able to develop these acquired drives and demonstrate the rewardingness of them and go on from there. The progressive school idea is "It's fun; you get something out of it."

Frank: Just on that one point about unlearning. The thing that I was concerned about is that unlearning is a way the individual continually relates himself to life as he grows and develops and meets the necessary transitions of maturation. That doesn't mean unlearning the basic patterns that are inside him; under regression, under stress and strain, they may be reinstated; but the earlier ways of relating himself to life have to be unlearned in order that a more mature pattern, more compatible with his developing capacities, can be learned. I'm looking forward to the time when we will stop talking about drives and motivations, because that is a unilateral conception of something operating inside the individual which ignores the surround or field. As we get more of a transactional conception, the concept of motivation, drives, and so on may be very considerably modified, if not given up. This is the same kind of revision in thinking that Galileo made, when he gave up the Aristotelian idea of a force from behind and replaced it with the conception of inertia—that a body remains at rest or continues to move in a field, unless interfered with.

Keesing: I just would like to bring out the relevance of this whole discussion to a field which is being rapidly developed in a very reformulated form in anthropology and which we usually call cultural dynamics, or cultural change. This is an area where a great deal of what was said by Dr. Taba and others shows how the educator can make an important contribution to anthropological theory, as well as providing factual data. Historically our theory in this field developed around the concept of "invention," or "innovation," as we have more recently tended to call it. When we examine the case materials on innovation, we see that the anthropologist in general has been dealing with acts largely completed, and so recorded from the past. This is true of all types of innovative experience, both those we think of as original creativity, or "primary" innovation, and those involving cultural transfer from one cultural setting to another, or "secondary" innovation. We've paid very little attention until recently to the larger learning-theory context, such as has been brought out here, as over against these arbitrary acts.

I wouldn't quite agree with Dr. Taba, however, about ruling out age and sex factors so thoroughly. One of the lines merely at the exploratory stage in matters of cultural manipulation, for instance, involves this biographical approach—or whatever you might want to call it—that Dr. Frank mentioned. If you were an administrator, say, rather than an educator and you wanted to introduce a new agricultural technique, would it be more effective if you took it to the young adult men who face the subsistence problems most urgently, or to the old men who tend to command the lore, or to the children who are the future manipulators of economic behavior? Or if you wanted to alter basic values, would you try to manipulate the ideas of the old men, who hold largely under security conditions in many cultures the more implicit value system and are quite capable, as we have seen again and again, of making it over suddenly and dramatically when it suits their own prestige and other motivational purposes? And what would you take, in terms of that line of reasoning, to children and expect that they can effectively be motivated or brought to learn, unlearn, and relearn? We know very little about the incidence within the life cycles in given cultures of the lodgment of tenacity and mobility. This applies to the sacred things and to art and play elements, which I think are of great importance as an area of elective behavior and have not had enough attention.

Cultural Alternatives and Intercultural Learning

Siegel, Frank, Mead, DuBois, Taba

Siegel: I think possibly we might think of still one other dimension of this problem of intercultural dynamics. In any monocultural situation we can think of certain types of learning reactions geared to the scheme of means and ends. And within both means and ends we have a variety of alternative responses for doing things in order to get things—in order to achieve satisfaction. There is a problem of choice, then, which the individual faces in selecting from among the various alternatives and means presented to him, and this problem is particularly important in intercultural situations.

In the bicultural or multicultural situation, there is a proliferation of alternatives and the problem of choice then becomes complicated for the individual. At least some of the problems that we're concerned with in the learning and transmitting process are the processes by which changes do occur in the patternings of choices, in the reorganization of choices as individuals see them. For the monocultural person who acquires an awareness of other cultures the problem is different from that of the bicultural or multicultural person, who must make some kind of adaptation. In other words, a sense of urgency may be lacking in the first situation and there may be simply a curiosity and an interest of some sort—maybe even intellectual. But in the case of the bicultured person the crucial thing becomes the degree of sensed urgency of reorganizing possible response patterns, and of re-evaluating the degree of allowability and desirability of following certain means to achieve certain goals which are in a state of flux. This is what W. I. Thomas speaks of as crisis—the redefinition of the situation becomes an on-going process in a person's life. Each one of these points, some of them very crucial and urgent, some of them not so urgent, becomes a point of crisis in this sense. Now, the problem, as I see it, that we would like to investigate is what happens when a person comes to see new alternatives in given means for achieving either the same ends he has already held, or new ends that are presented to him as valuable in one way or another.

If the values in a person's own culture become depreciated, or if he is not allowed for one reason or another to give them up and yet comes to value the way others do things and is able to participate in making new choices only to a limited degree, the resultant frustration may become a barrier to new learning even though he has acquired, in a bicultural situation, a feeling for the desirability of new values, new ends, and new ways of achieving them. I just want to throw this out as another way of looking at the problem.

Frank: As we develop more programs of intercultural education, people are going to be aware that other cultures have devised different ways of meeting these life situations. It's already apparent that some people who've read Margaret's (Mead) *Coming of Age in Samoa* have concluded that the way to meet the adolescent problem is to permit premarital sexual relationships. Some people have read Murdock's book and quote him as saying that everything is completely relative; it doesn't make a bit of difference what you do. We should develop a more sophisticated concept of cultural relativity which will indicate that every pattern is relative to the total cultural context in which it's found and can't be taken out of it and introduced into another culture without some difficulty—that every culture pays a certain price and gains certain advantages for what it permits and what it forbids. Are we willing to pay the price of the Samoan premarital situation; are we willing to pay the price of the French extramarital relationships? And then, second, we may emphasize that cultural relativity means that every pattern, every institution is relative to the time, the stage of historic development in which it arose, and it may be anachronistic, if not archaic. Those are two sophisticated interpretations of cultural relativity which would serve to guard intercultural education from misinterpretations and misapplication.

DuBois: Certainly a great many of the young foreign students who come to this country—particularly, I would say, women who come from countries where the status of women is less favorable than in the United States, and our Austrian and German students—quite realistically appraise their life chances at home as opposed to the life chances that they see in this country. They become what the State Department would call alienated—they want to stay on here. Now though I agree with your general proposition as an intellectual formulation, psychologically there is a distinction to be made between realistic life-chance appraisal of oneself as an individual in one society as opposed to another society, and simply the reaction formation where you're sore at your own society and everything in the other society is fine.

Taba: To extend this point, the same kinds of questions need to be raised in connection with importing of one piece of culture into another: What is the life chance of that importation and what does it do to the total culture? The UN in its work in retarded countries is beginning to face that problem. Their difficulty is that people who are technically qualified are often extremely monocultural, hence are in no position to assess either the life chance of these improvements or the negative cultural consequences that may flow from the introduction of a given piece of technology.

Another remark which applies to the problem of choices. There are some young people in our own society who for practical purposes—e.g., for survival—need to be trained in a double culture, such as using one kind of language in school and another one at home. Actually learning to conduct oneself in two different cultures is almost a necessity in the process of acculturation. Persons learning a new culture, such as lower-class children in a middle-class-oriented school, have to adopt two different sets of behavior to maintain communication in both. Some children need to learn to say "thank you" in school to be accepted there, and to refrain from saying it in their street gang to avoid being considered a sissy. While maintaining this double way is a burden to an individual, it is also a practical necessity. The difficulties in school occur when schools forbid an individual a way of behaving (e.g., fighting to maintain status) before he has learned a suitable alternate.

Mead: The point I want at least to get on the carpet is that almost everything we've said here has been emphasizing slowness, correct sequence, not learning big lumps that don't fit with other lumps, and so forth. But speed may be of the essence—it may be easier to learn a whole pattern than a piece of a pattern. If—and here the whole question that Fee (Keesing) was raising about whom do you teach, the old men, the young men, or the children, is relevant—if you teach them all at once, you may be able to move the whole society with a minimum of personal damage; if you learn a whole pattern at once you may be much less troubled by it than if you learn pieces. Therefore one of the things we may want to learn, which is implicit in what Hilda (Taba) has been saying, is how to teach children, in a sense, the nature of learning about different patterns; the cognitive learning they have to have today is that things are different in different places and at different times and that you can learn them. There are places where you throw peanuts on the floor and there are places where you don't; and in one it is right and in the other one it is wrong. But there's a much bigger right and wrong that's included in it. We can use speech as one of our possible models, using as living models the sort of things for instance that happened in old pre-Soviet upper-class Russian education, where children were expected to learn several languages and they learned several languages, and they learned about learning languages.

Hart: I would like to make just one comment. It seems to me that at this stage somebody ought to remind everybody here that people live not only in cultures but also in social systems. I think most of this has rather tended to suggest that the individual is a completely free agent, free to learn irrespective of his position in the social structure, and I don't think that would be a sound basis to go on.

Frank: Here again, we face the question of the difference between society and culture. Now, it is conceivable that we may develop a social order in this country—a technological civilization—which is not incompatible with a multimodal culture. For example, Charles Morris' studies have shown that there are a large number of college students in this country who, when presented with the poetry, the art, the religion, the philosophy, of other cultures, express a spontaneous empathy, a decided preference, for Zen Buddhism, Taoism, Mohammedanism, or other cultures. If we want to develop healthy personalities and have more social order, we could permit and even foster more idiosyncratic, individual cultural preferences, within a social order, which individuals could accept because they were not torn by frustration of their individual, temperamental orientation.

DuBois: If this value judgment is generally agreed to here, and I think it's good, then what we must really discuss as crucial is the social order in which we live—the change is from culture to society.

Section V

CONTRASTS BETWEEN PREPUBERTAL AND POSTPUBERTAL EDUCATION

C. W. M. Hart
University of Wisconsin

General Introduction

Anthropologists are expected to know anthropology and to base their conclusions upon anthropological data. Even when in the unfamiliar position of being called upon to contribute to a joint conference with educationists it would be a mistake if the anthropologists, in their desire to say something useful to the educationists, should attempt generalizations which do not arise out of the general corpus of accepted anthropological data. The fact that the corpus of anthropological data appears to be sadly lacking in specific and concrete information about "education" does not justify anthropologists in scrapping or ignoring it.

This paper, then, represents an attempt to use the body of generally accepted anthropological information as a baseline for considering the educational process. It might be paraphrased as "the educative process, anthropologically considered." I assume that "anthropologically considered" is equivalent to "cross-culturally considered," and I assume that education refers to any process at any stage of life in which new knowledge is acquired or new habits or new attitudes formed. That is, I have taken the question which forms the core problem of the conference and tried to develop a few generalizations about that problem from the general anthropological literature. But it follows that since they are anthropological generalizations their usefulness to education is a matter of opinion. All I claim for them is the old basis upon which anthropology has always justified its preoccupation with the simpler societies, namely that by studying the simpler societies we gain perspective and proportion in really seeing our own society and from that better perspective comes better understanding of common human social processes. I hope that the material in this paper will at least enable the educational participants in the conference to see our own educative process in better perspective and help them separate what is distinctively American in it from what is general-social and general-human.

My starting point is a distinction that is made by Herskovits. In his chapter on education in the book called *Man and His Works* (1948) he finds it necessary to stress that the training of the young in the simpler

127

societies of the world is carried on through two different vehicles. The child learns a lot of things knocking around underfoot in the home, in the village street, with his brothers and sisters, and in similar environments, and he learns a lot of other things in the rather formidable apparatus of what is usually called in the anthropological literature the initiation ceremonies or the initiation schools.

Herskovits stresses that initiation education takes place outside the home and is worthy to be called schooling, contrasts it with the education the child receives knocking around the household and the village long before the initiation period begins, and decides that the main feature of the latter is that it is within the home, and that it should therefore be called education as contrasted with schooling. There he, and many other writers on the subject, tend to leave the matter.

This tendency, to leave the problem at that point, is rather a pity. Further exploration of these two contrasting vehicles for training of the young will pay rich dividends, and it is to such further exploration that the bulk of this paper is devoted. But before going on, certain unsatisfactory features of Herskovits' treatment must be mentioned. To suggest, as he does, that preinitiation education is "within the home" is misleading to people unacquainted with the character of primitive society. While initiation education is very definitely outside the home and—as we shall see later—this remoteness from home is a very essential feature of it, it does not follow that the other has to be, or even is likely to be, "within the home." The home in most primitive societies is very different indeed from the connotation of "home" in America, and the type of education to which Herskovits is referring takes place in every conceivable type of primary group. The young child in primitive society may be subjected to the learning process in his early years in his household (Eskimo), or in a medley of dozens of households (Samoa); his parents may ignore him and leave him to drag himself up as best he can (Mundugumor); he may be corrected or scolded by any passer-by (Zuñi); his male mentor may not be his father at all but his mother's brother (many Melanesian cultures); and so on.

I do not intend to explore the social-psychological results of this variety of primary-group situations; all I mention them for here is to demonstrate how misleading it is to lump them all together as comprising "education within the home." About the only things they have in common is that they all take place in the earlier years of life and they don't take place within the formal framework of initiation ceremonies. I propose therefore to call all this type of education by the title "preinitiation" or "prepuberty" education (since most initiation ceremonial begins at puberty or later), and the problem I am mainly concerned with is the set of contrasts that exists between what societies do with their children in the preinitiation period and what is done with them in the postinitiation period. In other words Herskovits' distinction between education and schooling becomes clearer and more useful if they are simply called prepuberty education and postpuberty education.

One further explanatory comment is necessary. Not all primitive societies possess initiation ceremonies of the formal standardized type that anthropology has become familiar with in many parts of the world. How "schooling" or postpuberty education is handled in those primitive societies which lack initiation ceremonies and what the results of such lack are for the adult culture are interesting questions, but they are outside the scope of the present paper. What we are concerned with here is the set of contrasts between prepubertal and postpubertal education in those numerous and widespread societies which include formal initiation ceremonies in their set of official institutions.

Prepubertal and Postpubertal Education— How Do They Differ?

If attention is directed to the ways education is carried on in the prepuberty and postpuberty periods in a large number of simple societies— viz., those "with initiation ceremonies"—some very impressive contrasts begin to appear. They can be dealt with under four heads—(1) Regulation, (2) Personnel, (3) Atmosphere, (4) Curriculum; but the nature of the data will require us to jump back and forth between these four divisions, since they are all interwoven.

1. *Regulation.*—Postpuberty education, in such societies, does not begin until at least the age of twelve or thirteen, and in many cases several years later than that. By that age of course, the child has already acquired a great deal of what we call his culture. How has he acquired the things he knows at the age of twelve or thirteen? The traditional anthropological monographs are said to tell us little or nothing about "early education." I suggest that the reason the older literature tells us so little that is definite about the early prepubertal training of the children is basically for the same reason that we know so little about preschool education in our own culture, or did know so little before Gesell. Until the appearance of *The Child from Five to Ten* (Gesell and Ilg, 1946), the information on the preschool "enculturation" of the American child was just as barren as the anthropological literature. Whether Gesell has really answered the question for the American child and whether a Gesell-like job has been done or can be done for a primitive society are questions which need not concern us here except to point up the real question: Why is it so rare to find clear information as to what goes on in the learning process during the preschool years, in any culture?

One possible answer is that preschool education is rarely if ever standardized, rarely if ever regulated around known and visible social norms.*

* *Editor's note:* Nonanthropologist readers should be aware of the fact that Dr. Hart's statements concerning the lack of uniformity in prepubertal child training would be contested by many anthropologists, though the same ones might accept his basic position that in comparison to pubertal and postpubertal training the earlier years of experience are *relatively* less structured and less subject to the pressure of public opinion. This problem is treated in the discussion following Dr. Hart's paper.

It is an area of cultural laissez faire, within very wide limits of tolerance, and society at large does not lay down any firm blueprint which all personnel engaged in "raising the young" must follow. If, instead of asking for a "pattern" or "norm," we ask the simpler question, "What happens?" it seems to me that the literature is not nearly so barren of information as has been argued. It tends to suggest that anything and everything happens in the same society. For instance Schapera's account of childhood among the Bakgatla is pretty clear: "The Bakgatla say that thrashing makes a child wise. But they also say a growing child is like a little dog and though it may annoy grown-ups, it must be taught proper conduct with patience and forbearance" (Schapera, 1940). As Herskovits has pointed out, this mixture of strict and permissive techniques is also reported for Lesu in Melanesia by Powdermaker, for the Apache by Opler, and for the Kwoma by Whiting (Herskovits, *op. cit.*). This list can readily be added to.

There is no point in counting how many cultures use severe punishment and how many do not. The explicit statements of the fieldworkers just cited are at least implicit in dozens of others. Do the natives beat their children? Yes. Do they fondle and make a fuss over their children? Yes. Do they correct them? Yes. Do they let them get away with murder? Also yes. All this in the same culture. I repeat that it is pretty clear what happens in the prepuberty years in the simpler societies. Anything and everything from extreme punishment to extreme permissiveness may occur and does occur in the same culture.

The fieldworkers do not tell us what the pattern of early education is because there is rarely any one clear-cut pattern. What each individual child learns or is taught or is not taught is determined pretty much by a number of individual variables. A few such variables are: interest or lack of interest of individual parents in teaching their children, size of family and each sibling's position in it, whether the next house or camp is close by or far away, whether the neighbors have children of the same age, the amount of interaction and type of interaction of the particular "peer-groups"of any given child. The number of variables of this type is almost infinite; the child is simply dumped in the midst of them to sink or swim, and as a result no two children in the same culture learn the same things in the same way. One, for example, may learn about sex by spying upon his parents, a second by spying upon a couple of comparative strangers, a third by getting some explicit instruction from his father or his mother (or his elder brother or his mother's brother), a fourth by listening to sniggering gossip in the play group, and a fifth by observing a pair of dogs in the sexual act. Which of these ways of learning is the norm? Obviously none of them is, at least not in the same sense as that in which we say that it is the norm for a person to inherit the property of his mother's brother, or to use an intermediary in courtship, or to learn certain important myths at Stage 6B of the initiation ceremonies.

In asking for a uniform cultural pattern in such a laissez faire, anything-goes area, we are asking for the inherently impossible, or at least the nonexistent. There are, of course, some cultural limits set in each society to this near-anarchy: there will, for example, be general outrage and widespread social disapproval if one family shamefully neglects its children or some child goes to what is by general consensus regarded as "too far," but such limits of toleration are very wide indeed in every society. The household is almost sovereign in its rights to do as much or as little as it likes—that is, to do what it likes about its offspring in the *preschool* years. The rest of society is extraordinarily reluctant everywhere to interfere with a household's sovereign right to bring up its preschool children as it wishes. And most primitive parents, being busy with other matters and having numerous children anyway, leave the kids to bring each other up or to just grow like Topsy.

There are other strong lines of evidence supporting this judgment that prepuberty education in the simpler societies is relatively so variable as to be virtually normless. One is the self-evident fact which anybody can verify by reading the monographs, that no fieldworker, not even among those who have specifically investigated the matter of child practices, has ever found a tribe where several reliable informants could give him a rounded and unified account of the preschool educational practices of their tribe comparable to the rounded and generalized picture they can give him, readily and easily, of the local religion, or the folklore, or the moral code for the adults, or the local way of getting married, or the right way to build a canoe or plant a garden. This difference can best be conveyed to an anthropologist audience, perhaps, by contrasting the sort of answer fieldworkers get to such questions as "Tell me some of your myths," or "How do you make silver ornaments?" or "How do you treat your mother-in-law?" with the answer they get to a question like "How do you bring up children?" To the former type of question (not asked as crudely as that, of course) the answers will come (usually) in the form of norms—stereotyped and generalized statements that don't differ a great deal from one informant to the next, or, if they do so differ, will always be referred to a "right" way or a "proper" way: the "right" way to build a canoe, the "proper" way to treat one's mother-in-law, the "correct" form of a myth or a ceremony, and so on. Even in the type of sentence structure the answers come in, they will have this official character—"We do it this way" or "It is our custom here to do thus and so"—and often in case of conflicting versions an argument will develop, not over what the informant himself does but over whether what he says is "right" or socially sanctioned as "the right way."

But given the opportunity to perform a similar generalized descriptive job upon "how children are or should be brought up," informants fail dismally to produce anything of this kind. They either look blank and say little or nothing, or come up with a set of empty platitudes—"All boys should be brought up good boys," "They should all respect their elders," etc.—which clearly have no relation to the facts of life going on all around the speaker; or (most common of all) they fall back onto their own life history and do a Sun Chief or Crashing Thunder sort of job. That is, they give in endless and boring detail an account of how they individually were brought up, or how they bring up their own children, but they clearly have no idea of whether their case is typical or atypical of the tribe at large. And the anthropologist equally has no idea of how representative or unrepresentative this case is. This happens so constantly that we are left with only one conclusion, namely, that if there is a cultural tradition for preschool education (comparable with the cultural tradition for religion or for tabu-observance or for technology), then the average native in a simple society is completely unaware of what it is.

This same conclusion is also supported by another line of evidence, namely, the complete change that comes over the picture when we move from prepuberty education to postpuberty education. Postpuberty education is marked in the simpler societies by the utmost degree of standardization and correctness. At puberty the initiation rituals begin, and perhaps the most universal thing about these is their meticulously patterned character. Every line painted on a boy's body, every movement of a performer, every word or phrase uttered, the right person to make every move, is rigidly prescribed as having to be done in one way only—the right way. A wrongly drawn line, a misplaced phrase, an unsanctioned movement, or the right movement made by the wrong person or at the wrong time, and the whole ritual is ruined. They belong to the same general type of social phenomena as the English Coronation ceremony or the Catholic sacrifice of the Mass; there is only one way of doing them, regardless of the individuals involved, namely the "right" way. By contrast that meticulously patterned feature throws into sharp relief the haphazard, permissive, and unstandardized character of the education that *precedes* the time of puberty.

(2). *Personnel.*—So far, then, our stress has been on the unregulated character of primitive preschool education. Certain further things become clearer if at this point we switch our attention from the focus of regulation to the focus of personnel—i.e., from the question of whether the education is controlled and standardized to the question of who imparts the education. Anthropologists are coming more and more to realize the importance of the "Who does what?" type of question in field work, and perhaps nowhere is it so important to know who does what than in the area we are discussing. From whom does the child learn in the simpler societies? As far as the preinitiation years are concerned the answer is obvious: He learns from his intimates, whether they be intimates of a senior generation like his parents or intimates of his own generation like his siblings, cousins, playmates, etc. In the preinitiation years he learns nothing or next to nothing from strangers or near-strangers. Strangers and near-strangers are people he rarely sees and even more rarely converses with; and, since learning necessarily involves interaction, it is from the people he interacts with most that he learns most, and from the people he interacts with least that he learns least.

This is so obvious that it needs little comment. But one important point about intimates must be made. In all culture it appears as if this "learning from intimates" takes two forms. The child learns from his parents or other senior members of his family and he also learns from his play groups. And the interaction processes in these two situations are different in several important respects. The parents are intimates and so are the members of the play group, but there is the important difference that parents, to some extent at least, represent the official culture (are the surrogates of society, in Dollard's phrase), while the play groups do not. All the work upon play groups in Western society has tended to stress what autonomous little subcultures they are, each with its own social organization, its own rules, its own values. The family is a primary group, but one which is tied into the total formal structure of the society and therefore subject to at least some over-all social control. The play group is an autonomous little world of its own, whose rules may be, and often are, directly at variance with the rules of the home or of the wider society.

If, then, as suggested above, it is true that in most societies—simple or modern—each household is allowed a great deal of freedom to bring up its children pretty much as it chooses, and if this wide degree of tolerance leads in turn to a wide variation in the ways in which the culture is presented to different children, then obviously such variation is enormously increased by the role of the play group. Even if we were told of a culture in which all households rigidly standardized their child-training practices, it would still fall far short of being convincing evidence of a standardized child-training situation because of the great amount of knowledge which children in all cultures acquire without the household or at least the parents being involved in the transmission process, namely the knowledge which the child "picks up somewhere."

Once we recognize the influence of this second group of intimates on how the child acquires certain aspects of his culture, the case for wide variation in early child training is greatly strengthened. There seems to be no evidence that would suggest that the play group in simple societies functions in any notably different way from the way it functions in modern societies, but unfortunately we have few studies of the "subcultures" of the playworld in other than Western cultures. Among child psychologists dealing with Western cultures, Piaget in particular has some findings that are relevant to the present discussion (Piaget, 1929, 1932). These findings tend to show that at least by the age of ten or eleven the child has become empirical and secular in his attitudes toward rules and norms of play behavior, partly because he has learned by that time that each primary group has its own rules, so that there is no "right" way, no over-all norm—at least for children's games such as marbles—for all play groups to conform to. Piaget, of course, is describing European children, but primitive children spend at least as much time in unsupervised play groups as European or American children, and since their preschool period is certainly many years more prolonged, there is no apparent reason why this conclusion of Piaget should not have cross-cultural validity.

However, I am not trying to develop a theory but merely to follow through some of the difficulties that are hidden in the simple statement above that preschool learning is between intimates. There are different sorts of intimacy because of the child's dual relation to his home and to his playmates, and some of his culture is mediated to him by each. We don't know nearly enough about degrees of intimacy, and we may be forced by further research to start making classifications and subdivisions between the different sorts of intimate relationships (different "levels" of primary groups?) to which the child in any culture is exposed in his preschool years. Even if we do, however, the fact still remains that in his preinitiation years the child in primitive society learns nothing from strangers or near-strangers. And this leads to the second comment under the head of Personnel, which is that in his *postpuberty* education in contrast to that of *prepuberty* he *has to* learn from strangers or near-strangers and cannot possibly learn from anybody else. When puberty arrives and the boy is therefore ready for initiation (or the girl for marriage), his family, his siblings, his gangs, his village, all the intimates to whom his training or learning has been left up to now, are roughly pushed aside and a whole new personnel take over his training. Who these new teachers are varies from culture to culture, but a very common feature is that they be nonintimates of the boy, semistrangers drawn from other sections of the tribe (opposite moieties, different districts or villages, hostile or semi-hostile clans, different age groups, and so on), people with whom he is not at all intimate. Who they are and what they represent is made painfully clear in the ritual. An actual case will help to make clear the nature of the transition.

Among the Tiwi of North Australia, one can see the traumatic nature of the initiation period in very clear form, and part of trauma lies in the sudden switch of personnel with whom the youth has to associate. A boy reaches thirteen or fourteen or so, and the physiological signs of puberty begin to appear. Nothing happens, possibly for many months. Then suddenly one day, toward evening when the people are gathering around their campfires for the main meal of the day after coming in from their day's hunting and food-gathering, a group of three or four heavily armed and taciturn strangers appear in camp. In full war regalia they walk in silence to the camp of the boy and say curtly to the household: "We have come for So-and-So." Immediately pandemonium breaks loose. The mother and the rest of the older women begin to howl and wail. The father rushes for his spears. The boy himself, panic-stricken, tries to hide, the younger children begin to cry, and the household dogs begin to bark. It is all terribly similar to the reaction which is provoked by the arrival of the police at an American home to pick up a juvenile delinquent. This similarity extends to the behavior of the neighbors. These carefully abstain from identifying with either the strangers or the stricken household. They watch curiously the goings-on but make no move that can be identified as supporting either side. This is particularly notable in view of the fact that the strangers are strangers to all of them, too, that is, they are men from outside the encampment, or outside the band, who, under any other circumstances, would be greeted by a shower of spears. But not under these circumstances.

In fact, when we know our way around the culture we realize that the arrival of the strangers is not as unexpected as it appears. The father of the boy and the other adult men of the camp not only knew they were coming but have even agreed with them on a suitable day for them to come. The father's rush for his spears to protect his son and to preserve the sanctity of his household is make-believe. If he puts on too good an act, the older men will intervene and restrain him from interfering with the purposes of the strangers. With the father immobilized the child clings to his mother, but the inexorable strangers soon tear him (literally) from his mother's arms and from the bosom of his bereaved family and, still as grimly as they came, bear him off into the night. No society could symbolize more dramatically that initiation necessitates the forcible taking away of the boy from the bosom of his family, his village, his neighbors, his intimates, his friends. And who are these strangers who forcibly drag the terrified boy off to he knows not what? In Tiwi they are a selected group of his senior male cross-cousins. To people who understand primitive social organization that should convey most of what I want to convey. They are "from the other side of the tribe," men with whom the boy has had little to do and whom he may have never seen before. They belong to the group of men who have married or will marry his sisters, and marriage, it is well to remember, in primitive society is a semihostile act. As cross-cousins, these men cannot possibly belong to the same clan as the boy, or to the same territorial group, and since only senior and already fully initiated men are eligible for the job they will be men in their thirties or forties, twenty or more years older than he.

By selecting senior cross-cousins to conduct the forcible separation of the boy from the home and thus project him into the postpuberty proceedings, the Tiwi have selected men who are as remote from the boy as possible. The only thing they and he have in common is that they are all members of the same tribe—nothing else. If, then, we have stressed that all training of the child in the prepuberty period is carried on by intimates, we have to stress equally the fact that the postpuberty training has to be in the hands of nonintimates. Anybody who is in any way close to the boy—by blood, by residence, by age, or by any other form of affiliation or association—is *ipso facto* ineligible to have a hand in his postpuberty training.

I selected the Tiwi as my example because the case happens to be rather spectacular in the clarity of its symbolism, but if one examines the literature one finds everywhere or almost everywhere the same emphasis. Those who prefer Freudian symbolism I refer to the initiation ceremonies of the Kiwai Papuans (Landtmann, 1927), where during initiation the boy is required to actually step on his mother's stomach; when Landtmann asked the significance of this he was told that it meant that the boy was now "finished with the place where he came from" (i.e., his mother's womb).

Van Gennep has collected all the older cases in his classic *Rites de passage* (Van Gennep, 1909), and no new ones which invalidate his generalizations have been reported since his time.

I therefore suggest two reasonably safe generalizations about initiation rituals: (*a*) The rituals themselves are designed to emphasize in very clear terms that initiation ceremonies represent a clear break with all home, household, home-town, and friendship-group ties; and (*b*) as a very basic part of such emphasis the complete handling of all initiation proceedings, and initiation instruction, from their inception at puberty to their final conclusion often more than a decade later, is made the responsibility of men who are comparative strangers to the boy and who are thus as different as possible in their social relationships to him from the teachers, guiders, instructors, and associates he has had up to that time.

3. *Atmosphere.*—It should now be clear what is meant by the third head, Atmosphere. The arrival of the strangers to drag the yelling boy out of his mother's arms is just the spectacular beginning of a long period during which the separation of the boy from everything that has gone before is emphasized in every possible way at every minute of the day and night. So far his life has been easy; now it is hard. Up to now he has never necessarily experienced any great pain, but in the initiation period in many tribes pain, sometimes horrible, intense pain, is an obligatory feature. The boy of twelve or thirteen, used to noisy, boisterous, irresponsible play, is expected and required to sit still for hours and days at a time saying nothing whatever but concentrating upon and endeavoring to understand long intricate instructions and "lectures" given him by his hostile and forbidding preceptors (who are, of course, the men who carried him off to initiation, the "strangers" of the previous section). Life has suddenly become real and earnest and the initiate is required literally to "put away the things of a child," even the demeanor. The number of tabus and unnatural behaviors enjoined upon the initiate is endless. He mustn't speak unless he is spoken to; he must eat only certain foods, and often only in certain ways, at fixed times, and in certain fixed positions. All contact with females, even speech with them, is rigidly forbidden, and this includes mother and sisters. He cannot even scratch his head with his own hand, but must do it with a special stick and so on, through a long catalogue of special, unnatural, but obligatory behaviors covering practically every daily activity and every hour of the day and night. And during this time he doesn't go home at night or for the week end or on a forty-eight-hour pass, but remains secluded in the bush, almost literally the prisoner of his preceptors, for months and even years at a time. If he is allowed home at rare intervals, he has to carry all his tabus with him, and nothing is more astonishing in Australia than to see some youth who the year before was a noisy, brash, boisterous thirteen-year-old, sitting the following year, after his initiation has begun, in the midst of his family, with downcast head and subdued air, not daring even to smile, still less to speak. He is "home on leave," but he might just as well have

stayed in camp for all the freedom from discipline his spell at home is giving him.

The preoccupations of anthropologists with other interests (that of the earlier field workers with the pain-inflicting aspects of the initiations, and the recent preoccupation with early physiological experiences) have directed attention away from what may well be the most important aspect of education in the simpler societies, namely the possibly traumatic aspect of the initiation ceremonies. From whatever aspect we view them their whole tenor is to produce shock, disruption, a sharp break with the past, a violent projection out of the known into the unknown. Perhaps the boys are old enough to take it in their stride and the experience is not really traumatic. If so, it would seem that primitive society goes to an awful lot of trouble and wastes an awful lot of man-hours needlessly. Actually we don't know what the psychological effects of initiation upon the initiates are. All that can be said safely is that judged by the elaboration and the minuteness of detail in the shocking and disruptive features of initiation rituals, they certainly appear to be designed to produce the maximum amount of shock possible for the society to achieve.

This may suggest that our own exaggerated concern with protecting our own adolescents from disturbing experiences is quite unnecessary. If the grueling ordeal of subincision, with all its accompanying disruptive devices, leaves the young Australian psychologically unscathed, we needn't worry that Universal Military Training, for instance, will seriously upset the young American. But perhaps something in the prepuberty training prepares the young Australian and makes him capable of standing the trauma of the initiation period.

4. *Curriculum.*—What is the purpose of all this elaboration of shock ritual? Ask the natives themselves and they will answer vaguely, "to make a child into a man." Occasionally a more specific verb is used and the answer becomes, "to teach a boy to become a man." What is supposed to be learned and what do the preceptors teach in the initiation schools? Perhaps the most surprising thing is what is not taught. It is hard to find in the literature any case where the initiation curriculum contains what might be called "practical subjects," or how to make a basic living. (There appear to be certain exceptions to this generalization, but they are more apparent than real.) The basic food-getting skills of the simpler peoples are never imparted in the initiation schools. Where practical subjects are included (as in Polynesia or in the Poro schools of Liberia and Sierra Leone), they are specialized crafts, not basic food-getting skills. Hunting, gardening, cattle-tending, fishing, are not taught the boy at initiation; he has already learned the rudiments of these at home in his intimate groups before his initiation starts. This is a surprising finding because of the well-known fact that many of these people live pretty close to the starvation point, and none of them manage to extract much more than subsistence from their environment. But despite this, the cultures in question are blissfully oblivious of economic determinism, and blandly

leave instruction in basic food production to the laissez faire, casual, hit-or-miss teaching of parents, friends, play groups, etc. When society itself forcibly takes over the boy in order to make him into a man and teach him the things a man should know, it is not concerned with teaching him to be a better hunter or gardener or tender of cattle or fisherman, even though the economic survival of the tribe clearly depends on all the adult men being good at one or another of these occupations. The initiation curricula cover instead quite a different series of subjects, which I am tempted to call "cultural subjects"—in either sense of the word "culture."

Of course, there is much variation here from tribe to tribe and region to region, but the imparting of religious knowledge always occupies a prominent place. This (in different cultures) includes such things as the learning of the myths, the tribal accounts of the tribe's own origin and history, and the performance, the meaning, and the sacred connections and connotations of the ceremonials. In brief, novices are taught theology, which in primitive society is inextricably mixed up with astronomy, geology, geography, biology (the mysteries of birth and sex), philosophy, art, and music—in short, the whole cultural heritage of the tribe. As Pettit has pointed out (dealing with North America, but his statement has universal anthropological validity), the instruction in the initiation schools is "a constant challenge to the elders to review, analyze, dramatize, and defend their cultural heritage" (Pettit, 1946). That sentence "review, analyze, dramatize, and defend their cultural heritage" is very striking, because you can apply it equally aptly to a group of naked old men in Central Australia sitting talking to a novice in the middle of a treeless desert, and to most lectures in a college of liberal arts in the United States. It serves to draw attention to the fact that, in the simpler societies, the schools run and manned and controlled and financed by the society at large are designed not to make better economic men of the novices, or better food producers, but to produce better citizens, better carriers of the culture through the generations, people better informed about the world they live in and the tribe they belong to. It is here finally, through this sort of curriculum, that each adolescent becomes "enculturated," no matter how haphazard and individualized his learning and his growth may have been up to now. It is through the rigidly disciplined instruction of a common and rigidly prescribed curriculum that he assumes, with all his fellow tribesmen, a common culture. This is where standardization occurs in the educational process of the simpler societies. Everybody who goes through the initiation schools, generation after generation, is presented with the same material, organized and taught in the same way, with no allowances made for individual taste or choice or proclivity, and no substitutions or electives allowed. When we realize how standardized and rigid and uniform this curriculum is, it should help us to realize how variable, how un-uniform, how dictated by chance, accident, and the personal whims of individual parents, individual adult relatives, and the variation in peer and play groups is the "curriculum" on or in which the individual child is trained during the long impressionable period that precedes puberty.

General Conclusion

The above discussion has, I hope, provided the basis for some helpful generalizations about education in primitive societies, or at least has opened up some new avenues for further exploration. The main points of the discussion may be summed up as follows:

1. There are typically (though not universally) in primitive societies two sharply contrasting educational vehicles, the preschool process, lasting from birth to puberty, and the initiation procedures, beginning around puberty or a little later and lasting from six months to fifteen years. These two educational vehicles show some highly significant contrasts.

2. From the point of view of regulation, the preschool period is characterized by its loose, vague, unsystematic character. Few primitive societies follow any set standards or rules on how children shall be brought up. It is true that there are frequently, perhaps usually, pretty clear rules (which are actually followed) telling mothers how to hold a baby, correct methods for suckling or weaning, and standardized techniques of toilet training (though I suspect some of these are nothing but copybook maxims), but outside the "physiological areas of child-training" (which therefore have to bear all the weight the Freudians put upon them), it is rare indeed to find in primitive cultures any conformity from family to family or from case to case with regard to anything else in the child's early career. This is not, of course, to deny that there are differences from culture to culture in the degree to which children are loved and fussed over or treated as nuisances or joys. I am not questioning the fact, for example, that the Arapesh love children, whereas the Mundugumor resent them. What I am reiterating is that there is still a wide variation not only possible but inevitable in conditioning and learning between one Mundugumor child and the next.

3. If this view is correct, it raises certain interesting possibilities for theory. Because of the heavy Freudian emphasis in the literature on child training in recent years, there exists a strong and unfortunate tendency to talk of child training as if it were co-terminous with swaddling, suckling, weaning, and toilet-training practices. But these "physiological" areas or "bodily functions" areas are only a small part of the preschool education of the primitive child. Even if in primitive cultures the physiological areas of child training are relatively standardized (and this is by no means certain), there is no evidence that the nonphysiological areas are. On the contrary, the evidence points in the other direction. Among adult members of the same society there may be, for example, great variation in apparent strength of the sex drive, or in the overt expression of

aggressive or passive personality traits (Hart, 1954). Where does such "personality variation" come from? From childhood experiences, say the Freudians. I agree. But in order to demonstrate that personality variation in adult life has its roots in early childhood experiences, it is necessary to show not that childhood experiences are highly standardized in early life and that child training is uniform, but that they are highly variable. How can we account for the self-evident fact of adult personality variation by stressing the uniformity of standardization of childhood training? Surely the more valid hypothesis or the more likely lead is to be found in those aspects of child training which are not uniform and not standardized.

4. So much for the preschool training. But there is also the other vehicle of education and youth training in primitive society, the initiation rituals. The initiation period demonstrates to us what standardization and uniformity of training really mean. When we grasp the meaning of this demonstration we can only conclude that compared with the rigidities of the initiation period, the prepuberty period is a loose, lax period. Social scientists who find it necessary for their theories to stress uniformity and pressures toward conformity in simple societies are badly advised to take the prepuberty period for their examples. The natives themselves know better than this. When they are adults, it is to the happy, unregulated, carefree days of prepuberty that they look back. "Then my initiation began," says the informant, and immediately a grim, guarded "old-man" expression comes over his face, "and I was taken off by the old men." The same old men (and women) who sit around and indulgently watch the vagaries and idiosyncrasies of the children without correction become the grim, vigilant, reproving watchers of the initiates, and any departure or attempted departure from tradition is immediately reprimanded.

5. Who are the agents of this discipline? Primitive societies answer in loud and unmistakable tones that discipline cannot be imposed by members of the primary group, that it has to be imposed by "outsiders." The widespread nature of this feature of initiation is, to my mind, very impressive. Making a boy into a man is rarely, anywhere, left to the family, the household, the village, to which he belongs and where he is on intimate terms with people.[1] The initiation schools are directed at imparting instruction that cannot be given in the home, under conditions as unlike home conditions as possible, by teachers who are the antithesis of the home teachers the boy has hitherto had. The symbolisms involved in the forcible removal from the home atmosphere; the long list of tabus upon homelike acts, homelike speech, homelike demeanor, homelike habits; the selection of the initiators (i.e., the teachers or preceptors) from the semihostile

[1] In the original draft of this paper I mentioned the Arapesh as one of the few exceptions. At the Stanford conference, however, Dr. Mead pointed out that while it is true that initiation in Arapesh is carried out by intimates, they wear masks. To me this correction of my original remark dramatically emphasizes the main point. The Arapesh social structure is such that there are no "strangers" to use for initiation; therefore they invent them by masking some intimates.

sections of the tribe—all tell the same story, that the turning of boys into men can only be achieved by making everything about the proceedings as different from the home and the prepuberty situation as possible. Everything that happens to the initiate during initiation has to be as different as it can be made by human ingenuity from the things that happened to him before initiation.

6. This becomes pointed up still more when we remember that what is actually being taught in the initiation schools is the whole value system of the culture, its myths, its religion, its philosophy, its justification of its own entity as a culture. Primitive society clearly values these things, values them so much that it cannot leave them to individual families to pass on to the young. It is willing to trust the haphazard, individually varied teaching methods of families and households and peer groups and gossip to teach children to walk and talk, about sex, how to get along with people, or how to be a good boy; it is even willing to leave to the individual families the teaching of how to hunt or to garden or to fish or to tend cattle; but the tribal philosophy, the religion, the citizenship knowledge, too important to leave to such haphazard methods, must be taught by society at large through its appointed and responsible representatives.

In doing this, society is asserting and underlining its rights in the child. The fact that, for example, in Australia it is a group of senior cross-cousins, and elsewhere it is men of the opposite moiety or some other specified group of semihostile relatives, who knock on the door and demand the child from his mourning and wailing family, should not be allowed to disguise the fact that these men are the representatives of society at large, the native equivalents of the truant officer, the policeman, and the draft board, asserting the priority of society's rights over the family's rights in the child. Clearly in every society there is always a family and there is always a state, and equally clearly both have rights in every child born into the society. And no society yet—Western or non-Western—has found any perfect way or equal way of adjudicating or harmonizing public rights and private rights. The state's rights must have priority when matters of citizenship are involved, but the assertion of the state's rights is always greeted with wails of anguish from the family. "I didn't raise my boy to go off and get subincised," wails the Australian mother, but he is carried off and subincised just the same. "I didn't raise my boy for the draft board or the school board," says the American mother, but her protests are of no avail either. It is an inevitable conflict, because it arises from the very structure of society, as long as society is an organization of family units, which it is universally. The only solution is to abolish the family or abolish the state, and no human group has been able to do either.

7. The boy is not ruined for life or a mental cripple as a result of the harrowing initiation experience, but is a social being *in a way he never was before*. He has been made aware of his wider social responsibilities and his wider membership in the total society, but more important in the present context, he has been exposed to a series of social situations in

which friendship counts for naught, crying or whining gets one no place, whimsy or charm or boyish attractiveness pays no dividends, and friends, pull, and influence are without effect. The tribal tradition, the culture, treats all individuals alike, and skills and wiles that were so valuable during childhood in gaining preferential treatment or in winning approval or avoiding disapproval are all to no avail. He goes into the initiation period a child, which is a social animal of one sort, but he comes out a responsible enculturated citizen, which is a social animal of a different sort.

8. Primitive societies, then, devote a great deal of time and care to training for citizenship. They make no attempt to even start such training until the boy has reached puberty. But once they start, they do it thoroughly. Citizenship training in these societies means a great deal more than knowing the words of "The Star-Spangled Banner" and memorizing the Bill of Rights. It means exposing the boy under particularly stirring and impressive conditions to the continuity of the cultural tradition, to the awe and majesty of the society itself, emphasizing the subordination of the individual to the group at large and hence the mysteriousness, wonder, and sacredness of the whole individual-society relationship. In Australia, the most sacred part of the whole initiation ritual is when the boys are shown the *churinga*, which are at the same time their own souls and the souls of the tribe which came into existence at the creation of the world. Citizenship, being an awesome and mysterious business in any culture, cannot be imparted or taught or instilled in a secular atmosphere; it must be imparted in an atmosphere replete with symbolism and mystery. Whether it can be taught at all without heavy emphasis on its otherworldliness, without heavy sacred emphasis, whether the teaching of citizenship can ever be a warm, friendly, loving, cosy, and undisturbing process, is a question I leave to the educators. Primitive societies obviously do not believe it can be taught that way, as is proved by the fact that they never try.

9. One last point, implied in much of the above but worth special mention, is the rather surprising fact that technological training, training in "getting a living," is absent from the initiation curricula, despite its obvious vital importance to the survival of the individual, of the household, and of the tribe or society. Mastery of the food-obtaining techniques by the children is left to the hit-or-miss, highly individualistic teaching processes of the home, to the peer groups, and to the whimsies of relatives or friends. The reason for this omission from the socially regulated curricula of the initiation schools is, I think, pretty clear. In the simpler societies there is nothing particularly mysterious, nothing spiritual or otherworldly about getting a living, or hunting or gardening or cattle-herding. It is true that there is apt to be a lot of magical practice mixed up with these things, but even this heavy magical element is conceived in very secular and individualistic terms. That is, it either works or doesn't work in particular cases, and each man or each household or clan has its own garden magic or cattle magic or hunting magic which differs from

the next man's or household's or clan's magic. Dobu, for instance, is a culture riddled with garden magic; so is that of the Trobriands, but each group's magic is individually owned and comparisons of magic are even made between group and group. For this reason, garden skills or hunting skills, even though they include magical elements, can still safely be left by society to the private level of transmission and teaching. Public control, public supervision is minimal.

This leads to two further conclusions, or at least suggestions. (1) On this line of analysis, we can conclude the primitive societies, despite their marginal subsistence and the fact that they are frequently close to the starvation point, devote more care and attention, *as societies*, to the production of good citizens, than to the production of good technicians, and therefore they can be said to value good citizenship more highly than they value the production of good food producers. Can this be said for modern societies, including our own? (2) This relative lack of interest in standardizing subsistence-training, while insisting at the same time on standardizing training in the ideological aspects of culture, may go a long way toward enabling us to explain the old sociological problem called cultural lag. Everybody who has taken an introductory course in social science is acquainted with the fact that change in technology is easier to achieve, and takes place with less resistance than change in non-technological or ideological fields. I do not suggest that what we have been talking about above offers a complete explanation of the culture lag differential, but it may at least be helpful. I would phrase the relation between culture lag and education like this: that because prepuberty education in the simpler societies is loose, unstructured, and left pretty much to individual household choice, and because such laissez faire prepuberty education typically includes food-getting techniques and the use of food-getting tools (spears, harpoons, hoes, etc.), the attitude toward these techniques and tools that the child develops is a secular one and he carries that secular attitude toward them into his adult life. Hence variations from or alternatives to such tools and techniques are not resisted with anything like the intensity of feeling with which variations from or alternatives to ideological elements will be resisted. From his childhood, the boy believes that in trying to get food anything is a good technique or a good tool, provided only that it works, and he is familiar too with the fact that techniques and tools differ at least slightly from household to household or hunter to hunter. Therefore, as an adult he is, in relation to food-getting techniques and tools, both a secularist and an empiricist, and will adopt the white man's gun or the white man's spade when they are offered without any feeling that he is flouting the tribal gods or the society's conscience. The white man's ideology, or foreign importations in ideology, are treated in quite a different way. They are involved with areas of behavior which have been learned not in the secular, empirical atmosphere of the home and the play groups, but in the awesome, sacred atmosphere of the initiation schools, wherein no individual variation is allowed and the very notion of alternatives is anathema.

To avoid misunderstanding, a brief comment must be made about societies like that of Polynesia and the "schools" of Africa such as the Poro, where specialized technical knowledge is imparted to the adolescent males in special training institutions. The significant point is that in such societies ordinary food-getting techniques (fishing in Polynesia, gardening in West Africa, cattle-tending in East Africa) are still left to the haphazard teaching methods of the individual household, whereas the craft skills (woodcarving in Polynesia, metalworking in the Poro) are entrusted to vehicles of instruction in which apprenticeship, passing of exams, standardized curricula, unfamiliar or nonintimate teachers, heavy emphasis on ritual and the sacred character of the esoteric knowledge which is being imparted, and the dangers of the slightest variation from the traditional techniques of the craft are all prominent. In such societies, despite the inclusion of some technology in the "schools," basic food-getting techniques remain in the common domain of the culture and are picked up by children haphazardly—only the special craft knowledge is sacredly imparted. (Even as late as Henry VIII's England the crafts were called the "mysteries," the two words being apparently interchangeable.)

To conclude then, we may pull most of the above together into one final summary. In primitive society there are two vehicles of education, the prepuberty process and the postpuberty process. No Western writer has ever succeeded in contrasting them as much as they need to be contrasted, because they are in every possible respect the Alpha and Omega of each other. In time of onset, atmosphere, personnel, techniques of instruction, location, curriculum, the two vehicles represent opposite poles. Everything that is done in or through one vehicle is the antithesis of what is done in the other. Standardization of experience and uniformity of training is markedly present in the post-initiation experience: it is markedly absent in the prepuberty experience of the growing child. If this is accepted as a base line, it has very important implications for the whole field of personality studies, especially for those studies which seem to claim that personality is very homogeneous in the simpler societies and for those allied studies which allege that child training and growing up in primitive society are very different from their equivalents in modern Western cultures. It is suggestive also as a base for attempting to answer a question that nobody has yet attempted to answer: Why do individuals in simple cultures differ from each other so markedly in personality traits, despite their common cultural conditioning? And it furnishes us finally with another link in the complicated chain of phenomena which exists between the problem of personality formation and the problem of culture change.

All these things are brought together, and indeed the whole of this paper is held together by one single thread—namely, that childhood experience is part of the secular world, postpuberty experience part of the sacred world. What is learned in the secular world is learned haphazardly, and varies greatly from individual to individual. Therefore no society can standardize that part of the child's learning which is acquired under secular circumstances. My only claim for this paper is that the use of this starting point for a discussion of primitive education enables us to obtain some insights into educational and cultural processes which are not provided by any alternative starting point.

References

Gesell, Arnold, and Frances L. Ilg. 1946. *The Child from Five to Ten.* New York: Harper & Brothers.

Hart, C. W. M. 1954. "The Sons of Turimpi," *American Anthropologist*, LVI, 242–61.

Herskovits, Melville J. 1948. *Man and His Works.* New York: Alfred A. Knopf, Inc.

Landtmann, Gunnar. 1927. *The Kiwai Papuans of British New Guinea.* London: The Macmillan Company.

Pettit, George A. 1946. "Primitive Education in North America," *University of California Publications in American Archaeology and Ethnology*, XLIII, 182.

Piaget, Jean. 1929. *The Child's Conception of the World.* New York: Harcourt, Brace and Company.

———. 1932. *The Moral Judgment of the Child.* London: Kegan Paul.

Schapera, I. 1940. *Married Life in an African Tribe.* London: Sheridan House.

Van Gennep, Arnold. 1909. *Les rites de passage.* Paris: E. Nourry.

FOURTH SESSION OF THE CONFERENCE

Chairman: Robert Bush
Discussant: Lawrence K. Frank

Frank: This paper brings again into sharper focus the question of timing and the appropriateness of different kinds of experiences in the enculturation process to the developing organism. That's one of the major questions that this group has to consider. My own feeling is that we have not had an adequate picture of the sequential process of enculturation that takes place in the child in different cultures. To a considerable extent personality and culture studies have been focused on the development of character structure, basic personality; but to my way of thinking, we have not paid enough attention to all the other ways in which cultural patterning is built into the child, over and above those which personality theories have considered most important. For example, there has been little discussion, so far as I know, about the way the child develops a conceptual framework and how he learns to perceive the world in terms of the basic ideas, assumptions, the patterns of perception which his culture says is the way to view and understand the world in which he is going to live. One of the major needs of education which it is appropriate for the anthropologist to attempt to fulfill is for a systematic statement of all the ways in which from birth on, this growing, developing, maturing organism is subject to the patterning, channeling, transforming of the ways through which he becomes a personality, a participating member in that symbolic cultural world and the social order in which he lives. Dr. Hart's paper focuses attention on some of these questions, but before discussing them I'd like to make a few detailed comments on the paper.

Dr. Hart has made the statement that the methods of child rearing in the prepubertal period are often laissez faire, haphazard, and unpatterned. While these methods and practices of child care may be unpatterned—in so far as there may be many variations in what parents do—the objectives of the care and nurture of a child, even in our own culture, are highly standardized. That is, parents are taught, and are usually convinced, that there are certain things which must be done to and for a child, or the heavens will fall. Now, the way they do this may vary from parent to parent, from family to family, but the guiding convictions and purposes are similar. Therefore, preschool education in the home does not appear wholly unpatterned: There exists a considerable degree of patterning, almost a rigidity, in different socioeconomic groups in our own culture.

Another point is that in our society, and maybe this is largely by way of contrast to the cultures that Dr. Hart was speaking of, the child begins to learn from strangers quite early—the doctor, the man in white, for example, is a stranger. Children who go to a hospital have experiences very similar to those described as initiation ceremonies; strange people drag him away from his parents. It's often a traumatic experience, long before he's ready, like the adolescent, to want to be freed from his parents. Also the child going to nursery school, kindergarten, and primary grades is put into the hands of a strange teacher. In our culture the different *timings* of these experiences are important, probably highly significant for the child and for our society. We do this in our way; another culture does it in their way—it again goes back to this matter of timing.

Another point relates what Dr. Hart has said: In our culture, at three, four, or five years, before the child goes to school, we believe it's necessary, and most parents are firmly convinced, that we must indoctrinate the child with the basic theological conceptions of the universe. They also give him an image of himself, usually an image of a bad, wicked, boy or girl. There is also a series of basic patterns of perception and conception which are inculcated in the "why-because" stage, since in our culture children start to ask "why" and then mamma or papa says "because," answering in terms of *their* religion, their philosophy, their law, their science, and so forth—whatever it is that makes life meaningful for them. Thus the child begins to build up his way of seeing the world, his private frame of reference, at three, four, or five. Those early conceptions, those early patterns of perception and interpretation of the world, largely persist throughout life without being much changed or greatly revised. All later learning is largely fitting new materials, new content, into that basic frame of reference which the child builds up in the preschool period. Parents, unless they enter into a child-study or parent-education class, rarely revise, analyze, or review their traditions or change their child-rearing practices except for aspects of infant care.

This emphasizes one of the points we should be most concerned about in education. To a very large extent children are being indoctrinated with ideas that are already anachronistic if not archaic; these act as a self-defeating barrier to their growing up and learning to live in the world of today. May I read a short quotation from a book written about 1918, by F. J. Taggart, called *The Processes of History*? He says:

> While then the educative discipline tends to preserve what has been acquired, it presents a very real obstacle to further advance. In face of this consideration, the theory commonly expressed as—in the inheritance of the primary achievements of one generation by the next is the main factor of progress, that in fact human advance has been due to the maintenance of tradition, to the drillings by which the individual has been put in possession of the acquisitions of the group—will be seen to express but a partial truth. For if this process had been the only one in operation, advancement would manifestly have been impossible. This persistence of tradition is what produces that condition of sameness, stagnation, fixity, which has been dwelt upon by so many when they have occasion to speak of backward people. The operation of this process tends to the maintenance of the idea systems of the group or the individual as it exists at any given moment, and the study of man involves as its next step an inquiry as to how modifications and changes in idea systems have been instilled and brought about.

That statement, I believe, is very appropriate to our problem of education today.

In our society, the nursery school and the elementary school—at about five or six—begin to impose taboos on the child; for example, the child is forbidden to carry into the school many of the language patterns, the customs, the practices—even the toilet practices—that he has learned at home. These practices are relevant as showing the great variation in timing at which certain cultures impose on or offer a child their patterns. And I would say that an initiation ceremony might be considered as concerned with trying to supersede and replace the more or less idiosyncratic, idiomatic, childish beliefs and patterns and relationships with those of the public "consensual" world. This revision may occur when the child goes to school and is told, "That isn't so; that's what you believe," or it may happen at the puberty initiation ceremony, as Dr. Hart has described it.

One of the points Dr. Hart raised rather strongly—omission from initiation ceremonies of instruction in handicrafts or the technological, material culture—probably reflects the absence of technological change in a society. In our society, on the other hand, where we have very rapid technological change, it becomes necessary for us to establish schools—a great many kinds of vocational schools so that the adolescent can be inducted into the present state of the arts. Vocational education often lags behind because schools can't get the new tools and machines.

Dr. Hart has raised this question: If there is a common, standardized process of enculturation, how do you account for individual differences? If we reflect on what we've already discussed, namely the individual differences in receptivity, in sensitivity and capacity for learning, and especially in idiomatic ways of learning, that seeming paradox might be resolved. It isn't the standardization of the situation stimulus that governs the learning but what the child sees, hears, understands, and what the situation or treatment means to him. One of the fallacies in some of our educational theories, as well as in much of our psychological experimentation, is the belief that all you have to do is to standardize the stimulus or teaching and then you will get a common result; this ignores what the individual does in learning anything.

Now, in our own culture we should raise the question of how useful and important an initiation ceremony such as Dr. Hart has described would be. The adolescent, growing up in our culture, faces an extraordinary array of conflicts, contradictions, incongruities, and discrepancies in our traditions, which each boy and girl individually, with very little help from church, school, or otherwise, has to try to resolve or reconcile in some fashion, in order to come to terms with life. For example, most of our children have been brought up (there's some change recently) with the feeling that anything connected with genitals and sex is bad, dirty, nasty, indecent, something you ought to be ashamed of. At the same time, when they become adolescents, they read our romantic poetry and novels, see our movies, and learn that through sex and romantic love they will find the greatest happiness in life. All boys and girls face that conflict alone, and must try to deal with it "in the agony of their own souls." Another example: We have as a part of our ethical and moral traditions the teaching to love thy neighbor, to be generous, helpful, altruistic, but at the same time the child or adolescent may be urged to be ambitious, to beat everybody, even in school, to get his own—again each child and adolescent has to resolve this conflict.

We could go on and elaborate these incongruities in our traditions, but all I want to do is to point out that one of the major needs in education today, whether it is conceived as an initiation ceremony or not, is to establish some procedure to help adolescents to resolve those contradictions and conflicts so that they don't pay too high a psychological price, as many of them do, so that they don't suffer too much anxiety or guilt, trying to conform to our traditional teaching. You may remember Robert Browning's poem *Paracelsus*, in which he describes so vividly one aspect of later adolescence, that transient period of altruism that so often flourishes, which is one of the greatest dynamics for cultural advance that we're wasting—where Paracelsus says, "I seem to long at once to trample on, yet save mankind." An understanding of that ambivalent attitude toward society is probably one of the most insightful contributions that has been made to adolescent psychology. Could we say that the schools should recognize more clearly that during this period the adolescent is very much confused and perplexed, that he has many curiosities and he also has many aspirations? Therefore the school should build a curriculum, using the usual academic materials and experiences (because if there are any answers they're in the various disciplines) but focusing and presenting those materials in such a way that they are more responsive to these needs, aspirations, and perplexities of youth. In this way we might approximate something similar to initiation ceremonies, so that children could come through this period and take their places as participants in maintaining a free social order, with a greater degree of clarity and integration of personality than they have at the present time. Through such a curriculum they would be helped to integrate and clarify their relationships, not only to the world (which is their philosophy or religion) but also to other people and to themselves.

The relation to the self and the image of the self are probably of major importance in the adolescent goal, because at this period the individual sets his level of aspiration. The rest of his young adult life and middle-aged life will be largely in terms of what at that time he believes he should do or try to do and become, whether he's capable of it or not. More specifically, we can make use of the formulations that have been made by various people—such as R. J. Havighurst's *Developmental Life Tasks* conception. We can think in terms of how the processes of biological growth and development call for a revision of the image of the body and of the self, and we can try to help the youngster to develop a revised, new image of the body he has to live with. How does he learn to accept his own sexual maturation at that time? How—particularly today when there's so much change and confusion—does he define for himself the masculine or feminine role by which he's going to utilize and guide and pattern his sexuality, as well as all the other areas of life? It should be emphasized more than it has been that in our society there are two different patterns, a masculine and a feminine pattern, for almost every aspect and phase of living. The law, for example, almost always makes that distinction. Masculinity and femininity are not merely matters of sexual relationships; these roles permeate the whole pattern of social life.

The problem of helping adolescents to go through this second decade of life with a minimum of disturbance and trauma while undertaking more or less drastic revision of their childhood ideas about family, church, society, justice, and so on is difficult but crucial. After puberty, it's as if the child has been wearing special eyeglasses and takes them off and suddenly sees what has been going on all around him for the first time. That's one of the most convincing demonstrations of patterned perception— the adolescent's perception is enlarged and sharpened and patterned shortly after puberty, often before in some of the less protected adolescents. How can the adolescent revise his relationships to his parents so as to minimize the "cold war" or hot war that frequently takes place in families in such a way that he can achieve his independence and then later come back to the family? How can the youngster conform to the peer demands without losing his integrity?

One of the observations made in studying adolescent girls might be mentioned—namely, that conforming to your peer group is the only safe way to become an individual. In other words, at adolescence the girl or boy is confronted with the terrifying process of becoming an individual. Adolescents gain a lot of reassurance by conforming to other people who are going through this experience; and if the girl puts on cosmetics, lipstick, and dresses and acts like everybody else, still she thinks she's doing it "with a difference." Conformity is a sort of protective coloration under which you can develop your own individuality. There are some indications that those youngsters who before puberty have been given opportunity to make choices and decisions to discover their own tastes, to do things for themselves, often seem to go through the puberty period and the early adolescent teen-age conformity and come out on the other side with more personal integrity than those youngsters who have been under complete parental domination, who often get swept off their feet by the peer group, and who never apparently find themselves or become individuals later.

Today we put upon the adolescent this very crucial life task of proving his adequacy by meeting the demands of school and jobs, which to a very large extent we know are largely irrelevant to the teen-ager, and may be either premature or postmature in relation to his state of maturation. Again, in this adolescent period, as Dr. Hart's paper has emphasized, there are some very dramatic transitions. An initiation ceremony is a highly dramatic, almost traumatic, experience, in which the child gives up what he's lived by and for previously in order to accept and go on into the next stage of his development. When I spoke about unlearning, in our earlier discussion, I meant that the child unlearns his pattern of activity or relationships; he doesn't give up and unlearn and destroy what he has built up before, but he incorporates these functions and capacities in a new configurational pattern, so that the earlier functions are released for new uses. Most of our adult difficulties and personality problems are the "unfinished business" of adolescence and often early childhood. In other words, the individual was not able to make the transitions at the time; they came before he was ready, or he was prevented from making them when he was ready to do so. Therefore he goes on into adult life still burdened with the "unfinished business," as the psychiatrists are showing. This adolescent period of very extensive revisions, of necessary transitions, offers some of the major opportunities for a genuine mental health program—not psychiatric programs, but a mental health program. If we could see the developing adolescent facing these persistent life tasks which he has to deal with, trying to cope with these transitions, we could ask the educational curriculum makers to provide the educational experiences, the insights, the awarenesses, the understandings, and the skills and knowledge, which will enable the adolescent to face those life tasks more courageously and confidently, so that he can go on and be a more effective participant in maintaining a self-repairing, self-regulating social order—which is one way of describing a democratic society—and also can participate in the maintenance and advancement of his cultural world. Here again it may be desirable to emphasize the importance of analogical learning in adolescence, the significance of non-cognitive experience, especially aesthetic experience, for learning and for focusing the newly developed energies and aspirations of youth.

I hope these comments are relevant and I hope we can come back and take up some of them, because I am emphasizing the relevance of Dr. Hart's paper for educational programs.

Discussant: William E. Martin

Martin: As a way of reacting to this paper, I would like to pose two types of questions. The first type refers explicitly and solely to the paper itself. It is this kind of question: "Is it really true that . . . ?" It may be a little brash of me, as a nonanthropologist, to raise such questions. My purpose is not to arouse defensive reactions among the anthropologists but only to eliminate any possible misunderstanding and misinterpretation. If the naïveté of the questions shocks you, then I think this only emphasizes the task that you anthropologists face in educating the rest of us. The second type of question concerns the implications of Hart's paper: "If this is true, then what does it mean for education in our society?"

As an example of the first type of question, let me begin by asking:

1. Why do we know so little about the early education of the child in simple societies? Hart says, "The field workers do not tell us what the pattern of early education is because there is rarely any clear-cut pattern"; further he says, "No two children in the same culture learn the same things in the same way." I would like to suggest some alternative explanations.

The first one is that the reason field workers do not tell us—cannot tell us—about methods of child rearing in simple societies is that these methods are so simple that they are difficult to describe. For example, in Whiting and Child (1953) you find this kind of statement: "When one of us, doing field work among the Kwoma of New Guinea, asked about toilet training, his informants were puzzled as to why this was anything to ask questions about. All they could say at first was, 'Why, you just tell the child what to do and he does it' " (p. 76).

A related explanation, it seems to me, is that there may be a lack of awareness in a society of methods as methods. I am reminded that some years ago one of my colleagues in a parent-counseling service, tired of listening to parents who were having difficulties in rearing their children, said, "Wouldn't it be wonderful to ask some successful parents what methods they use in handling problems that arise in the home?" Well, we found some successful parents—believe it or not—but when we asked them about methods of child rearing, they had little or nothing to say. They were so successful they weren't even aware of what they were doing. They had never made explicit to themselves and could not make explicit to others what they were doing. It would seem to me that these explanations are acceptable alternatives to that which Hart presents for our lack of knowledge of early education in simple societies.

2. Is there no standardization of practice in rearing the young in simple societies? No pattern? No consensus? Does anything go? Hart says child behavior is "highly random behavior," that child experience is "random experience." Then, I have to ask: If anything goes in these simple societies, how can anthropologists describe, as they have done, differences among societies in methods of child rearing in these early years? For example, again looking at Whiting and Child's recent publication, they state two general conclusions they arrived at as a result of their analysis of ethnographic data. They say first that "child training the world over is in certain important respects identical" (p. 63). "The other general conclusion of a factual nature is that even in these important respects child training also differs from one society to another" (p. 64).

There is a conflict between what these people are telling me and what Hart is telling me in his paper. Are these differences that have been reported manufactured—I do not mean, of course, intentionally—by anthropologists? I remind you that we get very explicit statements from anthropologists. For example, "Holmberg reports that an unruly child among the Siriono is never beaten. 'At worst, his mother gives him a rough pull or throws some small object at him.' " (Whiting and Child, 1953, p. 101.) As I interpret that statement, that is a pattern, a rather standardized pattern, of treating the young in that particular society.

I have to ask in this same connection: What is the content of a pattern of child rearing? I remember reading in one of the Josiah Macy conferences on the problems of infancy and childhood that Erikson said that we have to distinguish between what a parent (or child) ought to do; what a parent (or child) does; and what a parent (or child) can get away with. Is there no consensus on matters of these kinds, even among parents in a simple society? Hart tells us that there is a mixture of strict and permissive techniques, but this does not necessarily imply that there is no blueprint, as he suggests. The mixture of strict and permissive techniques may, in itself, constitute a standardized pattern.

And finally, I ask: Is it not strange that (I quote from Hart) "the right way for a man to treat his mother-in-law or for a brother to act toward his sister" is a "cultural entity" but the right way for a parent to treat (or rear) a child is not? If I interpret Hart correctly, I must accept the fact— and it is difficult for me to do so—that here are parents, members of the same society, participating in the same culture, and yet any similarity in their child-rearing practices is not only coincidental—it does not exist.

3. Do physiological areas of child rearing have so little importance in the total process of growing up? Hart says that there may be "rules telling mothers how to hold a baby, correct times for suckling or weaning, or standardized techniques for toilet training." But certainly outside these areas "it is rare indeed to find in primitive cultures any conformity from family to family." Yet, as I read the anthropological literature, it seems that in the working out of these problems in the physiological areas, many kinds of learning occur that cannot help but influence later growth and development. For example, Whiting writes of the Kwoma: "When a child is weaned he may no longer sit in his mother's lap by day nor lie by her side at night. This is apparently felt as the most severe frustration experienced at this period of life. No longer is it possible to attain the vantage point from which all drives have hitherto been satisfied." (Whiting, 1941, p. 33.) I see a connection between this and later experience. But Hart evidently sees none.

4. What is the nature of the relationship between adult personality and childhood experiences? How can we explain both the similarities and the differences among adult members of a society? Hart asks: "Why do individuals in simple cultures differ from each other so markedly in personality traits, despite their supposedly [word inserted by Martin] common cultural conditioning?" I ask: Do these individuals differ from each other so markedly? Do they not on the contrary resemble each other markedly? Are not the ways in which they are alike of as great significance to us as the ways in which they are different? Is not this resemblance a consequence of a common experience that reflects, in turn, a consensus of opinion in a given society on child-rearing practices?

5. What is the significance of the play group? After Hart describes the great amount of variation in child-rearing practices in simple societies, he argues that "this variation is enormously increased by the role of the play group." But this argument seems to detach the play group from the society of which it is a part. In our culture, at least, child behavior in the play group reflects adult behavior, although the imitation may be exaggerated and distorted at times. So that, rather than looking upon the play group as increasing variation, we may see it as accentuating and strengthening standardization of behavior patterns.

Now I want to assume that all of my questions were really rather foolish, if not impertinent, questions and that we need not have any serious doubts about the contents of the Hart paper. Instead, we need to address ourselves to the meaning and implications of that content. These questions occur to me:

1. Have we ascribed to the process of development in simple societies a continuity that isn't there? Previously, I had thought that in simple societies we found a relative continuity of development, while in our own society, for example, we had discontinuity that made growing up a considerably more difficult process for our youngsters. But, according to Hart, puberty, in simple societies, is a break with the past: The strangers come in and take the boy away; it is a traumatic experience; it is the beginning of a new life and almost a turning-back on the past. I cannot help but be reminded of G. Stanley Hall's conception of adolescence as a rebirth.

But, more and more, those who study development in our culture stress the underlying continuity of the process: Puberty is only a point of transition. Adolescence is not a break with the past so much as a realization of the past. Adolescence is a period in which the individual only grows more like what he has previously been as a child. Is it possible that the discontinuity which Hart describes in simple societies is not as sharp as it seems? Could we not see the initiation ceremonies as making explicit a system of values which had previously been only implicit, instead of seeing postpubertal education as the first time at which the boy is brought face to face with the ideology of his society?

2. Taking a lesson from what happens in simple societies, is it possible that we, in our culture, standardize and formalize our early childhood education too much? Should we have more incidental learning in these early years and not so much planned experience?

3. Should we delay our training for citizenship to the years past puberty, as Hart says that simple societies do?

4. What kind of training ought we to have for citizenship? Here I would like to read a few sentences from the Hart paper, so that we may all recall the flavor of citizenship training in simple societies. "Citizenship, being an awesome and mysterious business in any culture, cannot be imparted or taught or instilled in a secular atmosphere: it must be imparted in an atmosphere replete with symbolism and mystery. . . . Whether it can be taught at all without heavy emphasis on its otherworldliness, without heavy sacred emphasis; whether the teaching of citizenship can ever be a warm, friendly, loving, cozy, and undisturbing process, is a question I leave to the educators. Primitive societies obviously do not believe it can be taught that way, as is proved by the fact that they never try."

5. Do we misdirect our attention, or misplace our emphasis, in the matter of educational goals? Do we give too much attention to technology, to vocational education, to life adjustment, and too little attention, on the other hand, to ideology, to a liberal education, to a philosophy of life?

6. What is the significance of standardization in postpubertal education? Is it a function of the kind of content to be mastered? And similarly, for the lack of standardization in prepubertal education: Is that too a function of the kind of content which must be mastered at that time?

7. In simple societies, according to Hart's paper, it seems that what is learned latest is what endures longest and resists change most strongly.

In our society, in contrast, we have long believed that what is learned earliest endures longest and resists change most strongly.

8. I missed hearing something about females in this paper. What happens to them in simple societies? Don't they acquire values? Don't they go through ceremonial inductions of some kind? Don't they get any kind of citizenship training? Have we been contaminating girls in our society by subjecting them to civics and American history and the like?

Hart: I can answer that one very quickly. To treat women I would have needed a separate paper. In other words, it was really limitations of space that explains the absence of women, not any innate hostility to them.

OPEN DISCUSSION

Variation and Uniformity in Prepubertal Education

Hart, Lee, Gillin, Mead

Hart: I would like to thank Dr. Frank and Dr. Martin for their comments. The juxtaposition of statements from Whiting and Child by Dr. Martin against statements from me was not so contradictory as it may appear. For instance, one of the quotations from my paper expressed a skepticism about standardized pattern existing in many primitive societies with regard to the uses of punishment. Dr. Martin tried to controvert that by a statement from Holmberg to the effect that the child is rarely punished in the tribe in question; the most extreme case would be where somebody threw a rock or a small object at him. Now that statement to me, merely on the face of it, implies a good deal of variation from parent to parent or from time to time in the case of the same parent; it does not prove standardization; it does not even say that in the case of a child's transgression the same technique is used by the same parent today, or tomorrow, or in the case of several parents that Parent A would do the same thing as Parent B.

I was maintaining that child training was not as standardized as the people who read anthropology books tend to think it is. In the original paper—I cut it out in the interests of shortening the paper later—I quoted a statement from Lloyd Allan Cook, a well-known educational sociologist. The statement when I first read it shocked me. It was to the effect that the child in our own society is brought up by a variety of techniques or subjected to a variety of different situations from household to household and from class to class. But, Cook goes on, as anthropologists are well aware, this does not happen in primitive societies. I looked immediately down upon the bottom of the page to see his authority for that, to me, astonishing statement about primitive societies, and his authority was Margaret Mead. Now, I know Margaret never said that in that form, but Lloyd Allan Cook thought she was saying it. And I think there are a number of cases of that sort where the type of statement about child-training practices in primitive societies which a number of anthropologists have been making, has been grossly misinterpreted or exaggerated by psychologists, educational sociologists, educators, and other people who read our literature and read a great deal more into it than the anthropologists intended.

Lee: I think that the fact that people are not conscious of child-raising methods does not mean that there isn't some kind of pattern there. I would like to bring in an example from language. I remember an apocryphal story that is told of an anthropological linguist, to the effect that the first time he went to the field he asked an informant, "What is the first person of the exclusive plural of the verb 'to go'?" Of course you can never get at grammar that way, even though the woman that he was interviewing always spoke her language grammatically. So I think that there is in culture and grammar a structure that is followed quite often unconsciously, undeliberately. Moreover, as in language, you have in culture what we call style—there are these general precepts, grammatical regulations; there is also, however, an individual style of putting these regulations into practice. If you read the writing of twenty people without looking to find out who the writers are you can identify the ones you are familiar with because of their style. And you know just the same that they are not speaking ungrammatically, and you know that they are using the grammar of a specific language. It seems to me that that's the kind of variation that we have in culture, a kind of variation limited to the interpretation of an already present grammar which may not be known as grammar by the person who's using it, but which is there in whatever he does.

Gillin: We must remember that the word "pattern" is an abstraction, and that there are several types of patterns. One is the kind where you can't make a single error, as in operating switches on railroad lines. Another type is comparable to a road in the countryside with a fence on each side, where you are allowed to wander about as long as you don't cross the fences. In other words, there is a range of permitted variations about the ideal pattern. What Steve (Hart) is talking about largely, I think, is the occurrence of variations in primitive societies, in the same way that we have them and that every society has them to some degree. And anthropologists in describing the pattern—because of shortness of space or something or other—have often left out many of the variations of native behavior; but in primitive societies there *is* variation. Nevertheless, there tends to be a pattern; and in every system of child training there are limits set to variation.

Mead: We can say that in most societies most of child rearing tends to be nonverbalized; and therefore you have to do a great deal more work to study it than you do to study initiation ceremonies. We can also say that when you study more than one initiation ceremony you find they vary, and they vary enormously; that when you study kinship behavior—and really study it, really know all your people, and really watch it—it varies; and that the only differences, therefore, in these two positions of puberty initiation and early childhood behavior are in degrees and types of verbalization and in the degrees and types of study that have been accorded to them. I don't somehow feel that Dr. Hart has been considering the evidence as much as he's been constructing a problem to pose to educators; and he has posed some exceedingly important problems. The first is the role of the stranger as educator.

There is a tendency to construct the presenter as a stranger, which is far wider than was even indicated, because, for instance, he said it doesn't happen among the Arapesh, but it does: The initiator is a close relative, but he wears a mask, and when in our culture father represents rewards and punishments as Santa Claus, he wears a mask. The general tendency is widespread, though not universal, that at different periods in life—early childhood or late childhood or puberty—you do have a point where the community value enters through the role of the stranger. I think that's a useful way to look at our own school system, where we have a tendency to eliminate the stranger. Look at what happens in nursery school where we've tried to bridge that gap: We're not quite sure what a nursery teacher is—a mother, or a nanny, or a teacher.

The second interesting point here is the role of dramatization, a dramatization of values, whether it's done at puberty, whether it's done at other points—the extent to which a culture depends upon dramatization.

I disagree with Dr. Hart's interpretation of the ethnographic data and I disagree on the basis of my own and everybody else's field work that we have, where people have actually worked on children in detail, because we have found that when we took the trouble to observe what parents did in detail, family after family, and knew them all and watched them—hundreds of hours of watching—we have found regularities of the same order which you can find in language. But I do think the problems he has presented are exceedingly important and worth our discussing.

Discontinuities and Conflicts

Hart, Frank, Mead

Spindler: I think it's fairly clear that Mr. Hart has chosen to use epitomes or certain kinds of ideal types for purposes of sharp contrast. I doubt very much if any ideal type or epitome in this sense can be literally true. For this reason I believe we should not discuss any further here the data or even the interpretation of the evidence. I think that we should at this point go on to the questions that have been raised, particularly the question of the role of dramatization in the transmission of values, the problem of discontinuity and continuity, and the functions of the stranger.

Hart: What I do want to say at this point is that in a certain sense institutions in simple societies are competitive. It's a point which has been made very well by Frank Tannenbaum, who is not an anthropologist but who, I gather from Margaret (Mead), was to some extent influenced by discussions with anthropologists. What I have tried to do in this paper is to bring out the fact that, from one point of view, the home and all it means and all it teaches is pushed out of the way by another agency or another institution taking over. And all this business about the stranger coming in and dragging the initiate out of home, family, and so forth makes most sense to me when it is seen in competitive terms. Now, throughout this conference there has been a pretty constant stress on the notion that somehow we must have everything nice and peaceful and harmonious between institutions. It seems to me that the whole ritual of initiation ceremonies symbolizes the conflict between the claims of the home on the child, the claims of the kin group on the child, and the claims of the wider society. If you think about it in those terms, I think it's helpful for educators or people dealing with education in our own society, because it may well be that we will never succeed in harmonizing or bringing into a friendly alliance the competing claims of all the institutions in our culture which have some sort of hand in educating the child.

And that brings me to another point—that many adolescents have traumatic experiences in going through adolescence in our society. I think Dr. Frank indicated that we ought to try to remove those traumatic situations, or whatever causes them. I suggest that in those primitive societies where there are initiation ceremonies the trauma has not been removed but has been standardized, made uniform, invested with drama, and therefore made bearable. In dealing with the trauma of adolescence, there seem to me to be three possibilities: One is to try to remove it because it's bad on an individual basis; it shouldn't be there. The second is to be more or less laissez faire about it and do pretty much the way our society does now—worry about it, but do little about it. The third is to symbolize it, ritualize it, socially control it, make it a group experience through which a bunch of kids go together all holding hands and thereby mutually supporting each other. It may well be that the initiation ceremony in that sense is a therapeutic device and a somewhat better one than we have achieved. We apparently hope to achieve an even better one by abolishing trauma entirely; I'm not sure if we can.

Frank: My comments were intended to suggest not that we should abolish problems and conflict—because that's the way the individual matures and faces his life tasks—but rather that we try to give the adolescent the strengthening, the guidance, the co-operation, and especially the insights that will enable him to cope with those situations with less of the personal defeat and anguish and distortion that so many adolescents experience today. Problems arise because we are personalities; if we were just organisms and not personalities with aspirations, we wouldn't have any problems except survival; we'd just exist on an organic level.

One other point is important: that while every adult alive today has gone through this adolescent experience and had that kind of enculturation which one gets from a slightly older group, no adult ever passes that kind of experience on to his own children. And as I have pointed out elsewhere, the young teen-ager is anxious to get into this middle teen-age group; the older adolescent is anxious to get out of it. Thus adolescence has a number of dimensions which we have not clearly recognized, nor have we realized the cultural process that accrues from the older adolescent to the younger, not from adult to child.

Hart: Might I try to make my point about conflict a little clearer? If I am right in thinking that institutions tend to conflict with one another, then the whole *rite de passage* problem is raised. The individual at some point is going to have to make the transition from one competing institution to another; he might leave home to go into the army, or leave home to go to school, or leave one profession to move over into another, or change his politics. But if institutions are competing and individuals move in their life history from where they're controlled by one institution to where they're controlled by another, then it seems to me that crisis is inherent in all of these situations and that raises the question of how crises of transition can best be handled. The *rite de passage* is a crude, primitive way of handling those transition points. Nobody's advocating that circumcision and subincision should be introduced into American society. But the implication for educators of all this old-fashioned type of anthropological stuff is, I think, to see what functions are performed by these primitive institutions and then contrast these functions with the corresponding functions in our culture and see how we handle them and how we might handle them better.

Mead: It's interesting in connection with the competing institutions that Steve's (Hart) talking about that the Soviet Union today is doing its level best to eliminate every sort of competition between institutions and to make absolutely certain that the schools and the trade unions and the Komsomols and the youth groups all say the same things all the time. The one institution that they haven't quite got into shape is the home, and the home is held responsible for everything that goes wrong—all the other agencies are responsible for everything that goes right. If a child doesn't do his lessons in school, the Komsomol goes to the trade union of the father, which bullies the father into helping the child to do lessons so he does his lessons well at school. This system is set up as an iron ring around the child, with every effort to prevent this kind of competition between different institutions.

There are two possibilities: Discontinuity between different age periods may provide the leverage for either desirable or undesirable change, and the competition among institutions may also be a point of leverage for change. It's a point of leverage that's being very heavily utilized by the Communists in China, for instance, where the family—in Frank Tannenbaum's terms—the family represented by clans of several hundred people—was the dominant institution, at the expense of the state. It was exceedingly dominant, and one of the things that the Communists have exploited has been the desire of the individual to pick his own wife and to have a wider community of interests between groups. In this case there was an overbalancing within a competitive set of institutions, and this was used as a point of change.

Hart: I think that raises a very interesting issue. The way I would formulate it would be to say that unless we recognize not only that competition between institutions exists but also that it's highly desirable to preserve that competition, we are heading for a monolithic society like Russia, rather than a pluralistic society. In other words, if you decide that competition between institutions is undesirable, then you're opening the door to wipe out that competition by coming out with essentially one dominant institution and the others eliminated. This is what the Russians are doing. So that leads us on to the old argument about pluralistic versus monolithic educational practices.

Mead: I think that one of the things we have to be very careful about here is this "either-or" position. There is the monolithic state; there is a pluralistic state or society with a variety of types of competition. Bali represents a third possibility of a completely different order, where you can't even talk about competition between institutions or about a totalitarian state, where the major premises of the society are built in a quite different way. And probably if we explored a series of other models as carefully, we'd find many other models. I think it's awfully important that we shouldn't be trapped into the position that the Communists have made every effort to trap the world into for the last twenty-five years, and that is that there are only two solutions to everything—"You're either this or you're that." One of the contributions that a pluralistic society ought to be able to make is a plurality of possible solutions or alternatives.

The Function of the Stranger

Keesing, Mead

Keesing: Could I broaden somewhat this concept of "the stranger"? I'm a little uncomfortable about the idea that the school necessarily has to produce a condition of strangeness and sacredness and so forth. There are further dimensions that appeal to me from certain field materials with which I am familiar. Take the case of the eldest son in an elite family within a society counting seniority as important. He may be taken at quite an early age and subjected to the continuity of quite a highly specialized training to develop the responsibility and authority role that will go with his status. In Hawaii, as I know from certain cases even up to modern times, the oldest son in an important family might be turned over immediately to the grandparents on the male side to be reared in this special way from the first, without any sudden break or shift at puberty. Here would be an exception, and I would suggest as an aside that probably in our own system of values everybody's son is a "chief's" son—that is, we treat our children as having that sort of a role. Now, I don't think just saying a stranger has to handle this training would be enough. I would like rather to broaden it out to say that our concern is with understanding in any given society what persons in what statuses take role responsibilities for cultural continuity and transmission. The grandparents in the Hawaiian case represent cultural transmitters on a generation basis, with a generation being skipped to provide maximum continuity. At certain stages in the child's education there would be expert attention to the arts of spear-throwing, dancing, etc. In other words, a variety of specialists would be brought in, comprising kinsmen and perhaps others. Then there would be the authority figures and sacred figures who would also bear in upon this child who is to carry heavy responsibilities later in these fields. In other words, it is not just "the stranger" in this case, but a number of cultural-continuity-role figures who are brought into action. I would not like the educators in the room to think that they have to be strangers, but rather specialists assigned to cultural-continuity roles along with other figures—perhaps authority figures, specialist figures, nurturing figures, kinship figures, and so on.

Mead: In a sense I emphasized the stranger more than Steve (Hart) did, so let me do a bit of taking back. I think that instead we can say that there's a certain amount of official halo, some sense of difference—I would originally have used the word "distantiation" but I've used it to two people who thought it was jargon, so I dropped it. Nevertheless, it is useful to see that in certain teaching situations a degree of formality, ceremonialism, distantiation, occurs. Now, I know I was very shocked—and I don't know whether I should have been shocked or not, this is intracultural shock— that my child wasn't a bit upset the first time she had her teacher home to dinner. I thought, in terms of my childhood, that having the teacher to dinner was an event; you worried about what you wore, you thought about whether you were going to show her your room—all sorts of things. And my child, coming out of a modern progressive school, thought her teacher was just somebody she knew and she treated her exactly like a member of the family. Now, I think the great usefulness about the point that Steve has presented is that it gives us a model for looking at the ways in which we handle this kind of situation—the degrees of distantiation, the extent to which teachers wear a mask, the degree of ceremonialism of the occasion. Do we want, for instance, the teacher to be always a teacher? Or do we want the teacher to be also a friend of a different sort out of hours, a companion, a picnicker, a shoulder to weep on, and a whole series of other things? Is blurring these roles a congenial answer for our particular culture? If we use this as a question from that point of view, not overdefined and overphrased, I think it will be useful.

Some Problems for Future Exploration

Quillen, Cowley, Hart, Siegel

Quillen: I've been trying to think of the meaning and significance of what we've been discussing tonight for American education. It seems to me that there are three kinds of problems that have been presented. One of them is: How do you meet the developing needs and provide continuing satisfaction for the young child and at the same time prepare him to assume the tasks of adult life? Because obviously the tasks of adults go beyond the tasks of the child. This is a problem in American education: Do you build education on the basis of children's needs alone, or on children's needs plus some kind of adult preparation in terms of contents, skills, and the like? Some people say that you don't need to pay any attention to children's needs at all, that you impose an adult pattern on the child. I don't think very many people support fully either of these two extremes at the present time. Most educators realize that there is a way of satisfying children's needs and at the same time providing for the development of the understandings, skills, values, etc., which are necessary for competence in adult life. But there are still a number of conflicting points of view.

The second thing that we've raised is also quite important, and that is the extent to which you can get reciprocal reinforcement of learning in the different institutions in which the child is having experience as he grows up; the extent to which you can get reciprocal reinforcement between the family, the school, the peer group, the political state, etc. A question that grows out of the question Steve (Hart) has posed is: Is full reciprocal reinforcement desirable? Would it lead to a totalitarian society? Don't you need some discontinuity, some competition, in order to maintain pluralism?

This leads to the third question, which is the relationship of co-operation and competition in education. Many people pose this as a dichotomy, but it seems to me to be a false dichotomy. I think that both co-operation and competition are important. Educators question whether or not it's necessary to have destructive competition. You can distinguish between constructive competition—which actually, in a sense, reinforces co-operation, and builds greater creativity—and destructive competition, which leads to the breakdown of personality. The extent to which we have either co-operation or competition or a blending of the two is, I think, a very important problem in education which has been posed in the anthropological material that has been presented tonight. These are the three types of problems that I think are important.

Cowley: It seems to me there's a fourth that needs to be discussed which comes out both in the paper and in Mr. Frank's discussion, and that's the place of ceremony in American education. What has the anthropologist to tell the American educator about the place of ceremony? My concern is with universities and colleges rather than with the schools, and it seems to me that people on this level ignore the fact largely that we perform a lot of ceremonial functions and that these functions have a great deal to do with the importance of the college in the life of the nation. Football is a ceremonial occasion to many people. The pattern of behavior between the halfbacks and all that goes on there is much more important to many people than the game itself. We have initiation ceremonies in fraternities; we have hazing enterprises, which are ceremonies of a sort; we have commencements in which the faculty put on multicolored millinery, etc. Now, we know relatively little about this as far as I know; I should like to know what help the anthropologist has to offer the educationist concerning ceremony as a function of social structures.

Hart: If I were an anthropologist from Mars who came down to study the American school system, when I wrote my monograph on my return to Mars I would say that the most important part of the American school system was the gymnasium or the athletic field because of the much greater amount of ritual and ceremonial I found there than I found, say, in the civics courses or in the library. I'd make a second comment too, and that is that Americans are under the impression that they have no ceremonies, that ceremonial is somehow something that goes with feudal societies or peasant societies or primitive societies, and are opposed to the building of ceremonials on constitutional grounds. That attitude ignores the fact that we do have all these ceremonies. We dislike where the ceremonies are now placed, but our problem is not how to develop them. Ceremonial has developed in America; our problem is how to place it in what some of us would regard as more important places.

Cowley: Well, first we need descriptive studies of them, as far as my level is concerned.

Siegel: I think we've been confusing two types of ceremonials or rituals, one being a kind of temporal ceremonial that occurs on exceedingly important occasions, the other being rites of passage, which occur at critical points in life crises. A proposition has been advanced by Ralph Linton that is worth testing further if we want to understand something of the functions of ceremonial and ritual, and that is simply that you will find the greatest elaboration of rites of passage at those points in the life cycle where there is, first of all, the greatest amount of new learning, and second, the highest degree of crisis; very important must be the fact that the ceremonies do involve presumably a considerable amount of new learning. He was making this proposition in trying to evaluate why we find in some societies a great elaboration of puberty ritual and a small elaboration, let's say, of marriage ritual, whereas in other societies we find quite the contrary. And I wondered if we might perhaps throw this out as a proposition for further comparative testing to see if it stands up at all as a usable hypothesis, to see whether ritual designates or symbolizes in any way critical points in participation going on in the new learning of the individual.

Section VI

DISCREPANCIES IN THE TEACHING OF AMERICAN CULTURE

DOROTHY LEE
Merrill-Palmer School

The study on which this paper is based was initiated in an attempt to discover what cultural values, concepts, and attitudes are presented to the growing generation in the school.[1] The subject matter included in the Home Economics program, and occasionally under Family Life Education, was chosen because this includes generally most of what anthropologists cover under the term culture. It is concerned with helping the student to develop a healthy personality through participation in human relations in the home and the community and to develop into a mature and healthy adult, who will establish a home where democratic, happy co-operative living will prevail. Skills and understandings and knowledge necessary for homemaking are taught under this program. Behavior at home and outside the home is discussed, as well as personal ethics, social intercourse, friendship, and marriage.

The study was made through an analysis of teachers' manuals and guides;[2] and early in the study it became apparent that often there was a wide discrepancy between the objectives of the program and their implementation. A similar discrepancy was present in the presentation of areas of culture, as, for example, between the skills of homemaking and the relations and values in homemaking, or between the self and society. The family of one's birth and the family to be made through marriage appeared to contain discontinuous values. Work and leisure, duty and fun, the given and the chosen were presented in an exclusive dualism of opposition.

It is these discrepancies which form the subject of this paper. I believe that none of them are intended, since sometimes the implementation runs counter to the explicitly stated objective, and sometimes what is presented is obviously at odds with the general principles of the manual. The discrepancies are there apparently as a result of the revolutionary change in the function of the Home Economics program, as well as of the enormity

[1] This paper is a by-product of a pilot study on American values and concepts made possible by a grant from the Humanities Division of the Rockefeller Foundation.
[2] The manuals and guides used for this study are referred to by code number. The list will be supplied by the author of this paper on request.

of the task it has undertaken. In the early part of the century, and often even in the mid-'thirties, Home Economics concerned itself only with the skills and operations of housekeeping. Home economics books, dealing with "home management" and "housewifery," referred to husband and children only by implication, as when they spoke of cleaning the "master bedroom" or when they spoke of the "children's room." Human relations, in the earlier books, were recognized only in the administration of maids. People trained in this subject matter were suddenly confronted with the need to include in their teaching material on personality development, community responsibility, personal ideals, human relations. The other element was already there; it was the basic core. To this was added the social, affective, value aspect of the home; and if there is discrepancy at present, it is because this new addition has not yet been fully incorporated.

In addition, Home Economics has now undertaken to teach not only a woman's skills but also a woman's role to the growing girl; and the courses in Family Life may teach the adult role to both boys and girls. In this era of social mobility and second-generation immigrants it has proved excessively difficult to avoid an implication of discontinuity between the student's present family and the one he hopes to make through marriage, between family values and the ones he is taught in school.

As *A Guide to Planning Units in Home Economics* states:

The success of the family is dependent upon spiritual values as well as material things. Attitudes and beliefs originate in the home. . . . *When home influences are not what they should be, the teacher has double responsibility.* [The italics are added.] [2]

Again, the school cannot guide a girl to learn to become a woman through sharing the life and work of her mother, even if the factor of social mobility did not make this difficult. In the main, the school itself makes it impossible to teach the student in this way. The girl is required by law to absent herself from the home during the time when the everyday work of the home is carried on. The mother, well taught, has learned to wash dishes, clean the house, make beds, bathe and sun the baby, market, and even start dinner, before the daughter returns from school. Homework—whether given to the student by way of involving the parents in her schooling, or by way of keeping her occupied and out of mischief, contributes to this cutting off from the life of the home. In rural areas where schools are consolidated, the child may be absent from home for ten or eleven hours daily. Clubs in the school encourage the student to further absent herself from the home and its life. In addition, technological progress, the new time-saving devices, the new theories of human relations and personality make it necessary for the girl to learn in school about the home, the family, and herself. As a textbook in common use puts it:

We cannot assume that we shall learn all that we need to know merely because we grew up in a family. We cannot afford to overlook that part of our school training which contributes to successful home living. . . . Home Economics gives us improved techniques for home living. . . . We need training in home-making if we are to be successful homemakers.

To make the study, I analyzed some fifteen state and city manuals and guides for the teaching of Home Economics or the related field of Family Life Education. One textbook used as basic in one of the programs was also analyzed. The manuals come from the West Coast, the Middle West, the Southwest, the South, the East; they were written for teachers in these areas, although the writers may come from other regions and may thus represent certain cultural variations. I have analyzed the latest manuals I could find from each region; these cover a span of nine years. Since this is a study of discrepancy in the manuals, and not an investigation of what is taught today, no attempt was made to find out exactly how the manuals are used, how much freedom of interpretation a teacher has in using them, and to what extent she is free to use them only as guides suggesting procedure.

The writers of these manuals have undertaken, to a large extent effectively, the enormous task of clarifying human relations in a society of unclear roles; of maintaining belief in the dignity of work in an era of mass production; of presenting the American way with simplicity and conviction to a generation coming from a variety of cultural, social, religious backgrounds. My paper gives no indication of the great extent of what has been already achieved. Again, in presenting the material, I suspect that I often pass judgment on what I find, instead of giving an objective statement of fact. If I do so, I am subject to the same criticism which I make of the manuals: I do not implement my objective adequately. My intention is to be merely descriptive, and to draw conclusions without bias. When I speak of externality as dominant, I intend this to be sheer statement of fact. If I state it with dismay, it is because, as a Greek by birth and rearing, I regard externality as deplorable. I give this autobiographical item, because I believe it may be a factor in my perception and selection, as well as in the tone of my presentation.

I

The discrepancy existing between theory and implementation, as well as between the areas of home living and of homemaking skills, is expressed variously in discontinuities and dualisms, which, though more pronounced in the older manuals, are still present to an extent in the newer ones. A discussion of family life and marriage from a course of study designed for high school, published in 1950, will illustrate this point. This course is offered because:

We are living now in a changing society. The family patterns and traditions of yesterday no longer hold true in the world of today. . . . Plainly, people do need help in understanding the real values of life; in appreciating the very real treasure of the family . . . they need help in preparing for marriage in order to live fully, richly, and satisfyingly. The justification for the teaching of courses in the schools in human relationships is found in that last sentence. [3]

The main objective of the course is stated as follows: "To promote the founding of . . . ideal homes. . . ." For this the individual needs a healthy personality; and the basic social needs for the personality are best met in the family unit. The family is of "immense importance in the emotional development" of the individual; therefore, the course includes units which are to help the student develop his personality through the human relations in the home. The lesson on Family Relationships has as its first objective to "help the student to understand the meaning of the cooperative, the sharing; the democratic home. . . ."

How is the student's home life actually to be used in helping him found an "ideal home"? In the lesson on Family Relationships there are three more objectives stated:

2. . . . To realize the purpose of restrictions.
3. . . . To realize his contribution to family conflict.
4. . . . To help the student know ways of improving family life, of reducing conflict.

And the name of the lesson has as subtitle: "Family Relationships: Conflicts—Ways of Improving."

The lesson apparently attempts here to teach its material in terms of specific problems to be solved, specific things to do. And the problematic material is characteristically negative: not something had, to be enjoyed, but something to be achieved or solved or ameliorated. To teach in terms of problems has long been considered an effective method; the problem delimits, makes concrete, clarifies. But in selecting this method the manual necessarily suggests the presentation of family life as negative, thus going counter to its avowed intention. Family life is presented as not good and there is no suggestion that the student is to be helped to indulge in it and be emotionally nourished. He is to relate himself to it in terms of adjusting to it, correcting its evils, improving it, rather than enjoying it. Home life is full of conflict and restriction. In this lesson, the question posed as: "Why do parents act as they do?" is spelled out as "Why do they 'always' say no?" The brother-sister relationship is covered in one question, "What can a boy or girl do about a 'pesky' sister or brother . . . ?" and under one subheading, "Sister-sister, brother-brother, brother-sister conflicts." This is the picture which the course presents of "the very real treasure of the family" which it is to help the student to appreciate.

In using his family experience to develop into an adult who can found an ideal home, the student is to be urged to learn "to get along." He is to recognize restriction, improve relations, resolve conflicts so that he can "get along" with others and himself. Of the six "immediate and specific objectives" given for the course, four are to help the student "to get along." It is a negative objective, satisfied with a minimum which lacks positive value; it does not go beyond the elimination of the undesirable. It is corrective rather than creative. The most dynamic and positive phrasing in which this "getting-along" sphere of human relations is expressed is represented by statements such as the following: "A substitute for that tried and true method of getting along—desire and effort—has never been found. . . . Try to attain the live-and-let-live attitude, and see . . . the achievement in maturity it will mean, even its relationship to preparation for marriage." This minimal phrasing of goals is certainly not what this course of study wants to convey to the growing generation as American culture.

The American ideal of the maximum is expressed only when speaking of the future, of the homes which the students themselves will establish with a chosen mate. This future family life is presented in positive value terms, full of creativity. In the one lesson on Family Relationships, the term "get along" occurs seven times; in the eight lessons on dating, courting, engagement, and marriage, it occurs, I think, only once. And what is impressive here is the large number of times when the "get along" attitude is absent, replaced by terms implying spontaneity and value (the italics throughout the following are added): "You *enjoy* the thought of being his wife." "You work out disagreements as they appear, for your relationship is more *important* than being right." "You are *willing to do personally anything* to make it [the marriage] succeed." "You are *willing and eager* to share with him in everything." Now the student is to be helped to establish an "ideal home" where happy family life is maintained, by being helped to develop emotionally and mature through experiencing human relations in his family. How can the meager and stingy soil of the "get-along" relationships bring forth anything so vital?

"Family living" in the present and "marriage" in the future also differ in the way "sharing" is presented. "To be willing to share" is one of the signs of maturity listed in the course, and sharing is mentioned often throughout the course; the student is to be helped to understand "the meaning of the cooperative, the sharing." However, only in the marriage relationship is it *sharing in*, as in the last quotation given. In the life which develops the attitudes that would make this possible, it is always a *sharing*. And sharing, without the *in*, is diminishing and dividing; it is concerned with fairness, atomistically pitting one individual against another. It is in this respect the opposite of *sharing in*, which enhances in the very act of sharing.

The writers of this guide, faced with the task of presenting good marriage, give a picture of a warm, positive, creative, agentive relationship, full of value and without utilitarianism. But in trying to show the student how to relate himself with his present family, they face a dilemma. They would like to show him how to find emotional nourishment, value, and security here. Yet often this is a situation in which he is not accorded an agentive role, where he has no opportunity to create; it is a given, and often for him its predominant quality is one of dissonance and conflict. So the solution is to guide the student in resolving this conflict, understanding the basis of the restrictions, "getting along" with the least possible friction.

As a result, the course suggests that creativity in human relations be taught through the medium of situations which allow only of correction, and a positive attitude, through relations which are phrased as negative and restrictive. It has to teach the American ideal of the maximum— "willing to do . . . anything," "eager to share in everything"—through experiences phrased as minimal.

This type of unresolved dualism is found generally between the given and the chosen, the areas of the *must do* and the *free to do*. The skills used in homemaking are presented as a *must*, to be recognized and accepted. For example, a textbook tells the student "We must have a working knowledge of nutrition. We must know what foods. . . . We must apply what we know. . . . [1]"

The following are stated objectives for the "Clothing Unit" in one of the manuals:

Recognition that some seams need no finish.
Recognition of order of work as important.
Recognition of effect of laundry and pressing on appearance.
Realization of need for fixing good habits.
Appreciation of need for good habits. [7]

This, like the family of one's birth, is in the area of the given, to which the student is to be led to adjust minimally and not necessarily with joy. There is no social value in this, there are no "good times." Value and freedom lie in the chosen, the leisure-time activity, the hobby, the special occasion (the italics are added):

Problem 4: *Discuss* values of remembering family birthdays, other *special* days.
Problem 5: Discuss the *problems* of brother-sister relations. [4]

The chosen is something that I *can* do (I am free to do or not do) rather than something I *should* do (I am not free not to do). For example we have (italics added), "What responsibility in my home *should* I share?" and, farther down in the same section, "How *can* I help my family *enjoy* leisure time? [8]"

It is in the area of the chosen that value lies. During leisure time, one is free to choose one's occupation; this then may contain "fun" or other value. Consequently, there is a dualism between work and leisure. The word "enjoy" is used rarely, if ever, in connection with the regular work or life of the home. In one manual I found it used only once, when "to enjoy work [3]" is given in a list as one of the characteristics of maturity. In one guide, which suggests courses, lessons, and units for six grades, the word "enjoy [9]" is used twice to my knowledge, both times in speaking of hobbies. This guide suggests that the unit entitled Food for Family Fun be correlated with the unit on Family Relations; a year-long unit called Food for Family Health precedes this, but no suggestion is made as to its being connected in any way with family relations. In another manual, only leisure occupations are called "enriching [5]"; and only in connection with leisure did I find the words "joy" and "satisfaction" used.

The one value, apart from "nutritional value," implemented through the teaching of the skills needed for routine work in homemaking is "the value of saving time and energy," or the "value of time and money management." And this value is negative, tending not toward deriving satisfaction from the process, but toward the opposite. It helps shorten the process, what has been called a "meaningful experience" in the list of objectives, but is actually presented as preoccupation with the meaningless. In doing their work girls are urged to "perform housekeeping duties using both old and new equipment; compare results of experiment as to time, energy, and efficiency [8]." Relative enjoyment is apparently not to be considered as a factor in the evaluation. The human relations differential between the mechanical dishwasher and the family dishpan is not discussed. What is important is that the *must* be diminished, leaving more time and energy for the chosen.

It is so important, in fact, to diminish this *must* of everyday living that many of the manuals urge the "sharing" of work not as a good and rewarding experience in itself, but as a means of increasing leisure time, particularly, of course, for the mother. In one manual, the objective of "sharing responsibility" is implemented as "sharing household duties to allow for leisure [10]." In another we read,

Appreciation of fact that sharing home tasks means some leisure time for all.
    Problem: Report on sharing care of rooms in homes and on sharing mother's special tasks.
    a. How mother used that extra free time.
    b. Good times made possible by working together. [7]

Another way to escape from the valueless given is to make a special occasion of what is otherwise a routine task, for example, to prepare a picnic instead of the usual lunch. Instead of following established procedure passively, the individual can, in this way, exercise initiative and spontaneity, and be agentive in creating the special.

In all the writing there is repeatedly this suggested escape from the routine to the special, from work to leisure, when the good is to be introduced:

Housekeeping is an important part of the spirit that makes a home. . . . The end product of effective housekeeping is comfortable living. Comfortable living affords time for leisure. . . . [1]

Being without value the work of ordinary home life is not dynamic and provides no emotional nourishment, no feedback. This, like all the good, comes through leisure:

Happy family life is essential to the welfare of individuals and nations as well. . . . Total health, mental and physical, has its foundations in the habits established in home living. . . . Recreation is doing things for fun. Out of fun comes relaxation and renewal of energy for all we must do.

It is in the special that social values lie, and through these are they implemented. The section on Thinking of Others, in the seventh-grade homemaking course given in one of the manuals, states the following objectives :

1. An interest in doing things for others.
2. To learn ways girls can do thoughtful things for others.

[These are implemented through the following means :]
1. Events that call for special thoughtful attention to others.
2. Ways of remembering special times.
3. Simple refreshments for an "afternoon at home."
4. Decorations and favors for special occasions. [4]

The list continues through eleven objectives all dealing with the special. Another manual teaches "consideration for others and willingness to compromise," entirely through the problem, "Sharing facilities for entertainment : 1. Radio, 2. Other entertainment [7]." In one high-school course "Good Citizenship" is presented as "positively practiced [5]" only during one's leisure.

Family feeling, unity, loyalty, come through sharing occasions of fun. "The strong feeling of love and respect in a modern family is the result of playing together more often than working together," according to one textbook.

The greatest satisfaction is derived from the companionship of the people who live there [the family] and the pleasures they enjoy together. . . . It would be wise to adopt the slogan: "The family . . . that plays together stays together. . . . Good times shared by the family group result in a better understanding of each other and therefore promote family unity. [1]

At no time are the operations involved in everyday homemaking presented as areas where spontaneity might be given range. Initiative and creativity are listed, in one manual, only in the section on Fun with the Family, under the subtitle "Cultivating Hobbies [10]." In another manual, there is a leisure-time unit listed under "Clothing [7]" and only here is the development of originality mentioned.

"Work can be fun" but only in the context of the "special," or when one adds fun to it externally ; in itself, it contains no good. The manual suggests that the family "hang a bulletin board over the sink and put jokes and messages on it ; discuss plans together. This will add fun to the job of family dishwashing [7]." The work of homemaking will further be made bearable if you plan carefully so that it can be made as brief as possible and can thus give you leisure for creativity, fun, and the exercise of co-operation, consideration for others, and allied social traits. Working with others is good, because the work can then be completed faster. Working for others is drab, but you can adorn it with special acts of your own choice and initiative. Everyday life is grim because it is the given, and value lies only in private freedom of choice ; but you can always escape from routine work into the freedom of the special if you master your skills and learn to plan wisely.

The last manual, quoted above, states that one of its general objectives is "to develop an appreciation of homemaking as a valuable and enjoyable occupation." But it finds it impossible to show how homemaking in itself can be valuable. It attempts to teach "the value of a plan providing for . . . cleaning in which responsibilities are shared. . . ." One must "understand . . . the value of planning one's work" and the "value of planning for the care of the house." I think these are the only occasions when the word "value" is used. Several times the word "enjoy" is used, all except one in connection with leisure-time "Fun with the Family," as might be expected from the slogan quoted above. The exception is a "special" occasion, when girls were urged to prepare Sunday breakfast as a "surprise for daddy" and to "give mother a chance to stay in bed an extra half-hour [10]." The girls reported that they "enjoyed" this.

II

One reason why there is no value in the given operations of everyday homemaking is that the dualism between social relations and socially oriented operations is still unresolved, although much progress has been made since the two (family life and housework) have been put together under one program. There is an explicit attempt to merge the two, but so far it has not been entirely successful. "Both [skills and arts] are interwoven into what we mean by homemaking"; yet nowhere are housekeeping skills and operations presented as implementing the making of a home, which is "an emotional climate . . . [where] we are loved and wanted for ourselves. We find security and safety." Social value, warmth, love, human relations, or the inculcating of attitudes and values in the young child are not yet presented as implemented through any of the operations of housekeeping. One manual states the following in its introduction:

Learning to live, to share, to work and play together through wholesome and meaningful experiences in home and school living develops attitudes, abilities, appreciation and a sense of values essential for a democratic society. . . . The primary purposes [of Home Economics education] are satisfaction and efficiency in home living . . . [4]

The manual then proceeds to describe a unit on Family Meals for eighth-grade students. In this section the girl is taught what is appropriate kitchen dress, what are the nutritional needs of an individual, and how to save time, have an orderly kitchen, judge the results of her work, serve attractively, and select recipes. No "learning to live, to share, to work . . . together through . . . meaningful experiences" here: there is "efficiency," but no "satisfaction." The girl is "helping with the family meals," but the helped does not appear at all. She is asked to "serve family style"; but apart from these two instances, the "family" is not present or implied in any of the activities except when a girl is urged to "help younger brother or sister with eating habits." In all the manuals examined, home living as presented lacks value when proceeding on its usual way. For example, one brings up the subject under the following title: "Some Understanding of Factors Which Affect the Family: Friction and Strain in the Modern Family [7]."

The home economists are well aware of the need of introducing value into their picture of family living and homemaking. They speak of family values in their general statements. Out of twenty-four subjects suggested for discussion in one manual, two mention value:

Suggest round table discussion on: What values families cherish and how some values persist and others are modified as families grow up. . . . Find out how children and youth contribute to family's cash income. List values gained by such contributions.

Yet the very nature of the situation, the teaching of home life away from its context of social warmth, so far has presented an insuperable obstacle. When skills and attitudes are taken directly from the mother, while the child participates in her life, they contain the value of the social context. But Home Economics is given the task of adding value, human relations, and ethics of everyday living, to mechanically defined skills taught within the context of the sterile Home Economics laboratory. And even when the laboratory is a house or an apartment, it is one in which there is no pulsing life, where no one loves and grieves and rages, where none of the significant work of living is carried on. There is no continuity of daily living here; the acts performed fulfill no function apart from that of the teaching of an operation. Here we may find muffins baked at 1 :00, to be consumed by girls replete with lunch at 1 :35, because they have to learn not to waste food. The very situation demands that value be added afterward, externally, necessarily through the special. And when the skills and operations are discussed in their family context, this extraneous view of value persists, as it has been so firmly established.

What is striking here is that the consistent characteristic of the value-less, which apparently accounts for its lack of meaning, is that it is the *given*. All that the girl can do with the given in family relations is to improve them, adjust to them, correct them so as to make them bearable; or she can use them as an exercise in human relationship, by way of developing her personality. They are not nourishing in themselves or to be enjoyed for themselves. And she is not expected to find a creative role within the given. One manual mentions as one of its general objectives "helping the student appreciate freedom within the law [3]." But, as a matter of fact, nowhere here or in any of the manuals and textbooks examined is this objective carried out. It is never suggested that the student be given guidance in finding freedom *within* the law, the given relations, the routine of homemaking. To be free, to be creative, to exercise initiative and originality, to enjoy spontaneously, she is to be invited to escape into the chosen: into leisure-time activities, into the special occasion, the nonpatterned Sunday supper, the birthday party, the picnic, and away from the family of her birth into the chosen relationship of marriage. And here, also, it is only the relationship as wife which contains freedom and spontaneity; the mother's life then reverts to the routine procedures of the must.

III

Another dualism implicit in the manuals is that between self and society. The student is urged to develop herself by acquiring and developing, in the main, traits which meet with the approval of others: to achieve "a pleasing voice, a pleasant expression [5]," to find an answer to the question, "How can I be popular with others? [4]" This means that standards and criteria for personality and conduct are to be sought outside the self. The emphasis seems to be on the development of the "other-directed," to use Riesman's term. One manual lists a unit which "might be called personality and good grooming [7]"; and, in general, personality is defined largely in terms of manners, grooming, and adherence to accepted conduct:

Personality Development. Objectives: Desire and ability to know and use approved social customs and good manners. Make and keep friends. Possess good personality traits. Problems:

a. Get along with people by having good manners.
b. How to develop good manners at home.
c. Careful grooming to make you pleasing at first sight.
d, e, f, g, h deal with being a good guest and a good hostess and having a good voice.
i. How to be popular, and make and keep friends. Five points listed under this deal with good manners, two with dating procedures, five with how to behave in public. [4]

Such a person, who has good manners and behaves acceptably on social occasions, has "the ability to get along with people [which] not only increases your chances of having a good time but also contributes to success in every phase of living [4]." Another manual lists

General Objectives: [of unit which "might be called personality and good grooming."]
1. Realization of the importance of good personal appearance and the development of a good personality for successful living.
2. Knowledge of how to behave in a socially acceptable manner. [7]

One manual lists seven objectives for the unit which helps the individual in personality development. Of these, two are:

1. Understands the importance of knowing current customs.
2. Practices some ways of acting which are socially accepted. [6]

Another manual states as one of its objectives "Appreciation of and a desire for a pleasing personality." A "pleasing" personality is not necessarily good, or strong, or mature, or relaxed, one which satisfies an internal standard; it is an externally directed one, which succeeds when it pleases another. This stress on the teaching of good grooming and acceptable manners comes, to some extent, in response to a felt need and reflects the social mobility of this society; it will probably remain, even after the disparity between a good personality and a pleasing personality has been overcome.

There is another way in which society is presented as external to the self: it is to be used for the meeting of the needs of the self. A unit for the eighth grade, entitled "Being a Likeable Person in Your Own Home," states as one of its objectives the teaching of the student to look "for ways in which family life contributes to success." In the same manual, in a unit for the ninth grade, entitled "Feeling Successful in High School Years," the students are to become aware of "ways in which school and community are contributing to their success [6]." In another manual, relationships within the family, "contacts," and "cooperation" are urged on the student for the development of a "truly effective personality [5]." Consistent with this conception of the self, as external to society, a course is divided into sections on: *helping myself*, and *helping others*.

IV

The goals and values of the self are also phrased in terms of externality. Its qualities and traits are spoken of as possessed and acquired. Time and energy and even habits are mentioned as "managed" or "used" by the self. One manual states as its first objective

Ability to use wisely available human and material resources such as time, energy, health, money, attitudes, and understandings. [8]

It follows that the self, as presented here, is not an internally growing unit, but one which increases through accretion, so that personal development is a matter of "acquiring desirable traits."

In one manual, the unit on "Growing Up" lists the following among seventeen "needs and interests" (italics are added):

To *better* understand one's self and others.
Make *more* of own decisions.
Buy *more* of own things.
Assume *more* responsibility for behavior.
Find ways to *improve* personality.
Be *more* popular. [10]

Much of this is, of course, abetted by a language which makes it extremely difficult to refer to growth and development except in terms of accretion, increase, and improvement. Thus even emotional maturity itself may be phrased as external, a goal to be achieved, not a becoming. One manual which uses the phrase, "the child *grows into* [italics added] adult situations," nevertheless presents maturity as "a goal that pays the highest dividends." It speaks of the individual who "pays too high a price for the security he gains by withdrawal or by aggression," thus giving the impression that security, also, is something external to be bought at a price. Continuing this phrasing of externality it tells how some individuals maintain a discrepancy between the goals they set for themselves and "the energy they are willing to expend." An individual who has "a sense of values" knows that "there is a price to pay and is willing to pay for value received [11]."

The self is clearly conceived as external to its life process when we come to the discussion of planning. Managing the time and energy of the self by planning one's work is presented as one of the main objectives in a variety of areas. Out of forty-eight "behavior changes sought" through the unit on "Clothing" in one manual, seven mention "planning and the management of time [9]." In another manual, out of five objectives to be met in four to six weeks of teaching, one is "learn to save time [4]." In a unit on "Foods for Special Occasions," covering two pages, a manual mentions "plan" eighteen times and "time management" three: "Plan work efficiently, and manage time well" . . . "the value of planning" . . . "plan and carry out" . . . "plan time schedules" . . . "plan market order [7]" . . . and so forth. "Careful planning helps make the task easier," states another manual; *Value of Planning Care of the House*: 1. Saving time; 2. Saving energy [10]."

In general, planning is taught in connection with the given, the required work. Here there is to be no wasted motion or wasted time; no exploring and no randomness of operation. Time saved from this area is time for leisure and fun; energy saved means energy for leisure-time activity, and this may be used for exploring. One manual, however, carries planning into the chosen: leisure time itself can be planned and managed to the advantage of the self. A student can use leisure time to earn money, for example, and, in this way, meet three objectives:

1. Realization that what she does today is important to tomorrow's success.
2. Realization that success in the school, home, and community are related.
3. Finding out what are opportunities for part-time jobs.

The student is told, in effect, that if she wants to succeed tomorrow she should plan carefully so that even the leisure time of today may contribute toward this end. This manual quotes students' reports on how their free time was used, and lists some of the answers giving "satisfactory" ways (italics added):

Drove out in the country *in order to see the sunset.*
Read a book that *has been recommended.*
Did some typing for a neighbor for pay to build up a fund *for a definite purpose.*

No random driving in the country, nor exploring in lanes, no exploring in the realm of books, no building up a fund and then discovering something to spend it on. No exploration, no adventure is quoted as desirable, even in this "free" time. Time is "wasted" when one is "daydreaming instead of attending to the present"; when "one talks idly for long times." It is "not wasted" when "talking idly to someone in order to be better acquainted." Yet when does one discover that one wants to be better acquainted? Planning beforehand would save time, as "knowing what radio program you would like to listen to and when they come." Yet how does one discover the unknown and unpredictable?

V

The discrepancies, discontinuities, and unresolved dualisms listed in this paper are implicit in a program which is the result of accretion. The program is in constant process of revision and integration; when it becomes a unit some of these discrepancies will probably disappear. Others, however, are inherent in the very structure of a mobile society and in a culture which values change. It is possible, then, that in presenting the adult role in terms of discontinuity and exclusive dualism the writings examined here are merely faithfully presenting American culture.

FIFTH SESSION OF THE CONFERENCE

Chairman: Felix M. Keesing

Editor's note: Dr. Lee has revised the original paper submitted to the conference to the extent of adding an introductory statement on the research context, and attempting to eliminate what appeared to her, in retrospect, to be value judgments projected out of her Greek cultural background. In making this revision she incorporated certain suggestions by the two discussants, Dr. Mead and Dr. Shaftel.

Discussant: Margaret Mead

Mead: The written paper as it was distributed lacked the relevant cross-cultural context—of course all of us know that Dorothy Lee is a Greek; that is, the anthropologists knew it, and she has been accustomed to presenting material to us which we would read, putting Greekness in. This has been so, especially in the light of the study that she did on Greece for the UNESCO manual on "Culture Patterns and Technical Change" in which she looked at Greek culture from an anthropological view. The whole question for the educator is how we're going to handle this order of statement, which even if it is placed in a context (if Dr. Lee had either ironed her Greekness out of it or had put in a comparable cross-cultural setting, had discussed what a Greek, or a French, German, or English manual on home economics would say) would still raise quite serious questions in communication. That is, is this an order of analysis that educators find either congenial or useful? Now it *is* an order of analysis that the anthropologists use.

When I went to work on the question of food habits at the beginning of the war, my problem was to discover what anthropologists could offer to the nutrition program. I conceived it as necessary to find out what nutritionists were, who they were, what their version of our culture is—what some anthropologists would call their subculture. We fortunately had about a hundred very detailed case studies done by an education committee with psychological consultants on students of home economics, and I studied those case histories very carefully. I studied home economics pronouncements; I studied the principal home economists in Washington; I went to conferences and argued with them to see what they would and would not do; I studied age-grading within the home economics field, the documents that they produced and the procedures they use in the classroom. And I expected to come out with the value system of home economics, as approached by an anthropologist. I was primarily interested in nutrition, whereas Dorothy Lee's interest has been wider here.

From this piece of research we came out with such formulations as that one of the basic attitudes toward nutrition found among home economists was that shared by Northeast and Middle-Western culture in their attitudes toward food, which, summed up very briefly, is "If you eat enough food that is good for you but not good, you can eat a little that is good and not good for you." Furthermore we found that the entire profession had a simple type of moralistic bias, which meant that while you were learning to eat the right things you ought to be a little bit miserable and you ought to be doing it on purpose. They were very much opposed to any device that might have been invented by a social engineer so that you took salad without saying, "I ought to be taking it." We found that to set up eating situations so that people would just pleasantly and easily eat the right foods was unacceptable. The most we could do was to suggest that you say to people, "You ought to eat the right food" or "You ought to eat scientifically" instead of "You ought to eat carrots."

And in the course of this sort of investigation, I noticed the same sort of thing that Dorothy Lee did. For instance, I looked at model kitchens which had been designed as demonstrations for high-school-age girls and also for members of the community (older women who were to come in and learn how to do things). There was no place for the baby in the kitchen anywhere. I then would ask where the baby went and was told that "family life" was not fully represented in the Department of Agriculture—which is the reason there wasn't any place for the baby.

Now this is one way at least in which an anthropologist will go at this sort of material. That is, we look at a specialized form of education— whether it's agriculture or home economics or manual training in the schools—and we will look at who does it, where they came from, how they're trained, how they're selected, what their history is, what their value system is, and then what happens to them in the community. For example, one of the other things we did was to see what happens to the different kinds of home economists. There's a lot of home economics folklore—like "the blue eyes stay in the classroom"—which sums up a great many points. In this instance you had all through the 'twenties and early 'thirties certain kinds of pretty-prettiness about home decoration in which blue was the principal color; that got transferred to the eyes of the home economists. There is also a group of home economics women in business, the "*Hi-wibs*," who are strained off from home economics teaching; they're believed to be smarter—even slicker, perhaps cynical—so the group breaks in the middle, and on the whole the people with the simpler, less mobile point of view stay in the classroom and do the solid teaching. Another group—the ones who like to wear white coats and use slide rules and deal with life scientifically—become the hospital dietitians.

These are the kinds of things that we would mean by trying to fit something into the whole culture, and I might say that Dorothy Lee has done special studies of this type and had them as background when she wrote this paper. This paper made quite a lot of people very angry for different reasons—partly by accident, because Dorothy (Lee) presented just this short section of a larger operation. This was an accident but it became a good focusing device for some of the statements that anthropologists generalize from a little bit of something. This particular little bit is placed in the whole society, in the history of home economics, in the history of kitchen designs, in the history of home management, in the history of how family life came in—as any little bit can be. And yet I think even if an introduction of the sort that I've made were about five times as long, there would still be very sharp objections of some sort to this level of analysis of the cultural premises that are implicit in this material. I think it's important that these objections should be made. This should be a case study, if possible, in communication, and what I've said should not be regarded as a form of disarming criticism but a way of raising the problem.

Discussant: Fannie Shaftel

Shaftel: This paper has a different tone than the other papers presented here, from the point of view of a method of anthropology. It seems to me that it has a normative tone which up to now you people said you were not going to put into your work as anthropologists. I raise this simply as a question—I'm not saying this should *not* happen. Perhaps this is something we ought to talk about. Which will be of most service to education, an anthropologist becoming evaluative in terms of some kind of conception of what ought to be, or an anthropologist describing to us what we do so that we can see ourselves better, because sometimes it's hard to see yourself in this picture?

Now I think that some of the things that have been said about the history of home economics I would like to say again from an educational point of view. One has to remember that the home economics teacher was a "cooking" and "sewing" teacher until very recently. Her major emphasis was on "how to do" certain kinds of skills. Furthermore, this teacher was focused on the "how to do," in an educational system that is essentially moralistic, and upon improvement in terms of a rapidly changing and upward-mobile society. Thus the focus in home economics classes has always been on how to learn to do more nicely, more acceptably, so that you can improve your status in life. And this, I think, is reflected in Dorothy Lee's study and is demonstrated in most of the material which you see in the home economics textbooks.

I think we ought to remind ourselves that the school has been taking upon itself more and more functions which once belonged to other institutions in our culture, and that as women began to go out of the home to work and society became more urbanized, we in school have undertaken to bridge the gap between what once was and what we think might be in the way of family living. We begin to add more things to our curriculum that once were done in the home. As we move from a producer family unit, in which the child has a very real role, to a situation wherein most of our urban-living children have bystander roles and do not have any really creative participation in the basic life activities of the family, the school has tried to act as a supplementary agency. We have asked this cooking and sewing teacher to begin to work and talk in new dimensions; that is, to begin to restate the dimensions of family living in a new kind of society because what was ten years ago is quite different now. If you live in California you can go out and see entire communities that didn't exist three months ago; and you see people who've never lived in homes that had two and three bedrooms suddenly arriving at an economic status which enables them to move into a way of living they've never had before and now have to learn how to use.

Mead: Fannie (Shaftel), at this moment are you making an educational statement? It seems to me—this is just for purposes of our understanding—that you are making a descriptive statement that might have been made by any anthropologist or sociologist looking at the situation. You said when you started that you wanted to restate this from the educator's point of view; it seemed to me that the point where you said cooking and sewing were "how to do" was an educator's statement. From then on it seemed to me that you were making descriptive statements that might have been made by an economist or political scientist, or any trained person. What's *educational* about what you're saying right now?

Shaftel: What I was going to say is that all of a sudden we're asking the teacher of cooking and sewing to understand these new conditions and to take up a new role and a new function, which is teaching about what the family is and what is happening to the family and new skills for living, in a family that has new dimensions. Presumably this cooking and sewing teacher does not have the educational preparation or background to do this, and we educators come forth with in-service education courses and workshops, or we send her back to summer school and bring consultants in to try to give this cooking and sewing teacher some understanding of her new role. While progress is being made, the lag between training and expectation is often reflected in situations such as this one: We have nursery schools attached to some of our teacher-training institutions and some of our senior high schools and junior colleges. You will hear consultants say, "Don't go to that nursery school; it resides under the authority of the home economics teacher." They mean that the program you will find there is quite different from the one that is under the guidance of the psychology department, because you have an entirely different approach to child care with the teacher who has the older orientation as compared with the one who has had mental hygiene training, a child development point of view, as part of her general professional background.

I say this simply as an explanation of why we find some of the things we do find in home economics programs. Another thing we have to consider, I think, is that probably the cooking and sewing teacher is far more oriented to middle-class values than some other teachers—that is, she conceives as her function the teaching of these middle-class values. And when we have 63 percent of our children coming from lower-class homes she sees her function as that of teaching them how to get along and get by and improve themselves by acquiring the ways of behavior, the appearances, and the manners of the middle class. This is reflected in the material that Dorothy (Lee) has analyzed for us.

I'd like to make a few more comments. At any one time when you examine courses of study in the American school system you are examining something that probably is no longer completely applicable to the situation, because by the time it gets into print and is used, the schools are already changing their practices at the policy level. This is one of our problems: that our printed material is always obsolete in terms of our stated objectives and of our attempts to move ahead, because education is in movement all the time, changing all the time. In order to understand what is happening in home economics classes in relation to family life education, you would have to take many samples directly from classrooms as well as to look at printed material. Would it not have been good practice to interview some home economics teachers?

In public schools in America you can find anything and everything in the way of practices. We have schools that train teachers to teach with one year of normal school beyond high school; we have schools that require five years beyond high school. We have states that keep children in school until sixteen years of age, and others that do not. And within that range we have a great variety of practices, so you cannot talk about "the" home economics program when you are talking about American education. You can see everything from practices which are very experimental and very creative to practices which are very unimaginative and routine.

Perhaps one of the areas in which the anthropologist can give help to the educator is in thinking about a mass education movement in a mass society, where you are dealing with thousands of teachers and hundreds of thousands of children in many, many schools, and where the attempt to raise the level of planning and performance on the part of teachers often results in standardization. This may seem like a contradiction to my previous statement that we have many, many practices, but as I look at elementary schools in this country I think that especially in urban areas, as we try to analyze what we are doing and to make proposals for improvement, we are decreasing the diversity and increasing the standardization. The attempt at improvement has certain boomerang effects, from my point of view. This means that, to a certain extent, in the attempt to raise the poorer teachers up to a better level you are denying to many teachers the opportunity for creativity and the encouragement of interesting and delightful and new things which Dorothy (Lee) is asking for in her paper. And I find increasingly that experienced teachers in the field say to me when we discuss proposals for doing this kind of thing, "They don't let you do it; it isn't in the course of study; it isn't in the state framework; we aren't allowed to make these kinds of decisions."

It would be interesting to have the anthropologist help us to look at this kind of phenomenon. All the kitchens in all the home economics classes look alike, and they all are in terms of a middle-class kitchen and they are not in terms of the variety of ways in which families live and could live in America. Some of us have tried to tackle this when we take a little community like Oxnard (in southern California), which has a heavy Mexican-American population living in shanties, and try to think in terms of kinds of family living that could go on in better, more interesting, more imaginative dimensions within the realities of that situation. Hilda (Taba) in her work is demonstrating a reality-centered approach to this kind of thing that is positive in the sense in which Dorothy is asking for a positive approach to family living.

Dorothy talks somewhat critically about the discontinuity between what the girl experiences living in her own home and what she is taught in school *ought to be* in the family home she is going to create in the future. I'd like to raise the question, in the light of last night's discussion, that perhaps this is a necessary and even a good discontinuity in the light of the rapidly changing conditions of living in a technological society. Perhaps the best preparation for living in the home you are going to create as a young woman is *not* to learn it the way your mother did.

Finally, may I just say this: I wonder if Dorothy is right in being critical of the problem approach to family living for children in our culture. Teen-agers do view their situation as a problem situation and when you look at the kinds of things that teen-agers would like to have help in, it is "How can I get along better with my brothers and sisters? What do I do when my father says I must do it one way but all the kids I run around with do it another way?" When teachers really work with the concerns of teen-agers, they often get such questions as "How can I manage my situation when I am torn in so many different directions?" and I think that, increasingly, as we move into the mental hygiene movement, teachers see themselves as mediators between the child and the various institutions which impinge upon him in our kind of society. We are beginning to do some rather creative things, some very exciting things, in helping youngsters to understand and relate themselves to a number of different institutions in their culture in such ways that they can live with them in positive terms rather than in terms of anxiety or hostility. And I would, from this point of view, defend the problem approach to family living as perhaps a necessity in the kind of society in which teen-agers are growing up today.

Keesing: Would you like to reply, Dorothy (Lee), before we open the topic for discussion?

Lee: I tried to make it clear, but I realize that I didn't make it clear enough, that all I'm talking about is what I've seen that these manuals are saying. I have studied the teaching of these manuals as part of a larger study in home economics today, and I'm not saying here that this is a conclusive statement.

Second, about the fact that they become obsolete—two of the manuals I studied covered a number of years: they started out in a certain year and then they were changed through the years. For example, a unit was added on more problems and so on, but the manual itself was not changed. One manual was reissued about two months before I studied it; I had read it in an earlier version, I think published in 1948, and there was one fundamental change which I would like to mention here. In the earlier issue, it listed the objectives that were going to be met through the teaching of cooking. Among the objectives were No. 4—if I remember—which was the teaching of co-operation through cooking, and No. 11, which was the teaching that work can be fun, through the cooking procedure. Then it gave a large number of experiences to which to expose the student, and with every experience it told which objectives were to be met. Objectives 4 and 11 were met only through special occasions: the school picnic, the tea which you suddenly decided to have. The students were urged to read *Little Women* and discover how objectives 4 and 11 were met through a very special picnic that those girls had. In the 1953 edition, the same objectives were to be met by the same experiences but it does not list which objectives were met by each, and that is all to the good. It did not limit 4 and 11 to the special occasion. On the other hand, this is the manual which completely reprinted its section on leisure time, which must be used in such a way that every minute should count toward future success.

One more thing I want to say is informative. When I said that I got manuals from different regions I meant not that the manual itself expressed regional differences, but that it told me what each region officially offered its teachers as a guide. On looking through the list of people who wrote the manuals I found that in one case the manual was the result of a summer workshop which was under the leadership (this was a Southern manual) of one or two women, I think, from Philadelphia. Another manual in the Middle West had been written under the direction of a woman who was from Florida, and so on, so that I think the writers probably represent the country at large, and not the specific regions to which the manuals are addressed.

I want to thank both of you for a number of suggestions you made to move me forward in this paper.

OPEN DISCUSSION

Preliminary Considerations

Quillen, Gillin, Frank

Quillen: What I want to say has been said already in part, but I would like to underline it because I think it's very important from a methodological point of view. It would have been very important—you mentioned this yourself, Dorothy (Lee), but I'm just re-emphasizing it—for you to indicate what manuals you used, who wrote them, and the dates they were produced, for the reason that out of the hundreds and perhaps thousands of documents about home economics in the United States you selected fifteen, and you selected only one textbook. The textbook is probably a better indication of content than the manual in terms of what actually goes on in the classroom; but we have no way of judging here the quality of the person who wrote that textbook, when it was prepared, the extent to which it's used, etc., so that I think it's very important to have the documentation available.

The next point is in terms of the narrowness of the approach. I believe a social scientist is always normative; I don't think you can completely separate descriptive social science from normative and judgmental. But I do think it's very important for the social scientist to present a well-rounded picture of the descriptive material upon which he bases his normative judgment. I get the impression in this paper that you had a point of view partially formed, and then you examined the manuals and what you saw in them confirmed your point of view. Then when you wrote the paper, what you seem to have done was to select those things that supported your point of view, and included very little else. And not only that, but you have little parenthetical statements at appropriate points to make sure that no one misses your point of view.

In talking about education you at least should indicate that what you're giving is not the total context of the school situation. Now, take the matter of family living in the school. Home economics in most of our schools is for girls only; a few schools are including boys, but very few. In many schools home economics is not even required, although in most schools it is required of girls; consequently, the typical school does not depend on the home economics program to develop these values which interest you in the area of family living. That's done primarily in two areas in the public schools: first in the guidance program, which is becoming increasingly important and in which a lot of time is spent working on the positive development of human relations in the present family and future family living. The second part of the school program, throughout the United States, which emphasizes the improvement and enrichment of the values of family living, is the social studies program. If you go to the social studies textbooks and the social studies manuals, you will find a very positive interpretation of family life, although you could pick out from those materials many of the things that you've picked out here.

Gillin: I didn't think that in presenting this paper you had to read it as if it were written from the normative point of view. It seems to me that the normative content here has been injected to some extent by ourselves. For example, "joy" and "creativity" are loaded words. If this is true of what happens in the home economics classes in some communities, it is quite consistent with some of the basic themes in our culture. Work is work and fun is fun: let's do the dishes fast and get out to the bridge club (this is for the woman); the man thinks it's nice to get done with his daily occupation and get some golf in. School itself is unpleasant; you try to get through with school so you can get out on the athletic field. If that's the way our culture is, of course we have a perfect right to say that isn't good, that we ought to change it some way or another. But if these home economics classes are preparing girls to live in the culture that is, it seems to me that they're doing a pretty good job.

Frank: Listening to this discussion and having read the paper has aroused a number of suggestions and speculations in my mind, that might have some relevance to our larger theme of education and anthropology. In the first place, I want to raise the point of the difficulties of trying to inductively derive what are the values and goals in education from American textbooks and manuals, and home economics is a very good example. That is, the home economists had to follow the established textbook and curriculum pattern that utilizes an analytic fractionation of content and skills—you see the same thing lately in child development textbooks, where the textbook takes up physical development, mental development, language development; you see it in social studies. The curriculum makers have set up the thing in these particular kinds of units, and a series of objectives and goals which had to be achieved so that they could be tested and evaluated. To a large extent, unless you're aware of that, the documents produced look like spontaneous valuational statements, whereas they may be largely distorted in order to fit into what the educational authorities have demanded from textbook writers.

You see there's a learning theory involved here. The curriculum people have a theory that the only way children learn is bit by bit, just as we used to teach reading. This atomizing process, this movement toward a content approach, ignores very largely the need for a conceptual organization within which the content can be fitted. From the various units we rely upon the achievement of what you might call inductive generalizations, which may or may not be accompanied by a conceptual clarification.

Another point I would like to mention is that large parts of what have been historically and traditionally women's responsibilities—homemaking, child care and rearing—have been socially devaluated. Relevant here from the educational viewpoint is that if we're going to have anything that can be called preventive medicine or health care, it's not going to be done by doctors or nurses. The family as a primary agent of health care must practice preventive medicine to improve nutrition, to keep up vigorous activity, to protect against contamination and infection. This means dishwashing, laundry, housekeeping, the care of minor ills and so on have to be done *in the family*; there's no other agency that can do it. The same thing is true about the whole concept of mental health for developing healthy personalities. Psychiatrists, social workers, clinical psychologists can't do it; it has to be done in the home, the primary agent of mental health, through providing the kind of child care and rearing and interpersonal relationships which foster the healthy personalities we're concerned with. Now to the extent to which women's roles and functions are involved in this, it may very well be that if we are going to have an effective program of preventive medicine and mental health, somehow or other we've got to reinvest these practices with a value and a significance that quite transcend the skills involved. And I think that's just what we're trying to do in education at the present time, to see that they have a larger significance and are not just a matter of homemaking. It seems to me that anthropology as well as psychology may find some very useful lessons in what happened in home economics. And they can see in home economics, as well as in such areas as family living, physical and mental health— all these new areas that haven't become crystallized, that haven't a traditional content—the most fruitful opportunities to begin to infuse new ways of thinking as well as some of the concepts that are coming from psychology and from anthropology. We must avoid setting up little units in curricula and manuals—all these things that are fractionative and which destroy the very thing we're trying to do. And I believe that that's a very real responsibility of the schools of education, where so much of the pattern of curriculum-making is being determined. If the schools impose a conception of learning which says you only learn units bit by bit, and you have to test, time, and so on, then you're going to have curriculum textbooks and teaching that follow that pattern, for these are the markers of the channel of educational change. Now the thing that I am very much concerned about is, can we see ways in which we can communicate something to the home economists that will infuse their teachings? They're now established, they're supported by a state law, they've got incomes, they've got position and status; let's see how we can help them to be more fruitful in this whole situation, and do it in such a fashion that they won't become defensive.

Should the Anthropologist Make Value Judgments?

Thomas, Hart, Mead, Brameld, Lee, Keesing, Taba

Thomas: One of the troubles of lining up four or five to get a chance to speak is a certain discontinuity, so that my remarks are stimulated not by what Mr. Frank has said, but what was said four or five persons ago. So if you can shift gears that way . . . I was a little troubled by the objections raised by the educators to Dr. Lee's paper, because they seemed to me to take at face value what some anthropologists claim (and which, as you'll see, I doubt) : that you can describe cultural processes without bias, just report the facts that are there, and then introduce normative judgments and interpretations later. I think that this cannot be done and the best illustration of the impossibility of doing it is the two papers we have this morning. The paper by Dr. Lee has a very clear bias; I wish that all anthropologists wrote with such transparent and lovely bias as she does. And then Mr. Henry's paper has another bias on education as information-getting; all you do is turn around and look at education from that bias and you understand his remarks too.

Educators are very used to the idea that you have a bias when you set up a program, probably because they're practitioners rather than scientific researchers. And for that reason, I suppose, educational philosophy has grown in importance. It's probably too bad that there isn't a philosophy of anthropology to match the philosophy of education, one which would make explicit, clarify, and examine the biases that the anthropologists take to their examination of culture.

Hart: I think it's high time that anthropologists gave up this pose of making no value judgments; I think there was one phase in the history of anthropology when that was possible, and that was when anthropologists were primarily concerned with trying to reconstruct cultures which no longer existed. But as soon as the emphasis shifted from a concern with the past to a concern with present cultures, what I call here-and-now problems, then the possibility of not having any value judgments was completely removed, because all these here-and-now problems are controversial. It seems to me that even the older-fashioned anthropologists had some value judgments—I've never met an anthropologist who hasn't had value judgments about missionaries.

Mead: But we have a new invention that uses anthropologists' cross-cultural abilities, not in the avoidance of bias but in the creation of complementary and orchestrated teams. Ideally, I think, especially working in American culture, one always wants representation of at least three positions. What we try to substitute now is a statement by members of several cultures about several other cultures, with each position stated; e.g., this is a middle-class American making a statement about Greek peasants; this is an upper-class Frenchman making a statement about

Romanian gypsies, etc. You put several such statements together and provide a new kind of complementary cross-fertilization that balances the situation. All biases are stated very explicitly, and you are careful to have several of them.

Brameld: But the most difficult question of all has not been raised, and that is the question of *what* value judgments? That is to say, what judgments of a defensible theory of values that we can somehow agree upon, and from which we can rewrite our home economics manuals, and set home economics programs to work? Very frequently in educational discussions, and even in discussions among social scientists, one finds a tendency to say that "of course we have value judgments; of course we have biases," and then somehow or other we drop the topic like a hot potato—as though having said it, we're now being honest and frank about ourselves, and let's go on with the business of the day. The tendency is accelerated by the tremendous influence today of logical positivism in American thinking. This philosophy of science contends that there are no value judgments other than those which are purely arbitrary within the individual, that you cannot ground value judgments in any kind of validated agreement comparable to scientific judgments. So you get a dualism between scientific judgments and value judgments: the latter are admitted, but then after being admitted they're dismissed, and we've all been very pleased with ourselves for having admitted them at all. The real problem is whether or not there isn't a rationally defensible theory of values upon which, for example, to build a home economics program. I suspect that Dorothy Lee believes there is. Her paper is largely negative in that it says that the value judgments now operating in home economics programs are bad. If this is so, I gather that she has some opinion of what are good value judgments. And perhaps if we communicated a while, we'd even agree pretty well on what the good value judgments are. But could we also agree that these good value judgments are *defensible* value judgments, or simply arbitrary judgments which we both agree upon? Now it is exactly at this point that the anthropologist and the educator ought to get together. Here is a new horizon in interdisciplinary experience—the horizon of building a theory of values in which the contributions of the anthropologists and the educational philosophers are both needed. And the result is not necessarily going to be an arbitrary theory of values at all, but one which we can defend in the same way that we can defend scientific judgments about home economics. But this can never be done as long as the axiologist works by himself or as long as the anthropologist works by himself. That isn't the way to deal with the value problem anyway.

Lee: I think Dr. Brameld is right: I do have a value system. I will not defend it here; on the other hand, I think it is defensible in the light of material that's coming from research in mental health, personality, and so on. If I'm to express it, I think I can make explicit what is implied in my paper. For example, I said that life is presented in terms of externality in the manuals; I think it is good for it to be internal. It is good for the individual to grow into situations and through situations rather than have these added on; it is good for the individual from the very beginning to be accorded a climate, an atmosphere within which he can explore, within which he can discover himself. I define creativity as spontaneity and the ability to even see creatively; it doesn't matter whether the child or the adult produces a work of art; what he has seen is the creative moment, as far as I'm concerned. I think it is good for the individual to have creativity like that as a quality, as a dimension of personality, rather than as an externally seen and appraised thing. It is good for the individual to do those things which satisfy an inner standard—if that term is defensible—which contributes to the health, the satisfaction, and the further development of the personality of the person, rather than one which is set up to please or to follow good manners. And I believe that typically the rules by which society lives can be presented to the child as free. Yesterday I called it a recipe; I'd like to call it a map today. To me the child is in a jungle—society can offer the child a map, and this map is freeing because the child now can move on. Therefore I think that to present the child's society as constricting is counter to the values I have been presenting here. I believe that for mental health, for achieving the good in life, satisfaction must be found in the everyday, the ordinary, not in the special.

Keesing: I think, if I might make a remark other than in the role of chairman, that the conflict comes not in the right of an anthropologist to hold these opinions as a citizen, or in the humanities or philosophic mood. We could hope that no anthropologist would be entirely negative, especially to the point of being cynical. But the question comes historically, I think, as to whether this stand is admissible in terms of the scientific method: whether the anthropologist is here engaging in operations that meet the criteria of science, recognizing that the scientific mood, as many people have said, is a limited mood. There is of course the question here as to whether complete objectivity is possible, or whether normative dimensions will inevitably creep in or be admitted into what is conventionally the scientific mood. The problem is, really, at what point do you depart from the scientist's criteria of mental health and so forth, as they may be establishable at this point, and talk rather as a citizen or humanist?

Taba: It also becomes a problem of communication, and Jim (Quillen) hinted at it. If the talk or presentation or book, or whatever it is that we use for communication, is so stated that the next person who looks at it can for himself decipher where the facts are and where the judgments are, and then can get a clear idea of what biases are presented, and what his own biases are, then we at least have a road to thinking, and we don't need to say that on one hand you have no biases or value judgments whatsoever and on the other hand you only talk in value judgments and you don't need any evidence. The difficulty occurs when a communication does not make that distinction clear. Some judgments have to be factual, but when several facts are put together into an over-all generalization, one has to make a value judgment.

Thomas: It's become clear that that's the main thing. The problem of objectivity is not to avoid bias but to make explicit what your bias is.

Section VII

CULTURE, EDUCATION, AND COMMUNICATIONS THEORY

JULES HENRY
Washington University

Introduction

The present paper is an effort to develop a frame of reference suited to the study of education as a social process. When one confronts the avalanche of stimuli that strikes the child as he struggles up the Himalayas of classroom learning experience, one becomes aware that the aids that have been developed in the laboratories of learning theory require supplements that might ease the transition from the relatively simple choices of preliminary experiments to the relatively complex ones of the classroom. This is not to say that learning theory as developed by Thorndike, Hull, Tolman, Skinner, Miller, Dollard, and others may not be applicable in some respects to classroom learning. Rather the point is that a conceptual scheme must be found for the social transactions of learning also. I have tried therefore to make suggestions, some of them drawn *as metaphors* from communications theory, about what such theoretical supplements might be.

I said that I have found the frame of reference of communications theory suggestive, and useful in a metaphorical sense, in attempting to understand learning in social situations. When I say "metaphorical sense," I mean that it is helpful to me to think about social events in terms of communications theory, bearing in mind always that society is not an energy system like a working telegraph line or an electronic computer. As long as we remember this, we avoid the errors of those social thinkers who imagined they could apply literally the laws of mechanics or physiology to society.

With these reservations in mind, I have attempted an examination, partly within the framework of communications theory, of the storage of information in social systems.

Although in communications theory information is a mathematical measure of order (Wiener, 1950, p. 18),[1] it does not do too much damage

[1] I believe that the idea of attempting to apply communications theory to the analysis of classroom transactions came to me because of the discussions between myself and the other members of the Committee for a Unified Theory of Human

to that definition to use the word here to mean *that which is learned*;[2] for in society one important goal (though not always a consequence) of learning is the maintenance of social order (level of organization). In this paper I shall be concerned only with the *process* of storage of information in social systems, and not with content; nor will there be space for discussion of the important problem of the efficiency of the process. What I have to say derives in considerable part from observations made by my graduate students and me in elementary school classrooms in the United States in 1954. The conceptual scheme, therefore, while inspired in part by communications theory, is also empirically derived.

As a final note to this introduction, I would like to add that while the data used here place teachers in an inglorious light at times, I intend no fundamental criticism of teachers. I am a teacher myself, and though I am aware of many of our shortcomings, I am conscious also of the degree to which our profession has become the scapegoat of those who would place the blame for our contemporary desperation on teachers. Teachers, parents, and children can rarely be better than the total social system of which they are part.

A Note on Dichotomies[3]

In the following sections I set up a number of dichotomous categories, and since American scientific culture hates dichotomies, I do not imagine that mine will fare any better than anybody else's unless I point out that mine are formal models (Rosenbleuth and Wiener, 1945) which seem useful as organizing points for a great deal of previously unorganized empirical material. Thus I do not assume that my models cover all possibilities or are even found in the "pure" state in the data. In discussing their own work, Rosenbleuth, Wiener, and Bigelow (1943) point out that

It is apparent that each of the dichotomies established singles out arbitrarily one feature, deemed interesting, leaving an amorphous remainder: the non-class. It is also apparent that the criteria for the several dichotomies are heterogeneous. It is obvious, therefore, that many lines of classification are available, which are independent of that developed above.

These remarks apply, without alteration, to the present paper.

Nature of general problems in the behavioral sciences. Naturally Wiener's (1948, 1950) books have been especially provocative; but in addition Deutsch's (1951, 1951, and 1952) attempts to extend communications theory to the social sciences have been very stimulating to me. A valuable summary of communications theory is contained in Cherry's (1952) paper.

[2] Thus I am not concerned with the intake of isolated "facts" like the date of the discovery of America, or the Australian word for puddle, but with the general problem of those configurations of knowledge and/or awareness that form the basis for human social life.

[3] This note is written because Dr. Coladarci, in discussing my original paper, observed that I seemed to have set up a dichotomous world that did not account for the facts.

Some Principles of Process[4]

Target-seeking and diffuse learning.—Target-seeking learning is the expression I use for learning in which the child is taught to seek directly a human "target," which will deliver negative feedback. Here the child seeks out a teacher (as a parent, or the teacher in a classroom) who will correct errors or give goal-correcting signals. Diffuse-learning occurs where emphasis is not placed on the single target that constantly reflects corrective signals, but where, rather, *many* individuals correct behavior, and where the correction is frequently not sought directly. In target-seeking learning the individual is imagined to have, already built into him, a magnetic compass which automatically responds to the external magnetism of a single correcting source; in diffuse learning the individual is conceived of as wandering about in a random way, but pushed in the correct direction eventually by many impulses which he elicits by accidental "bumping." Target-seeking learning, so it seems to me, is so well known from our own culture as to be self-evident without examples. Since diffuse learning is not, perhaps, so well understood, I give below some examples from observations of the Pilagá Indians of Argentina.[5]

Darotoyi (male, probably in fifth year of life) is screaming because of a quarrel with an age-mate, Yorodaikolik. Adults in the village (not his parents, for they are not present) call out to Darotoyi, "Make your revenge." Yorodaikolik picks up two sticks and swings them at Darotoyi in a threatening way. Then Darotoyi is told by the adults to go home, and does so.

When Matakaná (female, probably in fourth year of life) is about to eat pig meat, two little boys yell at her, "It will bewitch you!"

A small boy is shooting at birds with a pellet-bow, and the men and boys around call directions.

Ethnologists give Deniki (male, in the second year of life) a small piece of biscuit. He immediately turns away from our tent and goes toward his house, where his mother and three adult female housemates (Nenarachi, Nagete, Araná) are sitting outside. As soon as he gets there . . . Nenarachi says, "Give me some!" and Nagete says, "Give some to me your grandmother, give some to grandmother!" Araná also holds out her extended hand. Deniki gives nothing to anybody. Then his brother Yorodaikolik (male, probably in fifth year of life) . . . comes to our door with Deniki and says, pointing to Deniki, "He's a stingy fellow."

One of the disadvantages in permitting many individuals to give signals is the confusion that may arise. The following is another sequence of diffuse learning events in which Deniki took part:

He goes toward Nenarachi. She shakes her fist at him. He smiles and moves away toward her husband. Then back to Nenarachi. She pulls him over

---

[4] In this connection—different learning techniques used in different cultures—see Bateson (1947).

[5] The writer and his wife lived with these Indians for a year. See J. Henry (1949 and 1951) ; J. and Z. Henry (1944) ; Schachtel and Henry (1942). All verbalizations were recorded in the native language, which was spoken by the ethnologists.

on her lap in nursing position (her breasts are dry) and he reaches for her breast. "It is torn," she says, referring to her blouse. He reaches again, and she sets him on his feet. Deniki is on his way back to his mother, when she asks Nenarachi for a pin. Nenarachi calls him, but he keeps on toward his mother. Then his mother sends him to Nenarachi, and Piyarasaina (ancient female housemate) turns him around by hand, he goes, gets pin, takes it to mother, who uses it to extract thorn from his foot. . . .

Situations such as these, in which the child is expected to be sensitive to signals from many sources at once, probably call for a different kind of alertness from those in which there is only one source of signals. Diffuse learning calls for a multiple awareness—an awareness on several levels at once—probably with a corresponding easy breaking of contact; target-seeking learning seems to require "single-mindedness," "concentration," and *high contact intensity*. People exposed to much tarket-seeking learning are good concentrators but may find rapid shifts of attention difficult.[6]

It is likely that both target-seeking and diffuse learning occur in all human societies; but it seems also that one method or the other is emphasized more in one society than in another. It is likely also that one or the other process is used in different degrees at different age levels and in different contexts. For example, on the one hand Dorothy Eggan (1953, pp. 283, 285) says of the Hopi:

From birth, a child in this extended family normally slept in a room with . . . his mother, father, mother's mother, father, or siblings. . . . All of these individuals . . . indulged, cared for, and disciplined him as he became older and required it, although he perhaps had most to fear in this regard from his mother's brothers.

Not only were there often several mother's brothers who divided the responsibility for the child's discipline somewhat, but in any case one of these was never the sole disciplinarian. . . . All persons . . . agreed that ceremonial parents, adopted relatives and paternal uncles, could and did scold them severely upon occasion. . . .

On the other hand F. Eggan (1950, pp. 31–32) says of Hopi fathers and sons:

. . . he [the father] is mainly responsible for preparing them to make a living. He teaches them to farm and herd sheep. . . . The position of father in relationship to his son is something like that of an older comrade and teacher. . . . The "ceremonial father" has the special duty of seeing his "son" through the various initiations. . . .

Thus it would appear that for different functions and at different times in the child's life among the Hopi, different methods of teaching are used. Specifically, in the case of four kinds of knowledge—values, interpersonal relations, subsistence techniques, ceremonial—the learning process and

[6] A comparison of these remarks with Riesman's (1950) statement of the difference between the *tradition-directed* and the *other-directed* shows areas of overlap and also subtle difference.

the person or group of persons who teach are different. Thus the first two categories are taught by a broad group of blood and ceremonial kin, and the process is diffuse learning. The third and fourth categories are taught by blood and ceremonial parents and the process is target-seeking. Hence what is learned, who teaches it, and the process employed are related to the underlying socioeconomic and ceremonial structure of Hopi culture. Meanwhile we may note that the Pilagá and Hopi observations of many people teaching the same child at the same time would be difficult to duplicate in our own culture. As a matter of fact, the effort by several adults to teach a child at the same time often creates tension in the group in our culture, and under such circumstances, "One at a time—he'll get confused," is quickly heard. Since traditional China and the United States seem to be cultures in which target-seeking learning is closely related to a compact nuclear family organization, while diffuse learning is related to cultures where the family organization is broader—where responsibility and authority are distributed among a relatively extensive group—these two models are seen to be associated with types of societies with different steady-state processes, and different internal boundary configurations.

Another consideration important to the difference between target-seeking and other types of learning is whether the culture's goals are in the past or in the future. Where, as in China, for example, or among American "upper-uppers," the culture is thought of as anchored in the past, then feedback is constantly available to enable individuals to steer their course, for all one needs to do to find one's bearings is to refer to past models. For instance, Chiang Yee tells us in his *A Chinese Childhood* (1952, pp. 11, 13) how, in the presence of the clan books, his father would talk about the family ancestors of two thousand years ago, and once pointed out

. . . how one of the fifty-first generation who did not follow the family rule as laid down by the first ancestor brought the family into disgrace. He was the youngest son, and being neglected, was always getting into difficulties.

In such situations there is no question of what to do about what: if the family history is contained in books that go back two thousand years, a precedent can always be found, somebody always has the answer, and target-seeking learning is feasible. On the other hand, where, as in our culture, goals are in the future and often not known, target-seeking becomes an increasingly difficult kind of learning to institutionalize, because nobody knows where the target should be anchored or, if it is moving, what its locus is. Hence, for a culture like the American ever since the settlement, it has become increasingly difficult to adhere to the more ancient forms of target-seeking learning. Thus boundaries are important determinants of the kinds of storage processes that are used: China's traditional culture has been bounded by a clearly defined past, so that targets—such as tutors, parents, and grandparents—could serve as excellent teachers of all things; but in contemporary America nobody knows where the boundaries are, so that children who begin by scoffing at their parents end by ridiculing their teachers.

Additive and spiraling learning.—Spiraling learning is said to occur when to the teacher's out-put the student is expected to respond with one that touches off a new response in the teacher, which in turn leads often to more information being forthcoming from the student, which then triggers another response in the teacher, and so on. The ultimate expression of this is the Socratic method, which fixes no limit to the discussion, but which theoretically can lead anywhere. Additive learning, on the other hand, occurs when the teacher simply adds one bit of information to another. An important difference between spiraling and additive learning is that the former requires spontaneous expansion of or response to an idea by the learner, while in additive learning this is generally not required. The following example of spiraling learning is taken from the protocol of an observation in a second-grade classroom:

Teacher: What would you think would be one of the *first things* to do for our play?
Students: Get scenery and conversation. Get kids who can memorize it. Tell the name and speak with expression.
Teacher nods head and replies affirmatively to each answer.
Teacher: But what is *the most important thing*?
Student: The characters.
Teacher: Name them.
Students: Billy Goat, Gray Pony, Red Cow, Calf, Jolly Pig, Mrs. Pig.
Teacher: What else?
Student: Scenery.
Teacher: Have you ever been in a play?
Student: No, but I've seen one.
Teacher: He's *using his head*; he's got *ideas*. Now what kind of scenery do we need?
Student: Apple tree, pies, house, sky, fence, ground.
Teacher: Would you have the outside and the inside of the house in one part? What do you call it when you divide a play?

It will be observed that even in this relatively simple situation, response to and elaboration of certain ideas take place. For example, in the teacher's requirement that the children state "first things" and "the most important thing" there is the cultural emphasis on hierarchy and order. The idea of order and arrangement is also carried through in the teacher's question about how the stage and the play are to be divided. She seems to be emphasizing the motto, "Each thing in its proper place." Thus, while superficially this protocol might seem to be an account of adding facts, important reasoning processes are taking place too.

The following examples of additive learning in China are among the "purest" examples I could find in a culture other than our own.

If the boys are beginners, they are brought up in a line before the desk, holding San-tsz' King, or "Trimetrical Classic," in their hands, and taught to read off the first lines after the teacher until they can repeat them without help. He calls off the first four lines as follows:

Jin chi tsu, sing pun shen;
Sing siang kin, sih siang yuen;

when his pupils simultaneously cry out:

Jin chi tsu, sing pun shen;
Sing siang kin, sih siang yuen.

Mispronunciations are corrected until each child can read the lesson accurately; they are then sent to their seats to commit the sounds to memory (Williams, 1883, Vol. I, pp. 526–27). Lessons of this sort are not accompanied by discussion of meaning, but all that is required is that the material be committed to memory.

No effort is made to facilitate the acquisition of the characters by the boys in school by arranging them according to their component parts; they are learned one by one, as boys are taught the names and appearance of minerals in a cabinet [p. 541].

Another example is Chiang Yee's description of how he learned to paint:

I do not remember that I ever had any proper lessons in painting from my father. He told me to watch him as closely as possible. I was allowed to try to paint what I liked and never given a subject or told which stroke to begin with for a bird or flower. I remember that after watching my father painting a few times I thought I knew just how to paint, but when I actually began I found I was mistaken. . . . I asked father to help, but he only smiled and told me to watch him again. He never pointed out where I was wrong and until I was about twelve did not attempt to correct my efforts. But from then on, when I produced something for him to see, he told me which part I must watch still more carefully [p. 58].

While all cultures employ additive learning, it is not yet clear that all use the spiraling type. Here a reasonable hypothesis is that the additive type is related to cultures that emphasize stability, while spiraling is related to cultures in a process of rapid autogenous change. Traditional China was a culture in which additive learning was emphasized in order to form a rigid, durable system. In China education was aimed at keeping information at the same level. In contemporary American culture a typical classroom routine is the brief informal discussion, in which the teacher, starting from the child's personal experience, so structures the interchange between himself and the child that he and the child mutually stimulate each other to higher and higher levels of awareness. But American culture is rapidly changing, particularly in the fields of aesthetics and pure science. American culture uses the additive type of storage too, but in terms of all existing accounts of Chinese education the latter did not use the spiraling type. Our storage processes generate a constantly increasing supply of information. *The storage process itself is such as to make of the information stored a source of new inquiry*. In this way the character of the in-put process determines in part whether the stored content shall remain stable or change by new increments.

The problem of out-put implicit in in-put.—In human learning it is generally assumed that the person's out-put is implicit in his in-put. Thus when a child is taught to spell cat *c-a-t* it is implied that the child, having learned that cat is *c-a-t*, will soon be able to reproduce the correct spelling. This is true of all formal school learning, and much of it is of this *simple, uninterpreted* learning. Another kind of storage in which out-put is implied in in-put is that in which the child, on a given signal like "Readers," uttered by the teacher, is supposed to perform a specific act, such as distributing the reading books to the other children in the class. Here the out-put, what the child does, is not the same as the in-put, but rather the signal calls forth a consequence which has been previously learned. I call this *simple consequent* learning. However, when a fourth-grade American child reads *The Wizard of Villeville* (Gray, 1947) and is asked to tell how one "wins people," he is presumably putting together complex past experiences into an interpretive system expressive of himself. This is therefore *complex interpretive expressive* learning.

The Wizard of Villeville is a story of a wizard who transforms himself into a rabbit and confers magical powers on Auntie Grumble, an old woman and the most unpleasant person in Villeville. Through the events brought about by these powers Auntie Grumble ceases to be "unhappy" and a "most unpleasant person." The following from a lesson on *The Wizard of Villeville* illustrates the problem of *complex interpretive expressive* learning, and also the process of *spiraling*:

Teacher (to class) : Why wasn't Auntie Grumble happy?
Pupil: Because she was grumbly and grouchy. People avoided her.
Pupil: She was mean.
Teacher: How did she win the people?
Pupil: She was happy.
Teacher: What did she do?
Pupil: She danced and laughed.
Teacher (to all the children) : Be Auntie Grumble. You know what a pantomime is—you've seen it on TV?
Children indicate they know what a pantomime is.
Teacher: Do a pantomime to show how she is going to be happy after being grumbly.
Children put on long faces, and then gradually change to a smile, and bounce around in their seats.

Cultures vary in the degree to which they emphasize one or the other of these forms of storage processes. In the last case the degree to which the child is really expressing himself rather than a generalized "other" is a problem related to the storage process also. For it is evident that in the American classroom the degree to which one is expected to or permitted to express one's self is strictly limited. When we reach the fourth grade, *complex interpretive expressive* learning is already the product of simpler forms of learning, whereby the child learns what his "self" has got to be in order that he may get along in society.

Since this example illustrates spiraling learning also, we ought to have a brief look at it from that point of view. In spiraling learning the question arises, *Where shall the "cut-off point" be?* That is to say, where shall the teacher stop asking questions, and when shall he cut off the students' questions? For example, in the present case the teacher could have asked, "What do you suppose makes people unhappy?" "What is happiness?" "Is happiness the best thing in the world?" "What does one mean by 'winning' people; and is this the finest thing in life?" Socrates was forced to drink hemlock for asking such questions, and thus we conclude that *spiraling learning is the most explosive form of education*. For not only may some teachers fail, as did Socrates, to set any cut-off point, but also the spiraling process may be internalized, so that the child begins to play question-and-answer with *himself*. Such "play," if engaged in by many people, can be threatening to the status quo. On the other hand what one observes in classrooms in our own educational system is that teachers—university as well as kindergarten—have *internalized the acceptable cut-off points*; for they know when to stop asking questions, and when to give no response to the questions asked them. Thus an interesting problem for students of education in all cultures is to discover where the cut-off points are in question-answer interchange.

Mono- and polyphasic learning.—Monophasic learning is the hypothetical case in which an organism learns one thing at a time. Possibly such learning occurs only in machines. In human beings, so it seems to me, the class of events in which only one thing is learned at a time would seem to have no members, but it is often helpful to imagine such a class, especially in connection with the human inability to learn only one thing at a time. On the other hand, just because human beings cannot learn only one thing at a time it does not follow that efforts have not been made to teach them as if they could. Let us look again at some examples. The first is from Williams' account of learning the characters of the Chinese language in traditional China (1888, Vol. I, p. 543). The first step involved simply committing to memory the characters themselves:

The tedium of memorizing these unmeaning sounds is relieved by writing the characters on thin paper placed over copy slips. The writing and reading lessons are the same, and both are continued for a year or two until the forms and sounds of a few thousand characters are made familiar, but no particular effort is made to teach their meanings. . . . It is not usual for the beginner to attend much to the meaning of what he is learning to read and write, and *where the labor of committing arbitrary characters is so great and irksome, experience has probably shown that it is not wise to attempt too many things at once.* No effort is made to facilitate the acquisition of the characters by the boys in school by arranging them according to their component parts; they are learned one by one. . . . [Italics supplied.]

Obviously this is not "pure" monophasic learning, for the children are not only being taught to recognize the characters by their shape; they are also being taught to associate specific sounds to them, and how to write them. However, the focus is on the single goal—the characters—detached from meaning or from any connection with the complexities of religion, the economic system, geography, etc. We shall presently see how different this is from polyphasic learning in a contemporary American classroom. Meanwhile let us look at a fourth-grade class being taught fractions in an American school:

Teacher goes to board: What is a fraction?
Tom: A piece of something.
Teacher sends Jim to board to draw "a piece of something."
Hands are up now.
Bill: A clock has sixty seconds.
Teacher: Each minute is what part of the whole clock?
Bill got confused here, apparently trying to divide a five-minute period into intervals.
Teacher: Can you help him? What part?
Child: One-sixtieth.
Bill explains his dilemma.
Teacher: Count them, honey.
Bill counts, and finds what part of an hour five minutes is.
Jim is drawing a rectangle at the board.
Teacher: Are other fractions possible?
Linda: The window [i.e., one of the window panes].
Teacher: Point out part of the window. . . . Let us see what Jim has for us. What is it, Jimmie?
Jim: It's a cake. [He has drawn a rectangle divided into four parts.]
Teacher: What do we do to change 3/4 to 6/8? Who remembers that? Good, which is which, James? The numerator is on the top. The denominator is on the bottom, which is the name of the fraction. (Teacher is at the board.) In adding and subtracting fractions forget it is a number. If it is apples or peaches or pears, you add them the same way. (She points to fraction on the board.) Can anyone see how you add them? You don't add the denominators, because that is the name of the fraction. How would we add chairs, chairs, chairs? So you wouldn't change them at all. I am going to let you copy the problem and add them. The denominators are going to be the same. That's another thing I'm going to help you with. Joey said the first fraction is 5/5. Is that right? It is one whole, and we are going to write it "5/5 or 1." Albert, what would make the denominator different?

Here again, though the children are being taught a number of extraneous matters, like mutual helpfulness ("Can you help him?"), and that the teacher likes some of the children ("Count them, *honey*"), the class is concentrating exclusively on trying to learn fractions.

Polyphasic learning is the process of learning more than one thing at a time. Normal human beings cannot learn only one thing at a time; rather they learn a pattern. This capacity to learn more than one thing at a time—to receive complex in-puts—is exploited in different ways by different cultures, and in different ways in various periods in our own culture. The present tendency in elementary school education is to *exploit consciously such polyphasic learning capacities*. In simple societies the storage processes often handle but very little information at a time; and even when information is relatively complex, the in-put process is not specifically developed with this complexity in the minds of the teachers. That is to say, for example, that while food-sharing among the Pilagá

Indians ends up being not only the process of giving away one's food, but also a way of operating a scale of social distance, food-sharing *as informa-tion* is not consciously taught as a social distance scale. It is the difference between saying, "Give food to people," and saying, "Give food to your first cousins through your mother." In the first instance the individual simply learns that he has to share food, in the second he is required to master a social system in connection with the giving of food. It is the second instance that is polyphasic in *intent*.

The present tendency in elementary school education in the United States is to exploit polyphasic learning capacities consciously. Thus a painting lesson becomes not only one in art, embodying the use of colors and brushes, learning the names of colors and how to mix them, and so on, but also a lesson in geography and human relations. A painting of the Sahara Desert becomes a vehicle through which to communicate in-formation about Africa, Arabs, and the Mohammedan religion *all at the same time*.

The following extract from a protocol of observations in a fifth-grade classroom will further illustrate the point:

Teacher: What does art do for us?
Student: It cheers us up.
Teacher: It cheers us up. Yes, beautiful things will cheer you up when you're feeling bad. What else does it do?
Student: It expresses yourself—I mean it's not just copied.
Teacher: What does it express about yourself?
Student: How you feel.
Students go on to say that a happy artist draws bright colors, and unhappy artists use dark colors or gray. Teacher points out exceptions: when the artist is producing a scene in which the subject is dark or gray. She says, "If a person is not disturbed, mentally or nervously, he tends to like bright colors, doesn't he?" Teacher announces she is going to play records which a student has brought, and the class is to listen to them, get the feel and the rhythm—whether it is active, soft, soothing, or what—and then express themselves in a picture. She says, "You know, the more intriguing your picture is the more valuable it is. You may have a five hundred dollar picture when you get through." (Both sides of the record are waltzes.)
Teacher stops the record, says, "Some of you are drawing before you feel the rhythm. You are bound to have a picture in your mind, but I'll make a bargain with you. Listen to the rhythm of the music, and then just cut loose and express yourself this time, and we'll draw the old-fashioned way another day this week." Teacher stops the music and says, "If you were in New York in an art class, you'd be paying ten dollars for this lesson, and if you talked, out you'd go. It's selfish to disturb your neighbor—now just be quiet." Plays more music.

From this example we see that what is ostensibly an art lesson is exploited, as a polyphasic learning experience, for the purpose of attempting to teach, among other things, the following: (1) The immorality and even disease of being unhappy. (2) Notions of economic life and the market. (3) The myth of the pot of gold at the end of the rainbow ("You may have a five hundred dollar picture when you get through"). (4) The importance of "cutting loose," but under the proper circumstances. (5) The relationship (?) between music and painting on the one hand, and "self-expression" on the other. We observe also efforts to control children's spontaneous expressiveness (dark colors should not be used) ; and above all, we can see that this art lesson is used to maintain level or organization in the American culture as a whole.

Since here, as in most of the procedures in these classes, spiraling methods are used, the reader should note the cut-off point. There is, for example, no inquiry about what "disturbed mentally or nervously" means ; yet the child with a desire to use dark colors may be left feeling he is quite loathsome because of his wish to use them. For a truly sharp contrast between this painting lesson, as a polyphasic learning experience, and what is almost its opposite, the reader may refer back to the painting lesson described by Chiang Yee.

When polyphasic learning is utilized as a *conscious* storage process, two questions arise: (1) At what point does it become self-defeating because of the sheer quantity and complexity of the in-puts? (2) When information about many things is given, let us say, during an art lesson, and all the information has *equal* emphasis, how does the storage mechanism in the head operate? Possibly all a child may retain of a painting lesson may be that you are disturbed if you use dark colors.

It seems likely that monophasic and polyphasic *emphases* in education belong to different kinds of cultures. That is to say that although it seems unlikely that any culture attempts always to teach one thing at a time, some cultures will *emphasize* monophasic learning while others will emphasize polyphasic. It would seem that monophasic emphasis will be found in cultures where few and simple factors require tight, indissoluble associations. Polyphasic emphasis belongs to societies where what is required is the communication of much information which can be "moved around" inside the head with relative ease to form new combinations, where the important thing is not fixity and simplicity, but rather change and recombination. Again I would like to offer the contrast between rural China, as a culture where relatively simple and rigid combinations of information were emphasized along with monophasic processes, and contemporary Euro-American culture, as one where change and recombination are emphasized, along with polyphasic processes.

The general problem of quantity.—As cultures become more complex and increase their content, more information has to be stored in their carriers. This must be accomplished by storing more information per unit of time and by increasing the number of methods employed. For the time being we beg the important question of *efficiency* of teaching methods. Now if n stands for the number of things to be learned, t for the time spent in learning each thing, and m for the methods used in teaching (f stands for, *is a function of*), we may set up the following model:

$$n = f\left(\frac{m}{t}\right).$$

This equation suggests that as the number of things to be learned increases, the time spent on learning each thing must diminish, or more methods must be devised, or both. We can then perceive from the equation that as the number of things in a culture increases, the culture may enter a cycle from which there is no escape except by arbitrary, authoritarian fiat. Since as n increases m must also, n receives a "double" increment, for a *new method* (m) *is itself another "thing"* (n). If, for example, we add a compass (n) to a culture that never had a compass, then one not only must learn about compasses, but methods (m) must also be devised for teaching about compasses, as there were no such methods before. Thus two "things" (n) are added to the culture, not one : the material object, compass, and the method for teaching how to use it.

It is also true that as teaching methods increase in number there is always the possibility that they will trigger new perceptions which will then add to the value of n.

As for t, it is a matter of common experience to elementary school teachers that as the number of things they must teach pupils increases, the teachers must devote less and less time to each thing. In such circumstances learning *how to switch* at fifteen-minute intervals from arithmetic to writing to geography to music becomes a new skill, which is also information.

Interesting data bearing on these points are available from *Life*, May 11, 1953, where a picture story is presented of a high-school teacher of English, who

. . . uses 102 teaching devices. His students learn spelling through a kind of baseball game, grammar through a variation on bingo [called Lingo]. He makes them keep journals . . . has them go through mock telephone conversations in class. . . . He knew all along that once he got his excited 15-year-olds "reading, reacting, recording" they could be coaxed into reading and thinking *about books they would otherwise shun.* [Italics supplied.]

Thus this story supports not only the hypothesis of the necessary increase in teaching methods when the number of things to be learned increases, but also the suggestion that there is a hidden danger in employing new teaching methods, new perceptions may be triggered, which in turn lead to new knowledge.

On May 24, 1954, *Life* published an article entitled "Why Do Students Bog Down on First R ?" The article, signed by John Hersey, was a summary of the findings of the Citizens' School Study Council of Fairfield, Connecticut. It illustrates the problems teachers, pupils, and parents have in coping with time and teaching methods. Throughout the article it is clear that speed, speed, SPEED in learning is the constant lash of teachers, students, and parents :

A basic principle of present-day public school education is that each child should be taken along at his own most suitable rate of speed in learning.

Children do not progress at the same rate of speed in all subjects.

In a public school classroom with from 25 to 40 pupils, the teacher simply does not have time to devote to special enrichment for advanced pupils; *she has a hard time getting through the basic material for all.* [Italics supplied.]

The fast learners are not always the fast performers; indeed they are prominent among the dawdlers, daydreamers, and out-the-window-gazers. . . .

Some educators now believe beginners could absorb as many as 200 words in the first six months provided words are used that the children want to learn.

If one were to ask, "What's the hurry?" the answer might be, "Because kids have to get on to the next thing, and the next, and the next." There are so many things to learn, and since speed itself is a cultural value, t is especially important in the equation in our culture.

The article emphasizes the pressure under which the American system places the teacher to develop her methods in order to meet the demands of cultural complexity and speed:

On top of *all her other duties,* the teacher who tackles reading is expected to be a psychologist, a literary tourist guide, a charming storyteller, a perfect grammarian, a steady workhorse with the mass of average pupils, and one with a special knack for bringing out the best in geniuses and morons. . . . [Italics supplied.]

The relevance of this paragraph to the equation is as follows: Psychological insight into the nature of children and reading difficulties is a methodological tool (m) added to the pedagogical armamentarium of the teacher in order to reduce the amount of time (t) needed to teach the child to read (n) and to reduce the number of so-called reading failures. A "literary tourist guide" is also a useful instrument (m) in awakening interest in reading in children. And so it goes. The reason the teacher has to be all the things mentioned is that they all are expected to add to her methodological competence. The article continues:

What does the teacher do in the face of such demands? She does what one of the teachers we visited does. "I like the manual," she says. "If you follow that you can't go far wrong."

But what does the manual urge? It urges a *multiplicity of techniques and procedures* that simply cannot be followed. The reading-readiness manual used by our teachers urges the keeping of a notebook containing a continuing checklist of the readiness of individual pupils. The checklist contains 52 items. A teacher who has 30 children in her class is therefore expected to keep running track of 1,560 items. . . . In higher grades the manual divides teaching instructions for every single lesson into the following sections . . . [The names of eight different sections are given. Italics supplied.]

While this article makes clear the close interrelation between the *number* of things to be learned, the *time* available for each thing, and the number of *methods* used, it suggests some further considerations. For example, when the aim is shifted from teaching a *mass* to giving attention to the *individual* child, then new methods have to be developed for getting at the idiosyncrasies of the individual child. This means in turn cutting down on the time available for other *subjects*. When attention to the *individual* goes hand in hand with a vast increase in the learning *population*, then new methods must be developed for getting at the individual child in *less time*, for the population of individual children is so much larger. Emphasis on the individual child, of course, goes hand in hand with individuality as a value. If the feeling in our culture or the structure of the economic system was such that large numbers of reading failures were of no consequence, the development of special methods for teaching reading to "geniuses" or "morons" would be a relatively minor source of concern. Thus the values placed on time and individuality are parameters that must be made explicit.

It has been pointed out to me, especially by Professor Coladarci, that there is no strict relationship between *n* and other elements in the equation, because so often related things are taught together. I believe, however, that the emphasis on polyphasic learning in our culture, in which the effort is made to teach several things at once, is related to the large number of things that have to be taught and the small amount of time there is to teach each thing.

Inadequacy of the mechanism.—In elementary school classrooms in our culture we have regularly observed that the child is given a problem that is beyond his *immediate* capacity to solve.[7] In engineering terms, the storage mechanism is not equipped with the parts adequate to the immediate storing job—something all good engineers avoid as a matter of course, for they know the capacity of the machine and they do not give it jobs to do for which it is unsuited. Furthermore, if they are careless the machine will break and be out of order for a long time. In the classroom, however, there often seem to be three assumptions at work: (1) that the machine, the child, cannot break; (2) that it is spontaneously flexible and will instantaneously adapt to the new storage operation; (3) that it can perform the operation. These assumptions are most obvious when the class is midway in the course of any new learning. Thus a child is sent to the board to subtract ⅔ from ⅔. In this case all the assumptions may be wrong in the case of a particular child, and the machine stops as visibly as a typewriter when several keys are pressed at once. Let us watch it happen in the fifth grade:

The child at the board stares at 2/3 minus 2/3. There is a faint titter, snicker, giggle or something (observer could not quite identify the feeling) as child stares, non-plussed by the problem. Teacher goes up to her and demonstrates with measuring cup: "If we have 2/3 cup here, and we pour it out, what is left?" Child remains baffled, and teacher says it again, seeming to try to force her presentation of the problem on the child in such a way as to cut out the distracting influence of the class, which is eager to be helpful. Child finally says, "Nothing," and teacher says, *"That's right."*

It can be seen here that not only is the machine jammed, but that the

---

[7] Ruth Benedict (1953) has discussed this and compared our culture with some primitive ones where the child is always given tasks nicely suited to his capacities.

culture is intolerant of jammed machines: the snickers of the children are an expression of the wish to kick and shake the machine in which the nickel has got stuck!

On the other hand, it should be borne in mind that the need to exploit to the maximum the organism's capacity for spontaneous expansion is a requirement of an expanding culture: though the process of putting the machine in jeopardy is dangerous to some, it is a steady-state requirement of one part of our culture. That such exploitation ultimately results in an over-all steady state is an open question. Meanwhile it is to be observed that *the capacity to rise spontaneously to the management of a new problem is again a capacity to be learned.* This underscores the circular character of the equation of which I spoke earlier.

It is to be noted that in the process of pushing some organisms toward new capacities we damage others. This makes us aware of the close relationship between social processes and human evolution, for those organisms that can accept the pushing, flow with the tide of evolution as it is at the moment, while those that are "jammed" by a fifth-grade failure may be forced to leave the field.

Noise.—In communications theory "noise" refers to the uncontrollable random fluctuations of the apparatus (von Neumann, 1951). Such things as the hum in a telephone line or radio receiver are noise, because such sounds have no relation to the actual message that is being transmitted. We thus deal with two problems: *lack of relationship* of noise to message, and *uncontrollability.* In discussing this paper Dr. L. K. Frank suggested that noise ought to be handled as I have handled other concepts from communications theory. This suggestion, taken together with Dr. Coladarci's that some account ought to be taken of the relationship between intended and actual learning, which is really the same as noise in many instances, makes it imperative that a section of this paper be devoted to the problem of the stimuli that impinge upon children from *areas of awareness not strictly related to the explicit lesson at the moment.* It can be shown, I believe, that from a psychological point of view the problem of noise is really *the* classroom problem in our culture, for the unintended learnings that children pick up, almost as a radio picks up static from the atmosphere, are very numerous, exceedingly subtle, and almost uncontrollable. Let us look at a game of "spelling baseball" in a fourth-grade class:

Children form a line along the back of the room. There is to be "spelling baseball," and they have lined up to be chosen. There is much noise, but teacher quiets them. Teacher has selected one boy and one girl and sent them to front of room to choose their sides. As the boy and girl pick children to form their teams, each child chosen takes a seat in orderly succession around the room. Apparently they know the game well. . . . Now Tom, who has not yet been chosen, tries to call attention to himself, in order to be chosen. Dick shifts his position more in direct line of vision of the choosers so that he may be chosen. Jane, Tom and Dick, and one girl whose name Observer does not know, are the last to be chosen. . . . Teacher now has to remind choosers that Dick and Jane have not been chosen. . . . Teacher gives out words for children to spell, and they write them on the board. (Each word is a "pitched ball," and each correctly spelled word is a "base hit." The children move from "base to base" as their teammates spell the words correctly.) With some of the words the teacher gives a little phrase: "Tongue—watch your tongue; don't let it say things that aren't kind; butcher—the butcher is a good friend to have; dozen—12 of many things—knee—get down on your knee; pocket—keep your hands out of your pocket, and anybody else's. No talking!" Teacher says, "Three outs," and children say, "Oh, oh!" . . . "Outs" seem to increase in frequency as each side gets near the children chosen last. . . . Children have great difficulty spelling August. As children make mistakes those in seats say, "No." Teacher says, "Man on third." As child at board stops and thinks, teacher says, "There's a time limit; you can't take too long, honey." At last, after many children fail on August, a child gets it right, and returns grinning with pleasure to her seat . . . (Observer notes: Motivational level in this game seems terrific. They all seem to watch the board, know what's right or wrong, and seem quite keyed up. No lagging in moving from base to base.) . . . Child who is now writing Thursday stops to think after first letter, and children snicker. Stops after another letter. More snickers. Gets word wrong. . . . (Frequent signs of joy from the children when their side is right.)

Here learning how to spell is made part of a competitive game in an effort to eliminate "boredom." However, what happens here, as may happen in the use of *mechanical* filters, is that one noise is substituted for another; while boredom drops out, *competitiveness* is *reinforced*. Another important noise is the desperation of the children who are chosen last—they learn they are cultural rejects; and their low valuation by the group is excruciatingly obvious, for the teacher even has to remind the choosers that these children have not been picked. Additional noise is provided by some of the teacher's short phrases: "watch your tongue," "get down on your knee," "keep your hand out of your pocket, and anybody else's," are suggestive. The child may learn from these phrases that the teacher thinks that people should sometimes get down on their knees; he may wonder why he should keep his hands out of his own pockets, and be frightened that the teacher should suspect that he wants to put his hands in other people's. He learns also, perhaps, that the teacher stands for morality. Finally the children themselves introduce noise into the system by snickering at comrades who find the tasks beyond their capacity. In all this the child is on public view; all the children in the class see that he is or is not chosen and when; that he spells correctly and quickly or that he is slow or fails. He *learns a conception of himself* in which failure and success, being chosen or rejected, being fast or slow, weigh heavily. Before closing this section it will perhaps be interesting to look at a situation from traditional China. The example again comes from Chiang Yee's *A Chinese Childhood* (pp. 81–82).

Once when [my] youngest uncle had, for some reason or other, offended the tutor, "Old Beard" made him kneel down in the middle of the courtyard. . . . To make him keep his back straight a huge square inkstone full of water was placed on his head. The tutor's seat being directly opposite him, he could not move for fear of spilling the water. [He had to kneel about half an hour.] My youngest uncle bore this punishment with remarkable patience. . . . He did not seem particularly exhausted. [On being questioned by Yee about his patience and lack of exhaustion, the uncle said it was because while he was kneeling] he remembered a story he had read in some book about a well-trained wrestler, and he went on thinking of this until he forgot about himself.

Here it would appear that while the tutor, "Old Beard," was trying to teach the child to be respectful, the child was learning fortitude, or even how to be a great wrestler. Significantly the story adds that the punishment was taken as a great joke by the children.

In the metaphorical sense in which the term is used here, we can think of the educational "apparatus" as including teacher, all students, and a particular child, who, let us say, is at the board trying to spell a word, or is kneeling with an inkstone full of water on his head. We can then see that there are noises that originate *inside* an individual's head (like a phantasy of being a wrestler), and noises that originate *outside* the individual student (like the snickering of the class at his failure to spell Thursday). It is clear, then, that different problems of control (of "random fluctuations") confront us, depending on whether we are concerned with one type of noise or the other.

One more interesting comparison between machines and human beings remains. In using a machine one makes a sharp distinction between noise and message, in the sense that the noise may be ignored except in so far as efforts are made to prevent it from interfering with the clarity of the message. In human learning, however, *the noise is often learned with the message*, and it is not ignored by the person; the child learning to spell, for example, does not, in our culture, ignore the deprecating snickers of his classmates if he fails to spell a word.

I have suggested that noise, in the sense of all those unplanned learnings that take place when human beings are educated, is one of the central problems of learning in any culture. As such it requires an extended treatment, which is quite beyond the scope of this paper, although I hope to give it extended treatment in a later publication. Here I have just tried to present enough to show the character of the problem and how it might be approached.

In discussing this section with Karl Deutsch he argued as follows: It is not quite proper to call noise the things I have characterized as such in the spelling lesson. He urged that the spelling lesson is, in a certain sense, a screen for the most important learnings, which I have called noise. He urged that what the culture is most interested in, and hence the most important part of the lesson, is that children should learn how serious it is to fail, how important it is to succeed, what they must do to stop being cultural rejects, that knowledge is power, that they must develop themselves so that they can function well as a team (as in baseball), that the culture hates slow people and rewards fast ones. These are the really important lessons to be learned, for when you are adult nobody really cares whether you can spell or not, but they do care whether you know how to co-operate, whether you know how important it is to succeed, and so on. I confess I am sympathetic to this view of Deutsch's, and his observations point up the great difficulty one runs into in transferring the frame of reference of communications theory from engineering to social science. Meanwhile let us note that this very effort has suggested some interesting cultural problems.

Conclusions

Even if we take the position of the "life adjustment" school of education, it would be difficult to show that education is anything more than the acquisition, interpretation, and integration of information. Hence the student of education cannot ignore the contribution of communications theory. But in education we also deal largely with information that is traditional and of a high level of standardization. Hence education comes within the purview also of cultural anthropology. Thus educative processes, communications theory, and culture theory ought to be brought together in a systematic way. This paper is an effort to show how this might be done, and to show also that simple, invariant categories of theoretical significance can be set up and used for the cross-cultural study of education. The equation is an effort to show how methods must change with content and how the time factor presses constantly upon us in our own culture as we increase the scope of our knowledge. While such formulations may not at present be considered laws, they are useful as heuristic devices and suggest a direction in which some laws of social learning may be sought.

Throughout the paper an effort has been made to show that what is taught, how teaching is done, and who does it to whom, are related to total sociocultural systems. A culture's values and goals, its social organization, technological developments, and the characteristics of its processes of change and stability all affect the What, the How, and the Who of teaching and learning. Even if the metaphors and their related categories could be shown not to suit the data, it seems to me that this contribution from the theoretical framework of anthropology—that educational patterns are related in complex ways to over-all cultural ones—is useful.

References

Bateson, G. 1947. "Social Planning and the Concept of Deutero-Learning," in T. M. Newcomb and E. L. Hartley (eds.), *Readings in Social Psychology*. New York: Henry Holt and Company.

Benedict, R. 1953. "Continuity and Discontinuity in Cultural Conditioning," in C. Kluckhohn and H. Murray (eds.), *Personality in Nature, Society and Culture*. New York: Alfred A. Knopf, Inc.

Cherry, E. C. 1952. "The Communication of Information (an Historical Review)," *American Scientist*, XL, 641–64; 724–25.

Chiang, Y. 1952. *A Chinese Childhood*. New York: The John Day Company.

Deutsch, K. 1951. "Mechanism, Organism, and Society," *Philosophy of Science*, XVIII, 230–52.

———. 1951. "Mechanism, Teleology, and Mind," *Philosophy and Phenomenological Research*, XII, 185–223.

Deutsch, 1952. "Communication Theory and Social Science," *American Journal of Orthopsychiatry*, XXII, 269–83.

Eggan, D. 1953. "The General Problem of Hopi Adjustment," in C. Kluckhohn and H. Murray (eds.), *Personality in Nature, Society, and Culture*. New York: Alfred A. Knopf, Inc.

Eggan, F. 1950. *Social Organization of the Western Pueblos*. Chicago: Chicago University Press.

Gray, W. S. 1947. *Time and Places*. New York: Scott, Foresman and Company.

Henry, J. 1949. "The Social Function of Child Sexuality in Pilagá Indian Culture," in P. Hoch and J. Zubin (eds.), *Psychosexual Development in Health and Disease*. New York: Grune and Stratton.

———. 1951. "The Economics of Pilagá Food Distribution," *American Anthropologist*, LIII, 187–219.

Henry, J., and Z. Henry. 1944. *Doll Play of Pilagá Indian Children*. Research Monographs No. 4, American Orthopsychiatric Association, New York.

Hersey, J. 1954. "Why Do Students Bog Down on First R?" *Life*, May 24, 1954.

Life, May 11, 1953, pp. 81–85.

Neumann, J. von. 1951. "The General and Logical Theory of Automata," in L. A. Jeffress (ed.), *Cerebral Mechanisms in Behavior*. New York: John Wiley & Sons, Inc.

Riesman, D. 1950. *The Lonely Crowd*. New Haven: Yale University Press.

Rosenbleuth, A., and N. Wiener. 1945. "The Role of Models in Science," *Philosophy of Science*, XII, 316–21.

Rosenbleuth, A., N. Wiener, and J. Bigelow. 1943. "Behavior, Purpose and Teleology," *Philosophy of Science*, X, 18–24.

Schachtel, A. H., J. Henry, and Z. Henry. 1942. "Rorschach Analysis of Pilagá Indian Children," *American Journal of Orthopsychiatry*, XII, 679–712.

Wiener, N. 1948. *Cybernetics*. New York: John Wiley & Sons, Inc.

———. 1950. *The Human Use of Human Beings*. Boston: Houghton Mifflin Company.

Williams, S. W. 1883. *The Middle Kingdom*, Vol. I (rev. ed.). London: W. H. Allen and Co.

FIFTH SESSION OF THE CONFERENCE, CONTINUED

Chairman: Felix M. Keesing
Discussant: Arthur Coladarci

Coladarci: I was pleased to find this paper here. Jules (Henry) is quite apparently persuaded, as am I, that communication theory can be a heuristic source for educational models. Further, he is to be commended for his temerity in undertaking to make such deductions, for it seems rather clear that, although the general systems and self-contained mathematizations of such people as Schroedinger, Wiener, and Deutsch have reached a rather high level of development, only a very few have attempted to focus directly on applied social contexts. It is somewhat uncharitable, therefore, to "criticize and run" and I hope that Jules will accept my reactions as a genuine sharing in his venture rather than as the "sniper's shots" that brevity makes them appear to be.

Some of the questions I had raised in connection with the original paper have been amply clarified in the present revision.* However, others remain and a few new ones arise. I will raise these as briefly as possible, using the organizing rubrics of *the value of the dichotomies, the assumptions about learning,* and *the implicit theory of behavior organization.*

The value of the dichotomies.—That dichotomies are valuable as formal models and necessary as analytical tools cannot be gainsaid. Further, I do *not* object to Jules's dichotomizations because "they don't account for the facts." The question I raised originally, and repeat here, is whether his dichotomies are the most heuristic ones in view of the purpose of this conference. That is, do they account for the most relevant educational facts? Do they relate to the *de facto* educational task? As an initial case in point, consider the "target-seeking–diffuse learning" categorizations. In one, the individual is thought of as seeking directly a human target which offers negative feedback; in the other, the individual is wandering about in a *random way* or pushed in the proper direction by many impulses *accidentally* elicited. These categories have considerable validity in the sense that some individuals at some times can be so categorized. I question them here on the observation that the greater part of the teacher's task involves learners who do not fall into *either* of the categories *nor, indeed, anywhere on any implied continuum for which these might be anchoring points.* The reference here is to the individual who is highly purposed, is *seeking out* multiple and differentially reacting targets, and does not perceive most of the "accidental bumping" noted by an external observer. Jules's response, I take it, is that he does not have to account for all behavior in a dichotomization. I agree. But, if the effort is to illuminate the educational process, why not account at least for *modal* behavior? If my criticism here has validity, then the "spiraling-additive"

---

* *Note by the editor:* Dr. Henry's revision of his paper took account of certain of Dr. Coladarci's first reactions and added new material for the purpose of clarification. Dr. Coladarci was subsequently requested by the editor to respond to the revised paper.

formulation is subject to the same difficulty. Finally, I wonder what is intended by the polarization, "monophasic learning–polyphasic learning"? The first of these classes is, the author notes, without members and, in the revised paper, the justification is offered that such a class is admissible as a defining category. I take this to mean that a continuum is represented here. If so, what is the value in a model that dichotomizes at the *end* of a continuum, leaving the remaining category with *all* the members? Jules's discussion at this point suggests that he finds such a procedure clarifying, but I need to be instructed.

Assumptions about learning.—Throughout the paper, Jules confounds the process of learning and the operations of the teacher. This makes it difficult to argue for the validity of my reservations here but I offer them on the suspicion that the error is not merely syntactical. Perhaps I can make my point most clearly by noting the assertion that n (the number of things to be taught) is a function of m (number of teaching methods) over t (time necessary for teaching). That is, as the number of things to be taught increases, the time necessary for teaching and the number of methods for teaching increase also. I call attention to the fact that the formula involves the necessary assumption that these "things" are *independent* of each other. While this condition is satisfied in machine models, the nature of the learning process precludes it. Indeed, it can be argued that, at any moment of time, a large and perhaps *infinite* number of "things" is being learned by many methods. The possible rejoinder that the model refers to *things-to-be-taught* is anticipated here with the contention that the meaning of curricula, or information, or communications is found in their *effects*. That is, the focus eventually must be on *"things-learned."* Once this frame of reference is taken, of course, the model further can be criticized on the grounds that any one of its "things" loses its initial definition in the very process of communication. That is, an "intended" message is continually modified during both the processes of encoding and decoding.

Implicit theory of behavior organization.—It is patent that when one is discussing information and communication theory he is also discussing behavior theory. While he is free to choose his theoretical locus in this regard, it is in the best interests of clarity that he explicate the conceptual frame of reference involved. It strikes me that the underlying *psychological* assumptions in Jules's argument are essentially those found in that general psychological system referred to as "associationism." This is a perfectly respectable view; what interests me is that such assumptions do not square with the *field*-oriented views he appears to espouse as an anthropologist. If my suspicion is correct, his general thesis contains contradictions at the theoretical level. I may be entirely incorrect in this criticism since it is equally possible that I am criticizing Jules's syntax rather than his ideas.

Implicit conception of the educative process.—There are many competing conceptions, among educators, regarding the relationship obtaining between subject matter (i.e., "information") and the learner. This is, essentially, the curriculum problem. Again, Jules is free to choose (within the limits of consistency) any one of them. My contention is that the one implicitly chosen here (i.e., curriculum is *entirely* selected by the teacher in advance of the learning act) accounts for only some of the educational outcomes. If Jules holds that the assumption *is* involved, then he should realize that he is addressing his models to a particular educational "camp"—and not a very large one.

In sum, I feel that this paper makes rather literal translations from communications theory (despite Jules's initial warning about the dangers of this). Such translations become major premises in a syllogism that leads necessarily to nonheuristic dichotomies, particular views about the learning process and behavior organization, and a particular conception of curricular organization. I suspect that he would not wish to go in these directions.

Since the foregoing response is almost completely drawn in negative terms, I wish to reaffirm my opening statement. Jules has attempted a commendable task and, should he continue with it, educators will profit immensely. The nature of my reaction stems from my interest in his paper and the assumption that, in the limited time available to me, Jules would prefer to hear the kinds of remarks I have offered. I can easily use as much time outlining supporting remarks.

Keesing: First, I think the author of the paper should have a chance to comment.

Henry: When Art (Coladarci) ties my discussion of education process to the teacher (by which I presume he means the *school* teacher) I feel he places too narrow a construction on what I say. My reference is to anyone who teaches—as my examples from the Pilagá, the Hopi, and the Chinese indicate. In regard to his reservations about the equation, the major one is accounted for in the text of the paper, where I say, ". . . since as n increases m must also, n receives a 'double' increment, for a *new method* (m) is itself another 'thing' (n)." Thus I specifically point out that m and n are *not* independent.

With respect to Art's feeling that my "associationism" does not "square" with my field theory, I see no reason why I have to tie myself to a single theory. One is useful to me in one part of the paper, another in another.

Much of our difficulty seems to revolve around logical problems and the view we have of models. For example, Art holds that one cannot anchor a line in a class that has no members. But this is a false problem, it seems to me. In mathematics, curves of energy (heat, motion, volume, etc.) are repeatedly anchored at the zero point. The issue is not whether or not you crowd all your cases into the cluttered classes, but rather, what is the quantitative variation in cluttering under different conditions? My paper throws, perhaps, a net of too wide a mesh, and thus lets too many fish slither through. I should like to remind Art, however, that my aim is to encompass not only the problems of our own culture, but also those of intercultural comparison. In this connection I feel that the data I have given from other cultures ought to be given closer examination.

Finally, I would like to say that there is something Art did not mention, but which as an anthropologist I think is particularly important. Art rightly concentrated on the problem of the applicability of the communications model and its possible inadequacy. As an anthropologist I was interested also in the relationship between teaching methods and the total situation, including social structure, world view, and conception of the person. Even if the whole structure were thrown out and the educators couldn't use it at all, I think this focus is important.

OPEN DISCUSSION
Wanted: A Model for Planning Multiple Learning
Hilda Taba

Taba: I start out with you, Jules (Henry), on the idea that learning is always multiple, whether we recognize it or not. But when we face it from a teaching angle, then it becomes important not only to recognize the fact but also to think how to *plan* for multiple learning. Too often learning experiences are planned around a single conscious focus with a result that other negative learnings go on at the same time. Models should be so constructed that they represent valid ideas about learning and also become incentives to thinking about learning.

When the idea of targets of learning is considered from the standpoint of multiple learning, and the possibility of planning for multiple learning, planning for learning of feelings and attitudes, and recognizing what negative effects might come in if you haven't planned properly, then one immediately faces the question of *open* targets and *closed* targets. To learn the multiplication table by rote is a closed target: you focus on it as if nothing else were involved.

Extending sensitivity to affectional relations in a family is a target too. It is not as explicit as the multiplication table is; neither is it so closed. When concentrating on the multiplication table as the target, you don't ask what else the child has in him except his capacity to learn the multiplication table, and you use a repetitive method. When you use a target like sensitivity to affectional relations among the family members, a range of perceptional levels and of responses needs to be taken into account in the very designing of the method. Exploitation of the varied current experiences of children is part of the design. These current experiences become the subject matter from which the next step is taken. Diagnosis of the gaps in current experience indicates the ways of filling in the gaps. For example, one class was dealing with the problem of extending sensitivity to various family relationship patterns by the method of open-ended discussion. They were reading *Mama's Bank Account* as one book in the series sampling relationships in a family. Each child brought to it whatever he perceived or had experienced before, and interpreted it correspondingly. I remember one child who, when they came to the incident of mama bringing meat balls to the school tea, asked, "What would you do if your mama did that?" One boy who had had some unpleasant experiences in facing differences in school and being laughed at said he would tell mama to go home as fast as she could. The next one said, "But mama would be hurt," to which the boy replied, "But mama was the kind of mama who wouldn't be hurt; I could explain to her but I couldn't explain to the kids." And so it went—each person responding to the situation in terms of his own experience but everybody's responses being extended because people with different reactions responded to them. The target was still there but it kept on growing and enlarging, and the growth came from the use of the current experience treated permissively as if the teacher were saying, "Well, there are these different experiences and it's O.K. to feel that way." Then openness and "O.K.-ness" gave the opportunity for each child to learn not only from the teacher or from the story, but also from each other. This to my mind is a different way of conceiving of a target of learning— maybe a very useful way for many problems of cultural learning.

The second problem is the misconception of the intent of teaching when teaching is based on a limited diagnosis of what the social learning of children is, regarding a given point in teaching. Furthermore, it is per- haps useful to think of how learning can occur in a heterogeneous group— by capitalizing on heterogeneity of experience as material for learning, as an occasion for learning, and as a stimulus for learning, rather than trying to eliminate it somehow and institute linear procedures. In the process of learning from the heterogeneous experiences of the group, the linear learning doesn't hold any water at all. In such an experience learn- ing is multiple, and the learning of one thing also teaches a method of learning. When children learn to work in groups with each other and respond to each other, they not only learn things like reading or painting or whatever they were doing—they also absorb a method of learning.

Now this puts the matter of spiraling learning in a different way. If the basic learnings are properly placed and properly planned, a cumulative sequence can be built in which the focal learning—in this case reading— can go on with great rapidity. This type of learning gives a kind of plus value. If we had models and concepts of learning which expressed this method of planning for multiple simultaneous learnings (such as focusing on reading *Mama's Bank Account* while stimulating many learnings), it would be possible to economize on time in learning or increase the quality and richness of learning. In my opinion, if we did this kind of planning of multiple learnings and used whatever we know about learning and cul- ture (including whatever the psychologists, anthropologists, and educa- tors now know), we could do what we now are doing in twelve years in at least ten. Or else we could get a great plus value out of the twelve years.

A Problem in Communication

Hart, Mead

Hart: I think this paper raises a very important point for purposes of this conference, and that is on the matter of communication between educationists and anthropologists. I think I can best put it this way. I believe I'm right in saying that Jules (Henry) has a very high reputation in anthropology for certain work he did on play groups and learning and child training and so forth in certain non-Western cultures. At this con- ference, however, he is talking scarcely at all about that, but instead is talking about learning theory in general and communications theory in particular. Quite frankly, I feel a great sense of an important resource person being wasted by talking about the wrong things. If I were an educationist, I think I would feel that while I had Jules here, I would like him to tell us a great deal more about the Pilagá or about the Chinese, and less about what happens in the American classroom. And the general question it's related to is this: when anthropologists are asked to communicate with nonanthropologists, how are they going to communicate what the people who are asking them to communicate want to learn from them? That may be a difficult question, but I think that the first step I would regard as necessary is that the anthropologists on the whole talk about anthropology, which is their field, and not too much about the fields of other specialists.

In other words, I think the title "Culture, Education, and Communications Theory" might have been differently distributed by having more culture and less communications theory, seeing that Jules is an outstanding anthropologist.

Mead: In this case, Steve (Hart), Jules understands models and Hilda (Taba) understands models. Jules, from his very wide anthropological background, comes in using all of it, but using the model and communication theory as a way of talking to Hilda with her wide background of educational experience; also, Jules knows something about school systems. He did study children and not just general anthropology, and he did study schools and is not just talking about the culture in general. The model becomes a vehicle of communication between Jules and Hilda, and it may be that we need such intervening types of communication.

Storage, Coding and Receptivity, Noise and Learning

Lawrence Frank

Frank: We should examine this communication model further. One of the concepts of information theory that Jules Henry has referred to is "storage." In information theory, used by communication engineers, storage usually functions as a place for referring relevant materials that are to be used later in solving the problem fed into the machine. We should recognize the extent to which the storage in children is not only relevant and useful but often is of either traditional, sometimes anachronistic, materials upon which they draw for solving their problems, or more or less neurotic, fixated patterns and beliefs which may block or distort their further learning.

We should also explore further the question of coding. In educational terms, coding means that each teacher codes her communication to the class, using specific kinds of words, phrases, figures of speech, diagrams, numerals, and so on; then each pupil has to decode this in his own terms. Between these codings many things may happen which are important for the educational process. We are becoming aware that it is not so much what is said, but what is heard and the way it is interpreted which is important. As Hilda Taba and others have pointed out, there is both an explicit and implicit decoding that takes place. To a very large extent, educators have been chiefly concerned with the explicit coding by the teacher of what she is trying to teach. Accordingly, they have largely ignored what the child may actually be learning from the lesson—the implicit decoding and idiosyncratic interpretation by each child. As we recognize the differential receptivity of children, realizing how each has his pattern of decoding and organizing experience, we will see that a teacher who uses a single standardized procedure for teaching may fail to communicate with many of her students. Some children will learn only what they receive visually, others auditorily, and so on; moreover, each one will fit what he does receive into his already existing frame of reference, and frequently his interpretation of the materials may be confused or otherwise distorted by his preoccupations and fantasies.

Jules Henry has pointed out on other occasions that much of the basic learning in a culture is communicated through fables and parables and metaphors, so that we may speak of this learning as analogical as contrasted with the digital, factual, logical type of information and learning upon which formal education largely relies. We should also recognize that there are probably basic differences, which have been largely ignored in teaching, in the receptivity and coding of males and females, but we should remember that every individual is a mixture or blend of maleness or femaleness in different proportions. Other significant differences in ways of learning, as Hilda (Taba) has emphasized, are found among children from different cultural backgrounds, different social-economic classes. These differences in ways of learning and interpreting experience are probably much more significant for education than the individual differences shown by standardized tests because they indicate these differing ways of participating in the communication process, more specifically in school learning.

Another concept of information theory is that of "noise." "Noise" is a generalized term for any interference or distortion that takes place between the communicator and communicatee. "Noise" may be of greater or less intensity for different recipients of a communication, making the teacher's message more or less confusing and ambiguous to each pupil. Also we should recognize the concept of "redundancy"—that is, the repetition (of information in a message) which may be necessary because there is a lot of noise or because the speaker believes the hearer may not be receiving or understanding what is being said. This is what occurs when we are not sure that we are saying what we intend and so we repeat and rephrase the message, saying, "I mean . . . , I mean . . ." For some children repetition may spoil the whole lesson, since they get bored; for others repetition is very necessary, especially repetition of the same information but expressed and communicated in different terms so that each one can learn in his own way. Whenever a message is not clear there is likely to be some repetition or redundancy of information. Furthermore, "noise" may occur not only in the transmission of a message but may be in the communicator or the communicatee. Thus we may think of noise in the teacher, in the sense that her own ideas and understanding of what she is trying to teach may be more or less confused and distorted, and hence her teaching by so much will be unclear. Then, as indicated above, there may be a "noise" in the pupil in the sense that what he is thinking about and what he is feeling toward the teacher or the subject matter may interfere with his receiving what the teacher is trying to communicate. We might also consider under "noise" a variety of other aspects of the situation in a class. One pupil may be sulky or resentful for having failed or been rebuked or humiliated, another—such as the class clown—may be engaged in trying to distract other pupils, while others may be preoccupied with their own reveries and fantasies and therefore are "not paying attention" to what the teacher is saying. There are also the many traditional preconceptions and erroneous assumptions which may function as "noise" in a pupil and interfere with his learning of any new ideas. One example of how this inner "noise" operates is observable in the many programs of health education for children and adults. Here we see often well-organized, scientifically valid material being taught with little realization that most individuals, children and adults, cannot accept much of the medical, biological information offered because of their preconceptions and often strong feelings about their own body and its functions. As long as we ignore these various kinds of "noise," especially the many invalid and often archaic preconceptions which children bring to school, teachers may utilize a variety of skillful teaching methods but fail to communicate with a student. What Kirtley Mather of Harvard has said in a recent article, "The Scientist's Responsibility for the Interpretation of Conceptions" (*Science*, March 5, 1954), may be appropriately quoted here. He says, "The fundamental concepts of even the most complicated of modern science can be comprehended by almost everybody. That indeed is one of the earmarks of the fundamental concept; it explains what appears to be complex and chaotic in terms of the relationships that give significance and meaning [to facts]. Concepts are mind-stretching; they enlarge the horizons of our mental grasp. They 'rejoice the spirit of man.'" Concepts, in other words, are the patterns or templates with which the individual organizes his experience. Instead of giving children an initial load of facts, figures, and empirically derived generalizations, it may be more effective to help them develop a conceptual orientation with which to integrate, organize, and interpret the content of facts and other materials which we expect them to master. Thus the statement that the number of things you have to teach increases the amount of time required may be valid only in so far as we insist upon teaching content without providing initially the concepts for handling that content. This viewpoint is contrary to the assumption in much of our educational theory and practice that children learn bit by bit, primarily by a digital way of learning; it seems increasingly clear that they learn primarily by an analogical process and then can master materials in digital fashion.

Section VIII

THE MEETING OF EDUCATIONAL AND ANTHROPOLOGICAL THEORY*

THEODORE BRAMELD
New York University

Although both educators and anthropologists have always been more or less aware of the theoretical underpinnings of their respective fields, it is probably true that never have they been as acutely concerned with the import of those underpinnings as at the present time. In both fields one finds growing attention to the assumptions upon which research and practice inevitably, if precariously, rest. In both fields, also, one detects not only an abundance of fermentation and fresh insight in the area of theory, but perhaps an equal abundance of uncrystallized thinking and unrefined terminology.

The reasons for this heightened concern are no doubt themselves cultural. Melville Herskovits (1948, pp. 314 f.), one of the few anthropologists who has thus far paid sustained attention to education as an institution of culture, suggests that one may easily distinguish between the way it functions for a people like the Zuñi and for a more complex civilization because the one is relatively stable by comparison with the other:

The homogeneity of the [Zuñi] culture makes for a unity of teaching objectives that reflect unity of cultural aims and methods of inculcating them in the young, and thus leaves little room for conflict between the directives given by different preceptors. . . . This conflict in directives is perhaps the source of the most serious difficulties in larger, less homogeneous societies, where the total educational process includes schooling as well as training in the home. Serious conflicts and deep-seated maladjustment may result from education received at the hands of persons whose cultural or sub-cultural frames of reference differ.

Although Morris Opler (1947) has pointed to the danger of oversimplifying this distinction, as Herskovits does also, it does seem obvious that today the divergence of educational methods and objectives in complex civilizations is widespread indeed—a divergence that is reflected not only in growing attention to and refinement of educational theory as a specialized discipline, but in deep-seated conflicts among its own spokesmen.

* Prepared in connection with a larger study on the same theme made possible by a grant from the Wenner-Gren Foundation for Anthropological Research.

Schools of all sorts are found to operate upon what I may call "meta-educational" assumptions, quite as fully as cultural beliefs and practices operate upon what the anthropological theorist, David Bidney (1953a) aptly terms metacultural assumptions.

Indeed, as might be expected in view of the ultimate if far from sufficiently delineated interdependence of education and culture, the same types of traditional philosophic categories may be utilized to characterize both fields of theory. Thus realism is an influential educational doctrine (Frederick Breed is a representative), but it is also influential in anthropology (Robert H. Lowie has been so classified). So too, among other doctrines, are idealism, historical materialism, neo-Thomism, and pragmatism. To be sure, these terms are not always manipulated with equal refinement, nor do the two fields always reveal exactly comparable meanings. Bronislaw Malinowski, to choose but one anthropologist, is undoubtedly closer to pragmatism than to any other current philosophic outlook; yet, as the philosopher Horace Friess (1950) has reminded us, his special way of adapting that doctrine to culture theory would scarcely satisfy the most influential American pragmatist and educational philosopher, John Dewey.

The difficulty with much of this kind of metacultural and meta-educational thinking, however, is that it claims more by way of explanation of the present struggles besetting both fields than it can easily justify. Bidney (cf. 1953a, pp. 25, 37 f.), for example, sometimes leaves the impression that he has satisfactorily interpreted, say, Alfred L. Kroeber when he labels this anthropologist as an objective idealist. The philosopher of culture, F. S. C. Northrop (1946), attempts a not dissimilar feat on a grand scale when he tries to explain Western civilization in terms of the philosophy of modern science, and Eastern culture in terms of aesthetic intuition. Similarly, various educational theorists seem to think they have finally understood Robert M. Hutchins when they classify him as an Aristotelian, or Alexander Meiklejohn as a Kantian.

Where these men frequently fall short is in failing to inquire carefully whether or not they have reached the limits of interpretation when they have discovered that educators and anthropologists, or even whole cultures, rest upon presuppositions that can be defined according to more or less established philosophic categories. Helpful, indeed indispensable, as these categories are, the problem that still remains is the nature of the intricate linkages between them and the cultural experiences with which they are properly associated. It is one thing, for example, to say that we have underscored the pragmatic premises upon which, to some extent, they undoubtedly rest. It is another thing to infer that we have thereby sufficiently revealed the origin, role, or practical significance of these premises. We still need to ask, after we have articulated them as clearly as possible, how and why pragmatism developed as it has in America. And we need to do so, I suggest, not merely by careful conceptualization or even by tracing it to earlier philosophies, such as the Hegelian, but by considering it as the symbolic corollary of a constellation of natural and cultural phenomena that are, in numerous respects, indigenous to the American milieu. In short, the crucial problem is the venerable but far from solved one of the interlacing of ideas, concepts, categories, on the one hand, with nature, human experience, culture, on the other hand. If another instance of reductionism is not to be committed, we must avoid what I may term here the "philosophic fallacy"—a fallacy to which some anthropological and educational theorists seem singularly vulnerable.

Just how far anthropologists have thus far become sensitive to the context of political, economic, moral, and other influences upon their own frames of reference I am not qualified to say. It is, I confess, surprising to note such relative paucity of attention paid to the bearing of that context upon anthropological theory in such an imposing overview of the field as *Anthropology Today*. And it is at least plausible to ask if there has been anything like enough interdisciplinary effort thus far to incorporate into their own viewpoints the perspectives of such diverse nonanthropological interpreters of American cultural assumptions as Charles Beard, Harold Laski, Vernon Parrington, Merle Curti, or Thorstein Veblen.

It would be, of course, a gross exaggeration to contend that educational theory has proceeded much, if any, further in such an effort. Here, too, the disregard of or at least insensitivity to the reciprocity of "inarticulate major premises" and environmental influences is far more typical than not. At the same time, the dim outlines of a more adequate approach are at least discernible—an approach no doubt due in considerable part to the immense influence of Dewey, who insisted throughout his long professional life upon the interaction of ideas and events, and in part also to the practical character of schooling as an on-going institution in everyday American life. Thus, the conflicts rampant in education today—conflicts now commanding frequent attention even in mass-circulation magazines—are occasionally assessed by theorists in terms of what may in general be called, after Karl Mannheim (1936), the sociology of knowledge. Here the aim is always to explore the environmental motivations of educational theory as essential to the nature of that theory : the conditions of economic and social tension and crisis, for example ; the technological and political revolutions sweeping our century ; the abnormal rate of change from, say, the "inner-directed" to the "outer-directed" types of character analyzed by David Riesman (1950)—changes themselves possibly the consequence of these revolutions ; and numerous other factors that are approachable only through a multidimensional interpretation in which conventional philosophic categories are a necessary but certainly not sufficient explanation of present educational bewilderments and struggles.

Granting that we have hardly begun to develop this kind of approach to any area of experience and knowledge, I wish nevertheless to illustrate what it might begin to mean in effecting a closer rapprochement between the two fields with which we are here primarily concerned. More particularly, I propose to select four among many more problematic concepts from anthropology and to suggest not only how these may be helpful to the tasks of American education, but how their consideration by educational theory viewed in the wider context referred to above may enhance their own importance and fruitfulness for anthropology. These four are: (1) the reality of culture, (2) process in culture, (3) values in culture, and (4) the integration of culture. In view of my purpose, it is obvious that I shall find it necessary to mention various facts and principles which, though familiar to members of one field, may be unfamiliar to the other. It is obvious, also, that each of these problematic concepts embraces so huge a territory that one can only hope at best to emphasize aspects of major relevance.

The frame of reference, if I may take the liberty of extending Mannheim's term, is an as yet embryonic methodology—the "metaculturology of knowledge"—metaculturology here being redefined provisionally as that encompassing discipline concerned with the assumptions of culture theory, and which accordingly includes not only the assumptions of anthropology, sociology, and all other sciences of man, but of the history and philosophy of culture as well.

II

The problem of the reality of culture refers to the disputes waged over locus, autonomy, and substance. The impression a layman receives from reviewing recent anthropological discussion is that, while in general there is now widespread agreement that culture connotes a level of human experience clearly indistinguishable from although related to all other levels of nature and humanity, there continues to be disagreement over its ontological status. If the anthropologist, Leslie White (1949a), is right in his historic survey, early pioneers such as Emile Durkheim were closer to the correct position than many recent theorists—the position that culture is a unique, objective level of reality, *sui generis*. White deplores, therefore, what he considers to be a retreat from this position by the majority of American anthropologists—Ralph Linton, Edward Sapir, and Ruth Benedict, to name but three—who, he feels, have reduced culture to merely psychological phenomena. Ironically, perhaps the two most vigorous American defenders of ontological substantialism are at opposite poles in their interpretation: White himself, who is sometimes called a historical materialist, and the sociocultural theorist, Pitirim A. Sorokin, who is a metacultural idealist. In passing, it should be noted that the *sui generis* position, however, subtle its ramifications, must also be assumed finally both by Marxian anthropologists (who consider the fountainhead of their doctrine to be Friedrich Engels' *Origin of the Family*), and by those subscribing to the metaphysics of Thomism (Father W. Schmidt no doubt being the most prominent).

Kroeber's long meditation upon the problem has led him to modify in crucial respects his own original hypostatic view of culture (1952, pp. 22 ff.). At least two recent statements (Kroeber, 1952, p. 121; Kroeber and Kluckhohn, 1952, pp. 148 f.) appear to take a clear-cut operational approach by holding that culture is not a reified substance but a functional abstraction by which certain kinds of human experience are delineated and interpreted. Despite certain inconsistencies, this is likewise the main direction pursued by Malinowski (1944), as it is of such diverse figures as the self-styled "philosophical anthropologist," Ernst Cassirer (1944), and the anthropological theorist-practitioner, Clyde Kluckhohn (1949).

Now it is surely interesting, though not really surprising, that much the same type of dispute runs through educational philosophy (cf. Brameld, 1950). Although culture is seldom precisely defined, the meta-educational attitude presupposed by the two groups of theorists often called essentialists and perennialists is that it is largely an objectively posited level of reality. Despite important differences among them(perennialists are Aristotelians and Thomists, secular or ecclesiastic, while essentialists usually are modern realists or idealists), both groups incline strongly toward a pre-existent ontology of the cosmos, and therefore of the world of social institutions and events.

The consequences of this attitude for education are enormous. Learning becomes chiefly a process of stimulus-response, mental discipline, or some similar practice devoted mainly to absorption of and/or training for unity with the already given cultural environment. The notion widely assumed by some anthropologists that education is established to guarantee transmission of the cultural heritage is welcomed by essentialists and perennialists as confirming their own predilections as to the relation of the learner to the reality that is learned.

Against this general orientation, educational philosophy in America is characterized today by at least two other viewpoints, occasionally termed progressivism and reconstructionism. Like their counterpositions, these also have a great deal in common amidst genuine distinctions. While reconstructionism, for example, tends to emphasize more strongly the need for clearly enunciated cultural goals, both accept the operational way of interpreting nature and culture. Therefore both also emphatically reject a *sui generis* position. Being concerned with educational methods as instruments of social control, they tend to deny that education, formal or informal, is properly characterized as an agent merely of cultural transmission. Since they are deeply respectful of science they do not ignore, of course, the anthropological evidence for such transmission. They do question whether the evidence is thus far complete enough to warrant the hasty generalizations frequently made, and especially so in view of the scarcity of systematic investigations by anthropology or education as a distinct institution of culture.

The conception of learning developed by this second pair of philosophies also tends to depart radically from the first pair. Malinowski's anthropological functionalism, for example, is by no means foreign to the educational functionalism now widely taught under such a label as organismic psychology. Here learning centers in the activity of mediating the immediacies of experience, to use the language of Dewey (cf. 1916, 1939). That these immediacies are, if you please, the "givens" of nature and culture, and that they are very real, very stubborn, and sometimes overpowering, is certainly true. The inference from these characteristics that they are *sui generis* existences in which man must either acquiesce or perish is, however, false—an inference plausible enough, in the face of long-standing unscientific habits and attitudes, but not therefore either logical or moral.

Education, in this framework, becomes normatively creative and re-creative rather than chiefly reflexive or reproductive. The major assumption is that habits of variation and exploration are cultivable, indeed that some cultures (our own most notably, perhaps) have to a considerable degree acquired amenability to habits of this kind at least as self-consciously as others have acquired alternative kinds. It follows that, since culture is entirely learned, education deliberately geared to modification or reconstruction can also be learned. The sociologist, Charles S. Johnson (1943, p. 4), speaking of "education and the cultural process," epitomizes the general view : "Education, thus is more than the transmission of culture from one generation to another. It is this transmission and it is also transformation of people who are more or less in conflict."

Although further examination would reveal certain overlappings between all four of the theories mentioned, just as there are overlappings between, say, White and Linton, a more important consideration here is whether we can detect any still wider significance for the problem of cultural reality as it bears upon both education and anthropology. Here, then, we approach the question of what a metaculturology of knowledge might begin to reveal as to the more pervasive reasons for the dispute.

One clue to an answer lies in the conflict within Western culture between what I shall call, in widest possible compass, an absolute-transcendental approach to nature, man, and society, on the one side, and an experimental-empirical approach, on the other side. This conflict is, of course, both ancient and multiple. While its most sophisticated formulation is philosophic, it is by no means merely or even primarily so either in origin or expression. Rather, it is religious, legal, industrial, familial, political, moral—indeed, one would have difficulty in sifting out any phase of Western experience which it has not invaded. Usually, we think of the Middle Ages as representing the dominance of the absolute-transcendental alternative, although we appreciate that this was by no means purely the case any more than modern civilization is purely experimental-empirical.

As a matter of fact, one of the most striking features of modern culture is that it has never emancipated itself from the heritage of medieval habits, beliefs, and practices—certainly not to anything like the extent suggested by Sorokin (1941) in calling our culture "sensate." Not only do most contemporary religious institutions perpetuate that heritage; so, too, do political institutions, including even American democracy with its anchorage of *a priori* axioms concerning equality, freedom, and the dignity of man.

Nor would we be wrong in recalling that modern science is far from immunized. On the contrary, as Jerome Frank (1945) among many others has shown, the mechanistic philosophy of science (first usually associated with Newton), which views the universe as an objective system of pre-

established law, is not only widely taken for granted even by some relativity physicists of our own day; it is, to an astonishing degree, assumed
as the model to be emulated by social scientists as well. Recently, in those
parts of the world controlled by communism, the absolutist outlook rationalized by dialectical materialism is officially espoused and enforced in
all departments of life: in the natural and social sciences, in political indoctrination, and in every type of school.

The relevant conclusion here is that the problem both of cultural reality
and of education's response to that reality is integral with the much wider
problem of alternative ways of believing and acting in cultural experience.
To be sure, these ways are made clearer both by anthropological and educational theories, just as they are by formal philosophies. One additional
measure of such theories, however, derives from perception of the underlying currents of influence, ideological and otherwise, which play upon
them at the same time that theories share in expressing and molding the
influences themselves. In the problem under discussion, this may well
mean, first of all, that the unresolved issue of the *sui generis* versus operational views of cultural reality, and likewise the unresolved issue of the
essentialist-perennialist versus progressivist-reconstructionist views of
education, are finally to be construed as metaculturological symbolizations
of, because integral with, absolutist versus experimentalist institutions,
attitudes, and habits that both precede and follow those symbolizations.

We need hardly be reminded, however, that any brief attempt to
sketch the significance of our first problematic concept on such a huge
canvas inevitably ignores innumerable qualifying factors. It should be
borne in mind that this attempt is itself strictly operational. The test of its
value lies in the extent to which it assists us in mapping a very large territory with a greater degree of potential and actual meaning, in developing
greater consciousness of the network of interrelations of the two fields
with which we are concerned, and in constructing the beginnings of a
framework through which to approach our three remaining concepts.

III

By concept of process I refer, in general, to the cluster of questions
centering in "the dynamics of culture change." That these are intimately
connected with the concept of reality is evident, but not at all in the sense
that the absolutist orientation denies change while the experimentalist
accepts it. No anthropologist, regardless of his premises, would defend
for a moment any notion of completely static culture; and no competent
educator would defend any notion of completely static education. To be
sure, the perennialist and certain essentialists regard time as subordinate
to the timeless forms of reality, and this regard affects their final outlook
upon the responsibilities of education. Even they, however, typically provide curricula and techniques that include recognition of changing events
and needs with which students must be prepared to cope during their
lives.

And yet, in an important sense, the absolutist view of culture approaches the problem of process from assumptions that tend to encourage consequences divergent from those of the operational interpretation; so, too, do conflicting philosophies of education. White, for example, still retains important features of the "evolutionary" thesis developed by such immortals of anthropology as Henry B. Tylor, Lewis H. Morgan, and Herbert Spencer—a thesis that presumes to detect in human history a unilinear progress from "savagery" through "barbarism" to "civilization." Despite differences, this is also broadly the Marxian doctrine— civilization in its highest form becoming the classless society of pure communism. In the history of American educational theory, the classical "evolutionary" position has never been more consistently expounded than by the neo-Hegelian philosopher and early United States Commissioner of Education, William T. Harris (1901), who, while scarcely hoping for the final emergence of a classless society, does find a melioristic trend in culture which it is the first business of the schools to reflect and reinforce. As Curti (1935) has shown, the Harris theory of education is accordingly traditionalistic in its cultural role. Change is not for an instant denied. But, as with the great majority of other essentialists and perennialists, the schools are charged with the first obligation to follow, not to modify or redirect, whatever course the institutions and practices of man as a member of society are destined to pursue.

As we have already seen, progressivists and reconstructionists are unwilling to settle for the Harris variety of policy and program. This is not to say that they conceive of education as *the* agency of cultural change—certainly not without careful safeguards to broaden the concept of education to embrace much more than formally organized learning and teaching. Their organismic psychology, however, plus their normative picture of democracy as a social laboratory engaged in continuous experimentation with every sort of human problem, enables them to argue that cultural change is not a mere epiphenomenon to which schools must passively adjust but is, in significant degree, a controllable process for human growth.

But operationalists in education could immensely benefit by further attention to some of the insights and discoveries of anthropology with regard to the meanings of process. For one thing, considerable evidence could be produced to show that progressivism, particularly, has underestimated or simply failed to cope squarely with the powerful resistances to consciously directed change that are typical of cultures. The frequent criticism leveled against Dewey, and even more his educational disciples, that they have inherited too generous a residue of faith in progress and rationality characteristic of the Enlightenment, may contain more than a grain of truth.

Thus, while it would be wholly inaccurate to assert that they have ignored the weaknesses of this traditional faith, progressivists do not appear to have given direct, careful attention to the importance of, for example, cultural patterns—to the kind of intensive investigations conducted by Kroeber (1944) and others to demonstrate the recurrence and persistence of such patterns throughout history. Greater awareness of this phenomenon would compel educational theorists to take into consideration a hypothesis such as cultural curves of upswing and downswing, and so to assess far more realistically their own sometimes overconfident if not naïve belief in the novelty, flexibility, and continuity of organized human development.

It is even possible that greater appreciation of anthropological theory and research would force progressivists to take a new look at their favorite concept of "creative intelligence." While they have never accepted anything like the "great man theory of history," neither have they adequately scrutinized the limitations of individual capacity to effect change. The "child-centered school," although occasionally a distortion in practices of progressivism in theory, and although now partly overshadowed by the notion of "community-centered schools," is still held up to thousands of teachers in training as an educational ideal. It is an ideal, I suggest, which to some extent is governed by individualistic biases that are in fact incompatible with anthropological knowledge of cultural structures and persistences.

At the same time it should be pointed out that in one still narrow sector of educational theory and practice, the impact of concepts of cultural process is considerable. I refer to the movement called intercultural education, itself largely the effect of progressivist influences. Such familiar and rewarding operational concepts as acculturation, assimilation, diffusion, and innovation have begun to take hold and have even been put to limited experimental use in certain school programs. I do not find, however, that the concept of enculturation is as widely utilized: it symbolizes the crucial fact, still far from adequately stressed, that learning is culturally motivated, conditioned, and directed, and hence that we are unlikely to construct any kind of competent educational psychology except in close co-operation with cultural anthropology.

Contributions to the problem of cultural process have been so numerous that it is difficult to resist the temptation to explore their educational bearings a great deal further. Here I am able to select only two concepts of unusual provocation. The first, neglected thus far by education, is "cultural focus"—the tendency, if Herskovits (1948, pp. 542 ff.) is correct, for cultures to organize certain variable clusters of traits in terms of dominant interests (aesthetic, economic, social, or others) of which members are likely to be especially aware, and hence which are more pliable. Assuming that the focus of our own culture, for example, is technological, it does seem true that in this domain we are readier to examine methods and devices, to strive for improvement and innovation, than in more peripheral domains such as organized religion. Granting that the concept is debatable, it suggests to educators that if they are to play any sort of creative role in cultural process, one of their first duties must be to determine as clearly as possible the precise character of the focus or foci of given cultures and subcultures, and then to construct strategies of change geared to this character.

The second concept is derived not immediately from anthropology, which is apparently unaware of it, but from educational philosophy: it is the theory of "practical intelligence" developed by Bruce Raup (1950) and a group of associates in the progressivist camp. Utilizing numerous principles from anthropology as well as other social sciences, they have sought to sharpen the function of intelligence as an instrument of cultural change by dissecting several components which they contend are neglected by those who define it in typically scientific terms. Thus they find that practical intelligence consists of three "moods"—the indicative, optative, and imperative—expressing respectively the surveying, normative, and programmatic phases of the total function. The major methodology of action emerging from their analysis is expressed in the discipline of an "uncoerced community of persuasion." It is this discipline which they hope can be put into widespread educational and social operation, as a way both to reduce tensions between and within cultural groups and to accelerate change in directions found to be desirable in the course of testing that methodology. The potential reciprocity of the concepts of practical intelligence and cultural focus in educational change is probably rich. Beginnings are, indeed, discernible in the greater perceptiveness of some educational leaders to the structures of local communities where schools operate, and which they must learn to carry along in any developments they undertake.

Raup and his colleagues proceed from a crucial assumption that is by no means as carefully considered either by educational or anthropological theory as it ought to be—the assumption that the present period of history is beset by abnormal strain, confusion, and a pervading sense of crisis. I select the concept of crisis for a moment of special attention because it is here perhaps most revealingly that one may place the problem of cultural process in the setting of a possible metaculturology of knowledge. Returning for a moment to the four philosophies of education in order to explicate the point, it is at least a legitimate hypothesis that these philosophies may be viewed not merely as significant symbolizations but as alternative diagnoses and prognoses of the present crisis in political, moral, economic, and other forms of national and international relations.

In very general terms, the perennialist formula aims to change culture by reacting against what it considers to be the ailment of materialistic and experimental habits and beliefs. Therefore it favors the restoration of aristocratic and/or theocratic principles and practices prevailing at a much earlier time in Western history—the Greek and Medieval periods, especially. The essentialist formula, exemplified by Harris, tends to utilize the *sui generis* ontology of modern idealism or realism in order to cultivate adjustment to the moving stream of history. Progressivism, symbolized by such concepts as practical intelligence, is committed to a democratic methodology which encourages gradual but deliberately planned cultural change with secondary regard for commitment to future goals. The reconstructionist, finally, builds his case upon the premise that progressivism, however potent, is no longer wholly satisfactory to cope with the deep-seated maladjustments of a crisis-age such as ours. Hence he contends that if the democratic values and institutions in which he believes are to survive, flourish, and expand, fresh and challenging designs for culture-and-education must now be constructed as well as implemented upon an audacious scale, with the fullest possible recognition of the obstacles and pressures which anthropology and other social sciences enable him to estimate.

It is only fair to admit that this metaculturological interpretation of American theories of education is by no means at present widely influential. Also, one ought to note that it is a way of organizing diffused masses of theory and practice that overlap in numerous ways, and therefore refuse in fact to be confined by such neat classifications. Nevertheless, if we remember that the attempt is entirely operational, this kind of approach may prove meaningful not only for the field of education but also for other fields.

It is interesting, for example, to examine the extent to which the concept of crisis in its peculiar relevance for the twentieth century is central to anthropological theory. Of course the concept is by no means ignored. Not only is it crucial to the work of such philosophers of culture as Oswald Spengler, Arnold Toynbee, Lewis Mumford, and Ortega y Gassett, but one also finds it receiving occasional attention by Franz Boas (especially in his writings for the layman), and by other leaders in anthropology. At the same time, one is struck by the fact that *as an explicitly treated concept* it is conspicuously absent from the index and content of *Anthropology Today*, from the recent technical "review of concepts and definitions of culture" by Kroeber and Kluckhohn (1952), from more than one widely read textbook in anthropology (e.g., Kroeber, 1948; Herskovits, 1948), and even from the invitingly titled symposium, *The Science of Man in the World Crisis* (Linton, ed., 1945).

I do not pretend to guess all the reasons for such striking omissions or peripheral treatments. Yet it would seem fair to inquire why a considerable section of anthropological theory finds the concept of crisis so uncongenial to its own systematic investigations. Surely, if it is held that we are now in the throes of world-wide cataclysm (the contention is itself debatable, of course), one would expect both its general meaning and bearing upon specific issues to receive sustained attention from anthropology. As is true of educational theory, I do not find this, by and large, to be the case. Perhaps even more than in educational theory, however, I fail to find careful attention paid to the question of why those theorists of culture who have explicitly dealt with the problem of crisis tend to react to it in alternative ways.

The issue here, in other words, is whether it is possible that anthropologists and allied scholars are themselves likely to vary both in their critiques and proposals according to their various locations on what might be called the continuum of a metaculturology of knowledge. To what degree if at all, for example, is Sorokin's anticipation of a new "ideational" culture motivated by his own metaculturological preferences rather than detached scientific judgments? Again, might further investigation show that the approach of functionalism in anthropology reflects, more or less, the same sociopolitically liberal orientation toward cultural change as does the educational methodology of practical intelligence? Similarly, is the *sui generis* position (cf. White, 1949*b*, pp. 344–47) likely to reveal or at least inadvertently to bolster attitudes and actions somewhat analogous to the conservative predilections of most educational essentialists? Is it even possible, finally, that those anthropologists, like those educators, who largely disregard the concept of crisis do so partly, at any rate, because it remains outside the range of their own ideological orientation—their own personal and professional status in the culture of their time?

The answer to such questions is far from self-evident. A meeting, however, of anthropological and educational theory at this juncture might benefit both fields in their endeavor to articulate and cope with the concept of process from their more deep-seated and pervasive assumptions.

IV

The problem of cultural values (anticipated, of course, in the issue just raised) is, if anything, a still more hazardous venture. One reason is that philosophers who specialize in axiology are themselves profoundly at odds. Another reason is that anthropologists have not until recently paid much careful attention to values. Educational theory is affected by both of these reasons. Its own widely varying theories support an equally wide range of opposing views of the role of values, but attempts to relate these views to the live issues of teaching and learning in real cultures have frequently been sterile. Still, it is my impression that today both education and anthropology are increasingly eager to penetrate the whole sphere of values, for both are coming to realize that indifference toward the problem can be tolerated no longer.

In anthropological theory, one of the most promising approaches may prove to be the personality-and-culture movement. The contributions of such diverse experts in the psychological sciences as Geza Roheim, Abram Kardiner, Lawrence K. Frank, Harry Stack Sullivan, Gardner Murphy, and of anthropologists such as Margaret Mead, A. Irving Hallowell, John J. Honigmann (1954), and others earlier mentioned, have widened and deepened the concept of cultural values even when they have not always sought to single them out for sustained examination. The immediate explanation, no doubt, is that values for all of these scholars tend, on the one hand, to be grounded in the energies of human beings—in what are variously referred to as needs, wants, drives, interests, desires—and, on the other hand, to be molded by the environment of nature and culture. Thus despite disagreement and uncertainty at many points, the personality- and-culture movement serves to locate the problem where educational theory is, in turn, only starting to cope seriously with it—in scientifically ascertainable realms of discourse and investigation.

So far as I have been able to pursue the concept of values in contemporary anthropological sources, two statements have impressed me most. The first, by Kluckhohn (1952) with the help of others, is weakened by repeated if possibly unavoidable terms like "somehow" and "in some senses" which often threaten to beg the precise points at issue. Nevertheless, the statement attempts painstakingly to formulate a theory of values based upon recent investigations both by philosophers and social scientists. I select only a few high lights.

Kluckhohn's key definition, in the context of a "general theory of action," is this: "A value is a conception, explicit or implicit, distinctive of an individual or characteristic of a group, of the desirable which includes the selection from available modes, means, and ends of action" (p. 395). Proceeding from the postulate that "normative and existential propositions" are empirically interdependent although logically distinguishable, Kluckhohn analyzes this definition to mean, among other things, that (1) values are constructs involving both cognitive and cathectic factors; (2) they are always potentially but not always actually verbalized; (3) while primarily cultural products they are uniquely expressible by each individual and each group; (4) because particular desires may be either disvalued or valued, it is essential to make sure that values are equated rather with the desirable, defined according to the "requirements of both personality and sociocultural system for order, the need for respecting the interests of others and of the group as a whole in social living" (p. 399); (5) selection among available alternative values are attachable to both the means and ends of action. This general conception has unusual significance for educators unwilling to settle for the easy notion of education as transmission of values: it invites them to treat value determination and implementation as, at least partially, also a conscious, selective, and creative enterprise of man in culture.

In trying to classify values, Kluckhohn finds that they may be grouped into such dimensions as modality, content, intent, generality, intensity, explicitness, extent, and organization. Of all these dimensions, perhaps the most pertinent for educational theory is that of "extent," which grapples with the old but lively issue of the relativity versus universality of values. Kluckhohn appears dubious of the position, popularized by Benedict (1934) and others, and influential today in programs of intercultural education, that values are purely relative to the particular culture which supports them. While recognizing that the problem of universal values has not as yet been attacked at all adequately by social scientists, he nonetheless contends that some values—reciprocity, control of mere impulse, respect for human life, for example—are in general considered desirable by all known cultures. His review with Kroeber (1952, pp. 174 ff.) is careful to insist that neither universality nor relativity is a sufficient category: "Both perspectives are true and important, and no false either-or antinomy must be posed between them." Nevertheless, "the phrase 'a common humanity' is in no sense meaningless." Judgments about value can be "based both upon cross-cultural evidence as to the universalities in human needs, potentialities, and fulfillments and upon natural science knowledge with which the basic assumptions of any philosophy must be congruent."

The importance of this view of the dimension of "extent" is made clearer by the second statement, prepared by Bidney (1953b). While there is much here, too, that cannot be summarized, I call particular attention to his repudiation of extreme relativism. After tracing "the concept of value in modern anthropology" all the way from Rousseau and other philosophers of the Enlightenment down to the present day, Bidney develops his own position (p. 698) :

The choice is no longer between a romantic cultural pluralism and a fixed evolutionary absolutism but rather between a world in perpetual crisis and a world order based on rational principles capable of winning the adherence of the nations of the world. . . . So long as anthropology remains at the descriptive stage, which is the first stage of empirical science, anthropologists may rest content with cultural pluralism, on the ground that they do not wish to overstep the bounds of scientific fact. But if anthropology is to attain the stage of making significant generalizations . . . then comparative studies of cultures must be made with a view to demonstrating universal principles of cultural dynamics and concrete rational norms capable of universal realization.

With a few substitutions, these words might have been written by an educational reconstructionist. Borrowing much from progressivism as always, he too rejects absolutist theories of value held by essentialist-perennialist educators and widely indoctrinated today both by secular and parochial schools. He too, however, denies that relativism is the only possible alternative to these theories. With Bidney, the reconstructionist searches for a way to build empirical and hence temporal universals amidst the admitted relativity of values—universals emerging with the help of cross-cultural investigations such as those of G. P. Murdock (1945) that search for the "common denominator of cultures."

While reconstructionism is a decidedly unfinished theory, I should like to select four features of its emerging conception of values (cf. Brameld, 1947 ; 1950, pp. 473 ff.) where close co-operation with anthropological theory would conceivably benefit both sides. It should be emphasized, however, that these features are selected not to proselytize for a particular outlook but solely to illustrate further how the two disciplines of anthropology and education may converge around a common issue. Other theories than reconstructionism might have been chosen to make the same point.

One feature is the effort of reconstructionists to define values as, in essence, "want-satisfactions"—an effort reflecting the influence of, among others, W. I. Thomas, Ralph Barton Perry, and Bronislaw Malinowski. Here Kluckhohn's treatment of the role of the "desirable" and of "selection" would, I am sure, greatly refine the reconstructionist conception. Also, the negative answer of Dorothy Lee (1948) to her own question, "Are basic needs ultimate?" should contribute further to its refinement by calling attention to the cultural values that underlie needs and wants themselves. One might then argue (to paraphrase Veblen's amusing dictum, "Invention is the mother of necessity") that values are the mother of needs.. Perhaps a still more precise formulation, however, would recognize the polarity of the two terms. For, as Kluckhohn (1952, p. 428) observes, "the relationship between a value system and a need or goal system is necessarily complex. Values *both* rise from and create needs."

A second feature is the normative generalization, "social-self-realization"—a high-level abstraction for the most encompassing universal value. This term might meet Lee's objection that needs are given merely as a list. Suggesting a Gestalt of want-satisfactions in which both personal and group values interpenetrate, it epitomizes much of the same affirmative viewpoint to be found in the culturally oriented psychoanalyst, Erich Fromm (1947). The concept of social-self-realization is not at all, however, an attempt to smuggle in an absolutist axiology under new disguise. Abraham Edel (1953, p. 565), in speaking of the problem of categories as one of the areas where philosophy and anthropology could profitably cooperate, puts the issue in a way that is equally relevant to social-self-realization as an empirically grounded norm:

Any such set of reference points, however well established, could not constitute a closed set defined once and for all; the elements would themselves change and grow with the growth of scientific knowledge. . . . Similarly, new "needs" may be added, as the need for emotional security has come to be recognized in our own time. The fundamental point in basing ethnographic categories [or normative generalizations] on universal elements would therefore seem to be their constant bearing to the best available *results* in the cooperative effort of the sciences of man. On the surface this seems to involve a paradox: the categories depend in part on the resultant pattern of knowledge, and the growth of knowledge depends in part on the types of categories employed. But the paradox is only on the surface; this type of non-vicious circle is a familiar characteristic of the method of science. The openness of the set ultimately therefore constitutes a practical but not a theoretical difficulty.

Third, reconstructionism emphasizes the role of "social consensus" in value formation. Social-self-realization, for example, always involves tacit or open agreement among participants in a culture that here, indeed, is the guiding norm of their conduct. The necessity of such agreement as intrinsic to the process and product of valuation is insufficiently considered either by anthropology or by education. It is only mentioned in Kluckhohn's statement, for example; and although consensus as an explicit concept more frequently enters into the writings of Herskovits (1948, e.g., p. 575) than any other anthropologist I have thus far read, even he does not appear to have profited widely from the research of Kurt Lewin (1948) and other "field" theorists in the social sciences who are centrally or tangentially concerned with the import of that concept. Yet, any effort to establish a defensible conception of universal values is, I suggest, singularly in need of the consensus principle. If Bidney is right in his demand for values "capable of winning the adherence of the nations of the world," anthropology and education will have to concern themselves with how and to what degree such adherence can be attained. Implicit in the concept is also, of course, the necessity and privilege of dissent.

Fourth, reconstructionism asks whether the concept of "myth" may not carry unassessed significance for a mature theory of cultural values. Here philosophers like Cassirer as well as anthropologists could provide additional guidance. Not only might they point to the dangers and limitations of mythical values in past and present cultures. They might help also to clarify the issue of whether there is still not a legitimate place for affectively toned, poetically expressed, but rationally defensible dramatizations of twentieth-century culture—dramatizations that could serve to magnetize the humane goals now so urgently required to neutralize the spurious fascination of totalitarian mythologies.

Little further need be said here of the relevance of a metaculturology of knowledge for the problem of values. It is implicit throughout the discussion above. Yet, as in the case of cultural process, it is difficult to believe that either anthropological or educational theorists are frequently concerned with the questions of how far and in what ways ideological motivations, for example, may be operating surreptitiously upon their own value judgments and commitments. One of Bidney's (1953b, pp. 688 f.) too rare comments on this crucial point illustrates the kind of needed interpretation to which I refer. Speaking of Benedict, Boas, and cultural relativists in general, he says:

In retrospect, it appears that American anthropologists continued to reflect the prevailing attitude of their democratic society. As liberals and democrats, they merely accentuated tendencies inherent in their culture but professed to have derived their "higher tolerance" from a comparative study of primitive cultures. They uncritically assumed the value of cultural differences and their mutual compatibility. . . . Had they thought in terms of the possible incompatibility and conflict of ideologies . . . they would not have labored under the naïve optimism of cultural laissez-faire. It has taken the impact of the second World War to shake this romantic cultural optimism and to awaken anthropologists to the reality of cultural crises and to the need for cultural integration on a world scale.

Cultural relativism, no less than cultural absolutism or any other theory of values held by educators and anthropologists, is itself conditioned by the cultural matrix of patterns and forces within which it is expressed, rejected, or espoused.

V

For the concluding problem, I have chosen cultural integration, referred to by Bidney above, mainly because it serves to tie together numerous strands earlier considered.

Although "integration" is itself a term of diverse meanings, the focal problem it generates is evident enough. On what demonstrable grounds, if any, can we hope to fashion a theory and program of education-and-culture that will organize, unify, harmonize the bewildering multiplicities of knowledge, values, practices, and beliefs that characterize an age of overspecialization, cross-purposes, and strife?

The concern of educators with this question is illustrated today by the current debate over "general education." There is widespread agreement that something must be done about the chaos of departments, techniques, courses, and standards that clutter both the lower and higher levels of the schools. Yet when one scans the specific proposals for curing the evils that flow from this chronic eclecticism and confusion, one is struck by equally widespread disagreement as to what kind of general education is most desirable. Perennialists advocate classical curricula based largely on "great books," a faculty psychology, and a more or less freely admitted metaphysics derived from Aristotle. Essentialists, as represented to a considerable extent by the Harvard Report on *General Education in a Free Society*, rearrange traditional classifications and tone them up with a few cautious concessions to recent trends in curricula and techniques. Progressivists and reconstructionists advocate various forms of the "core curriculum" which reflects the Gestalt influence: central concern is with clusters of problems regarded as vital to young people living in a period of rapid transition. None of these positions, however, seems to have inquired at all thoroughly into what anthropological theory might offer by way of fresh criteria, and this despite the fact that many would not deny that cultural experience should provide some or all of those criteria.

It is helpful, I believe, to consider the problem in two main dimensions—integration as spatial order and as temporal order—each of which is, of course, polar to the other. By spatial order, I mean the holistic relations of cultures and subcultures viewed in horizontal and vertical cross-sections. By temporal order, I mean those same relations viewed as historical and sequential continuities and discontinuities.

Of several possible concepts, two—"pattern" and "social class"—may be chosen to illustrate the spatial dimension of culture. Kroeber's (1952, pp. 92 f.) definition of patterns is authoritative: they are "nexuses of culture traits which have assumed a definite and coherent structure, which function successfully, and which acquire major historic weight and persistence." They may either cut across cultures, as in the case of "Hebraic-Christian-Mohammedan monotheism" and "plow agriculture"; or, as in Benedict's models, they may coincide with indigenous, whole cultures (pp. 90–92). The other term, social class, refers to status levels as developed most conspicuously by W. L. Warner (1941)—a social class being defined in major part as "the largest group of people whose members have intimate access to one another. . . . Class is present in a community when people are placed by the values of the group itself at general levels of inferiority and superiority. . . ." (Cf. Mayer 1953, 1955; Warner, Havighurst, Loeb, 1944, p. 19.)

Although educational theory has undoubtedly been influenced more by the second of these two concepts, one may doubt whether either pattern or social class has been considered seriously by educators to exemplify a fresh and productive approach to the problem of integration itself. Yet the need for this approach must surely seem axiomatic to any anthropologist: an ordered general education must first of all incorporate, cope with, and evaluate the orders discernible in cultures. Thus these two con-

cepts, combined of course with others, could help to crystallize new curricular designs dependent, first of all, upon the observable relations of real
people living in real cultures—designs cutting both horizontally through
groups and national boundaries (cf. Mead, 1953), and vertically through
layers such as status, class, and caste (cf. Davis, Gardner, 1941).

The polar dimension, temporal order, points to the dynamic factor of
integration. It is a factor that demands recognition of the endless flow of
cultural events through the past, into the present, and toward the future.
Most anthropologists today reject any semblance of inherent progress in
this flow, as indeed they have rejected the earlier "evolutionary" theory of
culture. Few if any, however, have ever denied the indispensable value of
history. The understandable reaction of Boas and his school against the
speculative character of "evolutionary" anthropology is now being qualified in the direction of more balanced views, such as those of the English
archaeologist, V. Gordon Childe (1951) and the historical theories of
Kroeber (cf. 1952, pp. 118 ff.). The latter has, indeed, gone so far as to
cite approvingly the opinion of Eduard Meyer that anthropology, being
"the study of the general . . . forms of human life and development," is
a more proper term for that study than the philosophy of history (p. 76).
Kroeberian contributions of great value include the effort to synchronize
history and science on a "sliding-scale," as opposed to the traditional
dichotomy of the two disciplines, and the hypothesis that one may profitably concentrate upon "cross-sectional moments" of history in such a
way as to subordinate time for purposes of characterizing the forms and
patterns of a given period of culture.

Both education and anthropology itself could, nevertheless, benefit
from the possibilities of enriching the concept of integration afforded by
recent philosophies of history. Some attention, to be sure, has been paid
to Spengler and others mentioned above. Also, it is interesting to note
that Kroeber, in holding that history is properly interpretative and recon-
structive, expresses much the same general view as the English philosopher of history, R. G. Collingwood (1946). On the whole, however,
interdisciplinary explorations of this sort remain in the future. In terms
of general education, the need for such explorations to revitalize the function of history in high-school and college curricula is acute indeed. The
sterile courses now littering typical programs should be discarded in favor
of creative, comparative interpretations of the great movements and struggles of cultures through time—interpretations that utilize Kroeber's
(1944) "configurations of culture growth," Northrop's (1946) "undiffer-
entiated esthetic continuum" of Oriental cultures, Mumford's (1941)
pendulum of "renewal," Toynbee's (1939) "challenge-and-response," and
many other galvanizing and synthesizing concepts that would invigorate
and stretch the youthful mind.

One final concept from anthropology—"configuration"—highlights
the dialectical character of spatial and temporal order. While the term is
often used synonymously with "pattern," it more often tends now to con-
note culture as a "way of life" or, as Sapir (1949, pp. 548 ff.) puts it,

"deep-seated culture patterns" that "are not so much known as felt, not so much capable of conscious description as naïve practice . . ." A configuration is the implicit aesthetic design, the theme, of a culture. Clearly, also, it relates to "value-orientations" discussed in Kluckhohn's (1952, p. 411) statement on values mentioned earlier; there they are defined as "a generalized and organized conception, influencing behavior, of nature, of man's place in it, of man's relations to man, and of the desirable and non-desirable as they relate to man-environment and interhuman relations."

Configurations then embrace and deepen, on the one hand, both the horizontal and vertical interrelations of culture, and, on the other hand, their historical interrelations. They apply more or less aptly either to a fairly homogeneous subculture, such as the Navaho Indian, or to heterogeneous culture, such as the Japanese. That configurations are one of the chief reasons both for the stubbornness and ubiquity of ethnocentricism is fairly obvious. With all their subtleties and complexities, however, they offer tremendous challenge to the concept of integration in educational theory. For one thing, they enable us to perceive that cultural reality, process, and value are all encompassed by that concept. For another, they suggest a possible fusion of the traditionally honorific notion of culture, laden as it is with the values of the "cultivated" carrier, and the scientific conception of culture as the inclusive view of the environment fashioned by man. For still another, they complement the concept of myth as a cautious aid in envisaging the needed goals of modern life.

But perhaps the most exciting of all implications in the concept of configuration is the likelihood that it can eventually assist anthropologists and educators in the formulation of an operationally incisive metaculturology of knowledge. The insistence of Sapir upon the unconscious or covert meanings inherent in culture as a way of life calls our attention in a different way to the elusive assumptions that govern all attempts to express those meanings. In our time, the problem of adequate expression is especially difficult. All of us are likely to be caught in the whirlpools of fear and uncertainty generated, in turn, by the speed of acculturation and the threat of totalitarian power, of moral disintegration, and of planetary war. But few of us are sufficiently aware of the grim contradictions between those explicit credos endorsed by governments and schools, and those implicit values and similar beliefs expressed in overt conduct (cf. Myrdal, 1944).

The question still remains, of course, (a) whether education is able to do anything fundamental about such contradictions, and (b) if it is able, whether it should. The first part of this question was anticipated in discussing the reality of culture. If one tends to hold a *sui generis* view of culture, then one is likely also to hold that education can accomplish little except to conform with and endorse already given cultural configurations. If, however, one holds an operational view, then it is entirely plausible to contend that education can play a constructive part in enunciating and acting upon the problems generated by those configurations.

The second part of the question brings us back to the statement by

Sapir with which our discussion of configurations began. After delineating the meaning of "the unconscious patterning of behavior" in culture, he concludes with the following passage:

No matter where we turn in the field of social behavior, men and women do what they do, and cannot help but do, not merely because they are built thus and so, or possess such and such differences of personality . . . but very largely because they have found it easiest and aesthetically most satisfactory to pattern their conduct in accordance with more or less clearly organized forms of behavior. . . . It is sometimes necessary to become conscious of the forms of social behavior in order to bring about a more serviceable adaptation to changed conditions, but I believe it can be laid down as a principle of far-reaching application that in the normal business of life it is useless and even mischievous for the individual to carry the conscious analysis of his cultural patterns around with him. That should be left to the student whose business it is to understand these patterns. A healthy unconsciousness of the forms of socialized behavior to which we are subject, is as necessary to society as is the mind's ignorance, or better, unawareness, of the workings of the viscera to the health of the body. . . . We must learn to take joy in the larger freedom of loyalty to thousands of subtle patterns of behavior that we can never hope to understand in explicit terms . . . [pp. 588 f.].

Now this is a disturbing argument, certainly, to anyone who takes a transformative view of culture and of education as an instrument of culture. It can be construed as an invitation to relegate efforts to examine and express the premises of any culture solely to experts. It can be construed as an invitation, also, to leave the rest of us blissfully ignorant of what our culture most deeply means, and hence insensitive to its disparities, its lags, its obsolescences. If Sapir were merely to mean that we cannot and should not always, at every moment, be conscious of cultural configurations he would, of course, be right. Cultural like individual experience is, in Dewey's terms, immediate as well as mediate or reflective. But it is clear that Sapir does not mean this merely. Rather, he implies a dualistic thesis: on the one side, there are the few who are alone apparently competent to delve into the mysterious depths of unconscious culture and on the other side, the many who are incompetent.

Such a position, the motivations of which might themselves benefit by exposure to a metaculturology of knowledge, is untenable in a democratic culture—or even in one that might become democratic. However, gigantic the task, however frequent the failures, a culture of this kind is one that must be undertsood, genuinely understood, by the largest possible proportion of those who carry its burdens, who hold ultimate responsibility for its failures and achievements, its means and ends. Hence utmost consciousness of configurational order is likewise their responsibility.

There are, I suggest, at least five norms by which education must be guided if it is to be seriously concerned with that kind of order. The first is for the schools of each culture to formulate as clearly and explicitly as they are able their present implicit premises—premises which are, of course, more or less precisely those of their respective cultures. The second is to consider wherein their resultant formulations appear outworn, inconsistent, or otherwise wanting in view of the transformations now occurring in the economic, religious, and other spheres of life. The third is to experiment with restatements that more honestly enunciate their actual as against traditionally professed configurations, and of course to implement these restatements through integrated policies and programs. The fourth is to provide for comparative studies of the results, by as many informal as well as formal educational agencies of as many cultures as possible. The final aim is to achieve not only a whole array of educational formulations that have profited by critical interaction, but also a unified international formulation that accepts common principles, common objectives, and common tasks for education everywhere on earth.

These five norms, difficult and gigantic though they are, may not be as idealistic as at first they seem. Actually, sporadic and fumbling efforts along similar lines are already under way, both in the schools of various countries and in commissions of the United Nations Educational, Scientific, and Cultural Organization. One trouble with many of these efforts has been, not that they are not well-intentioned or motivated by cultural disturbances, but that they have often been superficial because unwilling or unable to penetrate to the covert level where the real problem of configuration lies. Moreover, partly because of a dearth of close co-operation between educators, on the one side, and anthropologists, on the other, there has been a failure to perceive that any successful effort to reformulate a unified conception of education for our age must incorporate what we may now call three dimensions of cultural order. These are: the horizontal-vertical dimension of culture in space, the historical dimension of culture in time, and the "qualitative" dimension of configuration which compounds the first two into an integrated whole—an aesthetic design for a modern philosophy of education-and-culture.

References

Benedict, Ruth. 1934. *Patterns of Culture.* New York: Houghton Mifflin Company.
Bidney, David. 1953a. *Theoretical Anthropology.* New York: Columbia University Press.
———. 1953b. "The Concept of Value in Modern Anthropology," in A. L. Kroeber (ed.), *Anthropology Today.* Chicago: University of Chicago Press. Pp. 682–99.
Brameld, Theodore. 1947. "An Inductive Approach to Intercultural Values," *Journal of Educational Sociology,* XXI, 4–11.
———. 1950. *Patterns of Educational Philosophy.* New York: World Press.
Cassirer, Ernst. 1944. *An Essay on Man.* New Haven: Yale University Press.
Childe, V. Gordon. 1951. *Man Makes Himself.* New York: Mentor Books.
Collingwood, R. G. 1946. *The Idea of History.* Clarendon: Oxford University Press.
Curti, Merle. 1935. *The Social Ideas of American Educators.* New York: Charles Scribner's Sons.
Davis, Allison, B. B. Gardner, and Mary R. Gardner. 1941. *Deep South.* Chicago: University of Chicago Press.
Dewey, John. 1916. *Democracy and Education.* New York: The Macmillan Company.
———. 1939. *Freedom and Culture.* New York: G. P. Putnam's Sons.
Edel, Abraham. 1953. "Some Relations of Philosophy and Anthropology," *American Anthropologist,* LV, 649–60.
Frank, Jerome. 1945. *Fate and Freedom.* New York: Simon and Schuster, Inc.

Friess, Horace. 1950. "Philosophies of Culture," in Vergilius Ferm (ed.), *A History of Philosophical Systems*. New York: Philosophical Library. Pp. 588–97.

Fromm, Erich. 1947. *Man for Himself*. New York: Rinehart & Company, Inc.

Harris, William T. 1901. *Psychological Foundations of Education*. New York: Appleton.

Herskovits, Melville J. 1948. *Man and His Works*. New York: Alfred A. Knopf, Inc.

Honigmann, John J. 1954. *Culture and Personality*. New York: Harper & Brothers.

Johnson, Charles S. 1943. "Education and the Cultural Process: Introduction to the Symposium," in Charles S. Johnson (ed.), *Education and the Cultural Process*. Chicago: University of Chicago Press. Pp. 1–4.

Kluckhohn, Clyde. 1949. *Mirror for Man*. New York: McGraw-Hill Book Company, Inc.

——. 1952. "Values and Value-Orientations in the Theory of Action: An Exploration in Definition and Classification," in Talcott Parsons and Edward L. Shils (eds.), *Toward a General Theory of Action*. Cambridge: Harvard University Press. Pp. 388–433.

Kroeber, Alfred L. 1944. *Configurations of Culture Growth*. Berkeley: University of California Press.

——. 1948. *Anthropology*. New York: Harcourt, Brace and Company.

——. 1952. *The Meaning of Culture*. Chicago: University of Chicago Press.

—— (ed.). 1953. *Anthropology Today*. Chicago: University of Chicago Press.

Kroeber, Alfred L., and Clyde Kluckhohn. 1952. *Culture: A Critical Review of Concepts and Definitions*. Cambridge: Peabody Museum.

Lee, Dorothy. 1948. "Are Basic Needs Ultimate?" *Journal of Abnormal and Social Psychology*, XLIII, 391–95.

Lewin, Kurt. 1948. *Resolving Social Conflicts*. New York: Harper & Brothers.

Linton, Ralph (ed.). 1945. *The Science of Man in the World Crisis*. New York: Columbia University Press.

Malinowski, Bronislaw. 1944. *A Scientific Theory of Culture and Other Essays*. Chapel Hill: University of North Carolina Press.

Mannheim, Karl. 1936. *Ideology and Utopia*. New York: Harcourt, Brace and Company.

Mayer, Kurt. 1953. "The Theory of Social Classes," *Harvard Educational Review*, XXIII, 149–67.

Mead, Margaret. 1953. "National Character," in A. L. Kroeber (ed.), *Anthropology Today*. Chicago: University of Chicago Press. Pp. 642–67.

Mumford, Lewis. 1941. *The Condition of Man*. New York: Harcourt, Brace and Company.

Murdock, George P. 1945. "The Common Denominator of Cultures," in Ralph Linton (ed.), *The Science of Man in the World Crisis*. New York: Columbia University Press. Pp. 123–42.

Myrdal, Gunnar. 1944. *An American Dilemma*. New York: Harper & Brothers.

Northrop, F. S. C. 1946. *The Meeting of East and West*. New York: The Macmillan Company.

Opler, Morris. 1947. "Cultural Alternatives and Educational Theory," *Harvard Educational Review*, XVII, 28–44.

Raup, Bruce, George E. Axtelle, Kenneth D. Benne, and B. Othanel Smith. 1950. *The Improvement of Practical Intelligence*. New York: Harper & Brothers.

Riesman, David. 1950. *The Lonely Crowd*. New Haven: Yale University Press.

Sapir, Edward. 1949. "The Unconscious Patterning of Behavior in Society," in David B. Mandelbaum (ed.), *Selected Writings of Edward Sapir*. Berkeley: University of California Press. Pp. 544–59.

Sorokin, Pitirim A. 1941. *The Crisis of Our Age*. New York: E. P. Dutton & Co., Inc.

Toynbee, Arnold. 1939. *A Study of History*. New York: Oxford University Press.

Warner, W. L., R. J. Havighurst, and M. B. Loeb. 1944. *Who Shall Be Educated?* New York: Harper & Brothers.

Warner, W. L., and P. S. Lunt. 1941. *The Social Life of a Modern Community*. New Haven: Yale University Press.

White, Leslie. 1949a. "Ethnological Theory," pp. 357–84, in R. W. Sellars, V. J. McGill and Marvin Farber (eds.), *Philosophy for the Future*. New York: The Macmillan Company.

——. 1949b. *The Science of Culture*. New York: Farrar, Straus and Young, Inc.

SIXTH SESSION OF THE CONFERENCE
Chairman: Lawrence K. Frank

Spindler: I would like to say that this is one of the culminating phases of the conference—where we try now to regroup and generalize at a somewhat different level in our communication than we have so far. With that, I'll turn the meeting over to Mr. Frank, who will be chairman this afternoon.

Frank: I suspect in view of the discussions in the last three days that each one of us has come here with an educational philosophy as well as a theory of learning. They are implicit if not explicit in many of our comments. That's quite as it should be, and I think if we will recognize that, we may save ourselves some confusions. I suspect that each of us has a different conviction about the role of formal education in personality development, and in social and cultural change. If we put this on the record and acknowledge it maybe our communication will be facilitated.

We have three discussants: Cowley, Thomas, and Siegel. In that order, I am going to call upon them to open the discussion.

Discussant: William H. Cowley

Cowley: If I understand the burden of his paper, Mr. Brameld begins with a premise that we've been discussing this morning: that we cannot communicate with one another unless we make our underlying assumptions—which he calls metacultural and meta-educational—explicit. I want to confine myself to the discussion of the educational end of it from a point of view that may not interest many of you, but I'm going to throw it out in any event because it's where I live.

I've gone through Mr. Brameld's paper and have underlined every use he's made of the words "education" and "educational," and I've classified them. Essentially I am interested in educational taxonomy. When he uses the word "education," I want to know what he means by it. The group may recall Mr. Henry's observation of the first day that he doesn't know what education is. In my judgment, most educationists don't either because we use the term in many senses.

My classification of the terms Mr. Brameld has used—education and educational—falls into an order of occurrence in his paper. He talks about *educational process*, which I translate in my terminology into function—something that you do. Indirectly, in using the term enculturation, he talks about *educational purpose*. When he talks about formal schooling, he's talking essentially about *educational content*. He also talks about *educational results*, that which comes through from the educational process. Further, he talks about *educational personnel,* and then he discusses the professional discipline of education. Personally, I don't think that education is a discipline. I think, rather, that it's a profession made up of practitioners with very few persons concerned with its basic theories, Mr. Brameld being one. He also mentions *educational structures* in terms of the schools particularly. Here we have six uses of the word education, each one of them different.

Mr. Brameld also uses a seventh term again and again, namely, *educational theory*. I raised the question with him, in the course of lunch, as to *what* education theory; theory about *what*? General theory co-ordinating all of these six breakdowns? Or the theory about each of them separately? My own belief is that you must begin with the notion of a structure that performs certain functions for certain purposes to achieve certain results by means of certain content. I also believe that in the discussion of educational reconstruction you must begin with the question, "Who is going to reconstruct?" And if you ask that question, then you come immediately to the core question, "Who controls the structures?"

Consider the question, "Who is going to do the reconstruction?" Is it to be done by educationists? Is it to be done by the public at large? Is it to be done by pressure groups which have been mentioned a number of times? Is it to be done by the Bestors? Is it to be done by the McCarthys? Who is to do it?

I gather that Mr. Brameld believes it's possible—he ends on that note—for us to come to some consensus in the democratic process concerning the program of the schools. I'm a skeptic about this. I think, further, that it's undesirable that we should, that the merit of our democratic process lies in its diversity and pluralism, and that we are healthy because we have diversity and pluralism. In any event, the chief problems, it seems to me in Mr. Brameld's paper, are first, he's talking about the *reconstruction of what*—which of these seven facets of education, or all of them? The second is the problem of control: who controls the structures called schools?

Let me go on with control just a moment, although, as I say, I don't know whether this taxonomy question interests the group. We have long debates in American universities about who should control them. Should they be controlled by the professoriate, or should they be controlled by boards of trustees? And if somehow by both, then how should they communicate with one another, how should they be related to one another? Then we have other power groups including the alumni. Harvard University in the last analysis is governed by its alumni, since every major act by the Harvard Corporation must be approved by the alumni board called the Board of Overseers. On the other hand, Oxford and Cambridge are entirely controlled by their faculties with no structural relationship to the outside world except through royal commissions, of which there have been three in the last century. Between the times the royal commissions function there is give and take in various ways between Oxford and Cambridge and English society, but the policy-making group is the professoriate. This is a type of syndicalism. The new English universities, however, follow a variation of the American plan.

These problems of control are very involved problems. We can't discuss social reconstruction, it seems to me, without coming to terms with them. I gather from our talk during lunch that Mr. Brameld agrees with this, but whether or not the question interests the group will come out in the discussion. It seems to me, however, that we need to talk about structures and their control.

Discussant: Lawrence Thomas

Thomas: As I said this morning, it seemed to me that Professor Brameld believed there was a triangle of professional interests represented here. One was an interest in anthropological data—the practices, institutions, and values of cultures. The second was an interest in educational problems and policies, which also have their practices, institutions, and values. And third, an interest in what I would call a social philosophy of education. This last has two functions: one is an intermediary function of examining and clarifying the generalizations from anthropology before they are translated into the sources for educational policy. For example, Steve Hart in his cross-cultural summary last night of the ceremonials—education by kinsmen versus education by strangers—didn't declare that these ought to be policies of American education; but they tempt one to interpret them as "oughts," and this temptation should be resisted until you've philosophically examined them.

The second function of the philosopher is to identify and clarify the basic assumptions of both education and anthropology in this common task that we're talking about. And as Hal Cowley has observed, these basic assumptions might be called "metacultural" or "meta-educational," just to distinguish them from operating assumptions that any enterprise uses when it's trying to get some structure into its program. The nature of Brameld's argument seems to me to be in the form of a large circle with four distinct stages to it. In the first stage he talks about culture as perceived by the anthropologists. In the second, he goes to the philosophical orientations of the anthropologists, talking a good deal about David Bidney's book, *Theoretical Anthropology*, which identified the systematic philosophies underlying the view of anthropologists. Ted Brameld has observed that to stop here is to commit what he calls the "philosophical fallacy" of believing that your systematic orientation accounts for all of your behavior and your viewpoints. He has his own orientation—reconstructionism—which he has mentioned here, but it seems to me that he is much more interested in having us recognize that each orientation makes a difference than he is in arguing any particular orientation.

Then in the third stage, after citing these philosophical orientations, he went on to some philosophical issues in viewing culture which are not organized systematically yet. They include such issues as the character of change, of cultural dynamics, crises, values, configuration. Brameld protests a lack of concern on the part of anthropologists to the significance of these basic issues. At this point I would differ slightly and say that this job belongs primarily to the social philosopher, but he must work in very close concert with the anthropologist. I doubt if the anthropologists have the energy or the interest to develop very systematically the meta-assumptions behind these terms, and as social philosophers we're trying to do it. But we certainly can't do it in isolation; we have to work with anthropologists in some sort of environment like this.

Then Brameld goes on to the fourth stage, in which he takes up culture again, but in a new and deeper context. Here he contends that the anthropologist's own cultural orientation affects in some very subtle and profound ways his perceptions of any other culture. Now, of all social scientists, the anthropologists are the most sensitive, in my judgment, to the problem of shifting viewpoints. They have made a distinctive contribution by their insistence upon objectivity as you go from your own culture to that of a primitive, nonliterate culture and upon the avoidance of reading your own values into the different culture. But what Brameld has in mind is a sensitivity to assumptions that go much deeper than whether we respect the individual personality over the family or whether we believe that to make a good living is the most important value. The anthropologist is extremely sensitive to these values, but Brameld is talking about more basic ones—the conception of crisis and change, the matter of cycles in cultural trends—and develops a term which he calls a "metaculturology of knowledge." I admit I'm not too impressed with that term. I believe it would be much simpler to call it the philosophy of anthropology, and have it deal frankly with concepts like this.

I hope the discussion is going to deal with the third and fourth stages in this big circle, and to make an effort to facilitate that, I would like to spend a little time now on the second stage—the difference that a systematic philosophic orientation would make in how you view culture and education. If this second stage can be sufficiently clarified and understood, made common and current in our understanding, then we can pass on to some of the metacultural assumptions.

So I would like to take a few examples of the contrasts between two systematic philosophies. For this purpose, I'll group the Thomists and the essentialists in a generally classical orientation, and contrast it with the experimentalists, or progressivists as Ted (Brameld) calls them, leaving out his reconstructionism to some extent, although it would agree with progressivism on most issues. I hope these examples will give some clarity to his contention that your systematic philosophical orientation does make a difference in how you view culture. Here are the choices, and I would like to suggest you carry in mind two points: first, what is your bias?—because these all represent biases—and second, is your bias systematic? It is generally systematic to the degree that your choices of the following contrasts tend to be classicist or experimentalist. In each instance the first alternative presented is classicist and the second experimentalist.

1a. Newton's view of the universe—a system of objects and forces external to and unaffected by man's knowledge of them, and hence governed by pre-established laws.
1b. Relativistic view—the universe is a perceived pattern of events within man's experience, differentiated out of man's experience, and ordered by laws formulated and verified in man's experience.
2a. Outer reality (to which children should relate themselves) conceived as given and something to be accurately perceived.
2b. Reality as differentiated out of the flow of each person's experiences, greatly helped by others, becoming objective through intersubjectivity.
3a. Perception as ideally passive, taking in the given with a minimum of subjective distortion, as a camera.
3b. Perception as active, creative, interpretive, seeking equilibrium between the external and internal poles of experiencing.
4a. Change as occurring according to some cosmic design, hence teleological; progress is toward a pre-set goal.

4b. Change as infinitely variable and pluralistic in direction, and in which man can evolve guiding purposes genetically from the critical examination and testing of his on-going experiences.

5a. Culture as a particular kind of external reality (in Brameld's terms, a reified substance).

5b. Culture as a functional abstraction for identifying and delineating certain kinds of experience.

6a. Knowledge and values as relative to a culture but not properly relative to the child.

6b. Knowledge and values as relative to specific frames of reference and individual purposes as well as to larger groups.

7a. The child should be helped to internalize our culture. The teacher determines the kind and amount, while the child's purposes set the teacher's problem of motivation.

7b. The child should learn the culture by purposively utilizing and transforming his perceptions of the behavior of others in his own problem-solving and satisfaction-seeking. The child's purposes and goals (though not all of them) are decisive in determining the kind and amount of the culture he learns.

8a. In discipline, children are helped to discover the right limits.

8b. In discipline, children participate in the creation of mutually acceptable limits.

Now, if these eight illustrate adequately the grounds of bias in systematic philosophies, I hope that we can turn to more particular instances.

The main questions that Ted raises then in the third stage are things like this (he put them in the form of topics; I wish he'd put them in the form of questions. I'd like to try three of them to see if I express the sense of his interest and inquiry under these topics): The first topic was the reality of culture, and I take it he wanted to know in what sense and context does culture have reality. Then the second question dealt with cultural dynamics and process. I take it he meant to ask there: How might various concepts of cultural process — gradualism, crises, and cycles—affect the observance of trends? And third, in talking about cultural values: From various conceptions of the nature of value, can we get a generalized theory providing a universal human framework for studying values in any particular culture?

Discussant: Bernard Siegel

Siegel: I want to address myself more or less exclusively to the implications of what Ted Brameld has said concerning metacultural assumptions underlying our concern with the nature of culture, and what we can contribute in the way of understanding by virtue of these premises. I agree quite thoroughly with Ted that the kinds of premises that we have of reality condition how we think about culture and the way we verbalize it, and that as a result we are likely to be directed toward the gathering of facts and toward the interpretation of what we see. And I think it's very good to make this explicit.

I believe you have isolated four extremely important and crucial problematic concepts from anthropology, namely, the *reality* of culture, *process* in culture (cultural change), *values* in culture, and the *integration* of culture. I shall discuss the reality of culture first. I feel that if we think of culture as consisting of certain properties of human behavior, we might avoid the *sui generis* versus the operational point of view which seems to be causing such difficulty. For example, if we take as a basic property of cultures the element of sharing, then we can ask questions about the *degree* of sharing that exists within any population, the extent to which certain elements of behavior and expression, of having and not having, are shared. I think there is wide agreement among anthropologists that culture, from this point of view, does not behave autonomously. There is at least variation, even in the most simple cultures, around age and sex differences as they affect the interpretation and perception of patterns.

Now I do not think that an operational point of view (which means that we are defining our concept in terms of certain problems that we wish to study, for which our conception is relevant and functional) excludes the fact that the property of sharing certain modes of behavior is in part *sui generis*. That is to say, we can say certain things about the nature of shared beliefs and behavior that exclude certain types of reactions, variable types of choices that people might make with respect to new experience. If, for example, a people have come to share very widely a set of integrative, linked, or related propositions about the nature of man to the universe and man to man—and if, moreover, there is a sharing of agreements as to the enforcement of these beliefs by some kind of power relations within the group—then the kinds of choices that the members of that group can make in reacting to a new experience or threat will be correspondingly limited. On the other hand, there is a certain range of choices that they are permitted to make, but I would say from what we know empirically that this range of choice is finite. I believe this may have some implications for the reconstructionist point of view.

With reference to the second topic, *process*, perhaps it is a little unfortunate that you dwelt on the concept of *focus* as being important for a discussion of processes of change. I think it is unfortunate simply because—and others may not agree with me—I feel that this is a tautological concept. That is, one may ask how you arrive at the notion of focus (or what Herskovits means by an area of piling up of interests) except by simply finding it or observing it. So I find an area of behavior and belief in which there are all sorts of possibilities to talk freely and openly, in which people want to talk, and I label that focus. Then I say, people are quite willing and interested in talking about matters in focal areas of culture. And I am not sure where we can get from here. You suggest to educators "that if they are to play any sort of creative role in cultural process, one of their first duties must be to determine as clearly as possible the precise character of the focus or foci of given cultures and subcultures, and then to construct strategies of change geared to this character."

Perhaps if you were to expatiate for a moment upon what you mean by the last part of that sentence I wouldn't be troubled by it. If you mean that we should create strategies of education geared to supporting these foci, there my be certain dangers involved. It may be desirable, from some points of view, to attack the focus of a culture quite directly and quite abruptly. If we assume that the focal values are the basic value areas with which we must work in a culture, we are likely to produce what Goldenweiser once called a tendency toward involution—we elaborate the logical possibilities of a pattern exhaustively—a kind of development that doesn't enable us to deal very effectively with crisis situations.

And that brings me to a consideration of the notion of *crisis*, which I think is very important. I would like to point out in this connection that I believe there is a great deal more in the empirical literature of anthropological research, observation, and reporting which makes some use of the notion of crisis than is apparent. One can very easily overlook this concern because the word "crisis" is so seldom used. Sometimes it is substituted by the term "urgency," which essentially means the same thing in this context. But there is a very good reason, stemming from the social conditions in which anthropologists have worked, for the lack of use of the crisis concept. Anthropologists have frequently been in areas where crisis in the sense that we today are facing it has been faced by *other* peoples, but anthropologists have come in from the point of view of a member of *our* culture, even though they are sympathetic with the rights of the people. I believe there probably is some assumption on the anthropologists' part that continued crises for the so-called underdeveloped or primitive groups might be avoided or ameliorated. But I can assure you that if the anthropologist was a member of a number of the tribal groups who were "benefiting" from the contact with agents of white culture, he would interpret this immediately as crisis, and the notion would have occurred at least on every other page.

I think that if we re-examine from this point of view some of the literature coming out in the field of acculturation, we might get some insights for interpreting our own reaction patterns. I think there is, for example, an analogy between the patterns of reaction that often have been labeled "isolationism" on the American scene (retreat, conservatism, and so forth in its more extreme forms socially and politically), and what anthropologists term "nativistic reactions" in a great many other cultures that have undergone crisis situations. There is an important difference, of course, namely, that in cultures with more simple and primitive technologies, the realistic abilities to cope with the situation are limited.

Now I want to talk about the problem of *values*. It's a little difficult to discuss this as an anthropologist, simply because, as you pointed out, there has been so little attention paid to the concept of values. But on the basis of what we do know about the functioning of values and the nature of values as a component in most human acts, I would say that there is no single rubric under which we can meaningfully define what values are. I dont' feel, for example, that Kluckhohn's general definition is very meaningful in an operational sense. When we think about values and needs, and also think through the implications of these dimensions for the kinds of questions we can ask and the kinds of data we are likely to acquire, then we can formulate problems.

It's understandable that you should have singled out the issue of relativity versus universality of values. I would like to say, however, that there are probably other of these dimensions that are equally important to consider, from my point of view as an anthropologist. I will mention just two of these: namely, (1) the problem of organization of values, by which I would mean at least in part, and an important part, the hierarchy of values; and (2) the dimension of intensity, namely, the degree of commitment that the members of a society share with respect to the various values.

I think the problem of the organization of values is extremely important because it affects how people perceive all kinds of situations, old and new, and the way in which they organize their choice of behavior in terms either of avoiding certain kinds of possible reaction patterns or of taking advantage of certain kinds of choices. And I believe also if you think of the dimension of intensity in terms of commitment, that too suggests a wide variety of ways in which we may grapple with the concept of values and organize questions about it. We can no doubt formulate a number of hypotheses concerning what one degree or another of commitment in an organized set or system of values would imply, for the kinds of reactions to situations a, b, and c . . . n as ends with which a group might be confronted.

This is the end of my systematic observations. I thought your paper was extremely stimulating.

Frank: I'd like to have Brameld, if he will, make any comments now before we start the discussion; and then after that if we can entice Kroeber to say something at this moment and give him just a little extended space to speak without interruption, I think we would all appreciate hearing from him.

Author's Commentary

Theodore Brameld

Brameld: I'm very anxious to hear Professor Kroeber too, so I'll limit my comments here.

First, Hal Cowley's discussion of who controls the structure is of great importance; it is not developed in my paper. I'm not sure we can get the answer to the question from the anthropologists, although they can help; we need the help also of political scientists and psychiatrists and others. It is also important to bring the value problem in again by recognizing that if we are to attempt to deal with the power structure and the controllers of education, we have to do it in terms of a theory of values. Before we can decide who controls and should control the structure, we really have to decide—controls for what purposes? One thing that Childs, philosopher of education at Columbia, has emphasized for many years, and rightly, is that education is never impartial—that it always involves a theory of morality. Therefore teachers and all others involved in education must choose morally if they're to be effective. But they choose even if they don't choose, in the paradoxical sense that they will allow the stronger moral or immoral forces to control when they remain indifferent or neutral. I think it's possible to solve the problem of power and control only if we can build a theory of values sufficiently clear and having sufficient degree of consensus—not unanimous consensus but a majority consensus. If we can build such a theory in which we agree on our ends, then and only then are we in a position to make choices with regard to the question of who shall control, and to throw our own forces in behalf of the building of a power structure which will in turn enable the schools to become part of the larger cultural and social struggle to achieve those ends. I have tried to imply this, in part, by the hyphenated phrase "culture-and-education" or "education-and-culture." The four theories that are touched on in this paper are not theories of education in the last analysis; they're theories of life and theories of society. Education is a kind of microcosm of the macrocosm of life and culture which these four symbols represent. I often tell my students that when they choose a philosophy of education they're really choosing a philosophy of life, in which the school is integral with the total pattern of struggle for the ends to which these several philosophies are respectively committed.

Second, I appreciated Larry Thomas' supplementations. He used the metaphor of a circle and I was helped by his suggesting that my paper implied that you start with culture, move to the level of philosophy, then to the level of problematic concepts, and then back to culture. Perhaps the metaphor of a spiral would be better than a circle, because you don't go back to the original concept of culture; you move to a much deeper and more subtle conception of culture as you move through these various stages. Here is where metacultural interpretation occurs.

Third, as to Siegel's comments, knowledge of limitations in the range of choices that study of culture provides would be of great use to all philosophies of education. This is one of the weaknesses of the progressivists: they've often been rather tender-minded, I fear, in their faith that education can change the world. We learn from Professor Kroeber and others that it can't; the limitations are too tough. Reconstructionism, to which Siegel refers, is a fumbling, unfinished effort to build a paradoxical philosophy in the sense that it is, on the one hand, perhaps the most "idealistic" of the four major ones, and, on the other hand, the most "realistic" in the sense of attempting to be concerned with the toughness of culture, with the limitations and pressures against change. Possibly here the influence of Marxism is at least implicit; reconstructionism is not a Marxian philosophy, but of the four major positions it has been influenced perhaps more by Marxism than the others have. One of the strengths of Marxism is that it's pretty tough in some of its analyses, and it does call attention to the limitations of choice.

As to the concept of crisis, I would argue that the major alternative philosophies of education are really alternative diagnoses and prognoses of our age of crisis, and that it is the crisis which is ultimately motivating their respective formulations. That's quite explicit in perennialism, for instance: a man like Jacques Maritain is very conscious of the world crisis. Hutchins, whom I would also classify as a perennialist, is likewise conscious of it. He defines crisis somewhat differently than other people would, perhaps, but he constantly uses the word and he means something very serious by it. Now my point is that these philosophies of education that are warring for our allegiance today are themselves, at the deeper level, symbols of the several avenues along which people are invited to travel toward the future. They are alternative choices; they are deathly serious choices; and the great problem confronting education today is which choice are we going to make—if not among these, then perhaps some other? In this sense, philosophies of education are symbols of cultural choices at the metacultural level—a level that is not merely philosophical, but ideological, economic, religious, historical, *and* philosophical.

Frank: Dr. Kroeber, would you like to comment on that?

Commentary by Alfred Kroeber

Kroeber: Yes. I would agree entirely with Brameld's last sentence. I also agree with one of the first things he said about Cowley having developed an interesting situation; I'd very much like to hear further from him later on. I was much stimulated by Brameld's paper, and I was also somewhat fussed by it because of the way my name kept appearing and I saw myself portrayed in a role in which I don't see myself, either as a metaculturist or a systemic philosopher. As a matter of fact, I am an anthropologist; I'm an anthropologist who began with an interest in concrete facts and their organization, and little else. If I had any more general views, I wasn't aware of it: they were implicit. And presumably, as I worked on, and there was more material to be dealt with and more interrelations between them became evident, I began to think in relations or theoretical terms. I was nearing middle age, I think, before I had my first outbreaks of statements of a more general nature. As a matter of fact, it's only since my retirement from Berkeley that I find that I'm looked upon as a theorist. Certainly, people who knew me for forty-five years around the University of California never thought of me that way; if they did, they carefully kept it from me.

I think one reason why we anthropologists, and not sociologists or others, are here with the people from education is that anthropology has, so to speak, a triple parentage—three strands make it up. One of these is definitely humanism, and therefore deals with values. I need only point out how study of languages and archeology are classified as segments of anthropology: those come under the humanist side by general consent. For instance, my own entry was through an interest in language; and that is true, I'm certain, for a lot of other people. This humanist element cannot and must not be overlooked. Now, the humanist operates insufficiently from the point of view of the "total anthropologist," because he will not compare widely enough; he will not treat all cultures on one level of comparison. And consequently, whether he wants to or not, he is therefore making value judgments, with which I'm not quarreling. But he is making them from too narrow a basis; his judgments are in a sense predetermined because he doesn't know all the comparisons, as the anthropologist at least tries to know them.

A second component is the empirical, positivist, natural science ingredient, which I see as finding its closest analogue within natural science in what is ordinarily called natural history—natural history of the earth, natural history of animals and plants. There again, comparison is the dominant first approach, before we get further into interpretation. There is a large body of facts, and until they've been dissected and analyzed sufficiently so they can be compared in any deeper way, we cannot go on to anything beyond. I've often wondered, incidentally, why so few anthropologists have come into their science—because the older ones all came from somewhere else—out of the natural history part of biology. However, I hold a personal view which may sound paradoxical: the biologist also deals with value, although he has been taught as a scientist and naturalist not to make value judgments. When the biologist says a seal is a good swimmer, but a poor walker, or when he points out feature after feature of the structure of a bird which all have to do with swiftness of motion, the power of flight, and related capacities, he is then "evaluating" what a bird as an organism does, compared with a fish or a mammal. Ever since anthropologists have called themselves such, and have felt conscious of constituting a professional discipline with a separate subject matter, they have probably been dealing in values whether they knew it or not. Yet calling them values, discussing values in a theoretical way, is something that I have seen come up in recent decades, and particularly in the last half dozen or so years.

The third component, of course, is social science, and most often anthropology is for convenience classed primarily with the social sciences although, historically speaking, anthropology became a social science last of all; it's the latest of the three ingredients to have entered it. In the core social sciences—sociology, economics, and government—we do have a strong idea of utility, of being practical, of being of some use, at least sometimes of amelioration. Now such ideas were pretty foreign to the early anthropologists, whether they came in from linguistics and archeology on the aesthetic side, or from the natural history side of culture. They were not ameliorationists; they were not thinking that they had a program to offer the world for its betterment.

As to the factor of "sense of crisis," I mentally noted that Brameld spoke of Cassirer's emphasis on myth. The sense of impending crisis seems to be the myth of the day; it is the myth of the moment in our Western world. This appears to be essentially a temporary phase, a transient phenomenon. It might of course become permanent: that is, we might really bust up not because of atomic inventions but because everyone finally got so cumulatively panicky that he would have everybody else by the hair, and none would know what he was doing. I certainly would not consider the idea of crisis as being at all normal or natural to the human race. It seems rather a symptom of abnormality or pathology, which we would be much better off to get rid of quickly instead of indulging it.

If I may go back to Dorothy Lee's paper this morning, I have a sense that what she perhaps was protesting against (whether she knew it or not) was the tendency of people in the field of education to accept a role— which has been thrust upon them, no doubt—not of controlling, but of shaping such control as they have, in line with the pressures which come upon them from the larger public, from the community, or the world. They have got caught in the net of a democratizing drift which has helped bring about the very obvious revolution in education. The public seems to look upon them as put in control, and then expects their right answers to lead us all out of the woods. Further, I think the educationists see the jam they're in, or will soon be in if things keep piling up this way; and naturally they tend to call in others who can perhaps help extricate them— anthropologists or such. But personally I have no answer and little advice to give the educationists here. There are a lot of things none of us really knows, and I certainly am not ready to tell anybody else how to educate the nation or how the world should be saved.

Another point: the democratizing process inevitably brings with it a concern for what others think, "which way the drift is." In proportion as that concern is developed, there is less attention paid to inner development or stimuli. As internal resources are correspondingly diminished, one is more and more thrown on outer influences. That may be desirable, or it may be undesirable; perhaps it is inevitable. But it is a current I see as an undertow flowing through much in our public affairs, through education, through a great deal of science, through this meeting here. I call attention to it from a point of view such as Dorothy represented this morning from her more specific starting point. I expect Mr. Brameld is also conscious of the drift.

OPEN DISCUSSION

Sui Generis

Hart, Kimball

Hart: One concept involved with much that has been said is that of culture as *sui generis*. It seems to me there's a lot of misunderstanding of this position; the Latin phrase "*sui generis*" as far as I know was first used by Durkheim for social facts as distinct from individual facts, and I think if we go back and read Durkheim's initial formulation of the *sui generis* position you'll find he wasn't talking about culture as culture has come to be used in American anthropology in recent years. In trying to define his *sui generis* order of phenomena, he offered, among the criteria, the idea that social facts had coercive power over the individual. Now, as I see it, culture has no coercive power over the individual, except to the extent that there are enforcing agencies for various pieces of the culture. And I think it was these enforcing agencies Durkheim was talking about.

It's the pieces of social structure that have the coercive power—for instance, the army, as anybody knows who gets into it. There is a hierarchy of people who are paid to insist on certain regulations being followed, and that hierarchy of people is the social structure which we call the Army. And inasmuch as they're enforcing rules and insisting on conformity of the new recruit, they are coercing the individual to conformity in that area.

The social system exists, will continue to exist irrespective of the comings and goings of individuals. I think we can find enforcing structures all through societies, as I tried to illustrate in my own paper where I made quite a fuss about the change-over in personnel in the prepubertal and postpubertal enforcers. At puberty a whole new group of coercers takes over from the authorized coercers before: the authorized coercers earlier were family; the authorized coercers later are the strangers who come in and replace those of before.

Now, it seems to me that unless we're prepared to some extent to accept the reality of structures, there's not much you can do with social change. In this particular sense, I think not only is there a case to be made for the *sui generis* position—the reality of structure—but I find it very difficult to operate without it. Unless you have that *sui generis* position, I don't see how you can make a distinction between vague, free-floating changes in public opinion, and the changes that are represented by America before the rise of the C.I.O. and America after the rise of the C.I.O., or the American school system before the P.T.A. was formed and the American school system after the P.T.A. was formed, and so on. In other words, it seems to me that these structures channel and fix and give you permanent points in the free-floating public opinion change.

Kimball: I think Steve (Hart) has a point. In our discussion of learning we have hardly mentioned that learning takes place in social systems. We've been talking about cultural process, and I think we should also have talked explicitly about learning in the social context: the environment, the personnel, and the organization within which learning occurs. And if we don't talk about learning in this context, it floats around without relation to reality.

Hart: If Cowley is saying that he thinks anthropology should pay more attention to administrative setups, I thoroughly agree with him and say we are, but we call them social systems or social structure. And as an anthropologist I say that we can achieve social change much faster by changing the structure and not bothering about the people. The tendency to think of the individual as the causative factor, I think, is a bias in American culture.

Labels and Positions: More on *Sui Generis*

Coladarci, Kroeber, Gillin

Coladarci: Let me suggest that my understanding of the point of the paper and the discussion of it is not that one seeks his place in some present systematic thinking or identifies himself with available labels. Brameld offered us four and suggested the possibility of more. Rather, one inquires with reference to some very fundamental assumptions being made, some of which we have identified, and then, perhaps, he may apply a label if he wishes—a shorthand way of describing his thinking. There have been in the past some labeled positions that are internally consistent; it is not intended that one fits into any one of them.

My reaction to Steve's (Hart) point is the suspicion that, perhaps, he considers a *sui generis* position like that of White, with respect to culture, as a position which is intolerable *because it's factually incorrect*. But my understanding of Brameld, and as a matter of fact of philosophy (at a very superficial level), is that this *sui generis* proposition is not an *empirical* proposition: you can't test the *sui generis* proposition against empirical criteria. That's what makes one's position on this issue a fundamental point for inquiry, in Brameld's view. Am I correct?

Thomas: The point is the difference it makes when you have either one view or the other.

Kroeber: I have something on that I've been wanting to say. The *sui generis* has two sides: what it refers to, and what it means. Now,

Durkheim may have been the first to use the word, but Durkheim did not have the concept of culture. He called it social facts—which may be societal, which may be cultural, which may be both. Malinowski, on the other hand, spoke explicitly of *culture* as a "reality *sui generis*." Lowie has also spoken of culture as *sui generis*. I doubt whether I used the term, but at any rate I've been reckoned among the *sui generis* people. But Hart, I believe, was speaking essentially of social or societal structure.

Now, the other thing: What does the phrase *sui generis* mean or import? It can mean that culture is so wholly of its own kind that nothing else impinges on it; it is completely autonomous, and therefore if culture changes it is through immanent forces, through something predestined or predetermined. I think that is probably the view that Leslie White holds. As I look back, I see in myself in the past certain inclinations in that direction which, however, I hope I have purged. And *sui generis* may mean nothing more than that culture is an aspect of phenomena which has a certain uniqueness, without asserting that uniqueness involves absolute autonomy—that culture is something carved out of the universe and then set aside from the rest of it.

Gillin: In connection with this argument I don't see that we have to choose up sides or take a position, because for certain purposes a *sui generis* position—that is, in regarding culture as something unique within itself—is perfectly legitimate. On the other hand, for other purposes you have to realize that culture is a word for a set of phenomena that have theoretical connections with the whole universe.

The Anthropologist's Role

Lee, Henry

Lee: I have been very grateful both for the paper and for the discussants' comments because to me they have given meaning, sense, focus to everything that has gone on so far. I see on the one hand that I as an anthropologist am learning and getting an insight into the process which George (Spindler) has called, I think, "culturing," and that this process is not what we have called and what I have called myself the inculcating of culture—because that's too passive—but rather a creative, participating process in which the individual helps create his own enculturation. And I see that there is no line drawn between education and anthropology. On the other hand, I get from the paper itself a suggestion, a clue as to what my function as an anthropologist is in this combination that we have here. When I read from Brameld's paper, "one of the fresh and challenging designs for culture and education must now be constructed as well as implemented upon an audacious scale, and with the fullest possible recognition of the obstacles and pressures which anthropology and other social sciences enable us to estimate," I see that I'm asked to help in recognition of a conceptual framework. And there I feel that I have a function now.

Henry: There are certain situations in culture that look as if the individual had no choice but to drift with the organization (I say, *looks* that way). For example, let us take the engineer who gets a job in an aircraft factory and has no choice but to experiment with machines to get to the moon; if he doesn't want to do that, he's got to leave. Now, a somewhat similar situation arises in a hospital with a very complex social structure. The factors operating within the structure of the hospital are such that the worker in the hospital views himself as utterly powerless to control the factors that impinge upon him.

What the anthropologist can do is identify the areas of culture in which the individual is locked into a system which he views as if it could not be changed and he had no choice but to move along with it or leave. The anthropologist can therefore also identify the areas which have much greater flexibility, and within which the individual can manipulate the situation to a certain degree; of course there are small degrees and great degrees.

Limitations on Choice

Quillen, Frank, Keesing

Quillen: There are two points I've been wanting to make about this limitation of human choice. I think that there are always definite limitations on human choice, but when humans make choices they change the limits on future choices. So while the immediate choices are finite, it seems to me that future possibilities for choice are infinite. Consequently, while I accept limitations on free will or the capacity for choice in the immediate situation, I can't discern foreseeable limits in future situations. I know there will be limits in future situations, but I don't know what those are now; hence I will act within present situations toward goals which I think are desirable, hoping that the process of change will enable me to move closer to the goals. I think it's clear that we don't get changes in the exercise of power in human groups without changes in structures; but it's also clear that we don't get changes in structures without changes in human beings. In other words, you have a reciprocal reaction here, but the reactor is always the individual. He's the effective agent and he's affected at the same time.

Frank: I would like to bring out here that findings have been repeatedly made, namely, that the most coercive aspect of human behavior is not outside but inside the personality—if we're to understand what the psychiatrists and psychoanalysts are telling us. I wanted to bring that into our picture here because if we think only of outside coercion, we may have a very warped and inadequate conception of how culture builds patterns into the individual personality which become self-directing and coercing.

Keesing: Could I just say, apropos of Jim's (Quillen) use of the word "infinite" that I feel it is unnecessarily indefinite. I believe that Mr. Brameld is on a significant track in talking about universals in culture. Two million years from now, if man survives he will have a similar range of needs, problems, or whatever else we want to call them, to those manifested in cultures to date—man-to-habitat problems, man-to-man problems, man to problems of his inner world of the mind. One can block out a fairly comprehensive framework of universals and predict that all cultures must continue to involve behavior choices within the general conditions they set. I think in this sense the word "infinite" need not be brought in. Besides, following up that line of thought, we could supplement it usefully by an empirical search for high-frequency behaviors and goals in man's cultural experience to date (e.g., mental health), and possibly even set, say, goals for the planet two thousand years hence if we so wished, and then try to determine which among possible choices in behavior might best produce such end results with the greatest predictability (e.g., if we wanted internationalism, or greater isolationism).

Limits, Change, and Power

Taba, Shaftel, Mead, Henry, DuBois

Taba: I'd like to say something about the idea of limits in the light of what has been said here. Ted (Brameld) started out by saying that he liked certain viewpoints and certain attacks because they were tough about limits. Then we started talking about whether the limits were in the organizations or in individuals. Actually, if you look at a practical situation, limits and limitations are in both, and you can experiment with methods by which both are moved. Limits in individuals can be changed also. I'd like to give an example of a method by which this process of assessing limits can go on. We talked earlier in connection with Dorothy Lee's paper about what limits there are in home economics curricula, and what an individual home economist can do in the face of those limits and in the light of herself as a person acting as a representative of an area in education that is upward-mobile. Some of the limits of that individual are in his perception of what the limits are, which sometimes is mistaken, and sometimes is rationalization. Half of the limits that teachers think they have are rationalizations, mainly because they themselves don't have the skills by which to overcome them or substitute something else for what they're doing. Therefore one movable piece is to teach them the skills by which they can substitute so that they feel safe in doing it. When that happens, suddenly the limits aren't there any more. People see that they can make more changes than they thought they could. After this, one can move into changing the organization by creating a precedent.

So the steps are as follows: (1) work from individuals, (2) create a precedent that becomes in a sense an institution, and (3) use that precedent to make a little change in organizations which opens up the possibilities of change for the next teacher. We ought to investigate what these processes are, in what kinds of institutions, and by what methods they can be used. We can play the circular response, which Jim Quillen articulated, consciously and systematically and by stages of strategy such as not asking for changes in an organization before there are clearly perceivable and acceptable precedents for which to ask for it, and not asking for changes in individuals without helping them with the skills with which to accomplish the changes. These principles apply to hospitals also but in a smaller degree, because hospital organization is, as Jules (Henry) pointed out, much more rigid and much more articulated and much harder to change than is the school system.

Mead: On the other hand, you can change your nurses' organization—and it was done very cleverly when the new nurses' setup was made—by an organizational structure that puts public health nurses in a crucial place in the structure. They already had a slightly different character structure, a slightly different relationship to the culture, than the other group.

Shaftel: I'd like to comment that we are talking about change, but avoiding again the issue of "change for what." A number of comments here have put us educators squarely on the spot, especially Dr. Kroeber's and Dr. Cowley's, in that the suggestion was made that we teachers are meddling too much with some things we ought not to be meddling with. Can the teacher serve an innovative role in the culture?

Henry: What I'm concerned about is that that question should be asked at all. I think the issue is the anxiety behind the question, and not the answer to the question. As I look at what has happened to education through the ages, there is no doubt that the teacher has repeatedly been an innovator, not that he hasn't been conservative, too. For example, as changes began to take place in the Middle Ages, as power began to shift from the nobility and the church to the bourgeoisie, you had the introduction of the teaching of bookkeeping, the teaching of the vulgar languages, and the teaching of law, as law shifted from the control of the church to lay control. When one looks at the eighteenth century, as the vast changes consequent upon the Industrial Revolution began to take place, education of the well-to-do shifted—from the nobility, who used to take into their households the young men of the well-to-do, and train them in horseback riding and dancing, and so on—to the schools, and the kind of education that was needed for the development of the Industrial Revolution. So, as far as I'm concerned, therefore, the educator has consistently changed the kinds of things he has taught. The issue to me is not whether the educator shall be an innovator—for he has always kept pace with innovation; the issue is why one has anxiety about being an innovator, and I think this is the crucial issue. From where does this anxiety come?

Mead: I would say the anxiety comes from what's happening in the culture. It shouldn't be treated as just special to educators. In a hierarchical structure—if you limit or locate innovation in a hierarchical structure—you have certain problems that you don't get if you locate it in a wider co-operative structure. Now, we've seen this ever since the beginning of the New Deal in Washington—that the innovators were people who were low in the hierarchy. If you're low in the hierarchy and start to innovate, you have to subvert. I know that subversion is usually used for what people do who are bad; but subversion can also be what people do who are good. I think the problem that Fannie (Shaftel) has raised is very important and is connected with the problem that Hal (Cowley) raised and that Steve (Hart) raised: if we do not take into account the power structure, the teacher is spending her time fooling the school board or fooling the principal, or the principal is fooling the school board, or the professor is fooling the board of trustees, or the president of the college is fooling the board of regents. Then, instead of having a democratic procedure in which many institutions in the community are co-operating in the change, you get anxiety, because subversion always creates anxiety; even though the subverter is on the side of the angels, he's still pretty anxious.

Where are we going to locate those processes for change which do not put too much onus on people who are low in hierarchical power structures? And how are we going to set up parallel structures? You see, when the trustees of the American Museum of Natural History want a reorganization, they call someone like the president of the University of Michigan to do it; when Merrill-Palmer School wants somebody to argue with their faculty, they ask me to come from the American Museum of Natural History to do the arguing. So, if I've got any sense, I don't argue with the administration of the American Museum of Natural History. I help reorganize the rest of the country, and let the rest of the country reorganize us. That is, we have a great many good devices in a democracy for parallel and co-operative activity instead of subversive activity within hierarchies. And I think that if we look at our whole culture and we look at the anxieties that are aroused both in the people at the top of the hierarchy and the people at the bottom, Fannie's question is a very real one at present, and it's back of things like Bestor's attack. The teacher was not only subverted to the extent that she took responsibilities that her hierarchical position made difficult, but people even wrote books telling her how—handbooks of good subversion. Now handbooks of subversion are dangerous things to write, and they cause anxiety in the readers, even though they read them publicly.

Taba: Isn't that a curious connection with what we were saying yesterday about the use of a stranger in a primitive culture? You're using an outsider.

Mead: Yes, it's exactly the same point, Hilda.

DuBois: I think finally we're getting around to something that has some flesh on it. We are obviously dealing with a hierarchical structure in the educational system of the United States. The valuational changes and the techniques for those changes—the valuational changes have occurred at the bottom of that structure, I would assume. The techniques for changing individuals and for an altered educational system are beginning to be worked out, and are being applied more or less covertly, if you will. Now the problem arises as to whether or not the power structure can be altered coherently along with the valuational changes and the techniques for carrying them out. At that point the anthropologists have been called in as this initiating stranger, to an extent, and I think we have a very real role to play in giving that kind of support; it's the way we function in our society. And it's really the sort of thing, in a sense, that Mr. Cowley was talking about, that Steve (Hart) has been talking about. We have as behavioral scientists—and I'm speaking of psychologists and anthropologists primarily now—almost always consistently avoided facing up to it adequately when we've studied our own cultural or practical problems. I've sat in now on at least five conferences that I can recall where after three or four days we finally got down to the essence: What is the power structure, about which we've been called in for consultation? And it's the last thing anybody really wants to face because of the anxiety that all of this engenders.

Mead: It's un-American to emphasize power. We have to have three days of ritual behavior in which we do not primarily emphasize power, but emphasize our values rather than our practices.

Constructs: Culture and Society
Spindler, Quillen, Mead

Spindler: I would like to raise a question with Margaret (Mead). When we refer to hierarchies, I like to think of them as being in society and not in culture. I don't think when we refer to American culture and speak of hierarchies in the same breath that we're talking quite adequately; hierarchies involve patterning, to be sure, but they involve particular organizations, collectivities, aggregates of ranked individuals occupying positions within a social process. This is something quite different.

Quillen: George (Spindler), don't you think that social organization is a part of culture?

Spindler: I think that social organization in terms of expectations for behaviors connected with certain statuses and roles is certainly a part of the cultural directives. I think that the structures that are a function of both these expectations in part, plus other forces—ecological, political, economic, geographic, and so on—are structural, functional, societal entities.

Mead: But the units are people. And when you're talking about culture your units are not people but items of behavior of some sort, out of which you get regularities. When you're talking about structure, you're talking about organizations of people or groups. So your units are different. But they're two ways of abstracting the same thing: you can talk about the culture of a hospital; you can talk about the organizational forms of American hospitals; or you can talk about New York Hospital at a given moment in time, in which case every unit is a person. But they're all different ways of attacking a mass of phenomena; we just sort our observations in different ways.

Spindler: They are constructs we use to order our data, to be sure. But it seems to me that if you use culture as your exclusive frame of reference, you're automatically led to thinking about the internalized patterns of directives for behavior that are in the person. Or else you refer to the values that are floating about outside of the person, but not in any particular matrix of social action. Whereas if you refer to society you are forced to deal with systematic, structured organization. This leads to somewhat different kinds of questions. This is why the distinction might be quite important to the educator, because he's led to a different kind of research question if he wants to find out about these things, and to a different procedure if he wants to try to change things.

Reconstructionism, Power, and Values

Cowley, Brameld, Mead, Frank

Cowley: I'd like to take the discussion back to what seems to me to be a point we've neglected; and it's a point on which Mr. Brameld and I would, I think, disagree. He labels himself a reconstructionist. I raise the question, Who isn't a reconstructionist? It seems to me that almost everybody concerned with education is a reconstructionist. For example, the Roman Catholic Church is a power structure and has certain points of view about the topics just discussed. Clearly it seeks to reconstruct in so far as it's able in any community in which it can get the power. At the moment, McCarthy is a reconstructionist in terms of what he believes should be taught and who should be on the faculties of the universities in the country. Bestor is also demanding various kinds of reconstruction. In short, could you illuminate how you would distinguish yourself philosophically from other reconstructionists, since it seems to me that most of us are about the same business of reconstructing, even if from different points of view?

Brameld: I'm afraid that you have taken a word that has been operationally defined in a fairly definite way and decided to obfuscate it by treating it as a kind of blanket term for all kinds of things which it does not mean operationally for a person who chooses to use it in comparison with other operational terms, such as essentialism, perennialism, and so on (you could obfuscate these others in the same way, couldn't you?). There are a lot of people who are converging toward the reconstructionist kind of orientation all over the world; people who are dissatisfied with the Communist solution, who feel that there is still an opportunity to build a democratic philosophy that yet possesses something of the militancy and idealism of communism without itself being Communist—a democratic philosophy which the other major philosophies, even progressivism, have failed to develop fully enough. It is groping, but you will find among educators in a country like India, for example, quite a group who are moving in this general direction. They're not using the word reconstructionism, but that's unimportant; the word is just a symbol for a constellation of attitudes, of goals and means, which may be symbolized better by some other word.

Taking Fannie's question about strategy as a departure, I would say that first we must again go back to the value question, and try to formulate commitments, choices, purposes in which we can believe effectively. And in order to do that we need the help especially of anthropologists, who can give us definitions of value that are based upon understanding of real human beings living in real cultures. They can do so in a way that perennialists never can, because perrenialist values are "self-evident principles" that aren't grounded in the living experience of people at all. This struggle to build such a theory of values has hardly begun, to be sure, but there is considerable evidence that it is at least potentially available even now. Specifically, for example, "universal" cross-cultural values are beginning to be documented by anthropological research. If we can get those clear, and if we can reach consensus about them, we are on the track of a goal-centered philosophy which in turn will guide us in reconstructing the power structure by which these values can be implemented.

If we're going to generate any kind of power, however, it has to be done through powerful organizations; powerful organizations of teachers, for one thing, but also organizations of other community groups with which teachers must be affiliated. And these organizations are already emerging. I call them the "forces of expansion" as contrasted with the "forces of contraction." The forces of expansion are those forces in the community and in the world which are more and more articulate and united in their demand to share in the abundance of earth and industry and health which, even now, is available. India again is a particularly good place to exemplify them. The Communist movement has exploited these forces of expansion and that's why the world has a Red China today instead of the democratic China that it could and should have had. In other countries where this hasn't happened, the forces of expansion are still uncrystallized—still amenable to a program and a philosophy of democratic reconstruction. Here is our opportunity. Can we in time take hold of this opportunity to develop and channel the forces of expansion, as against the forces of contraction exemplified by McCarthyism, in behalf of those human values for which some kind of consensus can be attained? I'll be specific about the kinds of organizations I mean. I mean the labor movement for one thing. Despite all its limitations and despite such weaknesses as racketeering, nevertheless the labor movement in this country is a tremendous potential in behalf of the forces of expansion. I also mean sections of the farming community; I mean the co-operative movement; I mean some politically-minded groups such as the League of Women Voters—we could go down the list. Now these haven't sufficiently united, but meanwhile teachers and the rest of the educational profession could make a choice and say that they have to become "self-conscious" about their relationships with those forces of expansion that possess organizational potentiality.

Mead: It differs for the same person in different groups. That is, the same woman in the League of Women Voters may be a factor for what you call expansive change, and when she's a member of the woman's club, she's a factor for nonexpansive stability. Sometimes we're working with structures and persons only within those structures, not always in those particular roles, and sometimes with persons in every role that they're in when we attempt to build a group of people who will be working on a particular task. When you say "we" you mean that the articulate, thinking people as a group—a group of educators, anthropologists, trade unionists, all sorts of people—should begin to have some shared goals that they can communicate in terms of, which will then eventually result in new structures.

Frank: I have wondered throughout this discussion if a little historical perspective mightn't be found useful. If we look back at the development of the social sciences—economics, political science, sociology—what you find I think, from the eighteenth century on down, is that every social crisis initiated a new type of thinking. Adam Smith tried to rationalize the coming of industrialism; Ricardo had to deal with a lot of it. Economics has never been considered anything other than an effort to deal with social crises. Political science started out primarily to deal with the efforts to put limitations on absolute monarchy. Education to a large extent, I think, has been in the same position. In every crisis, war, depression and so on, educationists say, "What can we do so that this thing won't happen again?" As Taggart pointed out, it takes a war, a migration, an invasion, a catastrophe to shake people up, to get them out of their customary ideas.

I think we might get some illumination if we thought of culture very much as we're beginning to understand science. Up to 1900, physical science had a very strongly set limitation in its basic assumptions—you remember the story that graduate students had to go around trying to find some rare gas to do a piece of research because the only problem was pressure and temperature in some gas. And then almost suddenly, with Planck's exposition of quantum physics, and later on relativity, the whole thing blew up. And then you began to get in science a realization that science's laws and generalizations are primarily a body of assumptions and criteria of credibility. Now the criteria of credibility, and the assumptions of each culture, and how they can be changed, are what we're dealing with. As they change, people and power structures change; I think that's fairly clear. One of the things that's been implicit all through here is the doctrine of complementarity which physical science has been willing to accept, namely, that you can make two completely contradictory statements about the same thing, and they're both valid. For example, Bohr pointed out that you can talk about large-scale irregularities in classical physics, and you can also talk about the discontinuities of Planck—and both statements are right, depending upon your point of observation.

I think those things are relevant to our discussion here at this time. Students of education, and students otherwise, need to be made self-consciously aware of the basic assumptions of our culture, so many of which have become anachronistic and self-defeating, so that they can begin to see that a new series of criteria of credibility can come in, which the anthropologist, the psychiatrist, the sociologist—all are helping to formulate. To my mind that's the way a new climate of opinion begins to emerge; you can call it a product of culture, or not, as you please. Now, it seems to me that to the extent to which we recognize what Einstein pointed out, that it was a great mistake of nineteenth-century science to believe that theory could be derived inductively from facts; this gives us the point that we've got to have a conceptual organization and formulation to do the kind of research that will meet the criteria of credibility with which we're beginning to operate. And I think that at this point we need a theoretical foundation, as I said before, to develop an educational program which will be responsive to the critical urgencies of today.

Now, the other point that I would like to emphasize is that if we can begin to think in terms of values, and not in terms of problems but of aspirations and strivings, maybe we can begin to get some strategy. A large part of the conflict today of the essentialists is that their answer to the crises of the day is, "Let's go back"; and the reconstructionist says, "Let's go forward." I think you're quite right, that both are dealing with the same situations, but with different attitudes and assumptions. If we can begin to think in terms of—at least I like this as my concept—Western people having over the centuries cherished the aspiration of recognizing and making explicit in their social organization and education a conception of the worth of the individual personality and human dignity, then today with the implications that are coming from psychiatry, from anthropology, and so on, we're creating a new interpretation of what we mean by the worth of the personality. We're beginning to get a new interpretation of human dignity in saying it begins at birth. Now with that kind of strategy we can go to these people and meet them on their own ground. We can say, "Does your program of essentialism or reconstructionism genuinely recognize the worth of the personality and serve human dignity, or does it infringe on it, delimit it; does it prevent the development of the human potentialities which we're beginning to recognize are available because we can see other cultures have evoked potentialities which we haven't begun to touch?"

Kroeber: Isn't that a value system?

Frank: That's a valuing system. Yes, precisely. What I'm talking about is aspirations, not "values" as something out of the sky.

Section IX

AN OVERVIEW IN RETROSPECT

SEVENTH SESSION OF THE CONFERENCE

Co-Chairmen: Margaret Mead, George Spindler

Spindler: Today the purpose of this first part is to try to see what we have said, what we wish we had said, what more we might wish to say or do. To start us off in this direction, I'd like to tell you a little bit more than I have about how the conference came into being, and in so doing reiterate to some extent the purpose of it so that we may be able to measure our accomplishment in terms of that aim.*

In the first place, we assumed that the educators wanted some help from anthropologists; so anthropologists, with two exceptions, wrote the papers, and the educators took the role of discussants and reactors. We began to solicit suggestions from educators as to what they wanted help on rather early in the progress of the planning and through the operations of several different planning groups, and we found that they had some rather clear-cut ideas as to the topical areas they wanted help on, but they didn't always have a clear idea of the way in which the topical area should be put into problem form. This is because they were not, understandably, ready to take the role of the anthropologist so that the problem could be stated in their terms. So what we got were such general categories as the teacher as an innovator, the educative process as a process of innovation, intercultural and international understanding. These were rubrics; they were not always problems. Both the educators and the anthropologists tried to create problems out of them to which there could be a specific kind of address. We came up with a whole list of additional topical areas in subsequent planning meetings: the secondary school and the enculturative process; the sociocultural position of the teacher and the personal and social consequences; informal techniques of education; the contribution of anthropology in the design of the curriculum in primary and secondary education; school-defined groups as reference groups, and potential conflicts with other reference groups operative for the child; special problems of the children of foreign-born parents; the varieties of American culture as mediated by the school; and so on. So we ended with problematic areas to which anthropologists might address themselves, but few had sharp definition.

In contacts with prospective contributors and participants, these problems were made more explicit. Cora DuBois, for instance, was invited to write a paper, and Cora DuBois said, "Yes, I would be interested in writ-

---

* *Note by the editor:* The initiation of the project and the role of the planning groups have been described in the editorial Foreword, so need not be repeated here.

ing a paper on intercultural and international understanding." And then we began to correspond, and both of us said many things in the communications that didn't appear in the paper; but Cora formulated a preliminary approach to the problem of learning intercultural understanding, and I responded to it critically and gave it to the educators with whom I was working to respond to, and we corresponded with each other about it. Then we sent it back to her with some suggestions and statements and some more orientations, some of which were to the point and some of which were not. Then finally Cora came back with this very interesting paper which was formulated out of her own thinking but which had been channelized in part by the reactions of others.

The anthropologist was asked in effect to select from his point of view, from his perceptual system, certain kinds of relevant materials, and to organize those materials to answer what he believed to be the educators' questions, as they were formulated through the mutual collaboration of the anthropologists and the educators who were engaged in the planning. This was a very painful process for each of the anthropologists who did it. There were many reasons for that. One of the reasons was simply that the anthropologists were responding to somewhat amorphous stimuli, and that, to be sure, was not all bad. It was like giving the anthropologist a projective test, like the Rorschach. His perceptions, his field, his personal inclinations and experience found their way into his response in the form of a paper.

Our aim was to push on to new formulations, to be exploratory. This meant being selective in our focus, and not doing a number of potentially worth-while things. That is, for instance, we did not but could have spent a considerable amount of time criticizing and reviewing the contribution of the social class community work that has been done to date. We could have also taken up in detail the question of intelligence and cultural differences, an area in which considerable research has been done. We could have gone off in the direction of the Klinebergian race, culture, and I.Q. approach. And there are other things we could have done. We furthermore selectively rejected the strong feeling on the part of several anthropologists that we should discuss the educational role of the anthropologist in the elementary school curriculum, in the secondary school curriculum, in adult education, in general college education, in the use of anthropological materials in mass media, in museums, etc. We rejected these in favor of bringing the concepts, methods, data of anthropology, and the sensitized structure of perceptions which the anthropologist as a person brought to the situation to bear upon problems, within these topical areas, which had been formulated in planning and conceived as relevant by the educators. We decided in favor of this with the hope that both the educators and the anthropologists would get new ideas of their roles, new ideas about the function of the schools, and some new concepts about the relationships between the educative and the cultural process that would point to new kinds of research leads, that would add to and innovate with respect to educational and culture theory, and—although I think this was always a kind of third purpose—possibly help to solve some of the immediate problems that the educators face. We hoped further that the anthropologists would get some new research leads on cultural process and particularly on the process of cultural transmission, because we were rebounding our ideas and perceptions against a backboard supplied by the educators, who are specialists in cultural transmission. And we hoped also that the anthropologists would be able to test their concepts and their approaches at a high level of discourse in a particular kind of problem context that is very complex and that would be very rewarding because it involves most of the dynamics of the social and cultural process. In testing these concepts and approaches we hoped that there would be some reflection on them, and perhaps modification.

This concludes my introductory and retrospective remarks, and with that may I turn the meeting over to you, Margaret (Mead)?

OPEN DISCUSSION

Anthropological and Educational Roles: An Evaluation

Mead, Taba, Keesing, Gillin, Shaftel, Hart, Coladarci, Frank, Martin, Brameld

Mead: At this point I think we need more or less quickly to examine what has happened and deal with the gripes that are bound to occur in any conference. So far, the plan is that at the end of the morning I will give some kind of summary statement and try to pull things together. And then this afternoon we start life all over again and deal with segregation; having had closure, we go on back to life, so that we don't run that awful danger of not having had any catharsis. Now, in this intermediate period between George's (Spindler) description of what's happened, as he sees it, and my attempts to summarize certain elements of the conference, there are a bunch of things to kick around, I think. They are the feelings between the two groups. So far as I know, I haven't heard anybody talk publicly—that is, in any group of any size—about the educators having hogged anything. The cross-disciplinary comment has been, on the whole, "Educators didn't produce papers; why didn't the educators produce papers? Why were most of the papers by anthropologists; was it really a two-way interaction if the people behaved differently?" I don't think this particular point is very serious. George has given us a description: The reason that the anthropologists wrote the papers is because they were asked to write the papers, and the reason the educators didn't write the papers is because they didn't ask themselves to write papers. Those are historical facts.

Keesing: It would be interesting to speculate: if the educators had written all the papers and the anthropologists had commented, would not as much as 75 percent or much more of the same discussion have occurred? I have a hunch that it would, regardless of who initiated the formal data.

Taba: What happened actually was that we only took off from the papers. We had some discussions that stuck to the papers; in a sense we started making refined anthropological discussions, but if educators had done that the same thing would have happened from the educators' end. But we took off to generalities which were commonly communicated.

Keesing: And then we got to recurrent themes that appeared again and again as rather critical areas in our intercommunication.

Gillin: I think that occasionally there has been an expectation that everything was going to be settled here between these two fields. To be realistic about this, of course, it isn't. We have to think of going on from here. There are two things that anthropologists might be able to help with: one is the day-to-day problems which quite naturally preoccupy the educators. My own impression is that, at least on the basis of this conference and the personnel here, the anthropologists are not particularly good helpers in that respect: we don't know enough; we're not handy men in the educational institutions. But when it comes to the development of a comprehensive theory of goal values, limits, possible programs, the effectiveness of programs, the use of cross-cultural data, the anthropologists are and should be able to help with that if they're going to make any contribution. In other words, let's not kid ourselves that we, simply because we're anthropologists, can solve *all* the detailed problems of Centerville or some other specific communities until we know a great deal more about Centerville than I happen to, at least.

Mead: There were remarks made yesterday of the possibility of this conference being a precursor of some sort of more structuralized relationships between education and anthropology. The thinking in this conference might be precursor of such more formal institutionalization—a committee of some sort that then comes out with some kind of platform that you take to the Dean, and the Civil Service, and the Director of the F.A.O. team, and all the other people that have to be formally and administratively involved in any procedure.

Taba: I'm not making any institutionalizing suggestions, but I was thinking of what to me look like possibilities of common points of thinking and would make sense to educators. These are:

1. A fuller concept of cultural learning.
2. The comparative problems in cultural transmission.
3. The use of conflicting reference groups.
4. Case studies enlarged to include the cultural case study.
5. The limits and possibilities of the formal materials in understanding an explicit culture. What cues might we use in studying adolescents, teachers, administrators, in contemporary culture in the light of anthropological material?
6. Schools as systems having a culture. The difficulty of traditions—the school populations change while old expectations are maintained.
7. The kinds of alternatives for replacing institutions which no longer are functional.
8. The problem of teaching to treat feelings as facts—requiring people to step out of (*a*) their community culture, (*b*) their personal culture, and (*c*) their national culture—a mental discipline that has to be learned. Anthropologists would have much to say about the ways of learning here.

Shaftel: I would like to speak on the role of the anthropologist. I got a far broader picture of the ways in which anthropologists work and the kind of theoretical concepts which would be meaningful for us in education. And I feel that this conference served a very important function for an educator like myself in defining areas of work in which education can learn from anthropology and can team up with anthropologists in solving educational problems. I came with another conception of what anthropologists might do. I'll give you a concrete example: Roland (Force) is studying Milpitas, which is a little town across the bay from Palo Alto. It was just a railroad crossing with a little tiny country school. In that country school, which is now rapidly expanding because a Ford plant is being built in the town, there is a principal who is bewildered by the fact that he suddenly has a new community which is going to consist of people from all over the country with all kinds of problems. We need the help of the anthropologist in helping this administrator, or others in similar situations, to plan their school program and their own roles in the community. It seems to me that there is a research team kind of service, or a consultant role, where anthropologists could make studies, which would help educators, of some of the new phenomena in American life.

Keesing: You have stated the positive side. I'm sure you have also got a little clearer the negative side—what anthropologists cannot be expected to do, where they feel that their professional preoccupations and criteria would limit their participation.

Taba: It became obvious, for example, that anthropologists couldn't tell how to deal with a recalcitrant school board. The strategy is an educational problem. You can't give the administrator a recipe; you can give him some advice about what he needs to look into, or you can help him look into it.

Hart: I think Fannie's (Shaftel) statement was a very valuable one, at least to me—about where and how and under what circumstances anthropology might be valuable to the educator. I want to make one further comment on what she said. You talked about consultants and anthropologists doing some research in communities and so on. Does that mean you only see the use of anthropology to education by education hiring anthropological specialists? What about the other alternative— that a knowledge of anthropology might help educators themselves?

Shaftel: I assume that, Steve (Hart). This is just a special kind of relationship that I saw as a possibility.

Hart: If I might mention the comments on my own paper, I raised the question of the role of the sacred and the educators said to me: "Well, what about the role of the sacred in the schools—in American schools?" My inclination was to say, "That's your problem; you go and find the role—you go and use our concept of sacredness and what sacredness does, and see how it works out." Instead of which, apparently, the tendency would be to hire me to go in as a specialist and make a study of the role of the sacred in the American school—I think the teacher himself should.

Taba: What's wrong with you doing it—as part of a team?

Hart: Nothing at all; I'd love to do it. But why pay me a high salary to go and do it, when the teachers to some extent could do it themselves if they were anthropologically sophisticated?

Shaftel: I think that the teacher can develop a certain level of sophistication and a self-conscious use of anthropological material; but by virtue of being generalists and practitioners the educators will not be the people who will do the resource work which you people will do—that is, the really intensive studies of such topics as the ones you cited. Anthropologists could make such studies available in forms which educators could understand.

Frank: It may very well be that the most influential and valuable contribution to the educators will be not so much the content of anthropology as a way of thinking about, a way of judgment upon, the criteria of creditability that they bring, their way of looking at things—which can be infused all through education and not just applied to anthropological material.

Coladarci: That was illustrated here in many ways. I think that one very good example, whether it was by design or by nature, is the reaction of the educators to Fee's (Keesing) discussion of Bernie's (Siegel) paper. This was a high moment, process-wise, for me. So one would assume that an anthropologist can get outside his own shoes; it's part of his uniqueness, it's part of his training, one of his techniques. Fee did this; whether, as I say, it was by nature or design is immaterial.

Frank: We learned that from the mental hygiene people; their most important contribution is a way of thinking about children, which they didn't realize because they had to give specific clinical material which the teachers couldn't handle. I would hate to see anthropology making that same mistake by not learning from previous history that the thing to do is to give a point of view, a way of thinking, rather than too much specific content.

Brameld: Going back to the question of what practical values, what next steps, emerge out of all this, we must not overlook the fact that one of the most practical is the paradoxical step of being clear about our theory. The educational world today is in a state of appalling confusion with regard to its own conflicting theories. One of the practical contributions of this conference, therefore, would be to help educators in clarifying their theories. My impression is that in the last five years or so there has been a remarkable shift among some educational theorists, professional and otherwise, from a "psychological" orientation to what might be called a "cultural" or "social" orientation. But the trouble with the educators is that they get hold of an idea and then wear it to a frazzle until it becomes nothing but a cliché. Then it becomes an obstacle rather than aid to effective theorizing and therefore to effective practice. This happened twenty years ago when educators got hold of the concept of "felt needs." Now the cliché "culture" is beginning to replace that of "felt needs." This is unfortunate, as you would certainly agree. One of the values of this conference ought to be to try to prevent that kind of debacle from happening again.

At least three problems emerge from the culture concept that have both theoretical and practical importance, and that I should like to see emphasized. First is the values question. What can the anthropologist do to help us educators clarify our conception of values? I'm convinced no single science is available to the educator that begins to compare here with anthropology. Second is the area of resistances to change; how can the anthropologist help us assess and cope with resistances? Here various kinds of resistances need attention. One kind is the resistance that is present in the community, to which John Gillin's paper calls special attention, and which also received attention in connection with my paper— the power structure. Another kind resides in people themselves—what Larry Frank keeps calling our attention to. And still another may be called metacultural resistances: the underlying, deep-seated assumptions which are present in professional educators and, incidentally, in professional anthropologists. We somehow hate to admit them; they're painful to admit. We fight against them, and yet these metacultural resistances in some ways may be the most serious and important of all. The third general problem that I would like to see receive some attention is that of "general education." To what extent can anthropologists help us build an adequate design? Again, I believe that there is no science that can help anywhere nearly as much. There are designs for general education all over the map. Everybody talks about general education, but nobody knows what kind of general education. And nobody has seriously considered whether or not anthropology can really give us the basis for a new design. This problem is theoretical, yes; but too it is eminently practical.

Martin: Most of you seem to be wearing caps and you know what those caps are; I'm not sure what my cap is. But I will say what I think I have gotten out of this conference. I have learned something about anthropology. Is that too simple a thing for me to say?

I have not thought, however, that when the anthropologist ceased to be an anthropologist in these discussions he was any more or less wise than anybody else. In that sense, I am a little inclined to be on Steve Hart's side for a change: I want to know what the anthropologist knows, but, from that point on, what is done about it is the job of the educator, the man on the job, the practitioner. I originally resisted Jules Henry's distinction between fair and unfair questions. Now at the end of the conference I am heartily on his side because I thought the educators were asking questions to which the anthropologists do not have answers. They do not know any more than the rest of us know on some matters.

Now, who uses anthropological knowledge? Well, people like myself. And they use it within the limitations of their wisdom and training and skill in working with people. I don't come out of this conference feeling that if we just had an anthropologist at our side he could solve all our problems. I think he could help us by telling us what he knows. But how we use that information and when we use it, that is up to us practitioners.

Mead: I think that's fine; if people just learned that there isn't something called an anthropologist you can order from the grocery store, it would help a whole lot in every possible respect.

Coladarci: Or from the supermarket.

Kroeber: I want to confirm that sentiment. I consider the value or function that anthropology has in the world does not reside in delivering specific answers; it does some of that too, but most of the specific answers do not really interest the world; they are fairly technical or on limited areas. I think that what we probably have essentially got is an attitude, and if we can put that attitude across, it will be helpful to some other people. But then they must find their own specific answers, as we find our own. I agree entirely with what you say.

Comments by the Observers: Further Evaluation

Marie Keesing, Louise Spindler, Rose Wax, Roland Force

Spindler: The next thing I would like to do is to carry out a suggestion made by Ted Brameld as best we can in the limited time that we have. We have a number of observers here; people who have not entered into the flow of conversation and comments, but who are well trained or especially perceptive because of experience and background in the fields we have been discussing. I'd like to call on Marie Keesing, Louise Spindler, Rose Wax, and Roland Force for comments as to their impressions concerning conference processes and anything else that they would like to put into the record.

Marie Keesing: I am impressed by the enormous resource for the anthropologist who is studying culture change in the materials that the educators have under their control, in their case histories and so on, although these have been very inadequately used as yet for such purposes.

The second point I want to make involves the way some educators regard anthropology. I know that all the people here are thoroughly aware that the anthropologist who is interested in culture change is not a priest or a medicine man, but I hope that comes through in the report because I think that does tend to be the way many educators—not at this level, of course—look to the anthropologist, somewhat as the medicine man, expecting him to have his rituals ready at the drop of a hat on whatever they called him for.

With regard to communications, I perhaps have been one of the people who are particularly aware of the fact that the anthropologists have been doing an awful lot of communicating without benefit of words. And I've been interested that this has been extended to include the educators over the last few days. The interplay of personalities, the knowledge of what a person is going to say before he says it—you see that level of understanding operating below the verbal level.

I've further been very grateful, and I'm sure everybody else has, for the number both of educators and anthropologists here who use clear, simple language. All of us have some tendency to have an accent according to which discipline we've grown up in; the irritation with accents which I seemed to detect a little the first day now seems almost minimal. I hope that this simple language, that minimal use of difficult terms, will come through in the report.

I personally have to do an enormous amount of thinking for my own purposes, about this matter of values. I was so glad that we called the tune on this idea of the traditional anthropological approach as not involving the anthropologist in the normative and not evaluating. I think most of us here were aware that we do, and must do so, but it does us good to make that explicit.

Louise Spindler: There are two things that stood out very dramatically for me, one being very general and one quite specific. Primarily I've been impressed, perhaps because of my field work, with the similarity existing between the processes observable among an acculturating American Indian tribe and those existing here between the educators and the anthropologists. I'm convinced that the processes of change are regular and predictable, viewing this as an anthropologist would. There are the two subcultural systems interacting here—made up of values and concepts of the educators and anthropologists. After the initial presentation of stimuli, consisting of the papers and discussions, the process of selectivity took place in which both the anthropologists and educators in terms of their own perceptual set took what was meaningful to them. And then during the conference, a process of reinterpretation and contextualization—terms we use in anthropology—took place in which these introduced ideas were reworked in the context of the educators' and the anthropologists' subcultural systems. And finally the result, in anthropological jargon, was one of bilateral fusion (in contrast to unilateral fusion), which means that both systems rather equally contributed to a new system of patterned concepts in the form of new problem areas, which came out of the whole interaction process.

The other very significant thing which came out of the conference and which I consider one of the most fruitful ideas that I encountered, was from the educational philosophers. The anthropologists have been preoccupied with making cultural assumptions—both overt and covert—and cultural compulsives explicit, in an effort to avoid biases, but they have for the most part ignored their own basic philosophical assumptions in dealing with phenomena. For instance, they fail to make explicit the assumptions regarding relationships between persons and things, and I think the idea of whether they regard things as external to the person or whether they regard them as something that has been internalized is extremely important and that it influences everything that we have produced.

Rose Wax: I would say that from the point of view of interaction between two disciplines, I'm impressed by the fact that in the early sessions there was a tendency for people to talk, in a sense, at each other, rather than to each other, and a need to defend one's own point of view, and that this seems to have diminished through the days. I feel that this has reversed quite radically, and that now there's a great deal more openness, a feeling that there will be acceptance at the other end and something worth while come out of it.

From my own point of view, I think that I have become aware of what is meant by "cross-culture," in the sense that it isn't just a matter of going to a very different culture, but that people who speak different languages in a sense also belong to different cultures. And this awareness that it happens all the time, even though we don't realize it, is to me rather important. I think also the point that Dr. Mead brought up and that was brought up in various ways by other people, such as Dr. Taba—that learning in process is really the way you change people—was quite definitely brought out by the occurrences here.

Other things, such as what we do mean by values—we've been ignoring them largely, I think, in anthropology for various reasons; it becomes quite clear where they fit in, both at the most abstract level and also at the more practical level. And I have suddenly discovered that these two levels are not so far apart, that you cannot discuss one without the other. Also, I think that in regard to the original bias that I personally had— that education was something practical, and not particularly related to what we other people think we're doing—I have developed a more healthy respect for the complexities which applied problems have to face, and that in many ways it's more difficult than the clear theoretical statements; we're quite able to spin theories without having to be brought down to earth.

Roland Force: I find most of the things that I was going to comment on have been covered by the other people who have just spoken. There are a lot of minor points of personal observation that could be brought up, but I would rather convey an over-all impression. I've been reminded from the very first of an article that appeared in the *American Anthropologist* (April 1954), in which the author, John Bennett, commented on his own experiences in working in interdisciplinary research; and I'm afraid I brought some of his conclusions with me. I must say at this point, I'm inclined to be encouraged. The view that I had after reading Bennett's article, in which he related his own experiences which were not entirely favorable, was not a happy one. I see now where a number of issues have been resolved in terms of interdisciplinary communication here.

I quite agree with Louise (Spindler) that this is a good example of cultures in contact. This I think is a realization that we've come upon independently because we haven't communicated this conclusion between ourselves. I think it's worth saying that perhaps one of the reasons this may be so, that the bridge across disciplinary lines has been made, is the nature of the disciplines. The disciplines represented here are broadly eclectic, both of them, and perhaps this is particularly advantageous.

Spindler: Thank you for your comments. Now may I ask Margaret (Mead) if she will give the summary she has been planning as a result of an invitation by our Stanford planning group?

Summary by Margaret Mead

Mead: I am not going to attempt to summarize the whole conference. And I'm not going to attempt to repeat the things that have been said. I was asked to give a paper and decided not to, as long as I had to give this summary. Therefore, some of the things that I will say will be my points that nobody may have said yet, or that no one has said at this conference in this particular way. So that it will be a combination of some of the things I might have said if I had written a paper, and what I have distilled out of this conference. I suppose it could be described as what I've learned out of this conference, most of which I was not quite certain of before, and I'm going to try to put it in some communicable form.

First, this problem of co-operation between educators and anthropologists. This is a particularly complicated subject. Educators, after all, live in culture, change culture, work with culture, have students of different cultures, and so on, so that they feel *qua* educators a certain, sometimes very large, confidence in their understanding of cultural differences or cultural transmission, and so forth. And anthropologists teach, as Steve (Hart) pointed out, went to school, have children in schools, serve on school boards, and in a variety of ways are active participators in the educational system, sometimes are formal educators for large parts of their lives in many ways. And Fee (Keesing) as an educational administrator of a department in a complex university setting must spend almost as much time on educational problems as many educators here. Now laymen are bad enough in some ways when they're not competent; we all know about the amateurs who think that they know all about any subject involving human beings. We know about the people who know about marriage because they were married, and so on. But this is a still more complex problem, because we're both competent acting practitioners in the field of the other's area of competence. It comes up, for instance, in Bill Martin's statement that he wouldn't hire an anthropologist to do a particular job, in this case, deal with a school board. In that case, you wouldn't hire *an* anthropologist but you would hire somebody who knew about school boards, and he might be an educator who knew a lot about social structure and anthropology or he might be an anthropologist who knew a lot about school boards and education. As we work together in any kind of conference like this and in future discussions, these points need to be pinned down—the extent to which each person, each group, has competence in the other group's area of competence.

Now I want to discuss very briefly the formal possibilities of co-operation. This has been set up as a co-operation between the group called *anthropologists* and the group called *educators*. We've had some demonstrations in terms of preferences, of value, and of behavior here that there are many kinds of anthropologists: if you order somebody who's a Fellow of the American Anthropological Association you don't necessarily get anyone who can contribute to education except at the sheer content level of his particular area of professional specialization, whether it's archeology or physical anthropology or language, or whatever. It's very important—and I think this will help in the problem that Ted (Brameld) raised concerning stereotyping and clichés that are likely to occur—to distinguish between an anthropologist working in some field really relevant to education, either in content or practice, and just anthropologists. It is equally true of course—actually anthropologists are not in a position to do this as a rule because they don't command the enormous institutional structure educators do—that ordering an "educator" would be a terribly dangerous thing to do. It might even be more dangerous than ordering an anthropologist, because there's a certain amount of homogeneity of approach and attitude among anthropologists, whereas educators really span the earth. But I do think that this conference has raised the question rather seriously as to whether the communication is between *anthropology* and *education* as such. I mean, can someone defined as a pure anthropologist who has had no experience in education, who has not primarily studied education in primitive societies, who is not interested in teaching, and so forth—say, somebody out of a museum who is interested in band structure among primitive nomads and so has had no other contacts with educators—engage in a very profitable form of communication except at the book-reading source material level? There is one kind of communication that comes because the anthropologist has been working in the field of education, or the educator for a long time has been using anthropology. Lots of what Hilda (Taba) says is just soaked with anthropology, and it's far better than most anthropologists could conceivably do; but that is not without benefit of anthropology, because she's worked with anthropology and anthropologists and used anthropological material—she's absorbed it into her research approach; she's a research person from whom anthropologists can learn a great deal. Or when Cora (DuBois) writes about intercultural education—she's been working in intercultural education and dealing with it professionally and explicitly. So there's a possibility that the communication will have to proceed majorly either from anthropologists who have taken an active interest in education—an acting professional interest—or educators who've taken an active interest in anthropology. Ideally, it would be excellent to have a group of anthropologists who've done some very intensive work on education—the sort of thing that Jules (Henry) has done, having his students or research assistants do intensive observation in the schoolroom so that educational material becomes his research material. That is certainly one type of communication between us; I don't mean this to be exclusive. And educators should be very careful when they want an anthropologist to co-operate with them, either to expose such anthropologists to a couple of years of internship in the situation where they want them to co-operate, or get anthropologists who have really worked in a field that is relevant, and not order them from the supermarket, as I believe Art (Coladarci) said.

Another possibility is that we primarily communicate with each other successfully only when we are interdisciplinary people. Not bidisciplinary—which is an anthropologist who is a specialist on education, or an educator who has worked anthropologically—but when we also command a good many other things, like learning theory, like the use of conceptual models. If you look at the communication that's gone on here, for example, with Bernie Siegel's models, I think you will find that his organizational model bore some traces of sociometry, although he may not feel that articulately. The other model came from Kurt Lewin's channel theory which was developed in Lewin's psychology in answer to anthropological questions. And then Jules (Henry) used an information theory or communication theory model for communication, and that set up the communication between Jules (Henry) and Art (Coladarci). And Larry Frank all the way through has been using a very large body of interdisciplinary material out of which he moved in every sort of direction in this discussion. There is a high probability that one of the best ways of getting communication between anthropologists and educators is to use those anthropologists and those educators who are themselves interdisciplinary, and especially interdisciplinary in their use of psychology and personality theory— those areas where it is very important that the individual should be included as well as the society. Maybe this is *the* fertile spot of intercommunication.

When it comes to the question of areas in which we can have fruitful sorts of cross-disciplinary communication, I'm not going to try to make this list exclusive at all. We've had a whole series of suggestions; but I think it's probably very important to distinguish between the use of anthropology in teaching—the formal teaching to loosen people up, to widen sensitivity, to increase awareness—and the more systematic uses of anthropology, for instance, in the questions of where the educator is going to use research findings on such points as the relationship between adolescence and conflict as periods of choice. Somebody was worried that in this conference we had possibly given a picture of adolescence as a terrific *Sturm und Drang* period again, that the emphasis here was overweighted negatively. Adolescence is a subject on which educators need to have research findings of all sorts in other cultures; they need to have findings on importance of early learning, etc., that are of a different order from the problem of loosening up, increasing sensitivities, widening awareness in students. For instance, Hilda (Taba) made the statement at some point that anything that is learned can presumably be unlearned or relearned. That is a primary theoretical problem on which we need every inch of cross-cultural material that we can possibly get. It is possibly true that anything that is learned can be relearned, provided that it was learned in a certain sort of way. But the importance of how it was learned may be absolutely crucial. There are suggestions, for instance, that if people initially learn a language as one of many, they can always learn other languages. They have a different ability to learn other languages, to learn to think, read, fantasy, write poetry in other languages, compared to those who learn a language as the only language; and that learning a language as the only language is crippling from the standpoint of moving into other languages and needs at least a rehabilitation course before one is able to learn other languages. We've got a good deal of evidence of this sort about language, and possibly it's true of the whole of culture. It is possible that if one can learn one's culture as one culture among many, which is, incidentally, the way any New Guinea native learns his culture, then a type of flexibility may occur that is quite different than if one learns "this is *the* way to do things." There is also a possibility that we knew little about, that changing cultures may be like writing a piece of music in another key, and that there are possibilities of resetting the whole pattern. But every-thing that's being done in cross-cultural studies at present is relevant to that problem for the educator at a different level from the need to use anthropological material in order to increase sensitivity or widen students' horizons.

The same thing, I think, may be true of the whole question of social organization and social structures. We want the student to learn about different sorts of social structures and to become conscious of the ex-istence of social structures, so that a teacher knows she's in a school system, and she knows it is a system and not just an arbitrary set of pressures. That is rather different from the research level of what we know at present about institutional change, and the limits of institutional change. Jules (Henry) brought up the point about the areas where one feels one can't move at all—where one's position is perceived as a cog in a system and the only thing to do is to get out if you don't like it. Hilda (Taba) then showed that in teaching teachers she could show them that much of what they thought was being a cog wasn't a cog. That's one part of the picture, where the relative "cogginess" could be discussed; but there's another level that's closer to what Ted (Brameld) is interested in— that is, *where you can really make an institutional change*—and what do we know about social systems that could be used there? So I think in this conference from time to time there has been a confusion between these levels. When do you need an anthropological description of Centerville in order to operate in Centerville? When do you need an anthropological description of Centervilles in order to teach people who will go into a Centerville? And when do we need material on what happens with rapidly growing communities, at a quite different sort of theoretical level?

In terms of interchange or borrowing of methods from one discipline to the other, the whole emphasis on the natural history approach is one that I think can fit in very well with the history of education and what we teach students about it. But in the anthropological statements here, I think there's often been one striking omission, which may conceivably even be a very bad omission in the structure of the conference—or at least in a conference ten years from now. That is, I think that history ought to be here too. Ten years from now the distinctions between anthropology and history will not be such as they are now; those gaps are going to close, they are going to close very rapidly. It will depend on several things, such as how many historians the directors of the Ford Foundation Behavioral Science Center decide have anything to do with human beings; it will depend on how many historians have time to learn any biology. It will depend on a lot of things, but eventually a part of history and a part of anthropology are going to be combined in the sort of area that we've been working on here. Then the methods of anthropology, the methods of history, and the specific applications of natural history and of historical methods to education will fit in quite differently from the way they're fitting in now.

There's one other methodological problem, which I think has vexed educators and anthropologists for quite a while when they have worked together, that perhaps ought to be made explicit. It came up once or twice. I think Fee (Keesing) made it more explicit than anyone else here did; and it also came out of Professor Kroeber's statement about the different sources of anthropology. There is such a thing as collecting data in such a way that you minimize bias. But that does not mean you get rid of bias completely; it doesn't mean that you get rid of your perceptual modalities; it doesn't mean that your data on a particular society aren't going to be more visual than auditory. There are uncounted levels of the intervention of subjectivity into material. Nevertheless, with the adequate use of machine recording—with films and tape recordings and various devices of that sort—we're going to be able to get chunks of material that are multisensory, that are large enough. In such chunks, limits can be redelimited, so that even if the anthropologist did say, "I'm going to take a four-hour shot," somebody else could carve a thirty-seven-minute shot out of the middle of it that the anthropologist did not plan to carve out, and look at it later. We've had arguments in the past, severe arguments, as to whether introducing recording into the school system would interfere with the children's learning in some way, and then the educator had to protect them. With the growth of machine recording of various sorts, the participant anthropologist doesn't have to be so conspicuous and therefore such a thorn in the flesh of the local social system as he almost always is. If primitive people had school principals, probably no anthropologist would ever have been allowed to get in and study the native tribes. There is usually nobody in the native tribe who can say, "I don't want life disturbed," and so the anthropologist can get in. But anthropologists are not angels of noninterference and they usually make a certain amount of trouble in the village, and they can make a dreadful lot of trouble in the school system. But with the growth of machine recording we're going to be able to get away from that. We're going to be able to collect large chunks of material without too much active participant observer intervention in the system, on the one hand, and with increasing minimization of the distortion of the material from the point of view of the collector. In this way, we can separate the material from the interpretation, which is, I think, one of the points of view that the anthropologist, as a field scientist, is going to continue to stand for.

There's another use of anthropological materials that's been raised here also, and that's the use of anthropological records of primitive societies; or one may, from the point of view of a cultural analysis, look at ancient societies, exotic societies, and so forth, as living models that will widen our picture of the potentialities of what human society could be. One of the sources for new cultural invention is what other people have done. It is from that point of view that Steve (Hart) presented his material on initiation. This is something that cultures have done; this is the way it was done; these are the elements that recur. This gives us something to think about, not in order to transfer it directly, or to create a Utopia (for Utopias are extraordinarily deadly—no one wants to live in one after they've read about it), but it gives us an element that we might be neglecting at the present moment, or that we might combine with something else.

In the areas where educators and anthropologists are going to cooperate, inevitably these are normative areas. At the research level, you can call in an anthropologist to make a study of Centerville and give you the data if you want to. But the minute you want to change the teachers in Centerville or give the children in Centerville an experience their parents didn't have, this is inevitably normative. And I think it's important to make the difference explicit. The applied anthropologist must recognize when he's being an applied anthropologist that he's a practitioner and subject to the same sorts of pressures as those the educator is subject to—including in time, probably, various sorts of licensing and control—so that he isn't allowed to go and mess up Centerville without a minimum of control by the society that he's operating in.

Now, with respect to what Ted (Brameld) was calling for here, it seems to me he was calling for tough-mindedness and dedication, for people who were interested in change and who would take into account everything we know from all the social sciences about the difficulty of change, but nevertheless who wanted it, who had a positive motivation moving forward in a direction of social change. On the edge of that position, where the anthropologist, psychologist, educator—a whole group of people—will work on the problems of social change, there's the anthropologist who doesn't notice the lack of the kind of dedication that Ted (Brameld) was calling for, because he's majorly motivated by delight in curiosity, and he's more or less remained in the humanist position, and he's so happy being led from fact to fact, from theory to theory, that he's completely motivated, but his dedication is of another order from the necessary dedication to social change. Then there's the educator who is happy with that set of new faces in front of him, who's continually revived by the job of teaching a new group of youngsters—something new. So such educators in turn are not preoccupied with social change. They've got their own regenerative device. Now, Ted specifically, and to a degree this whole conference, need to direct their appeals not to the educator who finds sufficient reward in that fresh group of faces of any age, and not to the anthropologist who finds sufficient reward in discovering a lovely new kinship system—both of whom can be very happy—but to the group of people who care about change and who have a dedicated commitment to change in some way—enough so they want to work on it—and who are interested in obtaining the skills and research information that are necessary. I don't think the dedication of skill alone is going to be enough. Usually the expert who relies on technical virtuosity alone doesn't survive under the emotional pressures that are involved in the ups-and-downs of attempting to introduce change. This is a statement of opinion that I think can be pretty well documented with the breakdown rate for overseas technical assistance experts.

Next, I'd like to say a little about the question of lag. Some of the ideas that we've been working with here are on the edge of being superseded. I want to illustrate this by one point. Almost everything that we've said here today, in the last four days, takes off implicitly from the idea that change takes time. Even the most violent advocates of doing something will stress, "But you have to grow." Hilda (Taba) gave us a very clear statement of what she regards as the steps in change. Cora's (DuBois) paper discussed the periods, the steps that change has to go through, the trajectory of learning and change. I suspect that in the next five years our major emphasis is going to be on the fact that if you have enough speed you can have a great deal more change. That is an idea that was very unfashionable twenty years ago. It was unfashionable because the ideas of change were partial. We were trying to work with little bits;

we were trying to put a tractor into a medieval economy; we were trying to lead people to new hygienic measures where they were living in the same kind of house, going to bed in the same kind of bed, and yet wanting to give them a little bit of change. Now, what we see in many instances is that very rapid total change—for instance, where a population if they're going to work in a factory also go to live in a new kind of town—makes it possible to build new patterns extraordinarily rapidly. Take, for example, the present marriage pattern in the United States since World War II, which differs in about a hundred significant respects from the pre–World War II marriage pattern. It's been built under conditions of speed of migration and change in the whole social structure. There are a whole series of areas where possibly speed that doesn't give a chance to mobilize resistance, that doesn't give a chance for the partial learning to become pickled and crystallized, is going to be an important point.

Now I would like to discuss another problem that I don't pretend to understand well at all. This is the tendency of educators to take up fads or to produce things in cliché form, which, stated in more general terms, is the tendency to form cults rather than open-ended social systems. The little bit that we know about cults (and my recent Manus study is probably the most detailed study that's ever been made *in situ* of the fight between becoming a cult and remaining a part of the society, which struggle is what the Manus community is going through at present) suggests that the cult may be related to types of pressure. It may be related to the fact that the innovating educator has been under too much pressure, has been too much alone, and therefore has been on the defensive, and has tended to crystallize his thinking because he has had to fight so hard. We know that one of the things that leads to this crystallization of nativistic cults is the fight that goes on to get the particular new point accepted. But I think it's something, as Ted suggested, of which we as students of wider cultural processes should be extraordinarily aware—that educators have tended to settle down on clichés, to turn an insight into a cliché; and then of course they have to reject it later because it's become shorn of wider meaning, it's become isolated. For instance, let's take the sort of thing that's been said here quite often: "There was a psychological phase of education; now there should be the anthropological." That is a dreadfully dangerous thing to say, because every single valuable thing that came into education out of psychology needs to be kept, plus allowing for a continuous new stream, and anthropology needs to be combined with what is there. The danger of going from the child-centered school to the community-centered school and back again, which has been the sort of experience we've gone through in education, is one of which educators are extremely aware and in which cultural knowledge used by educators and by anthropologists interested in education might help.

Then we come to this question—the problem of the value of awareness. I think that there we have another angle on which anthropologists and educators are going to have to work together very closely. Radcliffe-Brown, a structural anthropologist, used to ask how much awareness can a *society* stand? Sapir was saying, in the quotation used in Ted Brameld's paper, how much awareness can an *individual* stand? If you are aware that the language you're speaking is one of seven languages, that as you use the word "cat" in a sonnet there are six other words for cat, that the structure of metaphor in English is different from the structure of metaphor in Russian, that when you're using an image in English poetry such as "He flew like an eagle" you get a very different imagery structure from "Not like an eagle he flew, but like a man" in Russian. If you think of all those things at once, can you ever write a poem? That was Sapir's position, and it was a very important one. There seems to be no doubt that people who have a lot of half-baked unindividually realized new scientific ideas in their heads produce very peculiar poetry, and very peculiar fiction, bad plays, and imperfect music. There is undoubtedly a process of assimilation that is necessary if we're going to have genuine aesthetic experience and genuine artistic work by individuals.

This is probably equally true of cultures in respects that we don't know. We don't know where the insight level operates. Now, I'm going to give you a kind of brief intermediate example, and that is McCarthyism. I think that if we could have found and invoked the analysis of the people who know most about McCarthyism, who know most about the Soviet Union, who started to think about interaction between the Soviet Union, Germany, Britain, and the United States in the late 'thirties, they would have been able to work out a series of predictions and we would have been able to give most liberals in this country the perfectly adequate prediction that (a) McCarthyism was predictable, and (b) it wouldn't be as bad as was expected; but this would have harmed rather than helped the vibrant furious indignation that has made the prediction actually work out. So that you lose, in communicating the insight, the very thing on which your prediction is based. Thus every time you communicate an insight or an awareness, you change the course of history. Do you actively want to change the course of history in this particular respect? Yet I agree with Ted that we are committed to building a society in which we have more and more insights and awareness. And Larry has made the point that we want a society that is regenerative spiritually in the sense that it continually reassays its goals, and at the same time, hopefully, will set up better mechanisms for reassaying its goals—of which, of course, a conscious educational system is one definite mechanism. But it's a problem we haven't solved. It's a subject on which a great many people are reacting today, and they're reacting in a variety of ways: some with a return to neo-orthodoxy, some with a desire for various and sundry sorts of control, some with a desire to return to the three R's. There are dozens of these reaction formations against uncontrolled insights that we don't yet understand.

We've kept saying, as an aim, "How are you going to get people to recognize that feelings are facts?" but we have not discussed methods at all. And this is an area where the anthropologist has traditionally been a specialist and where we are going to have to evaluate not only awareness, but the forms in which awareness can safely come: the places, for example, where it is safer to leave the awareness to the arts than to the expository, and the degree to which it is possible to direct the arts without making them the sterile, hopeless implementers of an economic or social point of view that they became in the 'thirties in this country, that they are in the Soviet Union today—in which they are so harnessed with some infernal social purpose that they lose all freedom. I think that's about the strength of what I'd like to say.

OPEN DISCUSSION

The Anthropologist in the School as a Field

Henry, Mead, Spindler

Henry: Margaret (Mead), I want to talk for just a moment on a point you raised. In this group we are emphasizing the importance of co-operation between anthropologists and educators, and one of the things that anthropology can do — you might say in a sense, its birthright — is to observe directly in a natural history way. And one of the things it seems to me you were doing was emphasizing the extent to which the anthropological observation itself could distort and upset the situation. Of course I was touched by this in my narcissism; I was also touched by this in regard to the profession. My students and I have observed in classrooms almost without causing a ripple, and these students were completely untrained for this. I would say that we paved the way very carefully throughout the whole school system before we went in to observe, and this may be one of the reasons why no trouble ensued.

The other point I want to make involves what has been called traditionally, and I think rather naïvely, distortion. And this insight came to me not out of my own perception of the situation, but from the people I spoke to when I went to Washington to talk to the U.S. Public Health Service. I said to them, "Now these are situations which I distorted," and gave quite a number of examples. And they replied, "Why do you call that distortion? These are situations which you observed, which because you observed them and recorded them can be exploited therefore as particular experimental insights." I think that you have taken a rather traditional position as to what a distortion really is, and also have over-emphasized how anthropologists can upset the situation.

Mead: Yes. I agree that we've experimented for years—feeding back into the group the results of the observation and making it part of the on-going process. And you can do that, and we've done it very many times. Nevertheless, the observer when he enters in does add to the situation and change it. Now, the word "distort" is evaluative. I've been in many experiences of doing research in such fields, and have listened to the educators, social workers, and psychiatrists complain about anthropologists or social psychologists (any kind of research worker, it isn't just the anthropologist), that they were interfering in some way. On the whole, if you can use forms of observation in which you don't have quite as active an intervention, it may be better: that's what I meant by machine recording, that we have now available means of recording that don't require quite as active intervention and therefore don't cause quite so much trouble.

Henry: It cannot be doubted that naïve and inexperienced observers can mess up certain situations; but I would be very much disappointed if this got into the record as an official anthropological point of view—that there's so much danger that the anthropologist is going to mess up the situation.

Mead: This is true of all social scientists, not just anthropologists. It happens whenever research is introduced into processes designed to teach, or help, or cure, or convert individual human beings.

Spindler: May I intervene at this point? I find myself in partial agreement with Jules, in that I think it's very important to keep the doors open in our own thinking regarding this kind of observation-participation. But I find myself in agreement with Margaret also. We have worked in a number of school systems through the Stanford Consultation Service. There are many things the same about going into this kind of situation that are also characteristic of going into a field situation; but the educational system is a relatively more defensive field and a very sensitive one. There are some kinds of things present there that are not present in the usual field situation. One of them is a rejection of expertism; that is, external expertism. You come in and say, "I am an anthropologist; I'm here to observe you"—now there's a value and some covert culture involved here. "Observe," to a teacher, does not mean just to watch and describe; it means to observe, evaluate, and supervise. Suddenly you have this outside expert who is coming in to do something that has a familiar kind of ring, and the teacher can go berserk about your particular role in the situation. That can all be avoided by the proper kinds of communication; but it takes a long time. You have to start at several different points at once and you have to talk to a lot of different people. You have to explain and you have to go in and refrain from "observation." You come in to learn as a "student." You assume a familiar role. You say to the teachers, "I'm a student; I'm trying to understand something about the situation; maybe you can help me to understand it." If you put yourself in this role, and do your participant-observation from that point on, I think usually you can become accepted.

Section X

THE SUPREME COURT DECISION ON SEGRE-GATION: EDUCATIONAL CONSEQUENCES

EIGHTH SESSION OF THE CONFERENCE

Chairman: George D. Spindler

Spindler: We have as our topical area for the last session of this conference the educative and social problems consequent to the recent Supreme Court decision on segregation. This was added to our program because it presents to anthropologists and educators reality problems and issues of significance that are of a crucial nature for American society and the educational system. We cannot expect, of course, to solve the complex problems subsumed within this topic, even at the symbolic level, but we can indicate what anthropologists would conceive as essential guidelines toward dealing with such problems, and what reactions educators may have to these guidelines.

I would therefore like to turn the meeting over to Sol (Kimball), who will present some materials he has organized for our reaction.

Analysis by Solon T. Kimball

Kimball: On May 17, 1954 the Supreme Court of the United States, as you know, handed down a decision of great import for the United States and of particular significance for the South. This was the unanimous decision which banned segregation in the public schools. This was the event which triggered this particular session.

I should like to tell you first how I shall organize what I have to say. Following the analysis I will open the meeting for discussion—and I hope that the general problems that we have been considering previously will have specific application in this case.

The sequence of my presentation will be, first, the Supreme Court decision itself. Second, I will present briefly the history of this issue and in particular the history of the relationships of the Supreme Court to segregation. This will be followed by a brief history of the South, which will be descriptive of the over-all pattern with which we are concerned. Last, I should like to talk about the South, as an anthropologist. (Such remarks should be considered as an example of the kind of specific material which an anthropologist might come up with during the course of his study, although we all recognize that types of anthropologists with different emphases see things somewhat differently.) Following that, I will open the meeting for discussion.

The Supreme Court decision was one which had two significant aspects to it. One was the decision itself to abolish segregation. The other significant aspect was that those who were affected by this decision had time to prepare plans by which they could carry the decision into effect. If I recall correctly, official representatives of the states directly affected were invited to appear before the Court, to indicate their plans for carrying the decision into effect. This particular aspect of the decision has been commented upon favorably by many persons. It is a recognition of the fact that the problem is not an easy one but that time and thought need to be given to it. It is recognition that there has to be considerable gradualism in the application of this particular decision. I assume that there are those who want the decision to be completely effective immediately.

There is one other aspect of the Supreme Court decision commented upon by James Reston in his article on May 18 in the *New York Times* in which he refers to the sociological aspects. His point is that the Supreme Court made its decision not on the basis of a legal technicality, but gave its justification on the basis of human beings and human beings behaving in groups. Reston points out that there were certain factors affecting human behavior and human development which impressed the Supreme Court as being of basic importance in their decision: that segregation impairs the ability of Negro students to learn; that it deters the development of their personality; that it deprives them of equal status in the school community; that it tends to destroy their self-respect; that it denies them full opportunity for democratic social development; that it subjects them to the prejudices of others; and that it stamps on them the badge of inferiority. He adds that the basis for this generally negative result of segregation practice is based upon the expert testimony of psychologists, sociologists, anthropologists, educationists, and others who gave testimony as to the unfavorable effects of the segregation policy.

I'd like to read some sentences from Justice Cardozo, quoted by Reston:

When the social needs demand one settlement rather than another, there are times we must bend symmetries, ignore history and sacrifice custom in the pursuit of other and larger ends. From history and philosophy and custom, we pass, therefore, to the force which in our day and generation is becoming the greatest of them all, the power of social justice which finds its outlet and expression in the method of sociology. . . . The final cause of law is the welfare of society . . .

You will recall there were five cases, some of them being in the judicial mill for as long as three or perhaps four years. The cases originated in four states, Kansas, Delaware, Virginia, and South Carolina, and the District of Columbia. The decision affects mandatory or permissive segregation laws in twenty-one states.

Let us turn now to the history of this particular issue and some of its aspects. Previous to the Civil War most of the Southern states where slavery was a prevailing institution had laws which prohibited teaching slaves to read and write. There were, however, in all these states a number of freedmen who had acquired a certain amount of education. In the Jacksonian period there began to develop a public school system under the same kind of democratizing influence that also had its effect in the Northern states and resulted in a great proliferation of public school education. Even so, education, except of the simplest kind, was primarily in private schools for the children of those who occupied the more favorable positions in the society.

After the Civil War, and during the Reconstruction era, there were two main influences in Negro education. One of these was the Freedmen's Bureau and during the course of its career it established four thousand elementary schools for Negroes. But there was another influence of considerable importance, which was the Yankee schoolteacher. One of the types to which Southerners sometimes refer along with the carpetbagger is the Yankee schoolteacher. She came primarily with a missionary movement of some of the Northern churches which established schools and provided personnel for Negro schools and also helped to establish a number of colleges primarily for Negroes.

The South, you will recall, was treated as a conquered country, and the last of the Federal troops were not withdrawn until the middle 1870's. Even afterward, the main currents in American life by-passed the South, whose allegiance tended to remain outside the immense movement in industry, commerce, and trade, and to remain with its agrarian tradition. The widespread poverty and adherence to the past was reflected in education. In 1900, less than 40 percent of the children attended school regularly; only one in ten reached the fifth grade; and 11 percent of whites and 48 percent of Negroes were illiterate. This was the situation half a century ago. These figures and other materials are taken from a recent book, *The Negro in the Schools,* by Harry S. Ashmore.

An event of considerable importance, about the turn of the century, was the provision of money by foundations for aiding public school education and specifically Negro education. As one example, monies were provided for subsidies and scholarships to bring young and able teachers from the South to teacher-training institutions in the North, and so between 1900 and 1950 a very large number of persons were given the best available education. These people are, in many instances, the ones who now occupy high positions in teacher-training institutions and in the educational systems in the South. It has been this group which has done such a magnificent job in the past half-century in improving Southern education.

The specific court decision which gave justification to the segregation policy was that of the famous "separate but equal" doctrine of the Plessy *vs.* Ferguson case in 1896. This case, which originated in Louisiana, involved traveling in Pullman cars. But the court in rendering its decision included a paragraph which gave sanction to a continuation of existing segregation practices, if separate also meant equal.

It wasn't until 1935 that we had the first specific application by the Supreme Court to education. This involved a case brought by Murray, in Maryland, who wanted to enter the Maryland law school. In this case the Supreme Court held that there must be equal facilities for Negroes and if there were not, then Murray could demand entry into white schools. Most of you are acquainted with such cases: they involve a series of decisions since 1940, mostly affecting Southern schools. As a consequence, many of the Southern colleges now have Negroes in them. As yet, there are no Negroes in schools of higher education in the states of Alabama, Mississippi, Georgia, or South Carolina.

In spite of the "separate but equal" decision of a half-century ago, there is still a gap between the facilities provided for Negroes and for whites. For example, in 1952 the per pupil expenditure for whites was

$165, and for Negroes it was $115. Here are some other figures which may be of interest. Concerning qualification of classroom teachers, in 1940 whites had an average of 3.4 college years of education, while Negro teachers had 2.7 years. By 1952 this gap had been narrowed so that white teachers had an average of 3.8 years of college education, and Negro teachers had an average of 3.5. In several states Negro teachers averaged a higher number of years of college education than did white teachers. The salary gap, which is partly a function of the number of years of higher education, has not been completely closed. Some figures will illustrate the improvement in salaries of Negro teachers relative to whites. In 1940 these were only 54 percent but had risen to 87 percent of white salaries by 1952. In Virginia, Tennessee, Oklahoma, and North Carolina, however, the average (mean) salary of Negro teachers was above the average salary of whites, indicative of change and the attempt to equalize.

There are some other aspects such as population characteristics, which are relevant. The South's population has increased, but not so fast as the remainder of the United States. For example, between 1940 and 1950, while the South's population increased by 13 percent, the rest of the United States increased by 15 percent. The white population has increased relative to the Negro population, owing largely to differential emigration. The figures show that in 1940 the South had 72 percent of all Negroes; the rest of the country had 28 percent. Ten years later the South had 62½ percent of all Negroes; the rest of the country had 37½ percent, caused primarily by migration to the Northern states—a migration which has exceeded a million people in the ten-year span 1940–50. But there is another aspect of population movement which is of great significance—the internal shift of Negroes from rural to urban environments. The figures show that in 1940, 51 percent of Negroes were rural but by 1950 this percentage had decreased by one-fourth to 37½ percent. The shift has also been heavy among the white population. It's a general rural-urban shift. The Negro movement, as I recall the figures, has been relatively greater than that of the whites. These figures give you some feeling for the extensive demographic changes.

Other figures show a tremendous increase in the amount of expenditure for public education. Southern educational leaders are, in fact, very proud that they have developed a first-rate public education system, and that the Negroes have begun to share relatively more as the years have gone on. There is a good deal of internal variation, of course, with regard to salaries.

Mead: This could also be read as an indication that the white teacher was still at a fairly low level, couldn't it? You're taking it from the Negro's side; it could mean, on the other hand, that there had been relatively less improvement compared with other states in the education of the white people.

Taba: Most of the white teachers get trained in a local teachers' college and stay with that degree because they're more assured of good jobs. But practically all Negro teachers come with Master's degrees from one of the Northern universities, so they get higher salaries.

Gillin: There are also Negro teachers' training colleges all over the

South. This is one of the few professions in which Negroes can get ahead, so they have the motivation to go for Master's degrees that the whites don't have.

Siegel: The fact of segregation, after all, made all schools, particularly white schools, less efficient, therefore less attractive to white teachers. There was not proportionally as much money to go into building them up or paying salaries as there was in the North. I should imagine that for the Negro teacher or potential teacher there would be much more incentive, because much more prestige is attached to that position than for the corresponding white teacher in the South.

Kimball: One should remember that the South has been traditionally agrarian in its civilization, which means that it has not had, nor did it produce the wealth which could pay for an expensive public school system. Nevertheless, the figures show that the Southern states are in the upper half, in terms of the percentage of total tax income that they apply to schools.

I should like to describe now some characteristics of Southern culture. Those who have lived in the South know that it is not homogeneous. They know that there are deep internal divisions. There are two main traditions. One tradition is Cavalier, the other is Calvinistic. The latter is a Puritan tradition, but not of the same kind that you get in New England.

This difference is also expressed in the two kinds of agrarian economy. The plantation economy originally utilized Negro slaves, but after the Civil War a system of tenancy and sharecropping for both whites and Negroes developed. It is a two-class system with landowning whites at the top and poor whites and Negroes at the bottom. The plantation areas included the rich level lands of tidewater Virginia and the Carolinas, the black belt of Alabama, and the delta of the lower Mississippi River states.

The subsistence, self-sufficient, small-farm pattern characterized the Calvinists. They occupied the highlands and were of English, Scottish, and Irish ancestry. When they came to this country, they migrated into the inland regions, to the hill country, and established a type of family and community pattern similar to the one from which they came.

The Piedmont is a third area which combines some of both the plantation and hill cultures. Presbyterianism has had a strong influence in terms of ethical code and the kinds of communities. For example, in Alabama you can identify a town of Presbyterian origin, because the landowners built their mansions in the town, while Cavaliers built their houses on their estates.

Differences in the pattern of settlement characterize each area. In the hill country the crossroads hamlet, with church, store, and later the school, was the main population concentration. But most of the people lived in the open countryside. In the plantation area you find the county town as the center of political and economic life—a pattern which is very similar to that found in Brazil, Ireland, and England. The differences between hill, plantation, and Piedmont are expressed in family, in politics, in religion, and in economics. They were of a kind that have influenced all of the significant events affecting the South as a whole. Jacksonianism found its support among the hill people, who opposed secession and in some localities favored the Union side.

Part of the emphasis which has been given to the conflict between North and South has been the struggle for the West, in pre–Civil War days. The immediate question was whether the West was to be slave or free. I think this oversimplified the issue, since the evidence also shows that the conflict was between two regional patterns. The military victory of the North and the subsequent reconstruction kept the South in its agrarian pattern for the next several decades. The New Deal and the Second World War accelerated the slowly developing industrialization, which has continued at a rapid pace since that time.

When one thinks of the South sociologically, it is customary to focus upon the relationship between the races, between whites and Negroes. But such emphasis oversimplifies the problem, for it is an area in which there are internal regional differences, and in which there are deep divisions within the social class system. There are, in effect, three social classes. There is an upper-stratum white group which—if you define it in terms of participation and not in terms of the ordinary categories of social class, such as characteristics of the size of the house or income—ranges through several economic levels. Family background and respectability are primary determinants of membership. Within this group there is great equality expressed by intermingling. A second major class is, of course, the Negro group, which is set off not only by virtue of its economic position but also by the fact of color and is further complicated by internal class division. And a third economic group, which has tended to increase with the growing industrialism, is represented by the migrants of the hill families in town. So the white mill workers, and more recently laborers in other types of new industry, occupy a position of comparable inferiority to that of the Negro; and for all practical purposes they are barred from institutional participation in the affairs of the community in the same way that Negroes are.

When you attempt to get at the kinds of things which give expression to the basic cultural values of the Southern scene, you are tempted, and I think you cannot avoid, referring to literature, because some authors have done a magnificent job. In particular, I refer to Stephen Vincent Benét's *John Brown's Body* and to his description of Southern women, of the genteel Southern lady, who, as she meets the world, meets it with composure, with equanimity, with graciousness, but who, behind this façade of easy social intercourse, operates an efficient household in which she takes care of and performs all the kinds of necessary functions for her house and for her family. Benét's descriptive verse goes, "The velvet sheathing the steel demurely / In the trained, light grip that holds so surely!" Although Benét's setting was of the Civil War period, his insights into the role of women are equally applicable today. The genteel Southern lady is a person of immense influence in the whole social system. This concept of "ladyness" extends through the entire upper stratum (gentility and middle class) of the whites, including the respectable but poor—but not the women of the mill workers' class. The "quality" Negro holds similar values and, as Faulkner and Mitchell have shown, sometimes enforces proper behavior upon his white folks.

The significance of the woman, I thought, was very vividly portrayed in *Gone with the Wind*. I attended the movie a second time a few weeks ago to see what I would see this time that I hadn't seen before, and the thing that impressed me was that Margaret Mitchell is really talking about the women of the South. She has all the main types represented. There is the "mammy," who was an important type in the old South; the poor white farmer's daughter who appears briefly, but as a distinct type; there is Melanie, who stands for the ideal genteel woman, and Scarlett O'Hara, who violates the values but who shows the conflict with her Irish ancestry; and then there are the grandmothers.

Another aspect which impresses one is the love of Southerners for children. This love for children is related to a family system in which the woman is the central figure; but it's not just mother and daughter; it includes grandmother and other kinswomen as well. Many times I have seen the three generations, grandma, mama, and little girls, going places together. In the relationship between the woman and her husband, the latter also has a central function. It is he who gives his wife babies, and in particular girl babies; because through females the system is perpetuated. Many a Southern woman looks upon sexual relations with her husband as something unpleasant, but as necessary in the production of children. She wants and loves children, and therefore she must have a husband, and hence sexual relations with one's husband can be justified. Another factor which complicates the picture is the association of freedom from sex restraint and prevailing beliefs about Negroes. It follows that if you enjoy sex, you lower yourself to the Negroes' level.

One must understand segregation in terms of family and gentility with values held and transmitted by the woman, with the man in the role of protector of the family and womanhood. The myth of Southern womanhood is no myth.

Within the Southern scene, there is among those who control the society a very real democracy. It is expressed by social intermingling among those who hold a similar view of life. Negroes and poor whites are excluded, so that any act which tends to break down the definition of acceptable social intermingling is a direct threat to the family system. And it is why the segregation decision has to be viewed in terms of the basic values as I've attempted to describe them. Will it happen again, as it did in the Civil War and the Ku Klux Klan days of Reconstruction that the males will feel compelled to protect their womenfolk by organization? With the control of the political system it will be easy, but times have also changed.

What can one judge from the reaction to the segregation decision so far? As nearly as I can tell, from limited contact, it's been extremely calm. This calmness should not lead us to believe there is acceptance. It may mean all kinds of things and I don't know what it means. One Southern woman said to me that this was the most important event in Southern history since emancipation. How many Southerners feel this way I don't know; but in the context of emancipation one should also remember that it was enforced from the outside. Southerners resent external interference so much that method of application is a consideration, because if the decision is interpreted as imposition of Yankee control, a situation which Southerners experienced previously, resistance will be intensified. On the other hand, if implementation is seen as a local responsibility there is greater likelihood of co-operation.

Let us examine one more factor. This morning Margaret Mead referred to the rise of cults and the relationship of the cults to certain kinds of internal conditions within a society. The Southerner has had the cult of womanhood, and this has been given expression in one formal organization known as the Daughters of the Confederacy. More recently, there have been two other groups that have come to include organized women. One of these is the League of Women Voters; how long it's been in North Carolina I don't know, but it's been in Alabama only three years. It was organized in Alabama by foreigners to the state, by the wives of the new managerial group, wives of professors, wives of others who have migrated from Northern states, carrying with them a cultural tradition at some variance from that of the Southern states. So the League of Women Voters is not yet part of the cult of Southern womanhood; it is a cultural importation.

But there are signs of another kind of cult behavior which may be very serious. The reaction to the Civil War eventually produced the Klan, which was led by the gentility and was finally renounced by the same group when the lower classes got hold of it. After the First World War there was a Klan movement of considerable proportions. After the Second World War there was another Klan movement, but this time it was primarily an expression of the common man and was quickly prohibited by law. There were about a dozen Klan acts in Alabama, only one of which was directed against a Negro; all the others were against whites. The Klan was a device which the rural white used to impose a code of morality on his own kind. A more powerful movement is found in the politically expressed stirrings of the Dixiecrat movement, which has cult implications. Dixiecrats were strongest in the plantation area and in those states with the largest Negro population. The movement was as much cultural as political and was a protest against social change. Those who were its adherents may be counted on to oppose desegregation and they may enlist many others on the issue. The decision can become a powerful symbol for rallying forces of white supremacy.

Let us now turn to some specific problems raised by the Supreme Court decision. What proportion of elementary school districts will not be affected because of existing patterns of separation in residential areas? In 80 percent (according to Gillin) of the already established school districts, there will be no change in attendance. The problem then is the other 20 percent. And one may expect that a good portion of the other 20 percent can be taken care of by gerrymandering. In the urban centers, the racial residential separation is so sharp that there will be very few cases, indeed, in which there will be mixed school systems, but these will pose acute problems.

What is the problem of intermingling Negro and white teachers? In some of the states which I mentioned, Negroes average more years of college education than the white teachers. This does not mean that they are better prepared as teachers, because many factors influence competency. Teacher integration is one of the problems. Another problem arises from the threat that Georgia, South Carolina, and Mississippi may move to meet the situation by new legislation. Proposals have been made to abolish the public school system and work through a series of publicly supported private schools.

One final comment: The social class factor is a very important one in terms of both the Negro and white groups. If there is resistance, will it be in terms of the stereotypes which whites hold about Negroes as being field hands, or is it possible that the class factor may overcome the color factor? In certain localities there will be no problem so long as the class values are not violated.

OPEN DISCUSSION

Gillin, Taba, Mead, Martin, Henry, Kimball, Shaftel, Frank

Gillin: There are, I think, though, some encouraging signs that the South is becoming modernized and perhaps its calmness is not just the calm before a storm. In the first place, the church has had a very strong influence; as you pointed out, it is Calvinistic for the most part. It is interesting to note that within the last six weeks the Southern Presbyterian Church in conclave denounced segregation, and that shortly thereafter the Executive Board of the Southern Baptists did likewise. The Bishop of North Carolina declared two years ago that segregation in the Catholic churches was out; he simply told the whites that if they didn't go along, they'd be refused the rites—so far as I know there were only a handful that were, that did get out of the church.

Furthermore, industrialization is the big thing that's happening in the South now; not only private industrialization, but public projects are mixing up whites and Northerners and different classes of Southerners to a degree that's never happened before, so I think that some of the traditional class lines are almost bound to give to some extent. The same happened in the big cities of the North when the immigrants came in—there was a general melting pot. It is interesting to note, for example, as you know, that the Air Force does not have segregation, nor the Army either; in North Carolina there is a very large base called Fort Bragg; there are several thousand students from these elements in the schools; not only the army personnel but the workers, carpenters, people who cut the lawn, and so on, send their children to the schools. There was a little trouble—I think six children were withdrawn—but now we haven't heard anything more than that little incident in a couple of years. This is merely an impression: there may be a big blow-up; but I can't help feeling that some of the statements recently made by Southern politicians are ritual statements—the politicians have to say something in order to make sure that the record's clear that they're against desegregation. South Carolina, as you know, passed a constitutional amendment giving the governor authority to abolish the public school system; but the governor has made no move in that direction and one gets the impression that this was at least partly a propagandistic move—another one of these sorts of dire predictions of what's going to pass—but when it comes to a showdown, most of the Southerners that I know, at least, don't see how to go about abolishing the public school system. The churches don't want to take it over; turning it over to private individuals would mean graft, bureaucracy. However, I do think that there are going to be a lot of private schools developed, and this could well be one of the results.

Taba: I'd like to add something from the standpoint of an educational worker—some personal additions on the constructive side. Officially so little was said and so little was done about Negro-white relationships except by organizations like the Southern Regional Council and so on, that we were always wondering how it came about that in some places things were happening. When I started working in St. Louis, and in parts of Georgia, there was a kind of ritual with people, where in effect you were led behind closed blinds, or in little bits of gatherings, from one corner to another—there was always an element of secrecy about it— and they were all workers for intercultural relations. When I inquired about the techniques, the role of the Southern lady came up very plainly, and it's epitomized in the writing of Lillian Smith, who is a Southern lady herself, I presume; or it is epitomized by a teacher from Birmingham who came to a workshop, and she was teaching a unit on race relations. We all asked how she got away with it, because presumably you didn't touch that subject in Southern schools at all. She smiled in a very ladylike fashion, and very softly said, "First, I'm a Southern lady; and second, I start with Christian principles." If she talks a Christian doctrine, under that heading she can say almost anything—being a Southern lady. She teaches the twelfth grade, and she uses very controversial material, which is discussed openly. That example is apparently multiplied all over.

Kimball: Yes, that's important. But they still don't want to be pushed around. If they're doing anything, they're doing it themselves.

Taba: They're doing it themselves and they're doing it quietly. They're not talking about it openly, and when they do talk, they talk to trusted ears only. Those are, in effect, hidden techniques—what you might call "subversive" techniques. That is what Southern ladies are doing in the South, apparently in large numbers. Second, there is the role of the Catholic church. They were accused of being politicians in taking Negroes into a Catholic church, but they did. They got into Catholic schools many Negro children who are being brought up as Catholics now as a result.

Mead: A lot of it stems from Boston. Just as the old white Protestant American used to let Boston alone and reform the South before the Civil War, now the Catholics in Boston give large amounts of money for Catholic missions in the South. That's a survival of a regional pattern.

Taba: The third factor is the role of the precedent, which I referred to yesterday; you create a series of little precedents that accumulate over a period of time. I wish some anthropologist would walk around in St. Louis among the workers that I know and piece together what that total precedent was; I have records only of some of the activities. But the sequence in the establishing of that precedent was somewhat like this. In the beginning the first meeting we had in St. Louis was of three people, of whom one was Negro; that was a committee on intercultural education. The school superintendent suggested the school cafeteria as a place to eat, knowing full well that school was out and that we could walk into it without anybody seeing us. We couldn't have anything intergroup, inter-school—Negro and white—because by law no white student could be in a class taught by a Negro teacher. So when we established our first prece-dent in interschool activity, we had two teachers in a classroom—one white and one Negro—all done quietly and planned carefully. When we wanted a mixed team to do something, we fished around a lot and finally decided to hold a panel on the atom bomb—picking the most scientific and pretentious of subjects, and included only three people but sent them to six different schools. Even at that, when the panel got into action one citizen had noticed a Negro boy walking up the stairs of a white school and called the school board. Fortunately, we'd foreseen that contingency and we had tipped off everybody so that it got explained and it didn't become a rumor. Then we used all the Southern ladies we could get hold of to promote a sponsor group that gathered up people in all schools and spent a day in mixed activities of various sorts. There was a five-year sequence of piecemeal planning of that kind of order, with the result that last year, on their own, the Missouri Teachers' Association opened itself to Negroes. A newspaper editorial put it that "public meetings say that in two years we're going to have to change to a desegregated school system." When a civic swimming pool, to be used by both Negroes and whites, was opened rashly by city officers without any preparation, and trouble occurred and they had to close it again, we had volunteers from among the teen-agers who had been trained in these groups who said, "We'll go and mix with them and we'll learn a way of preventing trouble if you again reopen the pool." That began in 1946; a creating of precedents is a very tedious, elaborate, calculated kind of job. I was always accused of being a gradualist, of not really wanting to go too fast—from both the Negro and the white side.

The next thing, which you hinted at, is in connection with Negro teachers. It happened in three cases in my experience where we wanted to change a segregated situation into a desegregated situation. There were Negro leaders who wanted segregation because, they said, "Now we have a Negro board. Several of us can be important in it. When it's mixed, how many of us are going to have such a chance?" And that's what many Negro teachers are going to say, and even some of the battlers for the Negro cause, because they have that fear that they won't have chances at important positions, which they now hold in a segregated system.

Mead: You get this from women in education too, who don't want to get rid of women's colleges because women's colleges are one place, at least, where women educators have prestige.

There is another half to this white lady position that isn't at all emphasized in what you were saying, Sol (Kimball). I recognize it because I've been in the position, as very few Northern women have and indeed very few Southern women have today. I have had to run a plantation—temporarily—with a couple of hundred native men right out of the bush. And I've also been all alone in New Guinea in native villages without a white man within a couple of days' march. In both cases if I made one single mistake I was endangering the lives of a very large number of people. That's the background out of which the present Southern position grew. And it's not pleasant for the white lady. One might think from this description that the white lady has something here that she has no reason to want to give up; but that's not so. The tension of never forgetting for one solitary moment the whole of the caste system in the South is carried by the white woman and the Negro man. They're the two groups that carry it, and they never can forget it for one single moment. There's a degree of tension in it, combined with guilt, as it goes with the Christian doctrine, that generates a very heavy drive toward being willing to give it up.

Myrdal's observation, which is based on hundreds and hundreds of case studies that we know at many different levels, has shown that you get the prediction of a riot—if such and such happens there's going to be a riot—and then it happens and the riot doesn't occur. This applies to one of the most significant generalizations that Myrdal has ever made—that every *anticipated* change in Negro-white relationships in this country was feared, and every consummated change was welcomed. One of the best anecdotes I've heard is that told by a woman speaker who was asked to go to speak in a white church in Georgia. In the white church there was a choir of Negro high-school children, a common occurrence in the South. But when they got through entertaining the white parishioners, a Southern lady prominent in the church led them all down and had them sit in the audience and the speaker lectured to Negroes and whites. The minister told her that if he had announced that morning that he was going to have a mixed audience there would have been a riot. But he didn't announce it; it was done, and done by somebody with prestige, and when it was done it went off. So in stressing all the forces against change—with none of which do I disagree—we also have to stress, as John (Gillin) has, the institutional decisions by the churches, and so forth, that there are very heavy forces in favor of change. The point Sol makes is that the South doesn't like to be pushed around; but Southerners have been terribly proud when they make these changes themselves, and they boast all over the South that they're treating the Negroes much better, that they've gone much faster in race relations than the North. And that is the point of pride. One of the big dangers here is the violation of pride, which isn't just the lady's; it's of the whole South.

Martin: Sol's (Kimball) presentation illustrates so well what I was trying to say this morning that I'd like to call some attention to it. Here we've had an anthropologist's report on the South. With that report and the knowledge of what he tells us about it, if I were an educator in the South I could make more intelligent decisions about what to do. In the process of doing whatever I decided to do, presumably the anthropologist might study that process and shed some light on what I was doing—whether I was doing it properly or what else I might do more effectively—and so forth. But I wouldn't expect the anthropologist to come in and do the job of education because that's the job of the educator. I think I see it as a simple division of labor. But if I didn't know what Sol has been telling me, I would be a much less effective person presumably.

Henry: I had something else in mind too. As Sol (Kimball) gave his report, in terms of my own value system, my heart began to drop lower and lower. It seemed awfully difficult for any change to take place. Then when John (Gillin), who is also an anthropologist, gave his evaluation, and Margaret (Mead) talked with her evaluation, then of course my heart began to come up a little bit. Now this is an exceedingly interesting problem; it's not a question of who's right or who's wrong, but rather a question of a very careful evaluation of the insights of the different anthropologists. This is the sort of difficulty we get into: one will evaluate it one way and the other will evaluate it another way. The administrator then may throw up his hands and say, "Well, I'd rather that I hadn't any anthropologists around at all."

Kimball: No, I don't think that's the case. I could have taken another twenty minutes and I could have run down all the things that have been said on the other side. (Gillin agrees.) Women are leaguing together in Alabama; the churches are doing certain things. . . .

Mead: But you chose not to, Sol (Kimball), and you would never have as long as you've had now to talk to any group of administrators. That's one of the things that I was conscious of as you talked—that the amount of background that has to go in from an anthropologist's point of view to give an adequate statement takes a dreadful lot of explaining. And you didn't have that extra twenty minutes and you would never have had it, so you made a selection within the time that you had of what you would say. And I think Jules (Henry) is perfectly right that if anybody had taken it sheerly, if they'd had nothing else to go on, the conclusion would have been, this probably is not going to work; it's either going to do an enormous amount of damage, or nothing will happen at all.

Taba: If you are interested in the process of interpretation, I responded differently. As an educator I said, "Aha! There is an explanation of one of the things that I have difficulty with, which matches up with something else." Or as I was working in my own mind while you were talking, I was saying, "Here are some of the negative factors that I may not have understood."

Mead: But, Hilda (Taba), you're an expert in the field; you've worked in it for five years.

Taba: But that's a process that we have to learn to carry on; we can't depend on one person to have the complete truth.

Mead: But isn't the point Jules wanted to put across that if Sol or if John (Gillin) had presented it only, and the people had had no experience, it would have looked as though they were presenting different things?

Taba: But presumably those people would immediately ask, "What else do you see; what possibilities?" They would have gone on.

Kimball: I think Hilda's point is a good one. Because in the accumulation of this knowledge which I presented I drew from several of us who continually added to each other.

Henry: I think that this is important: that two people, or perhaps three, can be very much more helpful than one.

Gillin: I'd like to make the point that if somebody called on Sol and me to make a report, and we'd had forewarning and time to get together, I don't think there would have been much disagreement. And that's the sort of thing that would happen in working with administrators; they're not going to ask for off-the-cuff statements; they're going to ask for considered opinion.

Shaftel: Maybe there is more sophistication among some workers than among others. I had occasion to consult with some school people from Phoenix very recently; they were concerned about the fact that the Negro community in Phoenix was now beginning to demand Negro teachers in the community, and the educators don't know how to handle this. They are afraid that the gains they have made are going to be lost by pushing too fast, and when we raised the question, "Did you consult with your Negro community leaders too?" they answered no, that they were not involved in the process in any way. So there's a lot of know-how that may be lacking in some of the areas where we would expect to have more sophistication.

Mead: In looking ahead and planning, I would think that one of the things we ought to consider now—and one of the foundations that is interested in the field should be asked to support—is a study of what is going to happen, for instance, to the Negro school principal—he's a more crucial person than even the teacher, because the probability of fitting in the Negro administrator is even lower. This whole group of people have got to where they are with great work and effort, and it means an enormous amount to them. They've sacrificed and studied and deprived themselves, and now a great number of them are likely to be thrown out in one way or another. There should now be some kind of educational move—new kinds of fellowships, new roles developed perhaps for some of the very gifted people, whom we can use in a lot of other places in the world. There are all sorts of ways of utilizing the highly educated and the gifted if there's not room for enough of them in the system when they make the shift.

Frank: In American cities there are a great many agencies engaged in trying to make improvements. They are very strong on the advantages of what they want to do, but rarely do they systematically enumerate all the different groups, opinions, beliefs, and so on, which have to be met, mitigated, countered, released, reduced in order to achieve their end. That's what I meant the other day when I was talking about developing a strategy of social change, and particularly educational change. We've been very remiss in trying really to see the things we have to work against, because we're so preoccupied in selling our goods. I think this discussion has made that fairly clear, that we've got to be more alert to, and aware of the kinds of things that are going to be encountered whenever you ask people to change.

Mead: Don't you think also we've got to be alert to the damage we do when we do good? There are going to be enormous by-products of this Supreme Court decision that are socially disrupting, and damaging to particular individuals, and we ought now to pick them up. The danger is that the people who are on the side of the angels are going to be so elated with victory that they may not have the energy or be able to divert the money fast enough (and there's not a very large amount of money for minority work at present) to pick up the pieces where the greatest damage is going to be done.

Taba: What particularly worries me is that the so-called specialized human relations agencies that have worked in this field have paid almost the least attention to those strategies. Each one of them has a gadget by which to work: one shows films, etc., and it's been very hard to juggle them into a position where their staff and personnel get the kind of training that these kinds of discussions would give them. Probably part of this occurs because they do feel unprofessional, and they aren't included in professional circles where this kind of discussion goes on. The professionals don't want to fool with them; they want to do the pure things and the good things, and so you don't have the interdisciplinary current even running in those directions. They're a sizable group and they spend considerable energy and money without any strategy.

Spindler: I am sorry that our time has run out. We have come to the end of this meeting, and the conference. I can't close without saying, of course, how grateful I am personally and in terms of our contribution to a very important field that all of you felt interested and committed enough to come and behave as you have.

AUTHOR INDEX

297

PARTICIPANT INDEX

SUBJECT INDEX

manistic aspect, 247; limitations on utility in education, 20; physical, 7; role in foundations of education, 11; role in teacher education, 30–33; as social science, 248; sporadic relationships to education, 29

Applied anthropology and normative problems in education, 80, 81

Audience for which conference intended, 27

Awareness, cultural and personal, 277, 278

Bicultural learner, in intercultural learning, 101, 102

Bicultural learning situation, in intercultural understanding, 93, 94

Ceremonialism in American education, 161

Channels model, in analysis of educative process, 45–48

Childhood education, 53, 118, 119, 136, 139, 151, 152, 154, 166 ff., 190 ff., 202, 203, 206

Citizenship education: implications, 153; in primitive societies, *see* Postpubertal education

Cognitive learning, in intercultural learning, 90 ff., 107, 108

Collectivities: critique of relations, 51, 52; in educational and social communities, 42, 43

Communication: additive and spiraling learning, 193–99; between anthropologists and educators, 212, 213; coding and decoding in teaching and learning, 213, 214; inadequacy of children's storage mechanisms, 202, 203; information model, 199, 200, 209; mono- and polyphasic learning, 196–98; "noise" in, 203, 204, 214, 215; problems in, between educators and anthropologists, 27; signals, 190, 191; target-seeking and diffuse learning, 190–92

Communities in United States, diversity of, 63, 64, 72

Concomitant learning, in intercultural understanding, 117

Continuity and discontinuity: in education, 153; in Home Economics programs and family experience, 163, 164 ff.

Cultural analysis in teacher education, 33

Cultural awareness: development of, 35; goal in teacher education, 11, 32, 33

Cultural change as factor in education, 25, 26

Cultural dynamics: as contribution to education, 8; culture and personality relationship, 113. *See also* Cultural integration; Cultural process; Culture concept

Cultural integration: 231–36; configuration, 233, 234; contradictions between real and ideal culture, 234; spatial dimensions, 232, 233; temporal dimension, 233

Cultural learning, not necessarily painful, 34

Cultural materials, intellectualization of, 35

Cultural process: change, 254, 255; choices and limitations, 245, 246, 251, 252, 253; crisis, 226, 244, 246, 248; focus and change, 224, 243, 244; intelligence as factor in, 225; myth, 231; perennialist vs. progressivist, position on, 223, 224, 225; perspective on, 259, 260; philosophy of, 222–27; resistance to change, 266, 267; speed in culture change, 277; transformative view of, 235, 236

Cultural relativism, 124, 125, 229, 230, 231

Cultural transmission, 7, 8; in American schools, 38, 42, 43; complex interpretive expressive learning in, 195; and cultural change, 97, 98; cut-off points in, 195, 196; dualism in American society, 167, 168 ff.; in past- and future-oriented cultures, 192; problem of quantity, 199, 200, 209; and social change, 57; social class effect, 67; and social organization, 191, 192; unintended learning, 203–5. *See also* Communication

Culture: changing of, in persons, 33; theory of, 217 ff., 243–45.

Culture change: and intercultural learning, 95, 96; speed of, 125, 126; transposition in, 273, 274. *See also* Cultural process; Cultural transmission

Culture concept: cliché tendency, 266; limitations of, 21; and philosophy, 243–45; problem of values, 227–31, 244, 248; shift toward, in education, 18, 266, 267; *sui generis* position, 219, 220, 221, 222, 225, 227, 243, 249, 250, 251. *See also* Cultural integration; Cultural process

Cultures, styles of learning, 118, 119

DATE DUE

10. 15. '86	
MAY 31 '89	

BRODART, INC.

Cat. No. 23-221